SPECULATORS IN EMPIRE

New Directions in Native American Studies
Colin G. Calloway and K. Tsianina Lomawaima, General Editors

SPECULATORS IN EMPIRE

Iroquoia and the 1768 Treaty

of Fort Stanwix

William J. Campbell

University of Oklahoma Press : Norman

Publication of this book is made possible through the generosity of Edith Kinney Gaylord.

Parts of this book were previously published in
Pennsylvania History 76:2 (2009) and *New York History* 89:2 (2008).

Library of Congress Cataloging-in-Publication Data

Campbell, William J., 1976–
 Speculators in empire : Iroquoia and the 1768 treaty of Fort Stanwix / William J. Campbell.
    p. cm. — (New directions in Native American studies vol. 7)
  Includes bibliographical references and index.
  ISBN 978-0-8061-4286-9 (cloth)
  ISBN 978-0-8061-4665-2 (paper)
 1. Iroquoian Indians—Treaties. 2. Iroquoian Indians—Land tenure.
 3. Iroquoian Indians—Government relations. 4. Great Britain. Treaties, etc.
 Six Nations, 1768 Nov. 5. 5. Great Britain—Colonies—America—History—
 18th century. I. Title.
  E99.I69C35 2012
  974.004'9755—dc23
                              2012018052

Speculators in Empire: Iroquoia and the 1768 Treaty of Fort Stanwix is Volume 7 in the New Directions in Native American Studies series.

The paper in this book meets the guidelines for permanence and durability of the Committee on Production Guidelines for Book Longevity of the Council on Library Resources, Inc. ∞

For Carrie

CONTENTS

List of Illustrations   ix
Acknowledgments   xi
A Note on Terminology   xiii

Introduction   3
  1. Exchanges and Transformations   14
  2. The Carrying Place, War, and the Ohio Country   26
  3. Converging Interests   67
  4. Boundaries   109
  5. The 1768 Treaty of Fort Stanwix   139
  6. Prospects, and the Collapse of Protocol   167
Epilogue: Revolution and Redefinition   202

Notes   213
Bibliography   253
Index   265

ILLUSTRATIONS

FIGURES

"Communication between Albany and Oswego," 1772   xvi
"A mappe of Colonel Romers voyage to
     ye 5 Indian Nations," 1700   24
"Carte de l'Amerique Septentrionnale," ca. 1688, and detail   30
Plan of forts at the Oneida Carry, 1754   55
The Ohio Country, 1764   81
Plan of Fort Stanwix, 1758   140

MAPS

Boundaries of the Royal Proclamation of 1763
     and 1768 Treaty of Fort Stanwix   155
George Croghan's Fort Pitt area land claims, 1749–1773   181

Acknowledgments

This book would not have been possible without the generosity and guidance of others. Given that this project has been almost a decade in the making, I have incurred a multitude of personal and professional debts. Accordingly, I must begin by apologizing for failing to mention all of those people who helped transform the underdeveloped ideas of a graduate student into a doctoral dissertation and, finally, this book—the shortcomings of which remain my sole responsibility.

For their editorial advice on many parts of this book or related articles, I thank John Weaver, Colin Calloway, Daniel Richter, Ian Steele, Alan Taylor, Daniel Barr, Laurence Hauptman, Carrie Dickenson, Michael Gauvreau, Trudy Nicks, and the anonymous reviewers of the University Oklahoma Press, Cornell University Press, *New York History*, and *Pennsylvania History*. I am particularly indebted to Colin Calloway for his patience and encouragement; and to Alessandra Tamulevich, Emily Jerman, and the production team at the University of Oklahoma Press.

Funding from a variety of sources provided much appreciated support as well. Without grants and the assistance of staff from the American Philosophical Society, Newberry Library, Library Company of Philadelphia (my special thanks to the benefactors of the Albert M. Greenfield Dissertation fellowship), Ontario Graduate Scholarship program, McMaster University, David Library for the American Revolution, Pennsylvania Historical and Museum Commission, and California State University, Chico, this project would have looked considerably different, and not for the better. I am also indebted to the administrators of McGill University's Department of History, whose willingness in 2007/8 to take a chance on a recent graduate student to teach courses in American history afforded me the additional confidence, experience, and just enough money to continue to pursue a career in academia. Thank you.

Finally, a special debt of gratitude is owed to those who keep us laughing, loving, and moving forward. In my case, I wish to thank my dissertation supervisor, John Weaver, whose superb guidance and approachability was the envy of many of my fellow doctoral candidates at McMaster University. My thinking and general well-being have also been positively influenced by conversations with Ryan "early morning wisdom" Fitzgibbon, Daniel Krebs, Patrick Spero, Marcus Gallo, Robert Jones, David Aycan, and Phil Morgan. To my family—John, Wilma, Colleen, Scott, Erin and Liam—my endless thanks for your generosity and kindness. To my partner in life, Carrie Dickenson, for her love, support, and inspiration, I dedicate this book.

A Note on Terminology

The spelling and reference of indigenous terms, places, and people posed as much of a challenge for contemporaries of early America as for commentators in the present day. During the colonial and revolutionary periods, and through much of the nineteenth century, there were no standards for transliterating indigenous words. Those who left written records were always subject to varying degrees of influence from their own language and culture; the linguistic differences between American Indian communities, tribes, and nations only exacerbated the problem. With regard to capturing proper indigenous pronunciation, there were also inherent problems transliterating indigenous languages using the Roman alphabet. These factors contributed to a slew of linguistic complications and misnomers, both then and now. In the North American context today, the commonly used indigenous expressions and references are largely the product of a hodgepodge of interrelated French, Dutch, German, Spanish, and English renditions of people, names, and places that would otherwise have linguistic variations from nation to nation, tribe to tribe, or even between villages. The Algonkians, for instance, called the Ganiengehaga "Mohawks" ("Man-eaters"); the English term "Iroquois" was a variation of what the French called the Haudenosaunee.

Decoding and correcting three centuries of linguistic variation and mismanagement is a monumental task, constantly under way. To maintain clarity and consistency, I have opted to use the Europeanized versions of indigenous nation and tribal names. Accordingly, I use "Iroquois" instead of "Haudenosaunee." The same can be said for the "Mohawks" (Ganiengehaga, or "People of the Flint"), "Oneidas" (Onyota'a:ka, or "People of the Standing Stone"), "Onondagas" (Onöñda'gega, or "People of the Hills"), "Cayugas" (Guyohkohnyo, or "People of the Great Swamp"); "Senecas" (Onöndowága, or "People of the Great Hill"), and "Tucaroras" (Karū'ren, or "Hemp Gatherers"). Furthermore, unless the names of indigenous peoples and places have been modified to avoid confusion, they appear as they did in the original texts.

Because the actions and motivations of indigenous communities varied not only between nations but also between villages, when possible I distinguish between communities on the basis of geographic- or village-specific actions. The Chenussio Senecas for instance, are often referred to as the "western Senecas." The same can be said for the "Ohio Iroquois," "Shamokin Delawares," and so on. Even though these groupings do not always reflect community complexities, establishing regional dynamics and perceptions as related to local and imperial strategizing is of principal concern to this study. Consequently, because a long history of regional differences and disputes among the Six Nations has complicated commentary on the history of "the Iroquois," I have opted to refer to the "Grand Council." Though Iroquois communities often pursued divergent strategies when coping with the forces of colonization, the Six Nations' Grand Council of Chiefs was well aware of perceptions, protocol, and the benefits of maintaining a diplomatic front given their relations with the administrators of their European neighbors.

Finally, unless otherwise recorded in the notes, all references to currency throughout the text are in Sterling.

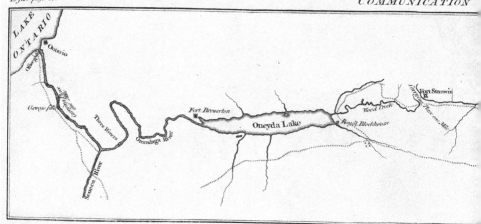

"Communication between Albany and Oswego," by Thomas Kitchin, 1772. From The Crown Collection of Photographs of American Maps Series 1, Volume 1 #48, #49, #50. Courtesy of the New York State Library.

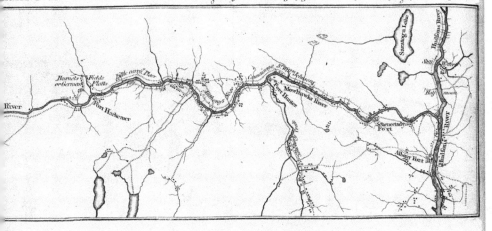

SPECULATORS IN EMPIRE

INTRODUCTION

In 1784, as the leaves began to change color, Joseph Brant (Thayenda-negea) made his way southeast from British Canada toward the land of his youth. Before traveling into the northern limits of the recently recognized United States of America, Brant stopped to rest and resupply at Fort Niagara. Despite the terms of the 1783 Treaty of Paris, the thinly garrisoned post continued to protect regional interests that clung to the hope of a resurrected empire. Notwithstanding having acted as important testing grounds for Brant during both the Seven Years' War and the American Revolution, Fort Niagara provided a brief point of respite for the aging forty-one-year-old warrior traveling toward an uncertain future. Just south of the great falls, he turned due east and followed the ancient Iroquois warpath (better known today as Interstate 90) across Six Nations country. About fifty-five miles west of Canajoharie, he stopped at the Oneida Carry, a three-mile portage that bridged the Mohawk River valley and the Great Lakes river basin in what is now New York State. Adorned by the burned and rotting timbers of Fort Stanwix, the Carry's primary fortification had been set ablaze and all but abandoned four years after American forces repulsed the Crown's army in 1777. In October 1784 the remnants of the fort again played host to a meeting of foes.

Brant traveled to Fort Stanwix to hold council with not only Oliver Wolcott, Richard Butler, and Arthur Lee—the commissioners plenipotentiary of the United States—but also with Iroquois kin against whom he had raised his hatchet during the American Revolution. The

Six Nations came to blows during the recent colonial rebellion, a crisis that many scholars argue brought to end the Iroquois Confederacy. To be sure, on 6 August 1777, a mere six miles east of Fort Stanwix, Iroquois warriors clashed in one of the bloodiest battles of the Revolutionary War. The subsequent fallout from what would become known as the Battle of Oriskany witnessed the plundering and burning of North American Indian communities by rival factions. The American Revolution engrossed the Iroquois in civil turmoil and redefined the place of the Grand Council in early America.

Despite the consequences of the civil conflict that erupted among the Iroquois during the colonial bid for independence, as in scores of gatherings between colonial Europeans and first peoples that preceded the negotiations, land and diplomacy, not cultural restoration, remained of primary concern. With the Confederacy in shambles and most of the self-proclaimed indigenous proprietors of the northeastern borderlands considered defeated enemies, U.S. representatives aimed to set a precedent and example not only for the tattered Iroquois and humbled English Crown but also for ambitious state politicians and land speculators who threatened to undermine congressional authority. By assuming the role of principal negotiator with the first peoples at Fort Stanwix, Wolcott, Butler, and Lee sought to establish firm federal control over the northeast. To do so, the agents were charged with confirming the lands ceded to the Crown during the boundary negotiations sixteen years prior, on the very same ground.[1]

The scene at the Oneida Carry looked considerably different in 1768, when more than three thousand people gathered at Fort Stanwix. Instead of a small collection of splintered sachems, chiefs, and warriors, the Six Nations arrived in droves, projecting an image of authority, unity, and confidence. As the hosted guests of the British Crown, they ate and drank heartily for over two months while chief negotiators privately met to discuss the terms of a land cession unparalleled in the history of early America. Interestingly, even though the conference held at Fort Stanwix in 1768 was one of the greatest spectacles of intercultural diplomacy, no artistic interpretations of the events have survived. But what scenes the council would have provided. With more than three thousand individuals gathered at the

Carry, a sea of makeshift housing, batteaux, canoes, packhorses, and goods would have dotted the landscape as a who's who of colonial America mingled, traded stories, and gossiped in anticipation of the formal proceedings.

The congregated first nations had much to gain by rekindling the fire of alliance with the Crown. In exchange for their blessings, it was believed a measure of security could be gained by maintaining a partnership with the European builders of empire. After all, time had taught the Grand Council that the Crown paid handsomely to obtain the legalities of exploitation. Thus, given the unparalleled scope of the 1768 negotiations, there was much to gain. On 5 November, within view of thousands of pounds worth of goods and mounds of cash protected by armed guards and the formidable walls of Fort Stanwix, in the largest assembled council in early America, Iroquois representatives extended the agreed 1763 boundary between them and European colonists by ceding millions of acres of land to the English Crown. For a king's ransom the Crown gained possession of what is today parts of western New York and Pennsylvania, Ohio, Kentucky, and West Virginia—lands claimed, but not occupied, by the Six Nations. Commenting on the events more than a century later, William Elliot Griffis declared that "thirty-two hundred individuals were present to witness the bartering away of their birthright for such pottage as the pale-faces had to tempt these Esaus of the wilderness."[2] And though time has helped revise such misguided depictions of American Indians, it has done little to stimulate further investigation into the events surrounding the negotiations and their contested significance.

Considering how vigorously scholars have toiled over boundaries and the relationship between first peoples and colonizers, it is surprising that not more attention has been given to events surrounding the 1768 negotiations at Fort Stanwix. Instead, the history of the treaty reads like many other land grab transactions during the late colonial era. Albeit with varying degrees of complexity, the treaty's events remain a passing reference to the myopic policies of the Crown on the eve of the American Revolution, or within the context of Superintendent of Indian Affairs William Johnson's land-speculating interests.[3]

For those investigators primarily concerned with tracing the causes of the war of independence, the 1768 treaty held at Fort Stanwix has represented little more than another example of a Crown-sanctioned irritant that contributed to colonial rebellion. "Neither reactionary nor radical," the negotiations have been depicted as "a compromise influenced largely by the failure of imperial plans to tax the colonies, [and] by the desire of the merchants interested in the Indian trade to be freed from restrictive regulations."[4] Overshadowed on one side by the Seven Years' War and on the other by the American Revolution, the events at Stanwix in 1768 have been summarized as "the last desperate effort of the British to create order west of the Appalachians."[5] Therefore, because of the shifting political landscape in early North America, the treaty is represented as an insufficient effort by Whitehall to "delay the entire absorption of Indian lands" by appeasing the indigenous peoples in an attempt to avoid another costly frontier war.[6] In fact, historians during the past century have agreed with the contemporary advocates of negotiations who insisted that the intention of the treaty "was to remove every cause of future quarrel with the natives."[7] But the treaty did little to calm indigenous anxieties over illegal settlements. In fact, it did the opposite. According to some scholars, Johnson's own greed can be blamed for the escalation of frontier violence following the 1768 council.

Writing about the treaty in 1944, Ray A. Billington suggested that William Johnson "mercilessly fleeced the Indians who trusted him as their protector" in order to line his pockets through the acquisition of land. Accrediting the Six Nations with little to no agency, Billington remarked that Johnson coerced his most trusted Iroquois allies while concluding "one of the worst treaties in the history of Anglo-Indian relationships." More recently, R. Douglas Hurt has followed Billington's lead, at least with the depiction of Johnson. Well aware of the opportunity, Johnson took liberties and seized "as much territory as possible under the guise of Indian support." Subsequently, Hurt maintains, the "result proved less a negotiated than a British-imposed treaty." There are reasons, however, to question this interpretation of Johnson and the treaty's historical significance.[8]

Johnson may have been required to formalize treaty proceedings, but much of the bargaining that took place in the years, months, weeks, and days prior to the opening ceremonies involved careful politicking. Johnson's actions must be considered in light of him having to "balance being a royal official, private speculator, and friend of the Indians."[9] Eric Hinderaker agrees, noting that Johnson may have "worked behind the scenes on behalf of other large-scale land speculation schemes," but his actions at the 1768 council did not conflict with his position as a devoted Crown employee or friend of the Iroquois.[10] In fact, the superintendent may have used his authority at the negotiations to the point of helping to enact revenge on the Ohio nations for their involvement in the so-called Indian Uprising of 1763 and general disregard of the Grand Council.[11]

Scholarly infatuation with Johnson and burdens of taxation has diminished the significance of the treaty and the agency of other participants, namely, the Iroquois. Instead of being passive sheep led to the slaughter, Peter Marshall suggests, "the Iroquois were well aware of [the treaty's] significance" and consented to its terms. Although Marshall does not elaborate on the motives of the Six Nations sachems, his analysis at least introduces them as essential components.[12] Since, a few scholars have speculated on benefits to the Iroquois of the land cession. Analysis has centered on the quandary the treaty imposed on the participants. The Iroquois were forced to retain their credit with the British by ceding control over the Ohio Country, even though their authority inconveniently "rested with the ability to preserve the boundary line."[13] In short, the cession allowed the Iroquois "to shed responsibility for what was becoming a violent and troublesome region."[14] In this vein, the 1768 Fort Stanwix treaty represents a remarkable diplomatic feat and should be hailed as an example of the influential extent of the perceived Six Nations–British compact in early America. More important, the treaty provided a venue for those people and nations willing to further the constructed prestige of the Iroquois Confederacy. Thus, the ability of the Iroquois delegates to push the treaty through signaled one of the Grand Council's last great successes. It would prove to be a fleeting success, however; the parties at the time could not have forecast the momentous events ahead.[15]

Complicating this line of argumentation are the inescapable realities of Iroquois sectionalism. In this book I draw attention to how localized relations bound the interests of British-sympathizing

Iroquois (largely guided by the Mohawks) and Crown officials (like Sir William Johnson). Such regionalism reinforces the idea that the "Iroquois spoke with, not one, but many voices" during the era of European colonization. As Daniel Richter points out, "seventeenth- and eighteenth-century Iroquois politics and diplomacy, like twentieth-century post-Einsteinian physics, was a confusing world of particles constantly in flux, combining and recombining in diverse configurations."[16] Some historians have addressed this element of Iroquois sectionalism and characterize the Grand Council as being politically dysfunctional and inept by the mid-eighteenth century. This reasoning applies when gauging the capability of the Council to dictate daily life in "Indian Country." But a distinction must be drawn when it comes to the impact of the privileged place of the Iroquois Confederacy in the affairs of British North America on the eve of rebellion.[17]

Simply put, there is more to the story than a land grab at the expense of a feeble Grand Council. For those who gathered at the Oneida Carry in 1768, there was nothing last-minute about the terms of the land cession or the treaty protocol the participants followed. The construction and perpetuation of both Crown and Grand Council authority had serious consequences for those peoples affected by both indigenous and European enterprising. As real as the stress was that Europeans placed on the first peoples without the social standing to speak on behalf of entire nations or even communities, so too were the benefits reaped by Iroquois negotiators who cultivated an image of themselves as continental overlords. To acknowledge this is not to validate the sea of bogus agreements between Europeans and the indigenous inhabitants of North America; nor does it suggest that Iroquois negotiators demonstrated shortsightedness when they met European representatives. On the contrary. When appointed indigenous headmen met European agents they often had to balance the needs of their communities with the demands of competing empires. It follows, as David Preston argues, that the "treaties, conferences, and diplomacy . . . of early America cannot be understood apart of this very local frontier world."[18] But local interests also led to sectionalism, as perhaps best exemplified by events during the revolutionary era. As we see by investigating the circumstances surrounding the largest land cession in early America, it also increasingly empowered those willing to perpetuate the idea of a united and functional Iroquois Confederacy.

In this respect, despite the realities of divergent strategies, the 1768 land cession agreement reveals the extent to which those seeking to create and project the authority of either the Grand Council or Crown benefited from working in concert. Many Iroquois may have laughed at the idea of their obedience to a European king, but the Grand Council was well aware of the benefits of appearances and collusion. In this respect, both authorities became dependent on the survival of the other. The 1768 treaty's minutiae support aspects of this claim because they cover an extraordinary number of outstanding Iroquois concerns. The circumstances surrounding the treaty negotiations also point to other, less indigenous, factors that also have been eclipsed by the history of the American Revolution.

Many North Americans lived long enough to witness a new American government reject not only the diplomatic protocol that maintained an exclusive place for the Iroquois but also those Europeans who had invested in the benefaction of the colonial system. Like an inherited throne, the kinship ties and manicured patronage that provided an opportunity for such figures to manipulate and guide imperial policy also connected many of them to what would become a replaced past. As a result, the extinguishment of Crown rule not only forced an outward migration of unwanted alliances and traditions but also snuffed out the dreams and fortunes of those individuals who had helped protect the privileged place of the Grand Council.

When Joseph Brant relocated in British Canada after the war, he brought with him the remnants of the kinship networks that embodied many of the excommunicated elements of the colonial past. These so-called loyalist factions have received considerable scholarly attention, particularly in Canada. But it is the unsuspecting history that can be traced through Brant's third wife, Catherine, that not only marks the replacement of one world with another but perhaps best exemplifies the degree to which Iroquois-European networking and enterprising shaped the Crown's borderland policies in North America during the late colonial era.

Catherine Adwontishon Croghan was the granddaughter of an important Mohawk sachem. Her father, Col. George Croghan, was a past deputy superintendent of Indian affairs and William Johnson's valued friend. Prior to the exodus of loyalists to Canada and the treaty of 1784, it was Catherine's father George who held the thousands of borderland acres in "Indian deeds"—land purchased directly from indigenous people but lacking Crown confirmation and, thus, clear title. Along with tenuous holdings throughout the Ohio and Illinois countries, sixteen years before at the treaty of Fort Stanwix Croghan stood to capitalize on a lifetime of scheming, bartering, and speculating throughout Iroquoia and beyond. Croghan's story has, however, almost exclusively been assigned a peripheral position in the annals of early America. Like that of his daughter, when mentioned Croghan's tale often assumes the characteristics of a subplot—an interesting but less important reference to his superior, Sir William Johnson. Adding to his apparent historical unworthiness is the fact that Croghan outlived his colonial patrons, both Johnson and the Crown.

Nevertheless, the history of Iroquois strategizing on the eve of the American Revolution cannot be appreciated without also mentioning Croghan. It was Croghan, after all, who traveled to London in 1764 and pitched the idea of a new boundary to the Board of Trade; it was Croghan whom the Iroquois rewarded with thousands of acres at the 1768 Fort Stanwix council; and it was Croghan who presided over key negotiations in the Ohio and Illinois countries that helped facilitate the designs of both the Crown and the Grand Council. Actually, a closer look at Croghan's dealings leading up to the first treaty exposes the reliance of a fleeting empire's administrators on a reckless Crown agent and manic player for acreage. More important, Croghan's yarn comments on Iroquois willingness to reward those players who promulgated the authority of the Grand Council. Croghan's abilities and aspirations were realized and exploited by both William Johnson and the Iroquois. In this respect Croghan, for a time, became an important mouthpiece of the Grand Council, and the Crown, as he spent considerable time perpetuating the myth of an "Iroquois Empire." Likewise, when Croghan realized the personal gains that could be made by extending the domain of the Indian Department, and thus the authority of the Grand Council, he carried not only the messages of his superior west into the Ohio, Illinois, and southern Great Lakes but also the merchandise of his "secret" trading partners and financial backers in the east. It should come as no surprise that Croghan did not always follow Crown directives. Above all, his loyalties hinged on opportunism. In fact, in 1774 he had turned his back on treaty protocol in a bid to secure lands that were, ironically, sold to him by the Iroquois.

Croghan's tale reminds us that the history of land speculation and indigenous struggles for sovereignty are not only related but also, at times, even codependent. During the late colonial period, Iroquois strategies and European speculator interests converged. Because the land cession of 1768 involved such a slew of interests, both indigenous and European, it reveals just how integrated the Grand Council had become in colonial affairs. Europeans and American Indians seeking to guide the course of the British Empire in North America used land speculators, traders, and Crown agents willing to uphold the authority of the Grand Council. This history of empire and speculation in Iroquoia, then, is at times as much indigenous as it is European.

That being said, the lofty ambitions and calculated strategies of the Iroquois should not be lost sight of in the history of European disagreements or land grab finagling. In fact, when negotiators met at the Oneida Carry in 1768, they sought to prepare for a future in a continental empire by closely following the traditions and procedures of the past. As chapter 1 details, before European contact the protocol that guided negotiation in Iroquoia was antediluvian, but in a constant state of flux. As European disease, goods, and concepts transformed and fueled a new era of conflict during the seventeenth century, the well-supplied Iroquois made the most of the situation. They raided their neighbors throughout the northeastern borderlands and extended their system of cross-cultural exchange. By the turn of the century, however, the Iroquois had overextended their power. In response, they adapted. With the modus operandi of cultural exchange entrenched, beginning in the early eighteenth century Iroquois negotiators capitalized on both the real and imagined place of the Grand Council in early America.

Set to this backdrop, chapter 2 details the evolution of two important places central to this study: the Oneida Carry and the Ohio Country.

Both locales were considered critical to the survival of people, identity, and empire. As a result, they both underwent a series of transformations that placed each at the heart of continental conflict during much of the eighteenth century. By the end of the Seven Years' War, however, it became increasingly clear to both Crown Indian agents and pro-British Iroquois that to maintain control of both locations, and the regional inhabitants, much more collaboration would be needed.

From here, chapters 3 and 4 continue, both Superintendent Johnson and his Iroquois backers sought to project an image of unity, thus metaphorically reinforcing the links of the Covenant Chain (the Iroquois-English alliance) and power of both parties. A strict adherence to treaty protocol solidified Johnson's position as superintendent of Indian affairs and that of the Iroquois as administrators of lands that stretched well beyond the Appalachians. Aware the cession would enrage Ohio Country and Great Lakes inhabitants, the long-time partners nevertheless pushed ahead with the prearranged details of the agreement as outlined by Iroquois negotiators in 1765. The indigenous representatives focused on establishing a boundary that would first and foremost secure the interests of, primarily, the eastern Iroquois. For that reason, clauses were woven into the contract that granted millions of acres of land to friendly European speculators, like Croghan, and provincial authorities with an interest in expanding the British Empire west into the Ohio Country and away from Iroquois homelands. In fact, many Iroquois, along with Johnson and Croghan, realized that their futures rested with maintaining the precarious authority of the Iroquois Confederacy. Thus, those first peoples willing to bow to the idea of Grand Council authority were promised handsome rewards from both Crown and provincial representatives. This resulted in an era of wild speculation for Croghan and his associates, further drawing parallels between those speculators in empire.

I explore the culmination of these converging interests in chapter 5, with a detailed account of the events at the Oneida Carry in the fall of 1768. Unlike other, well-documented treaties, the events of the Stanwix negotiations have long escaped the pages of history. More than just an exercise in addressing this void, so to speak, detailing the progression of events at the Oneida Carry in 1768 reinforces the notion that a series of interests converged to produce one of the most spectacular displays of diplomacy and negotiation in early America. But the agreed spoils, the Ohio Country, did not sit well with that region's inhabitants. In fact, for two decades after the treaty, wars of independence engulfed the Stanwix cession lands.

Chapter 6 details the collapse of this complicated relationship, a collapse accelerated by increased settler pressure in Six Nations country and imperial cutbacks that hamstrung the Indian Department and the enterprising of speculators like Croghan. By the time the Virginian governor, Lord Dunmore, marched his soldiers toward the forks of the Ohio River to lay claim to the region, the protocols and patronage of the colonial system that had benefited the Iroquois and their consortium of European allies were all but ruined; the American Revolution and the 1784 Treaty of Fort Stanwix, soon thereafter, laid waste to the last vestiges of an alliance that had helped transform a continent.

By tracing the web of interests that fueled negotiations at the Oneida Carry, I aim to expose past struggles for survival, independence, and empire that deemphasize many themes and events long associated with the creation of a republic in North America. In fact, by primarily looking to the imperial and regional positioning in the northeastern borderlands during the interwar years (1763–74), I seek to blur the lines between European capitals and the council fires of the Iroquois and Ohio nations. Of principal concern are the thoughts and actions of those people who sat and smoked to discuss borderland affairs, often angling to capitalize on an expanding empire. Of particular interest is the 1768 treaty held at Fort Stanwix. More than just a play for land and a forum wherein whites clashed over jurisdictional rights, the treaty exposes the importance and recognition of place and protocol in early American history. The treaty's history also illustrates the relationship between the Grand Council and British imperial authority and their collapse, thus underscoring the delicate and regional dynamic of a well-worn but fragile alliance system. In the end, the treaty should be held as a benchmark example for those seeking a context to view the interworkings of Iroquois-Crown diplomacy during the eighteenth century and those factors that made the relationship both convenient, and eventually, unsustainable.

CHAPTER 1

EXCHANGES AND
TRANSFORMATIONS

So long as historians confine themselves "to the records kept by white men," William Fenton once wrote, they are "bound—even in the most conscientious interpretation of Indian-White relations—to miss something of the Indian point of view."[1] There is merit in that claim, and it should keep us humble about what we know from a limited set of documents. It is true that mostly white men put ink to paper, but documentary sources can still reveal some things about indigenous perspectives. As important, to reject the notion that one cannot tease "Indian perspectives" from written records is to deny that indigenous negotiators grasped the evolving concepts of, and contributed to, the world around them. In the end, the records of the white men Fenton speaks of also unveil diverse participants with varied motives that simply do not fit well with a colonizer-colonized dichotomy. Some of the most convincing arguments illustrating the primary role of indigenous agency in early American history have focused on the clever fluidity and malleability of the Iroquois.

From the time of contact through the early national period, Iroquois negotiators carefully crafted and forged a place for their communities during a time of unprecedented upheaval. Their primary concerns were often regional, their conflict resolution patterns ancient. By the eighteenth century, however, Iroquois leaders faced new obstacles. With their homelands threatened and population on a dramatic decline, they met local concerns with strategies of continental proportions. In fact, when European negotiators met Iroquois headmen to discuss trade, land transactions, war, and peace, both sides angled with a firm understanding of the other's cultural characteristics, procedures, and intentions. Therefore, to write the Iroquois into the history of early America we must attempt to understand the origins and evolution of the methods of communication between the various groups. Appreciation of the historical agency of both European and indigenous populations cannot be complete without an explanation of the intricacies of cross-cultural diplomacy throughout the northeastern borderlands.[2]

The diplomatic mechanisms the Six Nations used to resolve issues "might well be an Example to the European Nations," colonial politician and intellectual Cadwallader Colden remarked in 1727.[3] The Great Laws of Peace, or He Gayanashagowa, have long remained a fundamental component in resolving conflicts among the Iroquois and a spiritual cornerstone preserving the history of a people.[4] Though the exact date remains debatable, oral and early written histories have preserved rich accounts of the events. According to nineteenth-century linguist Horatio Hale, the story of the Great Laws begins sometime during the middle of the fifteenth century.[5] In his account of the legend, Hale records that for centuries prior to the Great Laws the Five Nations fought with one another and the surrounding tribes. At the height of conflict, the eastern tribes (Mohawks, Oneidas, Onondagas) were suffering from an extended war with one another and the coastal nations, and the Senecas and Cayugas had similar problems with confederacies to the west. According to Iroquois oral history, the Indian Peacemaker Dekanawidah rose above the conflict and traveled with Hiawatha among the nations urging resolution. After the Mohawks and Oneidas accepted the Peacemaker's message, the prophet traveled to the Onondagas. When he reached the Onondagas, Atotarho, a ruthless headman who ruled the nation with an iron first, refused to relinquish his power. Compromising, Dekanawidah promised Atotarho that the Onondagas would forever maintain control over the Council Fire, keeping the oral record the Five Nations. After Atotarho agreed, the Dekanawidah called the five warring nations together, buried their weapons under the Tree of Peace, and set the foundation to a method of peaceful resolution—also known as the Great Laws. The spread of the Laws is worthy of further exploration, because it is the method of intertribal resolution the Five Nations of the Iroquois League agreed upon that remains central to this study.[6]

The call to assemble to resolve a dispute was initiated by a message carried on a string or belt of wampum, which cleared the road to allow peaceful passage to the designated council fire at Onondaga, or *katsihstakéhõ?*.[7] Singing would be heard as the approaching participants engaged in event-specific song. Often the chanting of the names of the Iroquois League's founding chiefs would be heard as the respected sachems arrived at the great council fire. According to some scholars, the traditional council consisted of fifty chiefs each representing a matrilineage within one of the founding nations of the League. The Senecas had eight representatives, the Mohawks and Oneidas nine, the Cayugas ten, and the Onondagas fourteen.[8] These "civil" chiefs, or sachems, were often distinct from their "war" chief counterparts and "were to be confirmed in their offices by the General Council of the League," also known as the Grand Council. Despite the obvious numerical disparity, the power of the Grand Council was, theoretically, equally shared among the original Five Nations when they met to discuss the affairs of the League.[9] To be sure, the number of tribal appointments varied between nations from time to time, but the principle of cooperation, guided by ritualistic protocol, remained the foundational principle of the Great Laws.

When the participants arrived, each tribe was greeted by the "At the Wood's Edge" ceremony, which offered condolences for the losses suffered by the respective tribe since their last gathering. The ritualistic "covering of the dead" played an important role in Iroquois culture and negotiation protocol. The "Three Bare Words" were spoken, metaphorically clearing their eyes, ears, and throats to allow for unhampered deliberations. This constituted the first part of the "Requickening Address." A roll call of chiefs soon followed, as did the "Six Songs," all of which called upon the strength and wisdom of the League's founders as the chiefs prepared for deliberations. This was followed by the installation of any new chiefs, who often took the place and name of past council chiefs. A wampum record of the events was prominently displayed and songs of peace sung. The process took those involved though a metaphorical transformation. Evil thoughts were purged and any obstructions cleared from the body.

The participants recalled past friendships, figuratively covered the dead, renewed camaraderie by shining the friendship chain, dispelled the clouds in the sky in order to restore the sun, and rekindled the council fire. In this respect, the Iroquois and their League would continue for time immemorial.[10]

After at least one night of rest and informal greetings, divided by intertribal association the appointed councilors sat on two opposing sides of the fire. The first moiety included the Mohawks and Senecas, the gatekeepers of the metaphorical longhouse, and the Onondagas, the "firekeepers." They addressed the congregated Oneidas and Cayugas on the other side of the fire as "you, our children," who in turn addressed the Mohawk, Seneca, and Onondaga representatives as "our father's kinsmen."[11] The Tuscaroras, the sixth nation to enter into the Iroquois union in the early 1720s, had limited and indirect input into the decision-making process.

Next, ancestral laws and customs were recited and forgiveness for past injustices requested. Negotiations then began with the Mohawk chiefs, the first nation to embrace the message of the Peacemaker. After agreeing on a statement, a Mohawk speaker conveyed their decision to the Senecas, the last nation to bury the war hatchet and join the Iroquois League. Once the Senecas agreed, or a compromise was reached, the speaker of the first moiety, usually a Mohawk, announced the decision to the chiefs of the opposite side of the council fire. Wampum belts and strings that encoded the message were held by the speaker and passed over the fire. The Oneidas and Cayugas listened, supposedly without interruption, and acknowledged the message by touching and returning the wampum to the speaker. In a similar fashion of deliberation, and often a day later, the Oneidas and Cayugas conversed and when they reached an agreement announced their sentiment to the Onondagas—the designated mediators of the deliberations. Officially, the Onondagas' decision stood as the final verdict unless they decided to resubmit the matter to the chiefs for another round of deliberation.[12] Theoretically, the council deliberations remained open until the issue at hand was resolved or an agreement of deferment reached. Finally, after formal condolences and treaty negotiations, a public feast and presentation of gifts were arranged to conclude the negotiations.[13]

The process of negotiation and deliberation no doubt varied depending on the immediate circumstances. Like the Iroquois union itself, protocol altered over time. Both were processes rather than organizations and events set in stone. This was especially the case after contact with Europeans. Mohawk influence among the Iroquois, for instance, grew considerably during the seventeenth century after contact with French and Dutch (and later English) traders. By the middle of eighteenth century, however, the western nations, the Senecas in particular, began to exercise more tangible authority among their brethren as a result of numerical superiority, land possession, and trade alternatives, among other factors. Thus, depending on the issue at hand, regional interests among the Iroquois impacted council negotiations, protocol, and the decisions of the Grand Council. That being said, the negotiation protocol, even if loosely observed and always evolving, increasingly provided the foundation for cross-cultural exchange patterns throughout the northeastern borderlands. And as this use of the method of communication increased, so too did the claims of its indigenous creators. To be sure, peace had brought power and security to five once-warring nations. Centuries later, many of those same nations sought to secure a future by making the most of their place at the council fires of the northeastern borderlands.

The roots of what Fenton unfortunately called "forest diplomacy" can be traced to an "entrenched piece of Iroquois political ritual, the Condolence Ceremony for the mourning of dead chiefs and the installation of successors." Although traditional greetings and expressions remained intact, instead of dividing by intertribal association participants would often separate into two lines, as dictated by one's affiliation with Europeans or with the indigenes, on each side of the council fire. The dynamic among the nations of the League remained intact as the Iroquois treated with the newcomers. Similar to traditional verbatim recall, each point made was repeated and summarized while the speaker confirmed the message on wampum. By linking proposals to answers, "wampum functioned to regulate the ongoing speech event, and, in the end, to leave each side with a mnemonic record of the proceedings."[14]

Essentially there existed four basic rules to initiating indigenous-European council procedures. First, the hosts delivered a ceremonial welcome. Next, the visiting participants answered the ceremonial welcome and expected hospitality. Then, the fire was kindled as the petitioners set the agenda of the council and proposed the first point of negotiation. Finally, the respondents answered all proposals made by the petitioners before introducing their own business. By the mid-seventeenth century, this basic protocol for treaty negotiations had spread throughout the northeast, southeast, and Great Lakes region. By then "plumed and painted Indian chiefs met frocked and bewigged white men in what must count as one of the most interesting examples of a contact phenomenon in the early history of Indian-white relations."[15]

Related to this, we must also not forget that the term "treaty" in early America did not exclusively denote the confirmation of a signed contract between the appointed representatives of two or more nations. A treaty, Francis Prucha remarks, also included the "'act of negotiating,' the discussion aimed at adjustment of difference or the reaching of an agreement, and by extension the meeting itself at which such negotiations took place." Consequently, for European and later American statesmen, the term itself also meant the process of "'holding a treaty,' 'inviting the Indians to a treaty,' providing provisions 'for a treaty' or greeting Indians as they arrived 'at a treaty.'"[16]

By the mid-eighteenth century, documented ceremonial and treaty practices throughout eastern regions of North America reveal the dissemination and use of Iroquois protocol and the multiple meanings of "treaty" itself. In Six Nations country, parameters had expanded to include a British element. Two fires officially burned—one at Onondaga, the ancient heart of the Iroquois longhouse, and the other at Johnson Hall, the impressive Mohawk River valley manor of Sir William Johnson, the superintendent of Indian affairs for the northern colonies. By building negotiations on a foundation of Iroquois language and rituals, indigenous delegates and middlemen created an acceptable "protocol of intercultural diplomacy" that British colonial rulers warmly welcomed.[17] The system was welcomed because it served not only the Grand Council's claim to vast territories and image of themselves as continental overlords but also those of the

British colonizers who sought alliances to advance their own imperial goals. Securing allies also entailed following elements of ceremonial etiquette—namely, gift giving, a practice that had become lavish with the arrival of Europeans.[18]

Gift giving among indigenous societies had a long and multifaceted history prior to European contact. Because gifts served a variety of functions in American Indian communities, they were regularly exchanged. Gifts were used to signify prestige and authority, to maintain loyalty and respect, to bribe, to pay tribute, to declare war, and to condole the families of those who died. The French were the first to adopt and redefine the practice of gift giving to solidify and establish friendships in the region.[19] As French and English authorities competed for empire, the availability, quality, and quantity of gifts became increasingly important. "Castor hats trimmed with lace, gaudy waistcoats, brightly colored strouds . . . scalping knives, bullet molds, and vermilion war paint . . . wampum, duck shot, tin pots, needles, thread and scissors" were among a list of items used to reaffirm or gain alliances. But gifts were costly, and British authorities conscious of the debts incurred during the Seven Years' War eventually tightened the purse strings.

The failure to maintain a fair and constant supply of goods for gifts had devastating effects.[20] One aspect of the Uprising of 1763 (known as "Pontiac's") showed the cost of curtailing gifts. When Europeans failed to distribute the appropriate gifts and respect indigenous land claims, Great Lakes and Ohio peoples interpreted neglect as a failure to maintain an alliance and viewed the inaction as European disregard for their important role. The strategic and economic benefits gained from cross-cultural trade and negotiations were not restricted to Europeans. The impact of European commodities and the Atlantic market on indigenous societies was widespread. Few first nations, however, both exploited and were exploited by the situation more than the Iroquois.

Of the multitude of concepts, goods, and organisms that transformed traditional patterns of behavior, European diseases, market economies, and concepts of ownership and husbandry created circumstances that fueled tensions between competing peoples. Those tensions often erupted into conflict, and conflict led to death. For the Iroquois, because the "killing of a member of one group mandated revenge on the perpetrator's people," clashes over resources also provided forums through which young warriors sought to address past grievances, fulfill tribal obligations, and elevate their social status by demonstrating their courage and skill during battle.[21] By the mid-seventeenth century, however, these objectives became increasingly difficult as populations rapidly declined and nations divided over how to best cope with dramatically altering circumstances.

During the seventeenth century, the economic importance Europeans placed on pelts perhaps had the most extensive implications for the Iroquois and their immediate neighbors. Indigenous social and cultural traditions were altered to gain useful goods by satisfying European demands for furs. Although the "individualistic, profit-seeking values of Western European capitalism" did not completely replace traditional economic patterns, the impact of trade was significant. By the beginning of the seventeenth century, indigenous societies found it difficult to survive without the materials gained by trade with Europeans. In fact, coupled with the ecological impact of European farming and concepts of property ownership, maintaining traditional life patterns throughout northeastern borderlands became increasingly problematic.[22] As a result, existing enmity between indigenous communities increased as fewer and fewer of them competed fiercely for control over natural resources.[23]

By the mid-seventeenth century the French alliances that had maintained a firm grasp on northeastern trade were under attack by expanding Dutch settlements along the Hudson. During the 1640s the fur-bearing animals of the Hudson River valley had been depleted. Seeking further resources and armed with European weaponry, Iroquois war parties who had learned to use musket from the Mohawks ventured into the Ohio River valley and parts of the Great Lakes region.[24] The depopulated, disease-ravaged indigenous inhabitants—Hurons, Neutrals, Eries, and Susquehannocks—were no match for the European-armed Iroquois. For the next fifty years what historians have called the "Beaver Wars" raged as war parties raided enemy canoes and villages along the St. Lawrence and throughout the Great Lakes region. The wars changed tribal alignments and disrupted trade to Montréal and Trois-Rivières. Many affected tribes fled west of the Mississippi and into the Pays d'en haut, while others solidified their relations with the French of Canada in an attempt to defend against Iroquois aggression. By the late 1660s thirty years of conflict, "punctuated by short truces, consequently prevailed between New France and various members of the Five Nations, particularly the Mohawk."[25] Before the turn of the century, however, the Iroquois firearm advantage that had caused such disruption "was being lost as enemies supplied from New France, New England, and the Delaware and Chesapeake Bays caught up in the Native American arms race."[26] Tribal domains once again began to shift.

In 1664, a year after Louis XIV ordered thousands of French soldiers to North America with orders to eradicate the Iroquois, the Duke of York's English forces took control of New Netherlands. Within a couple of years the trading supplies that had flowed along the Hudson dwindled, along with the number of Iroquois. Almost a decade of war had ravaged them and depleted their villages. In fact, by 1660 raiding for captives to integrate in their communities was as important as foraging for furs. Both provided incentive to raise the hatchet. The enemies of the Iroquois in Canada recognized their weakness and struck hard. Villages were invaded and burned, and the French and French-allied tribes seized control of the Great Lakes region. From 1664 to 1667, Five Nations representatives sued for peace on multiple occasions with the French. Seizing the opportunity, as part of the negotiated truce, the French required that the Iroquois allow Jesuit missionaries into their villages. After convincing some tribes to convert, or at least to accept the apparent benefits of Catholicism, dozens of Iroquois opted to relocate to two main mission villages near Montréal. By the mid-1680s, these Kahnawake Mohawks (including some Onondagas), as they were soon called, had been deemed defectors by the Grand Council.

Meanwhile, the English began reestablishing a trading hub on the Hudson, Iroquois confidence and supplies had been slowly increasing. As a result, the balance of power in northeastern America again began to tip. By the early 1680s the Iroquois had resumed a series of campaigns against the Great Lakes peoples, but their struggle became increasingly tied to European interests as well. To reestablish themselves as the primary trading partners of the new occupants of New Netherlands, the eastern Iroquois nations sought to strengthen ties with the English. An agreement between Charles II and Louis XIV, however, prevented the English governor in New York, Edmund Andros, from lending support to the Iroquois in matters related to war. That changed in 1688 when William III seized the throne of England and extended the War of the League of Augsburg to North America. Although terms of peace were negotiated between European nations at Ryswick in 1697, the Iroquois and their neighbors continued to clash. Outnumbered, the Five Nations suffered a series of catastrophic defeats during the final decade of the seventeenth century. Pulled between new relations with the English at Albany and the need for peace with the French to the north, from "1699 to 1701 Iroquois ambassadors . . . threaded the thickets of domestic factionalism and shuttled between their country and the Euro-American colonies to negotiate . . . 'The Grand Settlement of 1701.'"[27]

For two and a half centuries, the relationship between Europeans and the indigenous inhabitants of North America shifted because of four primary factors—restoration, trade, military allegiance, and land. According to Anthony F. C. Wallace, during the first half of the eighteenth century the major functions of Iroquois military diplomacy included the maintenance of "emotional equilibrium" for warriors seeking to avenge or replace murdered family; political influence over other tribal groups; and "to perpetuate a political situation in which the threat of retaliation against either party could be used to play off the British and the French against one another."[28] Realizing that neither the French nor the English had the ability to attain definitive control over the other, the Grand Council knew that "acknowledging any governor exclusively as greatest lord was suicidal—particularly if that meant getting involved in imperial warfare."[29] Evidence of the pliable diplomacy of the Iroquois was best illustrated at the turn of the century.

In August 1701, Five Nations representatives along with others met Louis-Hector de Callière in Montréal and assured the governor of New France that the Iroquois would remain east of Detroit and maintain a policy of nonintervention in any future conflict between European powers in North America. After a few further days of private

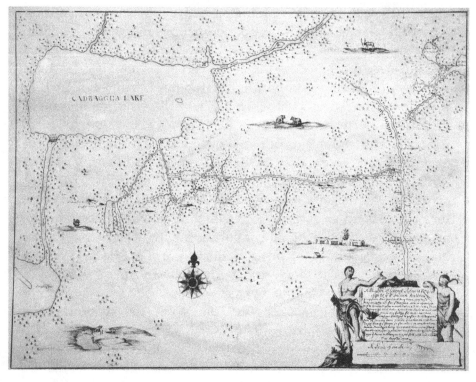

"A mappe of Colonel Romers voyage to ye 5 Indian Nations," by Colonel Wolf-gang Römer, 1700. Courtesy of the New York State Library.

deliberations, the then Five Nations agreed to terms of a Grande Paix.[30] At the same time, however, two other delegations of Iroquois headmen negotiated claim and trading rights over the same territory with the English at Albany and Philadelphia. The move was strategic, not coincidental. Daniel Richter elaborates: "In giving each imperial power an equivalent paper claim to the same territory (territory that the Iroquois themselves did not control), this 'Grand Settlement of 1701' promised to counter power with power and to preserve Iroquois independence through a new, far more subtle form of accommodation. In theory, each empire now had a stake in preserving Iroquois economic interests as well as peace between the Five Nations and its erstwhile Indian enemies."[31]

The turn of the century brought changes to Iroquois diplomacy. The negotiations of 1701 marked military defeat, but it also created opportunity for the Five Nations. Mounting tension between French and English allowed a reassertion of indigenous authority in the unfolding affairs. Instead of brute force, however, diplomatic schemers and clever cross-cultural brokers increasingly replaced raiding parties. A "Confederacy" of Iroquois emerged, and its mouthpiece, the Grand Council, increasingly armed itself with diplomatic mechanisms and language much more familiar to its European counterparts. It was a balancing act carefully calculated by the Iroquois, especially those communities still residing in the metaphorical longhouse—and those living close to Europeans, in particular. This tactic, however, came with inherent problems. The subsequent shifting between English and French imperial designs to situate themselves strategically meant that the words of the Grand Council often conflicted with actions of many Iroquois communities. But as the indigenous advocates of Iroquois hegemony increasingly realized the benefits of perception and a closer relationship with the English Crown, the marginalization of "dissident" regional actions paralleled the rise of the Iroquois Confederacy. As a result, by the middle of the eighteenth century the Grand Council had become as much an instrument of peacekeeping as it had of imperial enterprising. As we see in the following chapters, the Council's authority on the continent, both constructed and imagined, rested with that of the Crown. But without imperial backers it would wane along with the power of those Iroquois communities that allied themselves with the British.

CHAPTER 2

THE CARRYING PLACE, WAR, AND THE OHIO COUNTRY

The Five Nations' defeat at the hands of their European and indigenous enemies at the turn of the century may have set back the myth of a "Iroquois Empire," but it did not stop the Grand Council from perpetuating the idea of their irreplaceable importance. Meanwhile, the English, also having suffered a series of setbacks in North America, began to realize the increasing benefit of recognizing the Iroquois as primary players in the extension of empire. Chief among the potential indigenous benefactors were the Mohawks and other eastern Iroquois who had benefited from, and thus struggled to maintain, strong ties with European middlemen along the Hudson River valley.[1] Lands could be claimed and ceded through right of conquest, and the implications of this idea did not escape either party. If the British Crown intended to use past "conquests" to aid its continental ambitions, the Grand Council would make sure it took advantage of any imperial designing. A series of negotiations with the Five Nations at Albany, New York, during the first three decades of the eighteenth century confirmed the Crown's intent to work with the Grand Council to stake its claims to a larger New World empire. In fact, at the Treaty of Utrecht in 1713 the French acknowledged the Iroquois to be within an English orbit.[2] This formal recognition is telling of tribal realities given the existence of Catholic Mohawk settlements at Kahnawake, St. Regis, and Oka, along the St. Lawrence. But for French imperial planners, like the British, "Iroquois" usually referred to the pro-British communities, the Mohawk River valley communities in particular. Past conflicts and associations influenced perceptions and policy. Mending fences among indigenous factions in order to perpetuate certain appearances was left to Indian agents and missionaries. By the turn of the century the French realized that they needed to tread carefully while negotiating ground with the Grand Council. A wrong move could alienate their longtime Algonquian and Huron allies. The Iroquois had been humbled. For the time being, the neutralized threat south of the Great Lakes would cater to the expansion of French influence and trade in North America.

The prospect of losing their place as benefactors of commerce and trade in early America impelled many Iroquois communities, including many Oneidas, to foster closer ties with the British. In this vein, treaty negotiations between the Crown and eastern Iroquois representatives in the period 1727–54 can be better understood as regional maneuvering prior to the formalization of an agreement that would bind, by formal treaty if not widespread perception, the Grand Council and the English Crown. This union, in both perception and reality, was facilitated by the arrival of William Johnson and the events of the Seven Years' War. In this light, diverse council fire rhetoric that included mention of the Covenant Chain being broken must been seen as a part of two decades of jockeying between negotiators that ended with the formalization of an alliance in 1758 at the Treaty of Easton. The Easton agreement may not have been a forgone conclusion, but its terms underscored the mutually reinforcing needs of colonial administrators and most of their Iroquois neighbors.

This partnership, albeit problematic at times, was formalized during the Seven Years' War. With many of their homes and villages on the front lines, the Grand Council agreed to a British military buildup in the region and land cessions in the Ohio Country. Crucial to supply lines and communication was the Oneida Carry. Not surprisingly, the subsequent increase of a European presence created a growing sense of uneasiness at the Carry. The situation was compounded in March 1756, a year after Crown forces had erected Fort Bull on Wood Creek, when indigenous and French forces reduced the outpost to ashes. The attack widened the continental struggle that erupted between the French and the British two years before when a young Virginian colonel was beaten from the Ohio Country. The ensuing conflict may have curbed trade over the Oneida Carry, but it did not diminish the importance of the location. In fact, only two years after the French razed Fort Bull British engineers under the command of Gen. John Stanwix returned to the Carry to begin construction of what would become one of the most formidable English posts in colonial America—Fort Stanwix.

For centuries prior to European contact, the Oneida Carry bridged worlds. Known to the first peoples as Deo-Wain-Sta, the portage provided the shortest distance between the trickling headwaters of Wood Creek and the Mohawk River, thus linking Lake Ontario to the Hudson River. Because the two swampy flatlands between these headwaters connected the Great Lakes to the Atlantic Ocean, the location remained invaluable to the exchange of goods and information. Navigated by indigenous traders, marauding armies, and migratory communities since time immemorial, the portage rested in the heart of Iroquois territory. By the end of the fifteenth century, those first peoples who called the region home and exercised control over the portage were known as the Oneidas. Much as the Mohawk River valley helped shape the regional identification of the eastern gatekeepers of the Iroquois League, the Carry did the same for the area's local inhabitants. The Oneida Carry also provided an important resource for the overseers of the portage. By the middle of the seventeenth century, for a negotiated price seasoned indigenous navigators and pack carriers could be seen shuttling merchandise for European traders across what the Dutch called the Trow Plat. And, as trade increased along with the reach of European goods and people, so too did the traffic at the Carry.[3]

In the winter months of 1634/5, perhaps the first Europeans to traverse the portage (unknowingly) made their way northwest from the Dutch trading hub of Fort Orange. Guided by five Mohawks, Dutch West India Company agent Harmen Meyndertsz van den Bogaert, along with Willem Tomassen and Jeronimus de Lecroix, ventured in deep snow as far as the Oneida village of Onneyuttehage on the shores of Oneida Creek. Tasked with rekindling trading alliances and finding out why the flow of furs to Fort Orange had diminished, van den Bogaert recorded in his journal of the forty-day voyage the earliest known account of Iroquois communities west of present-day Albany, New York. A brief stay at Onneyuttehage helped to counter the recent overtures of French traders and emissaries, but it did not help answer the visitors' topographical inquiries. Van den Bogaert, and subsequent expeditions by Dutch investigators and renegade traders over the course of the next three decades, did not make specific mention of the Oneida Carry. In fact, according to Gilbert Hagerty, "until the English took over from the Dutch there are no records to show that Oneida Carry was known to the whites."[4]

However, sometime during the last three decades of the seventeenth century, the Carrying Place became a region of interest to both French and English colonizers. With peace in 1674 after the Treaty of Westminster that ended the Third Anglo-Dutch War came the expansion of trade throughout the northeastern borderlands. Interestingly, as early as 1688 a French mapmaker, Jean-Baptiste Louis Franquelin, made specific reference to the "portage" that bridged Lake Oneida and the Mohawk River. By the end of the following year, the French had built a small post to protect the location.[5] Aware that the extension of trade was crucial to securing indigenous allies, English authorities authorized several expeditions into the heart of Iroquoia to counter the growing French influence. One of the first voyages was undertaken by the Crown's chief military engineer, the Dutch-born Col. Wolfgang William Römer.

After spending a decade in Europe as a military engineer in the army of William III, in 1698 Römer found himself on his way to North America with the newly appointed governor of New York, Lord Bellomont. Two years later, after surveying the coastal region and Hudson River, Römer led a three-man expedition into western New York. They followed trading routes from Albany that now snaked themselves beyond van den Bogaert's earlier expedition to the shores of Lake Oneida. In September 1700, while on their way to the "Onondaga Castle" to search for a site to erect a British fort, Römer's expedition moved west along the Mohawk River. Before arriving at "Oneyda" the men had visited Mohawk strongholds at Schenectady and Canajoharie. On 20 September 1700, after meeting with the Mohawk sachem Onoronorum just west of Canajoharie, Römer's expedition arrived at Wood Creek. Tasked with recording "the country as you

"Carte de l'Amerique Septentrionnale," and detail, by Jean-Baptiste Louis Franquelin, 1688. Courtesy of the Library of Congress, Geography and Map Division, digital ID g3300 ct000668.

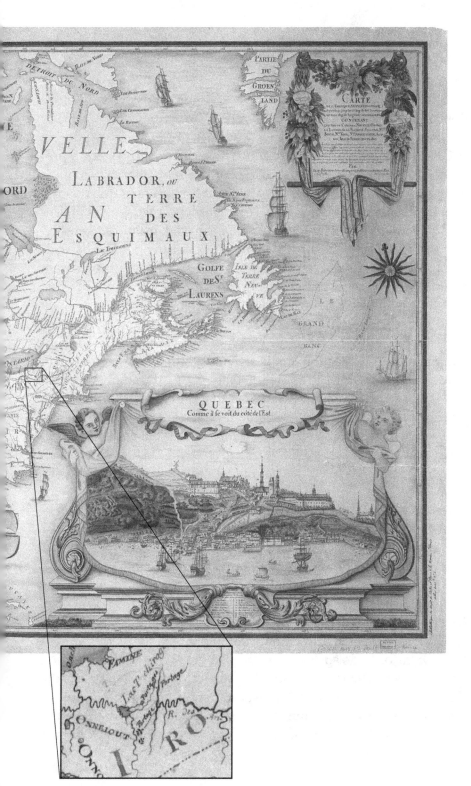

go and come" in order to assess the accessibility of the region, Römer noted the following: "We came by a most miserable path to the Carry Place."[6] He made no mention of a French trading post. Nevertheless, Römer could not deny the strategic importance of the Carry and made mention of such after slugging his way back to Albany.[7]

Less than two years later, in July 1702, Miami and Seneca representatives from the western reaches of the metaphorical Iroquois longhouse petitioned Edward Hyde, the third Earl of Clarendon and appointed governor of New York. No doubt concerned with establishing an easily accessible trade route to Albany, the Iroquois requested that the province blaze a permanent path over the portage by widening the passage and removing the fallen trees and brush from Wood Creek. The governor agreed and promised to cover the cost of guides who would bring the western traders to Albany. It appears that the governor kept his word. Four years later, Iroquois representatives wrote him, thanking the province for clearing and maintaining the Carry. Such action, the indigenous authors suggested, "will induce and encourage the far Indians to come to trade here which will engage them to be firmly united to us." The enlargement and clearing of the Carry paralleled similar trends taking place along the fertile flats beyond Schenectady and throughout the upper Mohawk River valley. And when traders began to cross the Oneida Carry much more frequently, the Oneidas did not let the new opportunities pass them by.[8]

As early as 1727, the province of New York endorsed the construction of a small, fortified trading post at the mouth of the Oswego River on Lake Ontario. Over the next two decades, as the importance of trade and regional domination increased, so too did that of the Carry. English engineers reinforced the post at Oswego and oversaw the building of stockades at the falls of Oswego and at both ends of Lake Oneida. To undercut French designs in the region, the English realized the need to maintain a strong foothold on the southern shores of Lake Ontario. To do so, however, they had to secure communication lines between Schenectady and Oswego. Consequently, the use of the Carry became central to the transportation of goods and a topic of interest at Albany. The commissioners for Indian affairs started paying particular attention to the area after forty-seven traders petitioned colonial authorities to intervene because the "Indians were making too much of a good thing of their situation at the Carrying Place."[9] To be sure, the Oneidas (along with local Onondaga and Seneca cargo carriers) recognized the value of their services and would not transport, or allow the transportation of, goods over the Carry without receiving proper compensation.[10]

In 1710 four indigenous representatives arrived in London with former Albany mayor Peter Schuyler. Known as the Iroquois Kings, or Four Indian Kings (only three were actually from the Five Nations), the visitors enjoyed the pleasantries of English society, including a Shakespearean play, cockfighting, and an audience with Queen Anne. Schuyler, concerned with Albany's vulnerability to French aggression from the north, used the publicity to press the Crown for aid. Meanwhile, the visitors took the opportunity to establish themselves of heads of state. Arguably, this marked the "heyday of the Iroquois," as the projected image of an authoritative Iroquois Confederacy increasingly found imperial backers in London.[11]

In 1747 a London-based publisher printed *The History of the Five Nations* by New York politician and scholar Cadwallader Colden. Written over two decades before, the brief history of the Iroquois in the New York region became a staple reference for colonial administrators on both sides of the Atlantic. In short, the work helped revive the idea of Iroquois authority. Colden, who wrote the first section of the two-part history in 1727, concluded the work during King George's War. He presented the Iroquois as exemplars of indigenous military and diplomatic ability. By referring to seventeenth-century wars between tribes and the "Great Laws of the Iroquois," Colden's rendition of events accented the history of Iroquois dominance over their indigenous neighbors. Moreover, the work employed an eighteenth-century European social model to describe—incorrectly—a people, society, and continent. Colden referred to "Indian Castles," "Kings," and "Conquest." As a result, *History of the Five Nations* not only represents one of the earliest documented accounts of these indigenous peoples but also expresses the willingness of the colonial administration to accept and perpetuate an inflated idea of Iroquois power. Each side viewed the other as an instrument for securing a degree of sovereignty

for itself on the continent. The reciprocal arrangement began to mate-
rialize in the late 1720s and 1730s, as both the Grand Council and the
Crown struggled to gain control over hostile neighbors.

Because neither the Grand Council nor the English Crown could
establish hegemony over their troublesome North American neighbors without the aid of the other, they had much to gain by working
in concert. The Iroquois needed the threat of the English to legitimize their authority and secure their future, while the Crown sought
an ally to curb French expansion, acquire lands, and pacify hostile
first nations.[12] The need appeared mutual, but maintaining the agreements that bound indigenous and white interests was often a delicate
task. Often brokering "official" agreements were middlemen versed
in negotiation and human exchange that forged alliances by traversing multiple worlds.[13] Among the most respected in Six Nations country during the eighteenth century was the superintendent of Indian
affairs, Sir William Johnson.

William Johnson has received a considerable amount of scholarly
attention.[14] In 1738, at the age of twenty-three, Johnson left his home
in County Meath, Ireland, and sailed to British America. He decided
to accept an offer from his uncle, Vice-Admiral Peter Warren, to manage an estate near Fort Hunter in the Mohawk Valley. With capital
supplied by his uncle, Johnson soon rose to prominence in the region
as a respected businessman. According to a biographer, "expan-
sive generosity came naturally to [Johnson]. He would instruct his
overseer to be strict in collecting debts, but respond in person to
every story of misfortune." Johnson's greatest asset was his ability
to traverse indigenous and white worlds with ease. He maneuvered
among, worked with, and employed mainly the eastern Six Nations.[15]
"Unlike most colonists, who disdained the original inhabitants of the
region, Johnson took pains to learn their customs and their words.
Remarkably accessible and relatively fair, he impressed the local
Mohawks, who ritually adopted him with the apt name Warraghi-
yagey, which meant "a man who undertakes great things."[16] Timothy
Shannon agrees: "Johnson spoke to the Indians in their own way in
actions and appearances as well as words. He made a constant effort
to transact his business in the Indians' cultural context."[17] By the end
of 1739, after Johnson purchased prime acreage on the Mohawk River

directly from his Iroquois associates, he commenced building a trading enterprise.[18]

Within six years he had another trading depot at Oswego, con-
tracts for imports, supply shops on the King's Road, and a close relationship with the local population. Johnson funneled thousands of
pounds worth of English goods through the Mohawk River valley.
He made a fortune by supplying the region and transporting goods to
New York, the West Indies, and London. He also built strong relations
with the regional Mohawks. In 1746, Johnson, the newly appointed
justice of the peace for Albany County and Indian agent, attended one
of the first documented Six Nations council fires on behalf of New
York governor George Clinton. Hoping to secure Iroquois support for
war against France, the governor sent Johnson with several Mohawk
representatives to Onondaga.[19]

Though the Iroquois officially maintained a policy of neutrality
during the War of Austrian Succession (1740–48; better known in
America as King George's War, 1744–48), Johnson's influence with the
eastern Six Nations grew considerably over the next decade. So too
did their influence over Johnson.[20] The king awarded Johnson a baronetcy for his role in the 1755 Battle of Lake George. Recognizing the
importance of gift giving and personal politicking, Sir William spent
a considerable fortune outfitting and supplying his indigenous associates to keep the eastern Six Nations happy and closely tied to the
English Crown. In 1747 alone, the Indian agent expensed more than
£3,500 on gifts—seven times more than the sum the New York assembly annually allotted their Indian commissioners in Albany. Most of
those goods were dispersed from Johnson Hall.[21] From 1748 to 1754,
as Johnson's fortune increased, so did his status. Alan Taylor hits the
mark when he states that, by the 1750s, "Sir William Johnson became
the most famous American in the British Empire. Not even the ama-
teur scientist and professional lobbyist Benjamin Franklin could com-
pare. George Washington, a wealthy planter and provincial politician
in Virginia, lagged far behind."[22] Johnson could not, however, have
risen to such prominence without gaining the trust of those around
him. Helping him considerably in his New World endeavors was his
1759 marriage to a prominent Mohawk woman named Molly Brant
(Konwatsi'tsiaienni and Degonwadonti).

Molly Brant became Johnson's publicly recognized partner after the death of his first wife, Catherine Weisenberg. Johnson first met Molly along with her bother Joseph at Canajoharie during one of his many visits there. In 1753, Brant Canagaraduncka, a well-respected Mohawk sachem and trusted friend of Johnson, married Owandah, the widowed mother of Molly and Joseph. Not long thereafter, Johnson and Molly became intimate. In 1759, Molly gave birth to Peter Warren Johnson, the first of nine children she would have with William. Widely recognized as Johnson's wife, Molly Brant acted as an indispensable conduit to the indigenous world Johnson, and many of his European contemporaries, depended on.

When Molly moved permanently to Fort Johnson, Joseph accompanied her. Acting as a father to Joseph, William Johnson took an early interest in the life of his wife's younger brother. In 1761, Johnson arranged for Joseph to be educated at the predecessor of Dartmouth College, Eleazar Wheelock's "Moor's Indian Charity School" in Connecticut. There, under the direct supervision of Wheelock, Brant absorbed British customs, learning to speak, read, and write in English. When Brant returned to the Mohawk River valley during the Uprising of 1763, he came armed with the tools to traverse multiple worlds. The relationship between Johnson and Molly, and later her brother Joseph, proved critical to the maintenance and extension of both Crown and Iroquois authority. But their authority did not go uncontested, especially when it came to projecting power. Few other places illustrate the impact of imagined authority and empire as well as the Ohio Country.[23]

During the early decades of the eighteenth century, the Ohio Country provided geographic and cultural security to several first peoples. Although claimed by the Iroquois, the region "was less an Iroquois empire than a refuge" for those nations dislodged and exploited by agreements reached between British and Iroquois negotiators. Resentment toward their exploiters, as a result, flourished throughout the Ohio and southern Great Lakes region. The Hurons, for instance, who had been forced to retreat from southern Ontario during the Beaver Wars, maintained strong ties with French traders and missionaries throughout the first half of the eighteenth century. Actually, in 1701 the Hurons pledged alliance to the French after Antoine Laumet de la Mothe Cadillac built Fort Pontchartrain and opened an outpost at Detroit to trade. In 1738 under the direction of Nicholas Orontony, a contingent of Hurons migrated to the Ohio Country and settled only a couple miles south of present-day Sandusky. They joined other displaced Petuns and together became known as the Wyandots. Furthermore, the Shawnees left for the region in the mid-1730s in response to pressure from increased European settlement in Virginia and Pennsylvania. Soon strong relationships were forged between these peoples and the local *coureurs de bois*. The relationship made English authorities wary.[24]

In 1732, Governor Clinton informed the Shawnees that he had heard of their recent visit to Montréal. When asked to move their wives and children from the Ohio Country back to Pennsylvania under the protection of Thomas Penn, the Shawnees declined. They cited anxiety over settler demands but assured the governor that their nation would not be swayed by French overtures. For the Shawnees, it was apparent that trade with the French had its benefits. The recently founded town at the mouth of the Scioto, for instance, flourished by the 1730s. In addition, the Shawnees organized themselves into a quasi-republic, kindled a council fire, and cast off all claims of the Six Nations to administrate their affairs.[25]

The Shawnees were not the only nation willing to subvert the authoritative claims of the Iroquois and their European allies. In April 1728, Delaware anger over trader abuses and settler encroachments filtered back to Governor Clinton. Instead of appealing to the Six Nations for their brokerage, as was expected, the Delawares took matters into their own hands. News that Delaware chief Manawkyhiekon sought Miami support to revenge the death of his relative Wequeabay worried colonial authorities about a possible rupture with the locals. Moreover, Sassoonan, "King of the Delawares," visited Philadelphia and complained about settler encroachments. Sassoonan lamented that he had grown old and was troubled by the lack of compensation the Delawares had received for the increasing Christian incursions. The chief called into question the sale of lands between the Susquehanna and Delaware rivers, sparking the examination of previous treaties.[26] Delaware efforts to secure their homelands were dealt a fatal blow in 1737 when Pennsylvania authorities established claim over hundreds of thousands of acres during the

infamous Walking Purchase.[27] In the end it appeared Manawkyhiekon had reason to question the quality of the Grand Council's brokerage, for Iroquois middlemen had supported the blatant play for
Delaware territory. Ordered by Iroquois and provincial proprietors
from their ancient lands, by the end of the decade many Delawares
sought refuge among like-minded communities in the Ohio Country.
Another faction headed northeast to Shamokin on the Susquehanna,
later to be widely recognized as the followers of the controversial
leader Teedyuscung.[28]

Distanced from the policies of Onondaga, Albany, and Philadelphia,
by the mid-1740s the Miamis, Wyandots, Delawares, and Shawnees
were thriving under increasing levels of socioeconomic sovereignty.[29]
As the region increasingly played host to English and French designs,
many of the loosely tied Ohio nations benefited from their newfound
positions of strategic imperial and economic importance.[30]

By the mid-1740s, the French had established a loose network
of trading posts that maintained vital lines of communication and
trade stretching from New France to the Mississippi. Supported by
the majority of the local indigenous inhabitants, a French presence in
the Ohio River valley threatened to hem in the English colonies by
blocking droves of traders and settlers from moving west beyond the
Appalachians. The dynamics of the Ohio Country began to change
significantly, however, after King George's War and the fall of Louisbourg in June 1745. French supplies began to dry up, which created a
lucrative opportunity for English traders and the Crown. Many Ohio
nations began to assume a fluid allegiance in order to gain the most
from a courtship by the two competing suitors. The availability and
price of goods went a long way to secure indigenous favor, and thus
imperial ambitions.[31] As a result, by the late 1740s more and more
tribes found themselves within the English commercial orbit, as traders such as George Croghan pushed deeper into the Ohio.[32]

According to Alfred Cave, "the story of Anglo-American Ohio
begins with George Croghan."[33] Born in Ireland, likely during the
early 1720s, Croghan emigrated to British North America in 1742, perhaps due to hardships.[34] Within a few years he had acquired almost
1,200 acres of land in the Condigwinet Valley with trader William
Trent and organized Pennsborough Township in Lancaster County,

in the province of Pennsylvania.[35] Not content with the prospect of a storekeeper's life and small landholdings, Croghan soon ventured to the northeastern borderlands with aspirations of gaining a fortune by trading with the local residents. By the fall of 1744 he had established a trading house at the Seneca village at the mouth of the Cuyahoga River, present-day Cleveland.[36] For the next decade Croghan traded goods with Ohio peoples and acted as an unofficial agent for the province of Pennsylvania. During this time he forged trading relationships with the indigenous populations in the region, learning how to conduct business in several Iroquoian and Algonquian languages and dialects. Similar to traders before him, Croghan wed a daughter of a Mohawk chief, named Nicolas. The union gave him further access to trade.[37]

Pennsylvania traders, led by Croghan, established a trading network that extended farther west than meaningful colonial authority. His post at the mouth of the Cuyahoga River challenged French claims to the trade of the region, and to their alliances with the region's villages. Croghan realized this and capitalized on the opportunity.[38] According to fellow Pennsylvanian trader John Patten, Croghan relentlessly urged those he traded with to destroy the French, not for glory or the English Crown but rather for economic concerns. "Self-interest," Patten later recalled, "was his sole motive in every thing he did . . . [as he tried] to engross the whole trade."[39] If personal financial opportunities fueled Croghan's commitment to represent provincial and Crown interests west of the Appalachians, it is also true that proprietary interests found his aggressive spirit useful. There were risks and prospects for all. In the end, those who dealt with Croghan were aware of the hazards of relying on such a "vile Rascal," as provincial secretary Richard Peters remarked in 1756.[40] Yet, given the circumstances of the mid-eighteenth century Pennsylvania and New York borderlands, Croghan was almost indispensable, and the best Sir William Johnson, colonial governors, and Whitehall could recruit. For those who wanted to influence and profit from the frontier but avoid venturing beyond the clearing, Croghan was the solution.

In July 1751 the Six Nations and Governor Clinton again met to discuss terms of cooperation to combat the growing tensions west of the Appalachians. Clinton warned the Six Nations delegation of French designs in the Ohio Country. He cautioned the Iroquois that they would "become weak . . . in the eyes of the neighboring nations" unless they combated the construction of French forts in region. In fact, Clinton warned that the "forts will be like bitts and bridles in their mouths, by which you and other Indian nations must turn, and go as the Gov. of Canada pleases." Furthermore, South Carolina representative William Bull Jr., son of the governor, pleaded with the Six Nations to plant the tree of peace among their southern neighbors, the Catawbas, Creeks, Chickasaws, Choctaws, and Cherokees. The English knew that peace among these populations would provide a stronger front against French expansion and calm an otherwise tense frontier. Well seasoned in diplomatic scheming, however, the Iroquois headmen were not easily goaded into action.[41]

After carefully weighing their options, the Six Nations representatives responded to the requests with bold (and perhaps strategically exaggerated) confidence. They informed Clinton that the French would not dare construct a fort without first approaching their chiefs. In fact, they did not hesitate to inform the English governor that a delegation of Iroquois had been sent to Montréal to meet with the governor of Canada to discuss the matter further. As for peace overtures with the southern groups, the Iroquois suggested that the pipe would not be smoked until the Catawbas returned all their prisoners to Canajoharie, as was customary. Furthermore, the Six Nations would also consider the provisional terms rendered void if the Crown did not appoint William Johnson as the conduit between indigenous and white worlds—a point Mohawk chief Hendrick (Theyanoquin) made quite clear: "We desire Col. Johnson may be reinstated; for as there is some of the six nations gone to Canada about the French building a fort at Oniagara; unless your Excellency appoints some person for us to go to, you can not expect to hear what answer they bring." Incapable of controlling the affairs of the Ohio nations through force, the eastern Iroquois were defining the place of the Grand Council in continental enterprising. It was a gamble, but the English could ill afford a complete break with these people.[42]

The Iroquois also attempted to utilize growing English presence in the area by pressing for the increase and regulation of trading goods.

In response, colonial administrators strengthened ties with traders in the Ohio Country. European goods arriving from the British empire were made available in villages such as Pickawillany. These villages had "half king" magistrates more receptive to the idea of an Iroquois Confederacy. Additionally, accessibility to goods bred regional dependence that might be exploited. Still, despite appearances and rhetoric, the Grand Council could not project hegemony over the region. In fact, rumor had it that even the Delawares of Shamokin were "open to a "favourable opportunity to throw off the Yoke . . . and to revenge the Insults that had been offered them at Philadelphia but two years before."[43] Thus, if the Grand Council decided to take part in a European war, they knew they risked open conflict with the Ohio nations and the Delawares as far east as the Susquehanna.[44] The Ohio nations and eastern Delawares, however, had to worry about the military might of the English. As a result of the temporary ascendancy of the British, between 1744 and 1754 the Ohio nations and eastern Delawares jockeyed for position by engaging in a series of treaties in an attempt to deal directly with the English Crown. Meanwhile, provincial authorities attempted to secure their own frontiers, while the Crown endeavored to formalize control over the Ohio Country and its inhabitants by bolstering the claims of the Grand Council.

On 4 July 1744 in Lancaster, Pennsylvania, Iroquois delegates met with representatives from Virginia, Maryland, New York, and Pennsylvania. In return for the resolution of land disputes in Maryland and Virginia, the Crown reasserted Six Nations' claims to overlordship of the Ohio River valley.[45] In return, along with £200 in gold, the Iroquois agreed to relinquish claim to disputed lands east of the Blue Ridge Mountains and into the Shenandoah Valley up to the Ohio River watershed. Aware that King George's War threatened to consume the northeastern borderlands, on the last day of the treaty Canassatec, the Iroquois speaker, made sure the assembled colonial representatives recognized the authority of the Six Nations. After mentioning that the Iroquois had forbade Onantio, the governor of Canada, from allowing soldiers to enter their territory to fight battles that could be conducted at sea, Canassatec paused, collected his thoughts, and "after some little Time" added: "The Six Nations have a great Authority and Influence over sundry Tribes of Indians in Alliance with the French, and particularly over the Praying Indians formerly a Part with our-selves, who stand in the very Gates of the French; and, to shew our further Care, we have engaged these very Indians; and other Indian Allies of the French for you. They will not join the French against you. They have agreed with us before we set out. We have put the spirit of Antipathy against the French in those People."[46]

Soon thereafter, Pennsylvania governor George Thomas "thanked [Canassatec] for the very agreeable Addition." By recognizing Iro-quois prominence, the council temporarily settled a brewing conflict between Virginia and the Iroquois that threatened to undermine the Crown's imperial designs, and Governor Thomas was also reassert-ing interest in trade and future land cessions in the region. But to minimize the threat of conflict, the Pennsylvanian reasoned, the prov-ince also had to deal directly with the Ohio nations. As a result, in November 1747 provincial negotiators engaged in direct discussions with the Ohioans. The move is telling, for it underscores the reali-ties of the northeastern borderlands. Fearful that an alliance between Ohio nations and the French would devastate provincial trade and threaten security, Pennsylvania presented the Ohio nations with £800 worth of gifts in return for a pledge of their allegiance and as a sign of goodwill to open up the region to trade.[47] The negotiations ushered in an era of extensive Pennsylvania-supplied trade, extending Eng-lish influence deep into the Ohio and southern Great Lakes region. Central to the supply of goods was the Philadelphia firm of Baynton and Wharton. In fact, aided by attacks on Saratoga and Schenectady, by 1748 Pennsylvania exports in fur to England surpassed those from New York.[48] But with increased trade came increased abuses.[49]

By the early eighteenth century, because waves of settlers followed close behind the advance of trade, the sale and acquisition of land began to dominate discussions concerning the northeastern bor-derlands. Indigenous ideas of land ownership and use were com-plex and varied across the nations. Nevertheless, the "intercultural" exchange of property occurred.[50] Conquest and sale were two of the ways tribal lands could change ownership. Both methods were often shrouded in ambiguity, confusion, and deceit. As a result, by the mid-eighteenth century a generation of disputes over the settlement and use of land in the heart of the Iroquois homelands created mistrust that spilled across the Susquehanna River and into the Ohio Country. Both Crown and indigenous players often insisted on having multiple written records of land transfers, transcribed and certified by the marks of the participants. Though both sides attempted to make appropriate negotiation adjustments over the first half of the century to curb points of contention, the continuous push of borderland settlers threatened to undercut Iroquois-British relations.

In the interim, the mutually advantageous trade arrangements between Pennsylvania proprietors and Ohio Country traders, and their diplomacy of influence, continued to erode French prestige in the region. "The English are more active than ever," one French administrator wrote, "not only spreading themselves over the Continent both in the direction of Louisiana and in the interior of the Canadian territory which unites the two colonies but moreover in exciting the different Nations of Indians against us."[51] In response, in 1748 when the governor of New France, Roland-Michel Barrin de La Galissonière, ordered Pierre-Joseph Céloron to the Ohio to rid the region of the growing British influence, he initiated a series of events that dramatically altered the political balance in the region. By reasserting control over the Ohio with a military presence, the Canadian governor had decided on an aggressive course of action. In June 1749, Céloron led more than 250 French, Canadian, and tribal warriors in a large flotilla south from Montréal. The force traveled to the southern shores of Lake Erie, portaged at the mouth of Chautauqua Creek to Chautauqua Lake, then followed the Chadakoin River and Conewango Creek, reaching the Allegheny River in late July. Along the way, Céloron nailed metal plates bearing the French royal arms and the following inscription to trees at each major tributary:

In the year 1749, of the reign of Louis the 15th, King of France, we Céloron, commander of a detachment sent by Monsieur the Marquis de la Galissoniere, Governor General of New France, to reestablish tranquility in some Indian villages of these cantons, have buried this Plate of Lead at the confluence of the Ohio and the Chautauqua, this 29th day of July, near the river Ohio, otherwise Belle Riviere, as a monument of the renewal of the possession we have taken of the said river Ohio and of all those which empty into it, and of all the lands on both sides as far as the sources of the said rivers, as enjoyed or ought to have been enjoyed by the kings of France preceding and as they have there maintained themselves by arms and by treaties, especially those of Ryswick, Utrecht and Aix la Chapelle.[52]

By claiming the soil in the name of the French king, Céloron's "Lead Plate" expedition "introduced European land ownership and sovereignty to the Ohio."[53] After the French captured a Virginia-built fort at the forks of the Ohio, the English scurried more zealously than ever for favor with the regional nations. Tensions mounted over the next three years.[54]

Because the English had been seemingly swept aside so easily, by the early 1750s Iroquois-British relations were strained. The 1748 Treaty of Aix-la-Chapelle did little to quell the anxiety between European powers on the American continent, and the French began making significant inroads with the Iroquois. Despite the fact that the French recognized a British protectorate over the Iroquois during the 1713 negotiations at Utrecht, by the middle of century regional concerns and appearances often fostered divergent Iroquois actions.[55] In response, New York governor George Clinton, the Iroquois, and the Ohio tribes gathered for a council at Albany in July 1751 to discuss the faltering state of affairs. Crown representatives stated that the French were building a fort on the lands near "Oniagara." In response, the Six Nations underscored that so long as the English guaranteed to build a fort, they would attend to the matter and halt construction of the French bulwark. Eastern Iroquois delegates again appealed to the Crown to "reinstate Col. Johnson . . . [to] Transact our Affairs . . . to whom we may bring our news, and from whom we may receive news."[56] Realizing the benefits that stemmed from personal politicking, the indigenous residents of the Mohawk River valley pushed hard to have Johnson commissioned. Writing to Governor Clinton shortly after the deliberations, Colden urged Clinton to consider commissioning Johnson as colonel of the Six Nations; "he made a greater figure and gained more influence among the Indians, than any person before him (so far as I have learned) ever did." Moreover, Colden pleaded that the Crown act swiftly, for the Six Nations had little confidence in the word of the English—a sentiment, the New Yorker reluctantly confessed, "our conduct of late has given them too good reasons to doubt of."[57] As time passed, the situation intensified.

On the morning of 21 June 1752, French-allied warriors sacked the ardently pro-British village of Pickawillany. Arguably, the event marked the onset of the Seven Years' War in North America. The reduction of Pickawillany placed further strain on the Iroquois-English Covenant Chain. The Piankashaws who founded the village in the 1740s were considered rebels by the French because of their trade partnership with the English—George Croghan being the primary supplier. The Piankashaw chief, Old Briton, or La Demoiselle, remained closely tied to British-backed ventures in the region even though the French continuously tried to dislodge his loyalty. After the June 1752 assault that witnessed the death of Old Briton, the Piankashaw and few remaining British-sympathizing Ohio groups sent the Grand Council wampum belts, calling for help to avenge the death of Old Briton. The Council refused. More concerned with the fact that the British and French clamored to lay claim to what they considered to be their property, the Iroquois officially withdrew from the conflict. In fact, when pressed by Pennsylvania representatives to intervene, the Grand Council declared neutrality. For the Iroquois, according to Richard White, "the English and French had merged into a single threat."[58]

But to speak of the Iroquois as a unified body is to miss important regional dynamics. By the end of the year, for instance, continued negotiations with the French, fear of English expansion, and the show of French influence in the southern Great Lakes and Ohio Country helped persuade some Iroquois to direct their efforts against the English. In fact, reports filtering back to Whitehall indicated that the French had made gains with the Iroquois as far east as the Oneida nation. Making matters worse, illegal squatting was increasing near Canajoharie, thus alienating the most pro-British factions of the Iroquois. The English needed to shine the Covenant Chain and began by appealing to the Mohawks.

Since the beginning of the century, the eastern Iroquois, led by Mohawks, had maintained close ties with the English. The former benefited directly from the Albany trade by acting as brokers and middlemen. In addition to the financial rewards, they viewed the concordat as an opportunity to solidify their position in future colonial affairs. By the early 1750s this relationship was under stress. Things had changed by the end of King George's War. Because William Johnson was no longer the appointed New York Indian agent, the flow of gifts to the Mohawks had all but dried up. No Johnson "meant no clothing, provisions, or arms with which to support themselves." It also meant that the Mohawks no longer received the same preferential treatment from colonial authorities. The inconsistency created doubt and social deterioration among the Iroquois residing in the Mohawk River valley. In fact, from 1748 to 1753 only one major council convened at Albany between the Six Nations and the governor of New York. Furthermore, despite repeated Mohawk requests, in November 1752 Governor Clinton reinstated Indian commissioners to handle grievances instead of reappointing William Johnson. The pressure of increased illegal settlements throughout the Mohawk River valley compounded an already strained situation. Thanks to a series of unfavorable judgments regarding land disputes, the Mohawks despised the fact that Governor Clinton expected them to negotiate with the Indian commissioners. Mohawk chief Hendrick made that point well known when he arrived at Fort George in 1753.[59]

In June 1753, Hendrick opened discussions at Fort George by reminding the colonial representatives of Mohawk loyalty to the British Crown during the previous war. After jogging the memory of the New Yorkers, Hendrick insisted that, had the war continued, the Mohawks would have "torn the Frenchmans heart out." He also called attention to increased illegal settlements on the Ohio River and throughout New York. The Mohawk chief voiced particular concern about the Canajoharie claim, remarking that if left unabated such intrusions accentuated English neglect of Six Nations authority. In fact, he warned that if mishap happened to befall surveyors in the region the British should expect "no satisfaction" from the Six Nations. Hendrick added that the "indifference and neglect shewn towards us makes our hearts ake, and if you don't alter your Behaviour to us we fear the Covenant Chain will be broken . . . and the rest of our Brethren the 5 nations shall know of it and all paths will be stopped." Shortly thereafter the Mohawk chief declared the Chain broken, and his delegation abruptly departed the deliberations.[60]

As Timothy Shannon suggests, Hendrick "did not break the Covenant Chain" but rather "recognized it as being broken." The Mohawk leader blamed New York colonial authorities for the deteriorating relations. By recognizing a rupture in the Covenant Chain, Hendrick threatened to jeopardize the king's continental aspirations. After all, the Covenant Chain "represented Iroquois dependence on the British Crown, which in turn legitimized British territorial claims in the Great Lakes and the Ohio Valley claims." If the English left the Chain in tatters, it "would be tantamount to renouncing those claims, admitting Iroquois independence, and capitulating to French expansion in the continent's interior." Determined not to become a "dog" of the English, Hendrick exploited the situation. He acted as much as a Confederacy spokesman as he did a disgruntled village chief. By the time Hendrick found his way to Johnson Hall a month later, his tone had altered as he prepared to meet an old friend.[61]

Well versed in the art of mixing subtle threat with negotiation and well aware of the anxieties of other parties, the Mohawk chief maneuvered between colonial representatives with skill. The deliberations at Johnson Hall in late July 1753 illustrate the scope of personal politics in eighteenth century borderland affairs. As Governor Clinton pondered the apparent flagging loyalty of the Mohawks, Hendrick and Johnson discussed the state of affairs on more friendly terms. By 1753 the men had become well acquainted. Although both answered to higher authorities, each realized the benefits of maintaining strong personal ties with the other.[62] Johnson distributed gifts and projected the idea of Iroquois supremacy, and the Mohawks provided Johnson with land and trade, and the English Crown with an avenue for continental expansion. During negotiations, both Hendrick and Johnson acknowledged the division within the Six Nations and the need to strengthen the Confederacy. The Mohawks reaffirmed allegiance to the Crown and pledged to urge the Senecas to help the English in their effort to gain influence among the Ohio Country residents, but both middlemen knew that the situation in the Ohio Country remained tenuous at best. Despite the agreement between Hendrick and Johnson, the Six Nations' disillusionment with European expansion continued.[63] During a visit to the Mohawks two weeks later, Pennsylvania agent Conrad Weiser recorded that Chief Abraham, Hendrick's brother, confided that because of the division among the Six Nations the Mohawks could do little to prevent "the French in their undertakings." In fact, the western Senecas stopped the message Johnson sent to those in Ohio to resist the French. They sent their own, demanding that they not engage the French and "sit still."[64] The eastern Iroquois began to question the intentions of the English. "We don't know what you Christians, English and French together, intend," Red Head told Johnson in September 1753. "In a little while if we find a bear in a tree there will immediately appear an owner of the land to challenge the property, and hinder us from killing it."[65] A month after Johnson met with the Six Nations, Thomas Pownall received word that "the Six Nations themselves are very backward to undertake anything against the French," and the Crown could not depend on the Iroquois unless appropriate steps were taken to brighten the Covenant Chain.[66]

In the Ohio Country, where George Croghan had forged strong trading alliances, tribes began to position themselves to best cope with competing claims to their lands.[67] The Ohio Delawares, in particular, who had earlier agreed to the construction of a British fort near Logg's Town, grew weary of a growing European presence in the area. When George Washington arrived in 1753 to begin construction of the fort and secure indigenous forces for a planned assault on the French fort Le Boeuf, the Delaware leader Shingas refused to comply. Shingas's unwillingness to accept the Virginian's demands enraged Colonel Washington. Tensions escalated when Shingas resisted the pressure of Tanaghrisson, the Seneca chief who would later bury his hatchet in the head of Jumonville and at times acted as a mediator between the Six Nations and Ohio peoples. Jane T. Merritt suggests that Croghan's quick diplomacy defused the situation and secured a council between Washington and Shingas. She cites the fact that after the seasoned trader intervened Shingas finally agreed to accompany Washington when the colonel returned in a year.[68]

If Croghan's diplomacy reconciled differences, it came with a price. After the council the governors of Pennsylvania and Virginia received records of the negotiations. The transcripts indicated that interest had been secured in the region. Interestingly, the records also stated that the Ohio nations agreed to compensate the local traders for recent losses by giving them land.[69] It marked Croghan's second attempt to gain a foothold in the region under the guise of Crown policy and protocol, the first occurring three years earlier. Croghan's play for land outraged both the tribes and colonial authorities. In late January

1754, while Croghan remained a captive of French forces, Tanaghrisson addressed Pennsylvania and Virginia representatives at Logg's Town. The Seneca chief denied that they agreed to compensate the traders with land, stating that the clause "must have been added by the Traders that wrote the letter."[70]

Thomas Penn, the principle proprietor, noted the problematic nature of Croghan's land acquisition practices sixteen months later. If this continued, Penn remarked, "we shall have Indians practic'd upon for the private advantage of every worthless fellow that goes among them."[71] The arrival of French forces on the Ohio in January 1754 temporarily ended Croghan's private dealings. French and tribal raiding parties seized almost all of Croghan's trading goods and killed or imprisoned dozens of his trading agents. The collapse of Croghan's enterprises paralleled the plight of the Crown designs. By the time the ice broke on the Ohio River in the spring of 1754, both English trade and speculation in the region were ruined.[72]

As the French and English moved once again toward an official state of war, the control of the northeastern borderlands depended on the Crown's ability to win the support of the eastern Iroquois. Meanwhile, the issue that could demonstrate to the rest of the Confederacy that the Mohawks had a special relationship with the British was the resolution of land disputes. The continued illegal European encroachments on Six Nations homelands throughout New York remained at the heart of eastern Iroquois grievances. Unless resolved, the complaints threatened to undermine imperial design. Competing claims to the Ohio Country did little to stabilize the situation. While the French, British, and Six Nations struggled to legitimize their own claims to the region, the Ohio groups increasingly ignored the demands resonating from the Grand Council. In fact, in May 1754 Croghan assured the governor of Pennsylvania that those in Ohio, along with some western Iroquois factions, would "actt for themselves att this time without Consulting ye Onondaga Councel." The Crown needed to act fast to retain their Mohawk allies and to reign in freewheeling colonial expansion. Eight months after the Lords of Trade ordered New York governor James DeLancey to convene a large council with the Six Nations, delegations met at Albany, New York, in an attempt to restore goodwill.[73]

Historical infatuation with the congress held at Albany in 1754 has perhaps made the deliberations the most famous in American colonial history. Because Benjamin Franklin and the Plan of Union have been mythicized over the past two centuries, however, most commentators have turned the congress into little more than "a dress rehearsal for the Constitutional Convention." But instead of depicting the event as a dry run of state making, recent literature depicts the congress in terms of British imperial expansion. To this point, the congress "marked a passage from a pattern of imperial and intercultural relations that was predominantly autonomous and commercial in nature to one that was decidedly more 'imperial' in the modern sense of the word: hierarchical and bureaucratic and dominated by a distant authority." Asserting an imperial design also required careful personal politicking.[74]

By the seventeenth century, Albany was playing a central role in intercultural relations. Located along the Hudson River in the Mohawk Valley, the region had hosted cross-cultural diplomacy ever since early Dutch settlers constructed Fort Orange in 1624. When the English assumed control over New Netherlands in 1664, the proposed Dutch village of Beverwyck was renamed Albany in honor of the future King James, Duke of York and Albany. By the mid-eighteenth century, the location had served as a crossroads of cultures for Iroquois and English diplomats for over a century. In the early summer of 1754, Albany residents again prepared to host deliberations.

From 19 June to 11 July, Iroquois and European delegates attempted to secure their interests on the continent. The English sought to stem the tide of growing French influence and firmly attach the Six Nations to the Crown. The Iroquois envoys looked to benefit from the heightened tensions. Interestingly, on 19 June when council greetings began the Mohawks had yet to arrive at Albany. Nevertheless, the Crown's representatives made it clear that they hoped the "threats of the Mohawks . . . have not been carried into execution." Regardless, the Crown continued, agents had been ordered to go among the Six Nations to distribute gifts and to investigate settler abuses and land complaints. As for a strategy to combat French expansion, it took a week of private debate before the colonial representatives finally agreed on a speech to read aloud to the assembled delegates. On 27 June, the colonies urged the scattered Iroquois to regroup and return to their ancient places of residence under the protection of the British. The colonies vowed to disperse the clouds that had built up and clear the road between the indigenous peoples and the English. For them to do so, however, the Six Nations had to agree to reject French overtures to the west and north and explain why the French had been allowed to build fortified palisades throughout the Ohio Country.[75]

Later that afternoon a Mohawk delegation arrived. As the rest of the Six Nations contemplated the message from the English colonies, the Mohawk speaker Canadagara addressed Gov. James DeLancey and William Johnson, among others. He thanked the English for convening the council but insisted that the Mohawks had recently been treated poorly. When pressed to detail Mohawk grievances, Canadagara cited the Kayaderosseras claim that stretched from "the half Moon . . . along Hudson's River to the third fall, and thence to the Cacknowaga or Canada-creek." The following day, on 28 June, Chief Hendrick, who arrived with the other tardy Mohawk delegation the night before, addressed the council. Hendrick dismissed the idea that the Mohawks acted only as William Johnson's minions, always willing to aid the English in their efforts to court the Six Nations. Hendrick stated that the Mohawks purposely arrived late to avoid being associated with the Crown's attempt to rectify grievances. The move reflected the divisions between the Six Nations and the Confederacy. It also hinted at the cause, namely, the English authorities' assumption that they could bully the Mohawks and take their allegiance for granted. After claiming that the Mohawks spoke for all Six Nations, Hendrick turned his attention to the colonial representatives. Instead of criticizing the construction of forts, he belittled English efforts to fortify their positions and likened them to women. His main concern rested not with the Ohio Country but rather with British claims around Canajoharie.[76]

Despite attempts to separate their objectives during the deliberations, the Mohawks and the English tried to reassert control over the neighboring tribes. By reigning in the increasingly independent actions of the western Six Nations and Ohio Country groups, the Crown would gain a stronger indigenous front against French expansion and the eastern Iroquois would enjoy the benefits of heightened status and protection from local land claims. But even if they agreed on the necessity of controlling neighboring tribes, the Mohawks and English could not agree on the future of the Ohio Country lands these tribes occupied. European claims to the region did not go unchecked. The Mohawks expressed dissatisfaction with both French and Virginian intentions throughout the Ohio River valley. They "are both quarrelling," Hendrick stated, "about lands which belong to us." If the Pennsylvanians or the Long Knives intend to build forts in the region, the Mohawk chief demanded that the chiefs of the Grand Council be properly consulted *and* compensated.[77]

After a few days of unsuccessful negotiations regarding the proposed Plan of Union, on 3 July 1754 veteran Indian agent Conrad Weiser responded to the Six Nations spokesman. He reminded the delegates that for the past thirty years the road of trade had been well traveled between the Ohio Country and the English colonies. In fact, Weiser insisted that in 1751 the Ohio tribes had called on Virginia to construct a fort in the region to protect them from French aggression and trader abuses. Soon after the Virginians arrived to construct the fort, however, the French with a force of "a Thousand and 18 cannon" took possession of the palisade. Thus, the English were not to blame for the deteriorating state of affairs at the forks of the Monongahela River. Weiser did not challenge Six Nations *ownership* of the region, but he made a firm stand regarding the intentions of the English colonies.[78]

Weiser's move did not go without reward. Two days passed before the Six Nations responded. When they did, a compromise had been reached. Hendrick brightened the Covenant Chain and vowed to resist French overtures. As would become evident during the forthcoming outbreak of hostilities, Hendrick's pledge included few other groups besides the Mohawks. For the time being, though, the Mohawk chief avoided further debate regarding Ohio Country lands by ceding thousands of acres lying between the Susquehanna and Ohio rivers to Pennsylvania. Hendrick's bold move infuriated the Ohio tribes and threatened to undermine Virginian claims to the lands south of the Ohio and west of the Monongahela. Complicating the situation, the Six Nations also negotiated a private transaction with John Lydius of Connecticut. In return for £2000 they agreed to cede lands on the north branch of the Susquehanna River in the

Wyoming Valley to representatives of the Susquehanna Company of Connecticut. The deal later acted as a primary instigator to the Pennamite Wars, because the cession overlapped with Pennsylvanian land grants and caused further friction.[79]

In return, and undoubtedly aided by the many private conversations that took place "in the bushes," Hendrick secured Crown support for matters closer to home. The Crown pledged to address contested land claims, along with problems associated with inadequate trade regulations such as excessive liquor trafficking. Furthermore, the Mohawks emphasized that they would remain discontented with Iroquois-Crown relations until the reinstatement of William Johnson as their primary Indian agent.[80] The Albany compromise may have cost the Mohawks "the ability to play several diplomatic hands at once," but it did lead to the replacement of the Indian commissioners with a royal superintendent of Indian affairs and guaranteed Mohawk brokerage in future continental affairs.[81] Hendrick maneuvered with great diplomatic skill and secured what he could for those of the Six Nations willing to work with him and the British. William Johnson later conceded to the Lords of Trade that the "eyes of all the Western Tribes of Indians are upon the behaviour of the Six nations, whose fame of power, may in some measure exceed the reality, while they only act a timid and neutral part." Johnson further confessed, "this I apprehend to be the modern State."[82]

In other words, Johnson realized that his Mohawk friends had bluffed and won for the moment, but tribes on the western fringe of the Six Nations would now be watching to see if the eastern Iroquois had the warriors and the will to fight. Plans to unify the colonies may have failed miserably, but by the conclusion of the 1754 Albany congress the colonial representatives had managed to brighten the Covenant Chain; and the shining of the Chain gave the Crown a dim light of hope as their position in the trans-Appalachian region continued to deteriorate.

By the spring of 1754, Ohio Company of Virginia shareholder George Washington had failed in his attempt to construct a fort at the forks of the Monongahela and Ohio rivers. When Washington returned with a Virginia militia later in July, his force proved no match for the French and Ohio warriors defending the newly completed and renamed Fort Duquesne. British regulars faired no better. In the spring of 1755, General Braddock led a disastrous campaign at the forks of the Ohio. Blaming what he believed to be inadequate indigenous support, Braddock turned against his man in the field, George Croghan. Based on earlier estimates from Croghan, the general had expected the freewheeling trader to meet him with close to four hundred warriors at Fort Cumberland. When Croghan arrived with fewer than fifty, Braddock demanded an explanation. Croghan attributed the poor showing to Washington's failure on the Ohio almost a year earlier. That defeat produced diplomatic stagnation between the Pennsylvania government and Shawnee, Delaware, and other Ohio tribes.[83] Croghan dispatched runners to the Ohio to gather support for Braddock's campaign. The trader reassured Braddock that in only a matter of days western Delaware warriors would meet English forces on the march toward the Ohio. Not only did those forces fail to meet Braddock, but factions of Delawares and western Senecas joined the Shawnees and attacked English settlements along Pennsylvania's borderlands.[84]

William Johnson's newly appointed secretary and aide-de-camp, Peter Wraxall, explained why the western Iroquois proved unreliable allies. Soon after Johnson received his appointment as superintendent of Indian affairs in 1755, Wraxall recorded, he requested council with a large assembly of the Six Nations. Many of the western Six Nations viewed the scope of the Ohio Land Company claims as threatening. They also expressed concern over the 1754 cession of land that drove the European speculation. Wary of the Virginians, many tribes west of the Oneida Carry viewed "Braddock as the Governor of Virginia and his armies as the people of that Province. . . . They looked therefore upon Mr. Braddock's Enterprise as one Encroachment making war upon another." The spoils of victory, many Ohio tribes judged, would be the lands they inhabited. After all, as Chief Hendrick boasted the same year, "we are the six confederate Indian nations, the Heads and Superiors of all Indian nations of the Continent of America." The tribes of the Ohio Country and the western Iroquois must have wondered what lengths the Grand Council would go to protect their own homelands and interests.[85]

As Braddock toiled toward the Ohio, Gen. William Shirley had been ordered to secure the Crown's position along the southern shores of

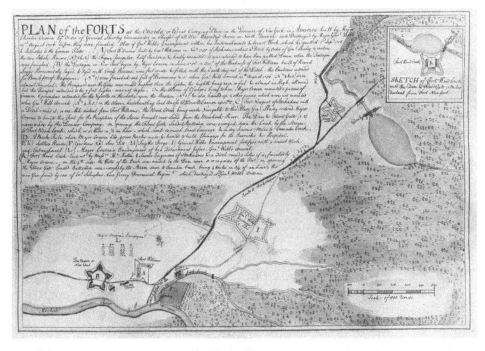

Plan of forts at the Oneida Carry, 1754. Courtesy of the Newberry Library, Chicago. Call # Ayer 136 H91 1907 Vol. 2.

Lake Ontario. To do so, Shirley turned his attention to Oswego, situated between two French lifelines: forts Frontenac and Niagara. In the late spring of 1755, Shirley marched more than 1,700 men of the 50th and 51st Regiments, along with Colonel Schuyler's "Jersey Blues," toward Oswego. Shirley recognized the importance of the Oneida Carry. William Johnson agreed. To keep communication and supplies open between Albany and Oswego, fortifications at the Carry required strengthening, and Wood Creek had to be cleared of all obstructions. As a result, by late May a contingent of soldiers and laborers from Shirley's force busied themselves with the first task. Directed by Marcus Petri from German Flatts, the workers began construction of two 35- by 20-foot fortified log storehouses, one on each end of the Carry. The only problem was that construction began without the consent of the Oneidas.[86]

By the time Shirley's men broke ground at the Carry, the relationship between the Oneidas and the English colonies had been

deteriorating for months. A year before Shirley's men arrived at the
Carry, reports of abuse at the portage had filtered to New York. In one
instance, English traders complained to Gov. James DeLancey that
when attempting to cross the Carry armed warriors "forced them" to
pay dearly to have their goods transported and "boldy robbed them
of their rum and stores with surly looks and storms of threatening
language." Fearful of their lives, the traders reported, they consented
to the terms but made sure to seek an alternative route on their return
to Albany. Correspondence from Johnson Hall confirms an increase
of abuses at the Carry and rumors that Oneidas were strengthening
their ties with western nations. Thus, when Oneida complaints filtered back to William Johnson shortly after the arrival of Shirley's
men, the soon-to-be superintendent of Indian affairs did not take
them lightly. Johnson urged a halt to construction until the consent of
the Oneidas could be secured. Shirley agreed.[87]

The construction of fortified storehouses may have been temporarily interrupted, but that did not stop Shirley from ordering Wood
Creek cleared of obstructions and the Carry's main road graveled.
He feared that the French and their indigenous allies "intended to
obstruct the passage . . . by falling great trees across it." But when
Capt. William Williams arrived on 28 June to oversee the clearing and
roadwork, he found the Oneidas openly hostile to the idea of any construction. As Gilbert Hagerty points out, relations "with the Oneidas
had now been strained to the where [Williams] not dare dig a trench
or cut a picket." Making matters tenser, without any form of protection those under Williams's command were at the mercy of the locals.
But within week of Williams's report Johnson managed to strike a
deal with the Oneidas. With the help of his Mohawk allies, Johnson
negotiated the erection of not only two storehouses but a fort as well.
In return, the Oneidas were promised a fort at their "Castle," continued control of trade over the Carry once the war ended, and that
no rum would be sold to their villages. Shirley also pledged "some
pieces of Artillery" to the Oneidas while negotiating at Oswego.
Thus, on 4 July 1755, five days before Braddock met his end at the
Monongahela, Petri recommenced construction of the storehouses.
By mid-August the project was completed, and Petri, now a captain,
was on his way to relieve the company at the western post on Wood

Creek. Meanwhile, Captain Williams was to remain at the eastern storehouse on the Mohawk River until Petri returned.[88]

Like Oswego, the British position at the Oneida Carry undercut French supplies lines and imperial designs in the Pays d'en haut. If left unchecked, French authorities reasoned, the British would be capable of pushing deep into the Great Lakes and up the St. Lawrence with the help of an increasing number of allies. French fears were not unfounded. In fact, when Oneida warriors helped Johnson during the Lake George campaign that September, the French threatened retaliatory measures that would take them and their allies deep into Oneida territory. Catching wind of the intelligence, and fearful that the Oneidas would retract from their earlier agreement with the upcoming scheduled arrival of more soldiers at the Carry, in October the now sixty-one-year-old Shirley ordered the construction of two forts to safeguard the portage, one at each end. How could Oswego be supported, Shirley lamented to William Johnson, "if the French should take . . . the Carrying Place." Five weeks later, Fort Williams, the largest and most fortified of the two, guarded the Mohawk River. Meanwhile, Captain Petri was at the trickling and marshy headwaters of Wood Creek overseeing the construction of a smaller palisade. Not a trained military engineer, Petri did not follow Shirley's plans and no doubt fell considerably short in reassuring the resident Oneidas that the fort would deter the French and their allies. In fact, when completed the fort at Wood Creek, "Fort Bull" as it became known, included "no loopholes, flankers, nor bastions of any kind." Also absent were mounted cannons.[89]

The apparent shortfalls at the Oneida Carry did not stop General Shirley from looking west from his post at Oswego with aspirations of marching on Niagara. Oswego, Shirley lamented, "is as much the key of these lakes and the . . . country lying around them, to the English, as Nova Scotia is of the sea coast and eastern parts of North America." If the French succeed in taking Oswego, it would "make them absolute masters of the navigation of all these lakes" and "let them into the heart of the country inhabited by the Six Nations." Not content with leaving the post without completing the needed repairs, and suffering bad weather and a dwindling number of committed Oneida allies, Shirley was forced to delay his expedition against Niagara.

Meanwhile, fifty miles away at Fort Frontenac, a force of 1,400 waited anxiously for Shirley to make his move. If the British general intended to attack Niagara, French forces would move on Oswego. By the end of October, however, it became clear that an attack on Niagara would have to wait until spring. As a result, Shirley departed for Albany, leaving Colonel Mercer in command of 700 men at Oswego and just a few dozen to guard the Carry. Soon the waterways froze and winter set into the southern Great Lakes. Starvation and scurvy nearly forced Mercer and Williams's ill-equipped, undersupplied men into a headlong retreat before the winter's end. By the end of February 1756, morale at Oswego and the Oneida Carry had hit an all-time low.[90]

As February gave way to March, the situation appeared to turn around. On 12 March a dozen batteaux loaded with supplies and food reached the Carry from German Flatts. Despite reports that the ice on Wood Creek had not yet fully broken and enemy war parties were camped along the supply line, Williams quickly ordered a relief column to take supplies to Oswego. Eleven icy days later, the relief party under the command of James Reade, the assistant commissary at Fort Williams, arrived at Oswego.[91]

In anticipation of renewed conflict, Col. John Bradstreet was tasked with recruiting and organizing two thousand laborers to trek thousands of pounds of ammunition and supplies over the Oneida Carry. By mid-March, arterial supplies critical to the British position in North America traversed through the Carry.[92]

Recognizing the importance of the supply line, French military leaders decided to make good on their earlier threats concerning the portage. On 12 March 1756, a company of soldiers and French-allied Iroquois (largely from Akwesasne, Kanesetake, Kahnawake, and Oswegatchie) and Huron warriors departed Fort de La Présentation. Opting to take the Carry by surprise, Lt. Gaspard-Joseph Chaussegros de Léry, a Canadian-born seigneur and commander of the two-hundred-strong French force, followed the one hundred-plus Iroquois and Huron warriors. Twelve days later they arrived and positioned themselves on the doorstep of the Carry. Early the next morning, after capturing some prisoners, de Léry chose to attack the poorly fortified palisade on Wood Creek. Soon thereafter they stormed Fort Bull, killing the handful of soldiers who garrisoned the post. Not long after, when de Léry ordered the fort to be set ablaze, the thousands of pounds of gunpowder ignited and blew the fort to bits. With William Johnson's force within striking distance and Fort Williams well equipped, and his allies having fulfilled their own independent objectives, de Léry opted to pull back. But the damage had been done. The conflict that had been raging in North America since the sacking of Pickawillany in 1752 finally became official. On 17 May 1756, King George II declared war against his "beloved" French rival, King Louis XV.[93]

As Whitehall prepared for a global war, Shirley kept his sights on refortifying the Carry. Writing to James Abercrombie in June 1756, he noted that "since early this Spring" a detachment of eighty workers under the direction of James Fairservice had been busy "Clearing the Wood Creek" in order to shorten the distance of the Carry. British engineers also built a new storehouse at Wood Creek on the site of the destroyed bastion and Fort Newport at the creek's upper landing. At the other end on the Mohawk River, under the direction of Maj. Charles Craven, British workers started work on "The Pentagon," or "Fort New" (later designated "Fort Craven"), with the hope of replacing Fort Williams by the end of the summer.[94]

Military operations along one of the Crown's most important supply routes in North America were not Shirley's only problem. By the spring of 1756, his command of the Crown's forces in America had come under scrutiny. Not long after losing the patronage of the Duke of Newcastle, Shirley found out that Daniel Webb and James Abercrombie were to act as interim successors until John Campbell, the Fourth Earl of Loudoun, was ready to take command. By July, Loudoun, Webb, and Abercrombie were sitting around a table in Albany debating an appropriate course of action. In the end, Loudoun opted to strengthen the British position at Ticonderoga instead of a preparing for a major Lake Ontario offensive. Still, like Shirley before him, Loudoun recognized the importance of protecting Oswego and the supply line over the Carry. As a result, he ordered Webb and the 24th Regiment of Foot to Oswego. But his orders came too late. On 15 August 1756, after Montcalm's cannon bombardment killed Mercer, Oswego fell to the French. News of the catastrophe reached Webb at the Oneida Carry five days later. Ill equipped and undermanned to defend the Carry from the rumored six thousand Frenchmen marching toward Albany, Webb faced a tough decision. Fresh off the boat, the British general began his North American command by leading a general retreat to German Flatts while the earthworks at the Oneida Carry burned to the ground behind him.[95]

Braddock's defeat in the Ohio Country, the sacking of Oswego, and the abandonment of the Carry did little to help British imperial endeavors and prestige in the northeastern borderlands. Along with the military defeats, it appeared that more and more indigenous allies were holding fast to claims of neutrality or, worse, taking up positions beside the French. In fact, Montcalm's victory on the shores of Lake Ontario induced many wavering Senecas and Oneidas to hedge their bets with the French. The English Crown needed to act quickly if it intended to turn the tide in the region.

Johnson began earlier that spring when in April 1756 he ordered Captain Petri and thirty workers to Canowaroghare, or the "Oneida Castle," to commence construction of the promised fort. Johnson also tried to mend fences during councils with Iroquois and Delaware leaders after Pennsylvania governor Morris placed a scalp bounty on all "Delawares." A few months later, Johnson dispatched Croghan, the newly appointed deputy Indian agent, to conduct peace talks between Pennsylvania and the Delawares.[96]

Animosity had been increasing between Pennsylvania proprietors and several nations because of the scalp bounty and contentious land claims, most of which stemmed from the infamous Walking Purchase scandal of 1737 and the land the Mohawks promised Pennsylvania at Albany in 1754. In fact, news that many Ohio Country Delawares had agreed to take up the hatchet against the English filtered back to Philadelphia.[97] Writing to Johnson in March 1757, Croghan remarked on the state of affairs: "There is good understanding between the Governor and me, as well as most of the gentlemen of the place, and every one seems fond of an inquiry being made into the Complaints of the Indians; except some of the Proprietary Agents."[98] Croghan's relationship with the Pennsylvania proprietors had deteriorated since the 1744 treaty at Lancaster. Thomas Penn, in particular, loathed Croghan's betrayal of protocol when he sought to secure Indian deeds for himself while employed as a Crown and provincial agent.[99] But Croghan's tune changed after 1757, and he too began to tout the authority of the Grand Council.

Interestingly, in the summer of 1757 Croghan initially sought to strengthen his alliance with the "Delaware King," Teedyuscung. If the proprietors' land claims were recognized, Croghan reasoned, it would make it very difficult for him to patent the Indian deeds he held, not to mention complicating his continued interest in acquiring land in the Ohio Country. Yet Croghan's plan to situate himself on the side of Teedyuscung during a council held in late August 1757 backfired. During peace discussions between Gov. William Denny and Teedyuscung, the "Delaware King" surprised Croghan by asking Denny to relinquish English claim over a land transaction dated and signed in 1718. Croghan, who possessed the deed in question and held other tracts included in the survey, insisted that the agreement was valid and in fact could be invalidated only by Sir William Johnson. Realizing that his future land interests rested with Crown control over the territories in question, he added that the Grand Council had also sanctioned the transaction. Enraged, Teedyuscung called Croghan a rogue and severed the alliance.[100]

By the end of 1757 things looked rather bleak for the English. The French controlled the Ohio Country, had sacked forts Oswego and William Henry, and with the help of Iroquois warriors had raided English settlements (largely consisting of German settlers) along the critical Albany-Oswego supply line. Commenting on the state of affairs late in the year, Marquis Pierre de Rigaud de Vaudreuil, commander at Niagara, stated: "I have ruined the plans of the English; I have disposed the Five Nations to attack them; I have carried consternation and terror into all those parts."[101]

Within months of the commander's remarks, however, the mutually beneficial partnership between many tribes and the French Crown that was critical to French success in North America began to erode. The British may have lost posts to French-led forces, but British naval blockades had halted the critical trade required to outfit the French and fuel their imperial ambitions. The fall of Louisbourg in May 1758 made things worse for the French. Throughout the Great Lakes and Ohio Country, many disgruntled tribes distanced themselves, or struck out against French garrisons incapable of providing "goods and services necessary to sustain the reciprocal relationship native alliances were built upon." By July, not long after a delegation of Ohio tribes visited Philadelphia to assess in person the validity of colonial peace overtures, Gen. John Forbes prepared to move against Fort Duquesne. A month later, Fort Frontenac on Lake Ontario fell to Col. John Bradstreet. By the end of the summer, English forces controlled the St. Lawrence River, the southeastern Great Lakes, and considerable ground west of the Alleghenies. Reports that even the Shawnees had relocated from Logg's Town up the Allegheny to be closer to the Senecas came as welcome news to British authorities.[102]

Eager to strengthen their position on the continent, imperial strategists again turned their attention to the Oneida Carry. In the early summer months of 1758, as British forces geared up for what would be a series of successful offenses, James Abercrombie ordered Brig. Gen. John Stanwix to reoccupy the Oneida Carry. At the same time, William Johnson struck another deal with the Oneidas to build a new palisade at the Carry. This time, however, their approval did not come without a promise from Johnson that, in addition to "plentiful and cheap trade," the fort would be knocked down as soon as hostilities ceased between the French and English. Johnson agreed. After engineers reviewed site plans and gathered the needed supplies, construction of the unnamed fort began on 23 August 1758, a quarter of a mile upstream from the ashes of Fort Williams.[103]

From the beginning, a series of obstacles plagued the timely construction of the new fort at the Oneida Carry. Despite promises to build a modest and temporary fortification, the initial plan agreed on by the lead engineers and favored by Stanwix called for a massive square fort with a 1,420-foot exterior circuit capable of "Lodging 200 Men, in the Winter, and for 3 to 400 Men in the Summer." The ambitious plan also called for "curtains, bastions, ramparts, barracks, magazine, and storehouses." To complete the task substantial manpower would be needed. Of the two thousand men assigned to construct the fort and defend the Carry, however, less than eleven hundred ever congregated at one time at the portage, with no more than four hundred working on the fort. Desertion, sickness, reconnaissance, a lack of ready supplies from Schenectady, and Bradstreet's renewed campaign against Fort Frontenac dwindled numbers further. Not helping matters, health problems plagued Captain Green, one of two lead military engineers overseeing the construction of the fort, eventually forcing Abercrombie to relieve him of duty before workers laid the first log.[104]

Despite early setbacks, Lt. John Williams, Green's replacement, made considerable headway in the first few weeks. But when a revised plan calling for a substantial scale-back of the fortifications in light of Bradstreet's recent victory at Fort Frontenac made its way to the Carry, another problem faced Stanwix and Williams. Determined to press ahead as planned, Williams convinced Stanwix to hold fast. Writing to Abercrombie in September 1758, Stanwix remarked that, if they continued as planned, "the Advantage of the Situation and guns sufficient for the post [would] make pretty Strong I am told every way preferable to Fort Edward." In response, Abercrombie consented but added that he expected a fort capable of lodging four hundred men completed by the end of winter. Failure to do so, Abercrombie added, "must be answerable for the Consequences." But it would be almost three years before General Stanwix could christen his namesake. Lucky for him, and Williams, "Mrs. Nanny Crombie," as his troops called him, had been replaced by Jeffery Amherst because of, among other things, the failed assault on Fort Carillon (later Fort Ticonderoga).[105]

As workers slogged away at the Oneida Carry, in October 1758 English authorities met with hundreds of potential indigenous allies for the third time in two years at Easton, Pennsylvania. Bringing together representatives from New York, Pennsylvania, and New Jersey, the Iroquois, Teedyuscung's followers from the Susquehanna (Shamokin Delawares), some Ohio nations, and scores of smaller tribes largely residing east of the Allegheny Mountains, the treaty helped turn the tide for the British. As Richard White notes, "direct peace negotiations between the British and the Ohio Indians proceeded rapidly after the appearance of [Delaware chief] Pisquetomen and Keeyuscung (or Delaware George)." Intent on finding terms of peace not only with the British but also among the Delawares, the men pressed for terms that would secure indigenous lands and open up trade. Interestingly, however, imperial endeavors at the forks were not of primary concern when the Delawares arrived at Easton. Far more concerned with patching up differences between the Iroquois and colonial authorities, those participants assembled even brushed aside Teedyuscung.[106]

Intent on securing his people's possession of the upper Susquehanna Valley independent of both Pennsylvanian and Iroquois

interference, Teedyuscung caused a stir. Perhaps not surprisingly, the
Iroquois and agents representing the Penn family and British Crown
joined forces against the "King of the Dealwares" and his Quaker
allies, marginalizing his influence over the proceedings. In fact, when
Croghan arrived at Easton to oversee the treaty, Teedyuscung and
two hundred Delawares were waiting for him. Before negotiations
began, Teedyuscung demanded a personal clerk. Nicolas Wainwright
suggests that the Quakers did not trust Croghan's minutes and persuaded the "Delaware King" to obtain an assistant. Teedyuscung also
distrusted Croghan.[107] The suspicion and innuendo of his duplicity
as an interpreter angered Croghan and marked a rift between the
two acquaintances. But there was real reason to be concerned. With
his own interests in mind, and as acting deputy superintendent of
Indian affairs, Croghan also began to tout the authority of the Iroquois
when it came to Delaware demands. In fact, when Easton concluded,
Teedyuscung's land grievances remained largely unaddressed. The
Quakers blamed Croghan for this situation, alleging that he kept
Teedyuscung too drunk to negotiate. Other evidence documents that
the "Delaware King" did not need much help. Whether or not it was
Croghan's strategy, Teedyuscung remained isolated during the negotiations. Croghan held thousands of acres in borderland deeds and
needed to play a careful hand given the Crown's promise not to settle
west of the mountains in return for support from the nations. Like
his patron Sir William Johnson, Croghan began to bolster the Grand
Council's authority over the Ohio region. The constructed image of
the Iroquois as overlords continued to gain ground as the Crown and
its representatives negotiated for allies. As for the assembled Ohioans, they acknowledged "a token of Iroquois hegemony" and agreed
to terms of peace only after the British promised to treat them as allies
and Pennsylvania agreed to relinquish claims to lands west of the
Appalachians. For the moment, a fleeting one at that, the European
negotiators agreed. When colonial agent Christian Frederick Post and
Chief Pisquetomen relayed the news west, the French did not waste
time razing Fort Duquesne and retreating back up the Ohio. By the
summer's end, Niagara too had fallen.[108]

Meanwhile, the war and Philadelphia debts had ended Croghan's
independence and made him beholden to a new patron. For this new

master he had to adjust his affiliations with Ohio tribes. To prove his newfound commitment, Croghan promised Denny and General Forbes that he would outfit fifty warriors in preparation for the planned march against Fort Duquesne. He secured £150 to do so before he left Easton. Croghan wanted allies with clout who could improve his own ambitions for western lands. When Forbes's forces occupied the forks of the Ohio on 25 November 1758, they encamped on land Croghan held in Indian deed. Croghan's commitment to the Crown was selective. He rightly saw that the war had turned and he could get back into the land game in his old region, but he now had new patrons and had alienated old friends, allies, creditors, and Pennsylvania government employers.[109] Shortly thereafter, General Forbes succeeded where Washington and Braddock had failed. In November, without a shot being fired, Forbes assumed control of what he renamed Fort Pitt.[110]

A month before Forbes took the forks, British victories in Africa, the Caribbean, and Europe were punctuated by General Wolfe's dramatic victory on the Plains of Abraham. Less than a year later, on 8 September 1760, Montréal surrendered. Six months later, with the French in North America defeated, the Indian Department cut frontier costs. Gen. Jeffrey Amherst now felt no obligation to maintain cordial relations with people he confessed he wished "to extirpate . . . root and branch."[111]

As the continent emerged from the Seven Years' War, control over the Carry once again promised to provide a measure of stability for the Oneidas. But because logistical and military setbacks delayed the completion of Fort Stanwix until 1762, the British did not intend to simply pack up and leave. Therefore, by the time terms at Paris officially ended the war, instead of being a defensive post against French aggression Fort Stanwix was a point of contention among the Iroquois. The fort, after all, had been built on the condition that it be demolished after the war. Not long after the cannons had ceased firing, William Johnson began fielding complaints originating from the Oneidas. As the Mohawks mediated, the abandonment of the recently completed palisade appeared even less likely by the spring of 1763. By then, with "Pontiac's Rebellion" raging, the "primary function" of the fort, according to one commentator, "was to provide for an imperial presence in the Iroquois country, particularly among the Oneidas."[112] But, as we see in the next two chapters, the end of Pontiac's so-called rebellion brought new problems to the footsteps of the Carry. Despite the terms of the Royal Proclamation of 1763, the relentless incursion of European squatters into the northeastern borderlands threatened to rip apart the Confederacy and ignite another war. It soon became clear to eastern Iroquois headmen and colonial administrators that the opening of a new frontier in the Ohio Country would serve to benefit a variety of converging interests—and what better place to convene to finalize an agreement than the Oneida Carry.

CHAPTER 3

CONVERGING INTERESTS

By the end of 1762, North America was reeling from the destruction, confusion, and betrayals of the Seven Years' War. Commonly referred to by colonists as the French and Indian War, the conflict that raged between imperial forces for nine years on the North American continent displaced and destroyed thousands of lives and all but bankrupt two competing European empires. When the war ended, the English Crown acquired a new extension to its empire as well as the hefty cost of its administration. In fact, Britain's national debt increased almost £50 million as a result of the global conflict.[1] Governing an empire with an administration plagued by financial and political instability bordered on futility. Whitehall needed to raise money and looked for relief from the colonies for which the war had been waged.

In addition to the friction caused by the well-documented perils of taxation without representation, a variety of problems contributed to the heightened agitation. Conflicting claims of indigenous sovereignty clashed with settler interests in western lands. Anxiously, colonial administrators on both sides of the Atlantic pressured the Crown to regulate borderland trade, European settlement, and land speculation throughout the colonies. In a bid to quell tensions, in 1763 policymakers in London made a fateful decision that would transform the continent within a decade.

The Guerre de la Conquête also served as the vehicle for rival indigenous nations and leaders struggling to secure a future in a complex world characterized by calculated and accidental misconstructions.

Despite "their council fire rhetoric of kinship and affection for their European 'fathers' and 'brothers,'" Colin Calloway reminds us, "Indians fought not out of love for the French or the British but in a consistent effort to keep their country independent of either."[2] In the spring of 1763, that struggle erupted into a widespread revolt against British positions and settlers throughout the upper Ohio Country and western Great Lakes region. After a few months of brutal frontier war, the uprising called Pontiac's did not rid the territory of the English. But it did stir the colonial administration to action. As winter snows brought respite from the conflict, messengers carried word west that the English king had created a new boundary line between indigenous populations and Europeans in North America.

News that the Crown intended to curb settlement west of the Appalachians and open trade with the "rebellious savages" did not sit well with many colonial authorities and borderland settlers, who sought to inflict their own rough punishment on the tribes. On one hand, the situation demanded some form of redress to quell hostilities; on the other, the Crown had to punish the rebels to dampen the growing anger of the settlers. As a result, from late 1763 to 1765 administration of the northeastern borderlands underwent several significant alterations. British responses towards the first peoples, however, were not spread evenly. While some nations and warriors involved in the 1763 Uprising were granted terms of peace and access to trade (Pontiac included), others met with English sword and musket. Such inconsistencies contributed to colonial resentment of borderland policy, often resulting in vigilante activity fueled by "Indian hating."[3]

Sir William Johnson figures prominently in this period. So does his deputy of Indian affairs, George Croghan. Both men, along with Mohawk and other Iroquois allies, reorganized and directed frontier policy. Many historians have convincingly argued that Johnson remained concerned with maintaining the integrity of the Confederacy and prestige of the Grand Council.[4] Tribal attitudes and diplomacy, Francis Jennings keenly remarks, were Johnson's "bread and butter."[5] Interestingly, they also came to be Croghan's. The reasons are palpable. The Grand Council's claim over all the lands east of the Mississippi River had many times proved quite useful to both indigenous and European interests. The benefits from trade and land transactions were reciprocal and obvious. The Crown secured rights to territory while the English-allied Iroquois reaped the material and strategic benefits from appearing as indispensable allies in times of European continental conflict. With an end to conflict in Europe, however, the Iroquois sought further resources to secure their tenuous future. The coveted Ohio Country, covering tens of millions of acres, remained chief among their interest. Both parties knew that where Iroquois authority could be established so too might a British colonial system be extended—and eventually an effective trade network established and land sold, settled, and improved. Without the appearance of a functional Confederacy, however, Johnson's legitimacy as a cultural broker waned along with Croghan's land interests and the Crown's claim to crucial resources.

That being said, by 1763 the weakness of the Six Nations claims to a vast territorial empire was nothing new. The extent to which the Grand Council had been disregarded during the Seven Years' War revealed just how fragmented the Confederacy had become. The Uprising of 1763 revealed the weakness of the British imperial system and highlighted the diminished power of the once powerful Six Nations. As a result, from 1763 to 1766 William Johnson did his best to guide resentment away from dissident Iroquois (the western Senecas, in particular) and to assign blame to the Delawares and Shawnees. With the integrity of the Confederacy in mind, Johnson wrote his superiors repeatedly to differentiate between "friendly" and "enemy" nations as the English prepared to march on the Ohio. Armed conflict caused rupture, and Johnson feared that if English resentment against the rebellious or disloyal tribes was not carefully directed the colonies might plummet into another local war—a war that would threaten to erode the precarious position both Johnson and the eastern Iroquois held in the imperial framework. At the same time, Johnson overestimated the persuasive power of the Iroquois and grew upset when he learned that Col. John Bradstreet sought a peaceful resolution with many western nations in 1764, nations Johnson deemed necessary targets for exploitation. Though Johnson was a crafty and adaptable diplomat, the mutual dependence he established with the eastern Iroquois often resulted in strategic confusion and stagnation. Neither party wished to disrupt the status quo, merely to reinforce traditions they viewed as faltering. Actually, the efforts to maintain the façade of an authoritative and united Confederacy consumed Johnson's attention, often leaving an opportunity for others to influence crucial matters, directly affecting the course of borderland events. The lull in colonial directive created opportunity.

Still, Johnson was no fool. A clever diplomat and influential broker, his actions did affect borderland policies. In the end, Johnson succeeded in deflecting English retaliatory actions (ca. 1763–66) away from the western Senecas and other Ohio Iroquois. By the end of 1765 he had also concluded several treaties with Six Nations representatives that seemed to confirm the future implementation of policy that both factions believed to be sound. The period from 1763 to early 1766, however, also suggests that other players influenced the course of empire along the imperial fringe while Johnson struggled with his borderland initiatives. Again, by turning our attention to Johnson's right-hand man, George Croghan, and Croghan's conduct in London and aspirations on the Ohio and Illinois rivers, we can see that in indigenous affairs Johnson followed as much as he led. A similar conclusion can be reached, as we see in this chapter, by calling attention to the persistent pressure placed on Johnson by Gen. Thomas Gage in terms of a shifting strategy that broke with Covenant Chain traditions, and also by the English-allied Iroquois who continued to protest encroachment on contested lands. In fact, Johnson was not the only, or even at times the most influential, borderland participant judging urgency and planning the next imperial step. As policy related to the first peoples evolved from 1763 through 1766, the Iroquois, colonial agents, and politicians manipulated the fluid situation to seek rewards from dishonest trade and controversial land cessions.

As the winter months of 1762 set in, few residents of colonial America seriously questioned the fact that French imperial forces had been defeated. Nevertheless, waging a war for empire proved to be a much easier task than establishing a lasting peace. The Peace of Paris "did more than shift cartographic boundaries; it set people and events in motion."[6] By the early 1760s the negotiated middle grounds that defined tentative coalitions and methods of acceptable interaction had begun to fragment. Nowhere was that more noticeable than the northeastern borderlands.

For many colonists, the Peace of Paris signed on 10 February 1763 "brought hopes for a change of fortune." For many European imperialists it represented an opportunity to return to speculating in lands in the trans-Appalachian region. With the French gone, enterprising speculators from Connecticut to Virginia obstructed by nine years of borderland conflict looked toward the Mohawk River valley and beyond the mountains to the fertile Ohio Country. Hardened by previous displacement, however, many of the indigenous residents living on the coveted lands did not relinquish the territory passively. The same peace that quieted cannons in Québec and Montréal also paved the way west for settlers, soldiers, and domesticated animals. By 1762, Iroquois concerns that the war had been mainly between rivals for their lands were substantiated as settlers lured by the Connecticut-based Susquehanna Company pushed deep into the Susquehanna Valley. The joint-stock land company formed in 1753 maintained that the province's colonial charter granted them sea-to-sea land rights. When Iroquois headmen met Johnson in April, they warned the superintendent that if incursions continued major problems would follow.[7]

The policies of Gen. Jeffrey Amherst also fueled tensions. "Arrogant and ignorant of Indian ways, the British commander-in-chief . . . viewed an empire as something to be governed, not negotiated and cultivated by giving gifts to Indians."[8] Amherst rolled back expenditures when most needed and demanded that Crown agents cease distributing gifts among the tribes. Such gifts not only showed respect for indigenous traditions and maintained the goodwill of the Crown but also provided many tribespeople with essential resources. Moreover, by withholding gifts and retaining a British presence west of the Appalachians, albeit scant, Amherst threatened indigenous autonomy on the Ohio.

In February, English trader Alexander McKee informed the Shawnees that the French king had given up all claim to the continent to the English. Angered at the notion that their previous "father" had relinquished claim to something he did not own, in April a delegation of Shawnees arrived at Fort Pitt to express their frustration. That winter, messages sent to Amherst and William Johnson from Ohio-based traders warned of increased disaffection of western nations toward the English.[9] The Iroquois, too, were complaining about squatters in the Mohawk River valley and as far west as Oswego. Reports circulated that factions of Seneca and Cayuga warriors were conspiring against the English; these and most Ohio and Great Lakes nations loathed the English as much as Amherst reviled the complications they brought him. By the spring of 1763 the message long preached from a Delaware prophet named Neolin had gained a wide audience of believers throughout the northeastern borderlands. Neolin insisted that during a dream-induced journey the Master of Life charged him with the task of ridding his people of the pestilence caused by the pale-faced colonizers. The prophet advocated the rejection of European drink and trading goods, and urged first nations everywhere to cease fighting among themselves. With racially charged terminology, Neolin promised a heaven without the ills of the European for those willing to cleanse their country of the white man and his abuses. Soon the "voices of militant warriors drowned out sachems' words of caution."[10]

On 7 May 1763, hundreds of warriors led by Ottawa chief Pontiac encircled and attacked British forces at Fort Detroit. A month earlier Pontiac had spread Neolin's message during a council with Ottawa, Wyandot, Potawatomi, and Ojibwa delegates at Detroit. The charismatic leader urged taking the hatchet to the English. Within weeks of the attack on Detroit, the infectious violent fervor had spread to the Ohio Country and seeped well into the metaphorical longhouse. By mid-June, British palisades at Venango, Le Boeuf, and Presque Isle, as well as the substantial Fort Michilimackinac, had fallen to determined war parties. At Venango, before the attacking Senecas murdered more than a dozen British soldiers they forced the garrison commander, Lt. Francis Gordon, to record their grievances. Inept imperial trading policies and high prices were cited, but the fear that the English planned to take possession of their lands topped the list. At Fort Pitt, Delaware chief Turtle Heart passed on the same sentiment while laying siege to the post.

In response to the swelling violence, British military leaders in North America sought a speedy resolution. As an acceptable means of reducing indigenous resistance to British occupation of the Pays d'en haut and Ohio River valley, Crown representatives conspired to "inoculate the Indians by means of blankets."[11] Before recorded in correspondence, however, the contagious idea had been played out at Fort Pitt. On 24 June, Delaware negotiators were given two infected blankets and a handkerchief by the leading commander at Fort Pitt, Capt. Simeon Ecuyer. "I hope it will have the desired effect," Indian agent William Trent noted in his journal later that day.[12]

Despite setbacks, bloody skirmishes continued well into the summer. In September a Seneca war party annihilated two British infantry companies and a supply train near Niagara Falls, killing five officers and seventy-six men. But by the end of October it was clear that the English would not be easily routed. Along with Col. Henry Bouquet's forces and the coincidental smallpox epidemic, supply shortages handcuffed the militants and reduced villages to beggary. Even Pontiac agreed to terms and withdrew to the south. Nevertheless, many warriors in the Ohio Country continued to resist British influences—and animosity between settlers and tribes festered.[13]

What historians have termed Pontiac's Rebellion has received significant attention and need not be detailed here. The struggle has even been considered the first American war of independence.[14] The indigenous residents may not have cleansed their lands of the English, but the hostilities did force the Crown to consider a new imperial strategy. The "rebellion" demonstrated the vulnerability of the northeastern borderlands and the need to address indigenous land concerns. The Crown realized that if unsanctioned trespasses continued peace would remain well outside imperial reach. As a result, the British had to uphold previous promises made at Easton in 1758 by extending protection to traditional lands west of the Appalachians.

On 7 October 1763, King George III signed a royal proclamation that set in motion a series of events that not only affected the lands and peoples along North America's colonial borderlands but also laid the foundation for rupture between Britain's colonies and the Crown. The Royal Proclamation of 1763 sought to centralize and organize the Crown's newly defined possessions in North America. The decree also aimed to neutralize growing violence over land. This was to be done mainly by drawing a boundary between European and indigenous populations that stretched along the back parts of the colonies, from the newly acquired Canadian territories to the Florida peninsula.[15]

The proclamation established a boundary that not only reflected an imperial policy of controlled interaction but forbid speculation and limited settlement west of the Appalachians on lands now reserved for its indigenous inhabitants. The terminology could not have been clearer: tribal lands "should not be molested or disturbed in the Possession of such Parts of Our Dominions and Territories as, not having been ceded to, or Purchased by Us, are reserved to them or any of them as their Hunting Grounds." As for continued colonial growth, Crown regulations would guide all further land sales. "No Governor or Commander in Chief in any of Our Colonies . . . do presume, on any Pretence whatever, to grant Warrants or Survey, of pass Patents for any lands beyond the Heads or Sources of any of the Rivers which fall into the Atlantik Ocean from the West and North-West, or upon any Lands whatever, which not having been ceded to or purchased by Us as foresaid, are reserved to the said Indians, or any of them." Moreover, for those tribes intending to dispose of their lands east of the boundary on lands not yet purchased by Europeans, the proclamation insisted that the initial sale must be to the Crown "at some Public Meeting or Assembly" to avoid fraudulent practices and future disagreements.[16] At its core, the 1763 proclamation spearheaded "enormous changes" that affected "many societies and countless lives in North America."[17] The year marked a turning point in early American history, particularly with regard to continental expansion and intercultural relations.

The Royal Proclamation of 1763 restricted speculation and Crown-sanctioned settlement but failed to curb unregulated trade or the irritating stream of European squatters. Encroachment by European settlers continued. Scores of renegade settlers persisted in seeking a livelihood throughout the northeastern borderlands. Because the proclamation restricted large-scale migration, however, it hindered European and indigenous enterprising. Squatters squatted, but speculators could not capitalize on the sale of land. This angered the indigenous inhabitants, and speculators like George Croghan and George Washington could not eject squatters from land they claimed because they could not secure clear title. Such frustration is an important element of early American history long eclipsed by the shadow cast by Frederick Jackson Turner's infamous Frontier Thesis.[18]

Perhaps more important, because the proclamation acted as a legal roadblock to the sale and partitioning of tracts beyond the Appalachians, it also stunted the resources and diplomatic mobility of the Iroquois. The redrawing of the 1763 boundary promised to open up Ohio and Illinois country to settlement, thus deflecting European interest in land away from the Mohawk River valley. Whether Europeans bartered, cheated, or stole, the result was universal: confusion and festering animosity. Illegal settlement throughout the northeastern borderlands challenged indigenous autonomy, created intra- and intertribal tensions, sidestepped provincial taxation, and undercut the enterprise of land speculating. With their French buffers ousted and support of the 1763 Uprising diminishing, many Ohio and Great Lakes tribes also engaged in scattered acts of resistance against Grand Council claims of authority as much as European occupation of land and illicit trade. Simultaneously, many nations attempted to procure Crown goodwill to avoid the wrath of punishment stemming from their alliances with the wrong sides in the recent war and rebellion. It was a balancing act that threatened to undercut the carefully constructed place of the Confederacy in continental enterprising. Consequently, soon after Jeffery Amherst made it clear that the Crown need not maintain costly alliances after the reduction of New France, the interests of the eastern Iroquois, a slew of colonial speculators, and select Crown agents converged. A new boundary meant the extension of imperial authority, and therefore the continued prominence of the Indian Department and the eastern Iroquois in an imagined empire. Thus, Iroquois headmen had as much to do with the demise of the 1763 boundary as did land jobbers, squatters, or imperial strategists in Whitehall.

Thus, for many concerned administrators on both sides of the Atlantic, the Royal Proclamation of 1763 represented only a temporary measure that was hurried through the political apparatus because of the urgency of frontier relations. The president of the Lords of Trade, twenty-six-year-old Lord Shelburne, "envisioned a boundary line as a device for regulating, not eliminating, frontier expansion." It was an apparatus that "would eventually be abolished as old colonies grew and new ones were created." Four days after the young George III signed the proclamation, the document's details sailed for North America. By the end of the year, Amherst had been recalled from North America and tribal delegations from throughout the northeast carried copies of the proclamation west.[19]

For many Europeans the scale of devastation wrought by the brief Uprising of 1763 created a combustible combination of embarrassment and betrayal. Before being recalled to London, General Amherst already had begun to set in motion his plan for retribution. In September he wrote Johnson, fixating on "The Punishment of the Indians" and insisting that Johnson contact Colonel Stephen, who commanded a Virginia volunteer force presently on the Pennsylvania frontier, and recommend that he strike hard against the Shawnee settlements on the Ohio. The seemingly impervious Iroquois Confederacy also appeared poised to fall victim to British plans for revenge. Along with the Shawnees and Delawares, the western Senecas remained a target of Amherst's call to arms. "I should think they ought not to be permitted to Come within your Doors," Amherst admonished Johnson, "but that they should be totally Despised as Ungrateful Villains, who Deserve the Severest Punishment." Caught between the impending fury of the British military and the perceived ancient Iroquois union, Johnson had to move fast if he had any chance to modify Amherst's plans to punish factions of the western gatekeepers of the longhouse.[20]

The rhetoric of Six Nations overlordship may have been far from reality on the Ohio, but to Johnson and the Grand Council it remained an active and essential ingredient "in the Crown's formula for postwar Indian affairs."[21] Wasting little time, Johnson wrote New York governor Cadwallader Colden on 20 September 1763. On behalf of English-allied Iroquois, Johnson informed Colden of the recent successes of the Six Nations in luring the "two first Seneca Castles to reason" and hoped to soon inform the governor of their bringing over to reason the rest of the Ohio nations.[22] Johnson worked toward securing the validity of the Confederacy by redirecting English hostilities aimed at the Senecas. Meanwhile, Amherst made his way to London in November 1763 to account for the recent rebellion.[23] As a result, the implementation of a decisive and aggressive frontier policy again lost momentum. Johnson did not miss the opportunity to further his cause. On 17 November he wrote to Gen. Thomas Gage and asserted the loyalty of the Iroquois in the Ohio Country. The local Iroquois were doing their best, Johnson noted to Gage, to dissuade the "Delawares, &ca., who are our Enemies," from continuing hostilities against the English.[24] Twelve days later Gage forwarded Johnson's message to the newly appointed Pennsylvania governor, Thomas Penn, and requested him to take "such measures as you think necessary to frustrate the evil Intensions of the savages."[25]

On 12 December 1763, Penn addressed the provincial assembly. The governor sought support from the largely Quaker group to raise one thousand men to aid Crown forces in the reduction of the Shawnees, Delawares, and other enemy tribes who had previously committed hostilities toward the colony.[26] These enemies included the Ohio Iroquois and western factions of the Senecas, known as the Chenussios.

Johnson again intervened. The principal cause of conflict, he wrote to Governor Colden, was the admitting of "Posts" in their country without the due procedure of gift giving. Johnson further noted, "I am of opinion their offers of a Peace arise principally from an expectation that they will for the future obtain their desired Ends which they could not get by any other means than by having recourse to Arms." Johnson urged Whitehall and the provincial governors to consider at length the nations' appeal for a peaceful resolution, since failure to do so might very well make them "dangerous Enemies."[27] Governor Colden too remained skeptical.[28] On Christmas eve the superintendent of Indian affairs again sent word to the New York governor, indicating among other things that the Pennsylvania Assembly had incorrectly remarked that the Six Nations had entirely defected from the British cause.[29] The situation continued to deteriorate. *All* of the Ohio tribes, Gage wrote Johnson in January 1764, have murdered settlers without impunity, and failure to reprimand them promised to spark "every puny Tribe" to take up the hatchet against the English, embroiling the empire in further conflict.[30] Gage demanded action.

Three weeks later, amid anxious discourse in the wake of the Conestoga massacre, Johnson attempted to curb Crown hostilities toward the Senecas and Ohio Iroquois before the ice broke in the spring. On 12 January he informed Gage that more than two hundred members of the Six Nations had gathered at Johnson Hall ready to "go upon any thing" he required.[31] Even though the party was almost entirely Oneidas, Johnson nevertheless did his best to convince skeptics of a united Confederacy, insisting that even the Senecas were "sanguine . . . and desireous . . . to go against our Enemies."[32] Furthermore, on 9 February Johnson wrote Penn that he had just outfitted a two-hundred-strong Six Nations war party and expected news shortly of an attack on the Shawnees, Delawares, "or those nest of Villans at Kenestio." Appealing to the governor's fear of the cost of continued conflict, Johnson ended the letter by insisting that the war party would secure the northeastern borderlands.[33]

It appeared that Johnson's heavy-handed tactics worked and his directive had taken hold.[34] In March he informed Colonel Bradstreet, General Gage, and Colden early in the month that on 26 February his party had captured Teedyuscung's son, Delaware chief Captain Bull, and forty-one other enemy warriors near a branch of the Susquehanna River.[35] Johnson also restated that Senecas remained committed to English efforts against hostiles on the Ohio.[36] As a result, historians have argued that Johnson "demanded that the Iroquois take up the hatchet" in order to force the Ohio tribes into submission.[37] A closer look, however, hints at the extent of Johnson's diplomacy and a dialogue between himself and his Iroquois allies.

Little is recorded of the Johnson's missions after the initial reports. In fact, few records indicate a rash of indigene-led offenses, and "there is no evidence that life on the Ohio was disrupted."[38] More suggestive is the point that Johnson concluded a peaceful council with western Senecas on 3 April 1764 at Johnson Hall, where the Senecas agreed to give up the Niagara carrying place—a tract about fourteen miles in length and four miles in breath from Fort Niagara to Fort Schlosser. The Senecas also promised to deliver some dissident Susquehanna Delaware leaders who had sought their protection.[39] Perhaps not as "humiliating" a peace as some scholars have suggested.[40]

Matthew Ward cites the inability of the Iroquois to subdue Ohio nations as evidence of the Johnson's misguided faith in the authority of the Grand Council.[41] This seems more plausible, but it may incorrectly put all initiative with Johnson and cloud the complex nature of the war party. Perhaps Johnson's war party may be better understood as a diplomatic delegation—a gesture of force supported by the superintendent. It was more likely a show of strength by the Grand Council in an attempt to rein in their Ohio "brothers" and "cousins." The English-allied Six Nations may have had the British on their side, but with their authority spread thin they were well aware of the need to tread lightly on the Ohio—a message Johnson tried to make clear to his European brethren.[42] In fact, given the extent of the proposed retaliations, the Senecas, momentarily, got off lightly. Johnson hoped to further contain the situation by protecting the integrity of the Confederacy. On 6 April he wrote both Governor Colden and General Gage attesting to the trustworthiness of the Six Nations.[43] Gage, however, remained skeptical. He disclosed in multiple letters to Johnson that he did not believe the sincerity of the Senecas and felt that nation had largely avoided punishment thanks to its close relationship with the rest of the Six Nations. Gage also insisted that the Senecas recent change in attitude was "rather suspicious." In the end, though Gage may have required Johnson's assistance in deciphering the details of some hostilities, he remained steadfast in his own belief regarding the untrustworthiness of the Ohio nations, the western Senecas included.[44]

Gage conceded to Johnson that the administration would likely be content with the actions taken against the Ohio Iroquois thus far. As for the Delawares and Shawnees, the general adamantly added, "nothing remains but a proper Chastisement."[45] Furthermore, he affirmed the British policy for the region west of the Alleghenies. "It's highly Necessary on many Accts. that we should become formidable on the Ohio," he remarked on 6 May. "Lands yielded to the King for his sole use in that spot, should be explained, that He may give it to be cultivated to whom He pleases."[46] By the spring of 1764, it appeared that Johnson had defused any planned hostilities toward the western Senecas. Furthermore, consent had been given to assert the colonial rights of conquest throughout the Ohio Country.[47]

Richard White remarks that in "this atmosphere of uncertainty, the British dispatched two armies to the *pays d'en haut* on a rather quixotic mission of conquest."[48] In August 1764, Colonel Bradstreet led an army west along the southern shores of Lake Erie while forces raised in Pennsylvania and Virginia marched to the Ohio River in

September under the command of Colonel Bouquet. White suggests that, because the commanders departed for the Ohio Country with vague orders from General Gage, they had "a great deal of discretion as to whether they should attack the Indians or conclude peace with them."[49] However, the fact that many of the anti-British groups remained hostile in spite of Johnson's earlier negotiations at Niagara, Senecas and Ohio Iroquois included, did not sit well with leading British officials.[50] Bradstreet made it clear that he sought bloody retribution.[51] Yet the colonel is said to have "lacked confidence" in his army, and "distrusted the [Iroquois, Caughnawaga, and Chippewa] Indians . . . whom Johnson had secured to escort him"—so much so that on 12 August when Bradstreet encountered a small party of Delawares, Wyandots, and Ohio Iroquois just east of Presque Isle he decided to negotiate a preliminary peace with them rather than attack. Bradstreet's peaceful overtures were again witnessed a month later at Detroit with Chippewa chief Wassong and at Schenectady with representatives of the Wyandots.[52]

Individual discretion may have played a role in the events, but Johnson's earlier intervention and the precarious situation of the British army should not be ignored. Some who entered into agreements with Bradstreet fell under the rubric of protected nations, and recent news of peaceful overtures being made by Delaware representatives made deciphering indigenous loyalties extremely difficult. Moreover, it had been made clear that misguided force might give way to another conflict. In the end, perhaps Bradstreet had little choice but to conclude preliminary negotiations with Shawnees and Delawares even after his indigenous escorts informed him that some of them were likely to be spies. News of peace offerings from Pontiac and Wyandots, Chippewas, and Ottawas likely halted the planning of military operations directed toward those nations. When Gage learned that Bradstreet planned to negotiate terms of peace, he was infuriated.[53] Apparently Bradstreet's pacifism created an opportunity that few renegades readily exploited. This point seems to have been confirmed in mid-September 1764, when Ohio Shawnee, Delaware, and Iroquois representatives failed to attend a scheduled council with Bradstreet at Sandusky to ratify their earlier offerings of peace. Word that they had failed to solidify a truce with Bradstreet further enraged

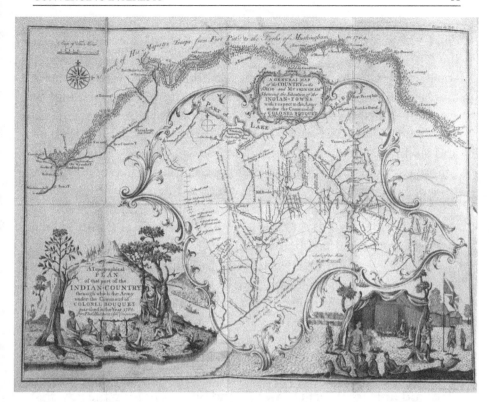

"A General Map of the Country on the Ohio and Muskinggum Rivers, shewing the situation of the Indian Towns with respect to the Army under command of Colonel Bouquet," by Thomas Hutchins, 1764. Courtesy of the Library of Congress, Rare Book and Special Collections Division, LC-USZC4–4809.

Gage. He renounced Bradstreet's earlier overtures and awaited news of Bouquet's expedition to the Ohio.[54]

By 5 October 1764, Colonel Bouquet had marched his army of 1,500 into the heart of the Ohio Country. On 17 October, on the Scioto Plains near the Tuscarawas branch of the Muskingham, about 150 kilometers from Fort Pitt, Bouquet issued terms of peace to the Ohio nations comparable to those offered by Bradstreet almost two months before.[55] The great Seneca headman Kiasutha led the Ohioans' delegation, most of whom Bouquet had fought against during the battle at Bushy Run in July 1763. Also in attendance was Chief Turtle Heart, who played a leading role in the 1763 siege of Fort Pitt. Only one Shawnee chief, Keissinautchta, took part in the negotiations. Nevertheless, for the Crown it was clear evidence that many Senecas and Delawares sought peace.[56] As a result, Bouquet again issued the terms of peace and demanded all hostages be returned to him. Again the English sword was sheathed.[57] To speed up compliance with the negotiated terms, Bouquet marched his army to the forks of the Muskingham and awaited the return of all English hostages. Meanwhile, as many "captives" reluctantly began to trickle in, a large portion of the Shawnees did their best to drum up resistance to the British demands.[58] A Shawnee leader named Charlot Kaské incited continued revolt by negotiating for over £1,500 worth of powder and lead with French traders throughout the Illinois Country.[59]

As the chill of another winter sent in, Bouquet had few options other than returning to Fort Pitt with his army and more than two hundred returned captives. After reaching the fort on 28 November, Bouquet pressed eastward toward the mountains. In the end, this mission marked a temporary conclusion to the hostilities stemming from the 1763 Uprising. Nevertheless, although thousands of pounds sterling had been directed at the Ohio problem, the Crown's show of force did little to deflect Delawares and Shawnees from the idea that the Ohio Country remained their homelands. They had given up a few hostages, but they had escaped the bloody chastisement Gage had envisioned.[60] For the moment, the Ohio Country remained out of the day-to-day control of senior British administrators. The return of Bradstreet and Bouquet to winter quarters, however, brought only a temporary respite for the villages in the region.

Although New France had been surrendered by the early 1760s, French-allied nations had not been conquered. Resentment throughout the Ohio Country toward the presence of Redcoats and English settlements continued. At this point in time, it has been argued, an impasse existed where neither the British army nor the Ohio nations could completely displace the other. This military stalemate then soon turned into an ideological stalemate.[61] Although this analysis remains well founded, it can be expanded. By July 1764 news was spreading among the Ohio nations of a new policy that promised to restore the tradition of gift giving and increase trade with them. These factors, along with a widespread belief that the British were planning to abandon their western posts, resulted in the lull in violence during the summer of 1764. The temporary truce established the Ohio nations as "victors in all but name."[62] To complicate the picture further, Johnson and the Grand Council had done their best to protect the integrity of the Confederacy and safeguard Seneca and Ohio Iroquois interests—sentiments and warnings that certainly muddled British policy. Meanwhile, borderlands strategy changed in the Indian Department. Johnson followed Gage's lead to accept the peace offerings of Pontiac's army in an attempt to cultivate division among the nations. The resulting situation was a confusing and unresolved set of British-tribal relations.

William Johnson sought to extend the Grand Council's influence over the Ohio region, but his approach reveals much about his skewed perceptions. He sought to protect the Ohio Iroquois and western Seneca nations, but the Delawares and Shawnees were another matter. A skilled Indian agent, Johnson first sought to maintain the façade of a united Six Nations by downplaying the role of any Iroquois in the carnage of 1763. Johnson knew that a British-led attack on the western nations of the longhouse could potentially result in devastating consequences for the colonies, and for his own position. Events sixty years prior had all too well demonstrated the double-agent nature of the Grand Council.[63] Johnson sought to tread lightly and reforge alliances based on the idea of Six Nations overlordship. Gift giving and grand councils were his chosen methods. On Christmas eve 1763, however, Gage quashed Johnson's idea of convening a conference of various nations to solidify a lasting peace.[64] Johnson followed the general's lead thereafter, laying the foundation of a new strategy for the frontiers.

On 26 December 1763, Gage offered Johnson the following advice. Avoid convening all the nations in council; rather, "raise up Jealousies of each other and kindle those Suspicions So natural to every Indian. . . . And all, which I can foresee must arise from this System is, that if they are Friends, they will join to cut our Throats." Regarding the recent peace offerings from Pontiac, Gage further suggested, "I think it is our Interest, if we find them sincere [in their push for peace] to close with them, and break the Confederacy; and be thereby enabled to turn our whole force against the Rest."[65] Johnson agreed and followed Gage's lead by conspiring to create mistrust and jealousy between the Six Nations and the western nations. He added that they could "prove very dangerous Neighbours . . . could they arrive at a perfect union."[66]

In late January, Johnson departed for the southern shores of Lake Erie to hold council. Rather than convene a large assembly, he prepared to meet only with the western tribes. Johnson wrote Gage confirming his intention to solidify the general's strategy. If the western tribes are led to believe they stood in British favor, Johnson confessed, "we should then have a right to claim their assistance on occasion, & they would hardly ever desire ours for any thing more than Arms & Ammunition which it would be our interest to give them in a War with one another." He further promised Gage that he would demand that the nations give up all their prisoners, deserters, and Frenchmen; agree to the removal of the Jesuits; and demand that the English have the liberty to establish trading posts and open the rivers to trade without interference from the inhabitants. Johnson urged the Senecas to guarantee the Niagara "Carrying Place" and, contrary to the Covenant Chain, demanded that those responsible for robbery and murder be delivered to the British to be tried under English Law.[67]

Johnson also addressed trade. By the spring of 1764, Gage had accepted the opening of a relatively unregulated trade system. He wrote Johnson indicting that the Crown should yield to the "immoderate Thirst which the Indians have for Rum, and let them have it" so long as consumption did not take place at the trading posts.[68] Only days later Johnson told Cadwallader Colden that all those who requested peace would be granted access to trade. Johnson hoped the "French Maxim of purchasing ye. Indians favour" would be adopted. Yet the superintendent knew well that there would be resistance to the occupation of some of the Ohio lands without compensation. He encouraged Colden to restrain traders "from holding any Meetings, or sending Belts to any Indians . . . [for they] have invented Storys & mentioned the names of Persons in power the better to obtain their End."[69] By the spring of 1764, Johnson waited anxiously while Whitehall mulled over his suggestions and attempted to reshuffle colonial affairs after the Uprising. In the meantime, other borderland players jostled to influence the state of affairs.

The reorganization of British imperial policy with regard to the administration of the northeastern borderlands had been an issue of concern among critics long before 1763. British thirst for land remained a nuisance to the effectual regulation of imperial policy. Speculation, squatting, clandestine dealings, and a lack of redress for indigenous peoples on the part of British authorities often created overwrought situations. As Benjamin Franklin noted in his address to the king's council in 1759, "if [the Indians] entertain any suspicion that they have been deprived of their lands without their consent . . . they usually conceal their discontent until an opportunity offers of revenging themselves."[70] Johnson agreed. He urged colonial administrators and provincial authorities to attend to a growing number of "reasonable & well founded" complaints of "enormous & unrighteously obtained Patents for their Lands" as well as the limitations of the provinces.[71] Although a system of indigenous-colonial relations had theoretically been exercised since the Albany Congress of 1754, it remained "strictly ad hoc."[72] Nevertheless, Johnson viewed the centralization of administrative power as the key ingredient to an enduring peace. The Uprising of 1763 revealed dangerous discrepancies in the British imperial system that exposed the arrogance of Amherst's policies and the cost of British diplomatic neglect throughout the northeastern borderlands.[73] Amherst's career collapsed, and many officials envisioned a new policy that would sustain a peaceful coexistence between first peoples and Europeans. Their ideas spawned the ill-starred "Plan for the future Management of Indian Affairs."[74]

In his "Native Americans, the Plan of 1764, and a British Empire that Never Was," Daniel Richter points to disputes over trade and land policies that required adjustment in order to address deteriorating relations with the tribes. Disruptions and ungenerous trade terms had caused disillusionment among the indigenous inhabitants of the Ohio. The unavailability and inaccessibility of British goods under Amherst's trading policy left many commercially oriented tribes starved and resentful of British occupation of the region. After the Seven Years' War, the English held a virtual monopoly on borderland trade. Moreover, because of heavy restrictions on "exported" merchandise, traders often illegally bartered throughout the northeastern borderlands. "Floods of rotgut rum and shoddy goods at high prices" Richter writes, "combined with shortages of officially sanctioned alcohol and of the ammunition crucial for hunting to convey an impression of British mean spiritedness, if not outright aggression." Corruption and fluctuating prices often sent indigenous entrepreneurs down the Mississippi to New Orleans to trade with the French.[75]

The boundary also remained a problem. Even prior to the Royal Proclamation of 1763, renegade settlers poured west in search of "virginal" lands. By the early 1760s illegal settlements infected Red Stone Creek, Cheat River, and the road to Fort Pitt. As the Ohio nations began to witness the ramifications of settlement, more and more eyed the homelands of the Six Nations. Although speculator schemes remained temporarily checked by the 1763 decree, the increase in squatter populations west of the Appalachian range revealed that squatters were completely undeterred. Settlement on lands not yet formally ceded to the Crown, however, not only skimmed from the pockets of eighteenth-century developers but also fueled indigenous resentment toward the British. The deforestation and fences that accompanied Europeans across the globe also trailed those frontier families as they penetrated new lands. It is not surprising that violence followed close behind.

The grave colonial consequences of borderland clashes demanded that the Crown not only seek to regulate trade and readjust the boundary but also search for a system of justice that traversed cultural and ethnic lines. Nothing could be resolved between conflicting indigenous and European interests so long as a cross-cultural communication remained hampered. By the early 1760s the once delicately balanced system of "policing one's own" that previously defined both cultures' systems of justice appeared to be on the verge of collapse. After 1763 the inability of the Crown to control borderland expansion, and thus violence, tainted indigenous perceptions of the British legal system. Those guilty of slaughtering tribespeople often went without punishment. Few instances brought the brevity of remedying this matter into focus than the Paxton riots in December 1763.[76]

On 14 December an armed gang led by Matthew Smith rode into Conestoga and slaughtered six resident Susquehannocks, including two women and a child. During the butchery, fourteen others managed to escape and later sought refuge in the Lancaster jailhouse under the protection of the provincial government. Their thirst for blood not quenched, the "Paxton Boys," whose numbers had swelled, resumed their murdering spree on 27 December. They broke into the county jailhouse and massacred the remaining fourteen Susquehannocks, leaving their bodies in the yard. Before departing, the mob vowed to eradicate indigenous people on Province Island and march on 125 of them housed by Moravians outside Philadelphia.[77] The Paxton gang never reached Philadelphia. In early February 1764, Benjamin Franklin, among others, convinced them to turn back while camped approximately six miles outside of the city in Germantown. Native grievances remained, however, as the murderers of the twenty Conestoga residents went without punishment. With tensions high, Governor Penn wrote Johnson and Gage on 5 January 1764 in search of a solution.[78]

It was not until 10 February that members of the Pennsylvania Assembly reconvened after the lingering rioters had reluctantly dispersed.[79] Four days later, compounding an already sticky situation, the governor laid before the Assembly the grievances of the frontier inhabitants. Of principal annoyance, according to the statement, was the government's willingness to protect those "Skulking parties" who "attacked and ravaged" borderland villages during the previous war. "They come, not as Deserters," the frontiersmen argued, "but as Friends, to be maintained through the Winter, that they may be able to Scalp and butcher us in the Spring." The complainants, some of whom may have been murderous rioters, called for the reimplementation of a scalp bounty. They argued that the measure would reduce the tribes to reason and requested the government to halt all trade of warlike provisions to them. Finally, the complainants blasted the Quakers for "openly load[ing] the Indians with Presents," which they believed taught them to despise the Europeans as weak and disunited.[80] Governor Penn and the Assembly needed to act. The government issued a statement that charged the backcountry settlers for being "grossly absurd [and] unrighteously burthened" in their lawless reprisals that "made [them] Dupes and Slaves to Indians." To quell tensions in hope of maintaining the veil of authority, the government maintained that only a few tribes remained outside British favor and blamed the poor practices of traders and squatters for aggravating the situation.[81]

Past adherents to Turnerian theory have depicted the Paxton riots as evidence of "sectional antagonisms" throughout the frontiers. Historian Wilbur Jacobs emphasized the regional and religious differences that separated the rioters from the eastern Pennsylvanian elite.[82] The slaughter of December 1763 must, however, be drawn into a wider narrative inclusive of not only various indigenous reactions but also a bigger picture characterized by the erosion of Crown authority in the borderlands of Virginia, Pennsylvania, and New York. As paranoia traveled unbridled through the northeastern borderlands, abuses abounded. The Paxton murders, although an extreme instance, typified how an absence of the rule of law brought European violence to the bordering tribes throughout the 1760s. To subdue and avoid any further violence, by 1764 many in Whitehall and throughout the colonies entertained Johnson's push for the centralization of power related to indigenous affairs in British America.

The reconfiguration of the policy—the 1764 Plan for the Future Management of Indian Affairs—included a scheme to regulate commercial and political interactions throughout British America.[83] It sought to repeal the various fragmented provincial methods of commercial and political regulation (or lack thereof). British possessions on the continent had been divided into two "Indian" districts since 1754—northern and southern—each with a Indian Department superintendent. As we have seen, the division favored the Grand Council and its claims over the northeastern borderlands. The commissioners of trade noted to the superintendent of the southern district, John Stuart, that the Ohio River was not suitable as a boundary because "several of the Northern Nations had not only *Claims and Interest*, but possibly actual possession and residence to the South."[84] Perhaps so, but the confluence of the Ohio and Mississippi rivers marked the natural divide. Previously, the power of the superintendents had been checked by budget restrictions on the military and the divergent diplomatic practices of provincial governors. The new plan sought to change this in accordance with the precedent established at Albany a decade earlier.[85] Thus, exchange between tribes and Europeans could legally occur only after official authorization. That authorization did not include the colonial commander-in-chief, governors, or any senior military figures but was to rest solely with the power of the super-intendentcy.[86] If adopted, the proposed plan would have dramatically reduced the powers of political and military officials in colonial America and in turn greatly increased the influence of the superintendents and their deputies.[87] Put simply, Johnson stood poised to inherit the key to a borderland kingdom. He envisioned a series of interdependent confederacies, with the Ohio River valley a mere extension of Iroquoia. Many Iroquois shared that vision.[88] Concurrent with Johnson's plotting, his subordinates envisioned the material benefits of their patron's management of the Indian Department.

With the French defeated, many old and new claimants did not want to miss their chance at western lands. Johnson's deputy, George Croghan, pursued such ends. On 2 May 1763, Croghan departed Fort Pitt and began a lengthy journey for London, leaving Alexander McKee to administer local affairs. Croghan sought, among other things, to clear title to thousands of acres of land he held in Indian deeds and gain compensation for trading losses incurred during the onset of the Seven Years' War. At Harris Ferry, Croghan received word from General Amherst to return to Fort Pitt. The "Uprising" had begun. Croghan learned that warriors had sacked Forts Le Boeuf, Venango, and Presque Isle.[89]

Despite direct orders to return to Fort Pitt and address the hostilities, a determined Croghan sought the first opportunity to sail for London. He excused himself from service on the grounds of poor health and resigned his position as deputy Indian agent.[90] News of Croghan's departure unleashed a barrage of attacks on his character. "One can not but regret that powers of so great importance to this country," Colonel Bouquet remarked, "should in this instance have been trusted to a man so illiterate, imprudent and ill bred."[91] Neither a gentleman nor an officer, Croghan, and his borderland dealings, did not sit well with many Crown and colonial officials. Johnson, on the other hand, did not appear unnerved or surprised by Croghan's exit. In fact, it appears that Johnson did little to deter Croghan from a hasty departure.[92] Croghan's private ambitions took precedence, and his decision to leave for London in the spring of 1763 did not meet with much opposition from his superior.

On 7 December 1763, Croghan met with eleven men at the Indian Queen Tavern in Philadelphia to discuss the reparation strategy of those who lost heavily in trade during the onset of the previous conflict. Among the concerned were a few of his oldest creditors and friends.[93] Making Croghan their agent, they decided to lobby the Board of Trade for 200,000 acres of land in lieu of their combined losses in 1754/5.[94] They gave Croghan and David Franks £210 and a memorial on behalf of the "Suffering Traders" drawn up by William Trent and Samuel Wharton.[95] Unofficially, Croghan secured the trust of Baynton, Wharton and Morgan by offering them a monopoly on trade. Decades later, an embittered Morgan recalled the appeal of Croghan's scheme:

> By and through him we were to have an exclusive contract to supply with Goods not only all the Natives within the District, to our immense Profit on the Skins and Furs we should receive in Payment, but also to furnish the prodigious Quantities of Merchandise which would be wanting by Sir William Johnson and Col. Croghan to conciliate the Affections of the Savages to the English and also supply all the back Posts with provisions. . . . I frequently lamented to him the unhappiness of Mr. Whartons disposition in regard to airy schemes, and his affectation of aiming at the great merchants, without attending to his real business; I pointed out to him the shameful situation of their books and many needless expenses.[96]

The Suffering Traders were not the only collection of speculators seeking to cash in on the fact that French claims had been removed and Crown reaction to the Uprising promised to solidify British control in the region. With time being of the essence, Virginia claimants and New York speculators also began to stir the pot. On 21 April 1763 a startling New York advertisement was reprinted on the pages of the *Pennsylvania Gazette*. It proposed the establishment of an Ohio colony, "New Wales," that included all of present-day Illinois and Indiana and most of Kentucky, with parts of Wisconsin, Missouri, and Ohio. The advertisement suggested that every family who decided to settle in the colony would be granted 300-acre lots, and 40,000-acre allotments should be sold to "Gentlemen Proprietors." All of the land was to be granted in patents. British officer and Methodist preacher Thomas Webb topped the list of supporters. Although swiftly withdrawn within a week by order of General Amherst, the message created a stir.[97] The speculative onslaught did not cease. In June, land speculators from Maryland and Virginia, George Washington included, formed the Mississippi Company. The company sought two and a half million acres on the Mississippi River and directly petitioned the Crown.[98] Although the Royal Proclamation of 1763 temporarily halted any immediate plans to settle west of the boundary, speculators queued in anticipation of an opportunity. Shortly after Croghan left Fort Pitt in May 1763, Virginia claimants too prepared to lobby the Crown to recognize Ohio lands that had been promised to soldiers by Governor Dinwiddie in 1755. By July 1764, Lt. Colonel Mercer, in London on behalf of the Ohio Company of Virginia, petitioned the Crown for patents to lands granted by the king prior to the Seven Years' War.[99] The rush was on.

While in London, Croghan courted the interest of the president of the Board of Trade, Lord Hillsborough. When his initial overtures appeared unsuccessful, Croghan addressed the Board of Trade and submitted "The Memorial of the Merchants and Traders relative to the Losses in the late and former Indian Trade."[100] In addition to pleading his own case at the Board of Trade, he did his best to encourage the board to reconsider the structure of the Indian Department and ultimately the boundary established by the Proclamation of 1763.[101] Croghan knew that the establishment of a new boundary "would be the first and indispensable step for land speculation on the Ohio and Mississippi."[102] The Crown would block confirmation of private land sales until then, but once the land was Crown land the governors could confirm title. Croghan hoped to capitalize. On 24 February 1764 he wrote to Johnson, keeping his patron apprised of the board's deliberations concerning Johnson's restructuring proposals.[103]

Meanwhile, Croghan waited anxiously to hear back any news regarding his land petitions. Two weeks later he sent a letter expressing his impatience to his superior, indicating among other things that the pressure he had placed on the Board of Trade for over a month had been to no avail. "The peple hear spend thire time in Nothing butt abuseing one a Nother & striveing who shall be in power with a view to serve themselves & thire friends, and neglect ye. Publick."[104] Restless and frustrated, Croghan arranged to deliver a message to the board in late March outlining reasons for reconsidering the Indian policy.[105] The Crown must take the appropriate measures to restore peace throughout the backcountry before the completely disaffected nations "cut off our frontier settlements, and thereby lay waste a large Tract of Country," Croghan cautioned. The clever deputy then refreshed the board's memory by stating that "in the space of four months the last summer in Virginia, Maryland, Pennsylvania and the Jerseys . . . [the Indians] killed and captivated not less than two thousand of his Majesty's subjects, and drove some thousands to Beggary and the greatest distress." Croghan maintained that they had murdered numerous traders and plundered more than £100,000 of their goods. "If the upper Senecas and few other Tribes settled near Detroit and Miscelemackena with the Shawnees and Delawares settled on some branches of the Ohio were able to effect this in part of a summer," he warned, "what must His Majesty's subjects dread from a general defection of the Indians?"[106]

Johnson's underling quickly offered suggestions. "First," he argued, "a natural boundary should be made between them and us across the frontiers of the British middle Colonies from the heads of the River Delaware to the mouth of the Ohio where it empties into Mississippi." Annual favors and good custom and policy must also take place, Croghan warned, "rather than enter into a general Indian War, which may be a consequence of a neglect on our side." He continued. The "lands west of such a line should be reserved for the Hunting grounds of the Six Nations . . . as they are the original Propriators of that Tract of Country for all the lands East of such boundary."[107] Conveniently, most of his 200,000 acres in borderland deed would fall within the new purchase—a fact Croghan undoubtedly knew very well. He also held much larger aspirations. To get the board to reconsider a new boundary marked only his first step. Croghan also pressed the members to liberate the Indian Department from military control, which would alleviate great strain between the Crown, colonists, and tribes.[108] The Crown's provision of money and gifts remained central to Croghan's message. When informed in April that his Indian deeds would not be confirmed by the Crown, his anger grew along with his interest in the establishment of a new boundary. He wrote Johnson, "I am Sick of London & harttily Tierd of [the] pride & pompe of the Slaves in power."[109]

Johnson's acceptance of Croghan's departure for London deserves further scrutiny. To be sure, Johnson knew that Croghan would do everything in his power to extend the boundary and centralize respon-sibilities under the Indian Department, as it was the only tangible means Croghan had to cash in on his deeds. Johnson also had much to gain, with regard to his own land dealings, if Croghan managed to persuade the board. But Croghan's effort to gain Crown approval for land Johnson held in Indian deed came a distant second on his list of things to accomplish while away. By early April word reached Johnson that the king's council would not authorize the transaction because it stood contrary to the 1763 proclamation. Instead of issuing additional instructions to his estranged deputy to push the matter further, Johnson followed proper procedure and wrote to Cadwal-lader Colden.[110]

If Johnson sought to traverse imperial regulations that bound expansion, he did not want to begin by challenging the power of the governor's office. He had little choice but to seek the support of those who could petition on his behalf. Not until mid-July did Croghan receive word on the reorganization of the department and his other failed attempt to gain compensation for the traders' losses of 1754/5. Discouraged, he again sent word to his superior: "they Make very Light of [the] Indian Warr. . . . the pople hear think you are Rich aNouffe and they heat to hear of any amerrican being Either popler or welthey." Moreover, Croghan complained, Hillsborough believed that "No Indian Agent Should Make any Contracks with Indians fer Lands or be Concern[ed] in Trade & no More than twenty thousand acres to one person fer which Grant there is to be paid hear a Sume of Money besides the Fees to the Governer." He explained to Johnson that neither his land claims nor Johnson's recent 20,000-acre Indian deed from the Mohawks would be granted until a new boundary could be established. Finally, Croghan noted that he had done everything in his power to respect the Mohawk complaints about the "Cayaderrussera patent," and the ministers agreed that if the New York Assembly did not "Disanul them patents," they would force such action by act of Parliament.[111] But there were other developments that may have pleased Croghan.[112]

When it became clear that he would not be granted a special act of Parliament to address his grievances, suggests historian Dorothy V. Jones, "the boundary negotiations became the vehicle through which a reparations grant was sought from the Indians." But, she continues, Croghan acted separately from Johnson in his push for a new boundary. Yet it is clear he had much to gain by supporting Johnson's plans of reorganization, along with that of Iroquois overlordship, when he first arrived in England. Exchange between the men confirms this point. In this instance, we should not separate the actions of Johnson from those of his subordinates.[113] It appears more likely that Johnson turned a blind eye to his deputy's tactics in order to press the Board of Trade to reconsider borderland policies. Perhaps Johnson knew that his deputy worked best when his own interests were involved. This was not, however, the first time Croghan's personal concerns were paramount. In London and on prior occasions, he exercised freedom of movement in plain view of his superior.[114]

Croghan departed London without an answer from the Board of Trade but had been writing Johnson optimistically on that head since March. As usual, he also included commentary on the prospect of settling an Illinois colony if all unfolded as planned.[115] By July the Plan of 1764 appeared to be on the verge of confirmation. When an elated Croghan arrived back in New York from London in August, William Johnson, in what became a regular occurrence, disregarded Croghan's earlier resignation and reoffered him the position. Croghan, short on resources and reluctant to face angry creditors, resumed his role as deputy to the superintendent of Indian affairs. During the 1763 Uprising Croghan's trading enterprise west of the Susquehanna had been ruined. By late 1764, records indicate that Croghan owed more than £4,000 to the firm of Baynton, Wharton and Morgan alone and had lost an unidentifiable amount from the trading post of Trent and Smallman at Fort Pitt. Croghan did not receive official confirmation of his Indian deeds or compensation for trading losses incurred in 1754/5 during his visit to London. It did not take him long to hatch a new scheme.[116]

When Croghan returned to North America, all seemed quiet throughout the northeastern borderlands. Reports filtered in from the frontiers of Pennsylvania, New York, and Virginia throughout June and July remarking on the respite in violence.[117] Jumping on the opportunity, Croghan instructed Alexander McKee to disregard military authority in all matters of trade under the authority of the forthcoming Plan of 1764. And only days after his ship docked in New York, the wily agent began illegally issuing trading licenses.[118] In New York he resided with George Morgan of Baynton, Wharton and Morgan, his major creditors. They had lost heavily the year before during the Uprising, and Croghan negotiated to keep their support. He offered the partners the exclusive right to supply a venture he planned while conducting negotiations in the Illinois region.

Croghan revealed to Morgan that General Gage intended to send him to the Illinois to hold a peace council in order to lay the foundation for future trade. He claimed to have a Crown credit of £2,000 to purchase gifts to smooth the negotiations but also planned to hide thousands worth of traders' goods in his pack train. Croghan planned to open trade with the goods supplied by the merchants, after settling terms of peace with the Illinois nations. His plan was illegal. He requested "an immense quantity of merchandise" from the Philadelphia men, "to make presents of/on account of the Crown." Croghan reassured them that his personal protection "would provide [the merchants] a safe Guard [of their] Goods and Boats" while transporting them from Fort Pitt to the Illinois. Croghan required an additional whopping £20,000 worth of goods for the transactions and urged the three men to make a quick decision. He threatened to look elsewhere for support if they declined.[119] Croghan convinced Morgan that he had approached him first with a flawless plan because of his desire to maintain their friendship. The value of beaver alone, Croghan declared, would amount to over £100,000 annually. The merchants took the bait, and together with Robert Callender and Robert Field a deal was struck. Croghan again had goods and resources by spinning visions of profits for men used to accepting risks.[120]

A flurry of activity surrounded Croghan as he prepared for his Crown mission to the Illinois. "So as soon as I gave my consent to this extravagant scheme," Morgan later recorded, "Mr. Wharton began to purchase large Quantities of Liquors, Sugar, Coffee, Chocolate and other articles to a very considerate amount. . . . The Goods . . . were tumbled from the shelves and made up in huge packages insomuch that for several days it was with difficulty we could get in or out of the store."[121] Yet Croghan knew that the only plausible way to obtain complete restitution for trading losses was through the establishment of a new boundary. A new boundary would enable the governors to confirm land titles based on Indian deeds. At Carlisle, former traders whom Croghan knew well petitioned William Johnson and the Crown for previous losses. The memorialists, including Robert Callender, Thomas Smallman, Alexander Lowry, Levy & Trent and Co., and Baynton and Wharton, among others, "demand[ed] of them, as the smallest Consideration they can make, That they assign, and grant . . . some part, of tract of [Native] Land, or Country, proportionate to their Losses."[122] The petitioners soon became known by the name of their forerunners, the Suffering Traders. Many of the new group were also members of the original petitioners.

Croghan did not bind his loyalty to the cause of his Philadelphia creditors. After Samuel Wharton learned that Croghan had left to treat with the Ohio and Illinois tribes, he wrote Benjamin Franklin. While mentioning that Croghan's terms of peace promised to assist the firm in a grand venture "to obtain Possession of the Illinois," Wharton also noted that he had recently confirmed his suspicion that Croghan sought the assistance of Anthony Bacon, an employed trader of Baynton, Wharton and Morgan, to introduce into Parliament his own personal losses. Croghan's actions on his own behalf angered Wharton. He appealed to Franklin "to call upon Mr. Bacon & explain to Him, the Justice of our sharing equally, with the first Sufferers, in any Restitution that may be made by Parliament."[123] But the persuasive Croghan knew how to appear indispensable.

Interestingly, Johnson knew well his deputy's multifaceted plan but exercised little resistance to the scheme. In fact, the superintendent appeared quite content with the perks. Johnson accepted the goods sent to him by Baynton, Wharton and Morgan in April 1764. All but beaver hats were supplied as requested, Samuel Wharton wrote Johnson apologetically, since "by their being illicit Articles; by an Act of Parliament, prohibiting the Exportation of them from one Colony to Another." Had it not been for the "Men of War at New

York, now much a strict and rigorous bunch," they would have sent the beaver as well. The letter also hinted at a business relationship between the superintendent and a consortium that included Croghan and the Philadelphia merchants. Earlier, Johnson had sent the influential merchants intelligence regarding the recent subjugation of the western Senecas. Scratching Johnson's back, so to speak, Wharton happily reported that he had taken the liberty "of indulging Our Printers" with the news about the handling of the Seneca nation "so the Inhabitants of this and other Provinces, might certainly know; To Whose Wisdom and unceasing Vigilance, They were indebted, for the present pleasing [state] of Indian Affairs."[124] The correspondence uncovers Johnson's willingness to overlook illicit trade practices that had caused plenty of borderland problems in the past in order to maintain the privileged position of his office and the Grand Council.

On 23 December 1764, after a council with 230 English-allied Iroquois, Johnson informed Gage that the Six Nations desired that the Senecas be pardoned and the "the Shawnese and Delaware, who, with the Ottawas and Pondiac, [be] represented as the principals in the war." In addition Johnson urged that the Proclamation of 1763 be reconsidered and a new boundary established to suppress any further problems. With his own expedition well supplied, Croghan made the final arrangements for his mission to the Illinois.[125]

On 23 January 1765, Croghan, his cousin Thomas Smallman, and Lieutenant Fraser departed Philadelphia, picked up sixty-five pack horses (in addition to an original sixteen) and goods in Carlisle, and headed toward Fort Pitt. Although given a Crown credit of only £2,000, Croghan managed to purchase £2,650 worth of goods from his cousin and charged additional expenses to the Crown's account for the purchase of goods from Robert Field and his old friends Baynton, Wharton and Morgan. In total, Croghan spent almost double his allowable limit. In fact, along with the Crown's gifts for the tribes, he transported more than £10,000 in goods supplied by Baynton, Wharton and Morgan.[126]

But mishap soon befell the intrepid Indian agent in a manner nothing short of karma. When a barrel cloaked as a Crown present broke and disclosed scalping knives to local onlookers, word of the incident spread like wildfire. The atmosphere could not have been worse.

Since July 1764, Governor Penn had succumbed to backcountry pressure and sanctioned a scalp bounty to quell frustration as many borderland settlers seethed about provincial reluctance to punish hostiles with official retaliatory attacks.[127] Peace treaties themselves annoyed the settlers, but when it was revealed that Croghan had purchased trading goods that could be used against settlers the situation eroded further. Settlers charged Croghan and the Philadelphia merchants with a trade violation, since Pennsylvania law forbade the selling of arms to hostile tribes.[128] The violation by an Indian agent made the incident especially scandalous. It infuriated not only Gage, who already mistrusted Croghan, but the settlers who had experienced the devastation of warfare. Consequently, borderland vigilantes from Pennsylvania, Maryland, and Virginia (the "Black Boys") in conjunction with local magistrates, who had been rioting throughout May and June over trade issues, commandeered the eighty-one-horse "Crown" convoy near Sideling Hill and set ablaze more than £3,000 worth of goods being sent to Croghan. When the blackened-faced vigilantes learned that some of the supplies had already reached Fort Loudon, they closed Forbes's Road, blockaded the fort, and threatened to kill Croghan.[129] Meanwhile, Baynton, Wharton and Morgan began pressing "Mr. C" for payment for the lost goods via the king's account. Gage insisted that he would not reimburse a cent of the cargo until he spoke directly with Croghan.[130]

Croghan's responded to the corruption charges predictably. "I have no concern in trade with any body," he wrote to Gage shortly after the incident, "nor has had since General Braddock's arrival in this country." When the general did not believe the lie, Croghan tried to pass the buck to Robert Callender.[131] Gage described the situation to William Johnson very differently. He insisted that Croghan had entered into "leagues with traders to carry up goods in a clandestine manner under cover of the business" contrary to provincial law. Furthermore, Gage blasted, "Mr. Croghan thought to take advantage of his employment to be first at the market." To make matters worse, Gage learned that Croghan summoned a large number of sachems to meet him at Fort Pitt instead of a select few representatives to meet him in the Illinois. Croghan's efforts to summon a large group for the purpose of trade did not go unnoticed. In fact, Gage complained to Johnson that Croghan had squandered considerable time and money as a result of his poor decisions. "This whole affair has realy been occasioned as I have before told you, by Croghan's Indiscretion. . . . I need not repeat what I told you concerning this Matter in my last Letter."[132]

Johnson did little to reprimand his deputy. Perhaps he had little choice but to defend Croghan given his own indirect involvement. Johnson forewarned his deputy of the growing controversy days before Croghan answered for his actions.[133] He also delayed his response to Gage for almost ten days after the first letter had been sent. He assured the general that he had examined the situation closely, including a report from Samuel Wharton, and concluded that it appeared Croghan *did not* have interest in the goods being transported. But the play for trade was obvious, and Johnson tried to distance himself from the clandestine partnership: "as to any other particulars concerning them I am totally a stranger."[134] Johnson the diplomat could be duplicitous too, if need be.

Illegal settlements, broken promises, and the impotence of English law inflamed the tribes; settlers throughout the northeastern border-lands did not want to see the Crown barter and trade with those they believed to have participated in the burning of their homes and scalp-ing of their sons and daughters.[135] On 6 April 1765, Croghan recorded that "Four Six Nation Indians arrived [at Fort Pitt], in a canoe down the Monangahela, with Five Cherokee scalps—they met a number of Virginia Hunters, on the Heads of New River, who had like to have killed them."[136] In June news reached Philadelphia that a mob of over a hundred men had freed from jail the backcountry butch-ers of six hapless tribespeople. Taking a page from the Paxton Boys, the hooligans threatened to march on the provincial capital unless their leaders were pardoned. "This was not Lancaster County, Penn-sylvania," Matthew Ward notes, "these were the 'Augusta Boys' in Virginia."[137] Richard Slotkin describes the rise in hatred toward the tribes as a means by which settlers exercised control of the affairs of the colonies.[138] The agency of the settlers should not, however, be overestimated; the resulting wake of indigenous and Crown reactions requires further exploration. By 1765 neither the British army nor the tribes could completely displace the other from the northeastern borderlands.

Luckily for Croghan, chance remedied his fragile situation. On 8 June, while encamped just below the mouth of the Wabash, a group

of Kickapoos and Mascoutens attacked Croghan's party. Wounded by
a tomahawk blow to the head, Croghan later remarked humorously
to Johnson that his thick skull led him to good fortune.[139] The attack
ceased when the war party realized that Shawnee delegates accompanied the traders. Confused, the Kickapoo and Mascouten warriors
divided the goods and imprisoned Croghan. Captive and facing an
uncertain future, Croghan could not ignore his fertile surroundings.
He later recalled that they "marched for three hours through a high
country extremely well timbered." Furthermore, after crossing the
Wabash on 10 June, Croghan recorded, they traveled the remainder
of the day "through fine rich bottoms overgrown with reeds, which
makes the best pastures in the world, being preferable to . . . Oats."[140]
When the war party arrived at Ouiatenon, the situation erupted in
confusion. While the marauders received punishment for the attack,
Croghan found out that a circulating wampum belt called for him to
be burned at the stake. After some debate, and with the help of the
French commander at Fort Chartres, Croghan bought his release with
sixty-four gallons of rum.

Ironically, Croghan's imprisonment turned out to be the root of
his greatest success during his Illinois campaign. Because of the mis-
calculated abduction, the local French inhabitants and traders reprimanded the five Wabash nations (Kickapoo, Piankashaw, Miami,
Weas, Mascouten). The Wabash feared what might be devastating
consequences if they faced the wrath of both vengeful Ohio nations
and English armies. As a result, they wasted little time suing for peace
with the Crown. Prisoner turned diplomat, Croghan negotiated the
terms. Never missing an opportunity, he underscored the importance
of trade and a British presence in the region. On 18 July, Croghan
departed the Illinois and headed toward the Ohio with Shawnee and
Delaware guides. Along the way he met the great Ottawa chief Pontiac. Croghan countered circulating rumors that the English planned
to seize land and give it to the Cherokees and enslave local populations. Then, on 17 August, Croghan arrived at Detroit and commenced treaty negotiations a week later. In metaphorical tradition,
he opened a road from the setting to rising sun, and those in attendance apparently pledged their loyalty to their new English father.
On 28 August, Pontiac addressed the Crown. On a pipe that was to be
sent to Johnson, Pontiac solidified peace and, in diplomatic fashion,

blamed drunkenness for his people's previous behavior.[141] Croghan returned to Philadelphia a hero.[142]

By the fall of 1765, Croghan was back in the Illinois Country. Ordered to collect intelligence and work toward the pacification of the region, Croghan, unofficially, addressed the growing concerns of his creditors and looked for ways to improve his fortune. He once again turned to the avenues of trade and land speculation. In November he wrote to Johnson, indicating that the Illinois nations feared that the English planned to take their country from them and "bring the Cherokees there to settle & to enslave them." To combat the growing anti-Anglo sentiment, Croghan suggested to his superior that trading posts soon be established "at proper Places" or the "French will carry the best part of the Trade over the Mississippi."[143] More important, Croghan remarked a month later, the establishment of a permanent Illinois colony would strengthen the British position in the region. It would be of importance, Croghan reported to Johnson, to gain a strategic position between the various nations. A strong British presence or colony would not only split the southern nations of the Carolinas from the Western Confederacy (a loose coalition of villages and nations in the Great Lakes region and Illinois Country) but promise lucrative benefits of trade with the Ohio and trans-Mississippi nations. Croghan maintained, if a "Civil Government is immediately established there (Fort Chartres) and the King's subjects are permitted to settle and mix there an Important colony in the centre of the Indian Country maybe immediately established without expense to the Nation, same favors annually to the Natives, whereby we may soon divide and balance, the Interests of the several Indian Confederacies." Croghan continued by stressing to Johnson the need for a swift decision. He suggested that the Illinois nations "had not the least objection" to the erection of English forts and trade in the region, "nor to our forming a Settlement and cultivating Lands."[144] He later expressed a similar opinion to Benjamin Franklin.[145] Perhaps Croghan's impression of the local indigenous residents had been blurred by the recent blow to his head. More likely, he was promoting a false impression to gain backing for a private venture in the region.

From late 1765 to February 1766, Croghan ceaselessly communicated with Johnson, his creditors, and colonial officials about his Illinois journey. Most of the messages urged the foundation of an

Ohio-Illinois settlement. He was enthusiastic about the lush terrain.[146] On his return he convinced Johnson to send a message to the Board of Trade recommending the establishment of an inland colony. The wax of Johnson's seal had not long dried before Croghan and eight of his creditors had drawn up the "Articles of Agreement" for the first Illinois Company, on 29 March 1766.[147]

According to Croghan's first biographer, Albert Volwiler, both Johnson and Croghan "were deeply interested in the success of this venture and in the ventures of traders." Volwiler depicts both agents hoping to launch a colony to check the growing French and Spanish influence in the region.[148] Croghan stood to gain from the evolving imperial strategy, and this analysis connects his scheming to a grand strategic design. And though it is useful to have imperial and indigenous alliances and tensions arrayed on a large canvas, it is excessive nevertheless to connect them to Croghan personally, as if he thought principally of balances of military power. He was more venal than this strategic description implies. With visions of new lands for speculative adventures, Croghan had to plot a way around the 1763 boundary obstacle.

The Illinois scheme, suggests another biographer, was "characteristic of Croghan, devious and dangerously speculative. . . . With Indian affairs in mind, he was convinced that a large and immediate trade was necessary to cement severed relations."[149] To be sure, trade between Europeans and the nations built mutually beneficial relationships, and the Illinois arena was no different. The Crown stood to gain valuable allies and trading partners. As for Croghan, he made sure to position himself to gain a fortune. But by the fall of 1765, Baynton, Wharton and Morgan had not seen one beaver skin or deer hide returned to Philadelphia in payment for the trading goods entrusted to Croghan almost a year earlier. Making matters worse, they were kept busy trying to secure compensation from Croghan's superiors for his outstanding Crown accounts.[150] In response, the Philadelphia merchants decided to send Samuel Wharton to Fort Pitt to directly oversee the return of goods. "In justice to Mr. Wharton," Morgan recalled, "I must say that I really believe that Col. Croghan did in a great measure deceive him into this mad scheme."[151] Trade on the Illinois constituted only part of Croghan's aspiration. He undoubtedly envisioned greater fortune for himself and had used the opportunity to make another play for land.

Earlier in the year, with the help of his trading partners, Croghan convinced Gage to recommend to Johnson that he schedule a council with the Six Nations to address traders' losses from 1763.[152] Johnson agreed. By 1765 a sense of urgency prevailed throughout the northeastern borderlands, leaving the situation ripe for exploitation. Contested European encroachments on Iroquois homelands quickly corroded the Covenant Chain, and acts of vigilante violence threatened to undermine the tentative peace. When the British presence on the Ohio was solidified in the wake of peace negotiations, an opportunity presented itself. The issue of land again took center stage. For those anxious to gain reparations or speculative opportunities, a new boundary seemed an essential step.

The renegotiation of a boundary had been a topic of discussion since word of the Royal Proclamation of 1763 reached the British colonies in America. The 1763 boundary did not reflect the realities of the North American terrain, and neither had the Plan of 1764. Contested land claims continued to undermine the authority of the Six Nations and Crown, and so did the independent actions of the Ohio nations. When newly knighted Sir William Johnson held council and treaty with Iroquois sachems and warriors in the spring of 1765, he entered the deliberations armed with the promises of a reorganized and centralized administration. The treaties provided Johnson with the first opportunity to affirm Crown initiative by negotiating a new boundary, and this council gave the Grand Council a forum to reclaim overlordship in the Ohio Valley lands.[153]

The Kayaderosseras patent had been a thorn in the side of the eastern Iroquois since the first decade of the eighteenth century. The land was originally patented in 1703 and 1708 by thirteen original petitioners and included more than 250,000 acres north of the Mohawk River and west of the Hudson—land that encompassed the heart of Mohawk homelands and traditional hunting grounds. Like most other contested land claims, these lands had been patented under questionable circumstances. The patent received special attention at the Albany Congress in 1754 when Chief Hendrick voiced Mohawk contempt for the claim and demanded its nullification. Set aside for almost a decade as a result of war and borderland turmoil, the issue resurfaced with a vengeance in the fall of 1764.[154]

When Johnson sent the Board of Trade an update in November 1764, he knew well the diminished capacity of the Grand Council to enforce their will on the Ohio. Nonetheless, he stressed the Crown's need to keep them in good favor. To do so, Johnson suggested, the troublesome Kayaderosseras patent must be settled.[155] Mohawk frustration with the patent had long been kept at the forefront of discussion at Johnson Hall. In February, Johnson wrote Colden, indicating that the Six Nation delegates gathered at his home were outraged by the injustice they had experienced. Johnson noted that he had urged them to pay little attention to the claims of the petitioners but added, "the Mohawks are determined to make public Remonstrance & Complaint, which I find I cannot prevent."[156] On 15 March, Colden informed Johnson that he had sent word to the Lords of Trade and held council at Fort George in an attempt to resolve the issue. He encouraged Johnson to inform the Mohawks that New York and Crown authorities had done all possible to seek justice.[157]

Johnson replied on 21 March. At great length he detailed the history of "Illegal & unjust Steps" that worked toward creating a situation ripe for rupture. "Annulling a Pattent is nothing new in this Province," a frustrated Johnson remarked, and warned that the Mohawks would not be satisfied "unless the means of relief are speedy."[158] Johnson relayed the spirit of the message to Gage a day later. He went as far as to declare that "unless a Method is fallen upon for obtain[ing] Justice . . . *a Superintendant has no business* to tell the Indians that they shall not be wronged or imposed u[pon]."[159] The tone of a document is difficult to judge, but it suggests that Johnson was annoyed. He also believed that, if the situation was remedied, the Six Nations would give up claim to thousands of acres of other westerly lands on their own terms.[160] Briefly derailed by the news of Croghan's Sideling Hill mishap, Johnson redirected his attention to Mohawk grievances as he and the Iroquois prepared for treaty procedures in the spring of 1765.

On 29 April 1765, treaty negotiations opened. For weeks before, Johnson deliberated with Iroquois and Delaware delegates.[161] The Shawnees were not present, but the Six Nations and Delawares gathered there happily spoke on their behalf. After a few days of deliberation, Seneca chief Gaustarax (Kayendarūnghqua) and Delaware chiefs Long Coat (Anindamoaken al) and Squash Cutter (Yaghkapoose) agreed to remain hostages until the terms of peace as described by Henry Bouquet eight months prior were met and peace restored. Then, only days after negotiations had commenced, matters turned to land. On 2 May, Johnson asked the delegations to consider the grievances of the traders who lost so much as a result of treacherous conduct of some the "ye Indians" and then conveniently noted, "Brethren, The last but the most important Affair . . . is with regard to settling a boundary." Johnson stressed the need to run a line between the tribes and Europeans to end disputes over land. It would be a boundary "which no White Man shall dare to invade." In his closing remarks, Johnson called on his audience to inform him of the intended nature and path of the boundary.[162]

For the next four days the Six Nations delegates and Johnson deliberated over the geographic limits of the boundary, and on 6 May 1765 the Onondaga speaker proposed that the line begin at Owego on the east branch of the Susquehanna River. Thence, "down the East side of the River Shamoken (or Fort Augusta) and running up the West Branch of Susquehanna on the South side thereof." From there "to Kittaning [Armstrong, Pennsylvania] or Adigo on the Ohio, thence along down the Ohio to the Cherokee River [Tennessee River], and up the same to its head."[163] As for the request of the traders, the Onondaga speaker declared that they would be given "some lands near Fort Pitt" as restitution. How much land was left unclear. Later that night, after a few hours of private deliberation, Johnson assembled the chiefs. He asked them for further clarification with reference to the lands "to the Eastward," that is, north of Owego. The eastern Iroquois took the opportunity to address matters closer to home:

> We think to continue the line up [the Susquehanna] River to Cherry Valley Lake, and from thence to the German Flatts . . . [as] you have no right or title on the South side [of] the Mohawk River above that place, however for the present we shall not extend the Boundary Line higher than Owego, but when the affair comes to be finally determined we shall think farther about it. . . . You know that We are Owners of the Land Westward of the German Flatts, we hope we are not to be cheated out of it. . . . Brother,

Since that is the case let us know what the White People claim, and we'll tell honestly what we sold.[164]

The lands in question lay at the heart of ancient Mohawk homelands and were well known to Johnson. The 1763 proclamation had done little to halt illegal settlements west of the line. But the situation of the Mohawks was even more vulnerable, because the line did little to protect their homelands. By 1765 the Mohawk Valley was dotted with European enclaves. Sensing the weight they carried as brokers, the Mohawks left the matter of the boundary readjustment north of Owego to future negotiations. They had as much to gain as they did to lose if the matter was not handled delicately. On one hand, they knew the Crown wanted to extend the line as far northwest as possible to avoid settlement and land claim complications. On the other hand, the Mohawks realized that an extension of the line would place their settlements east of the new boundary. They wanted time to ensure that they could negotiate the best deal with the Crown. To do so, they turned to the Ohio River valley to alleviate the increasing pressures of settlements to the northeast. The negotiators keenly detailed the extent of their claims by outlining a new boundary. Even though they remained ambiguous with regard to the northern extension of the boundary, Johnson expressed satisfaction with the proposal. After all, the Iroquois agreed to cede almost all of the northeastern borderlands. By 9 May, Johnson had concluded official negotiations.[165] The Delawares present had agreed to the terms laid before them, including the boundary. The Shawnees, who occupied and depended on the Ohio River valley lands that had been carved away, were not present.

In 1760, when Johnson first took up the Kayaderosseras cause, he was given land by the Mohawks "for continued care of them and their interests." Located near the Mohawk Upper Castle, the gift was situated in the center of the contested territory. By June, after Croghan had failed to get Johnson's claims realized in London, Governor Colden began to petition the Crown on Johnson's behalf. Colden reasoned to the Lords of Trade that the Mohawks would not transfer the rights to the land to any person other than William Johnson. To aid the petition, Colden noted that Johnson did not purchase the land illegally but rather was given the tract in return for his help from the Mohawk nation. He suggested that the Lords of Trade make a special case for Johnson, as they had previously done when granting land to British officers and their families for services rendered.[166]

Johnson's contributions perhaps demanded special consideration. Historians have pointed out that his deep interest in the Kayader-osseras dispute derived from the thousands of acres he stood to gain by getting the early patents nullified. Perhaps so, but the agency of the Iroquois ought also to be acknowledged. The Mohawks knew that Johnson would be an important ally in their struggle to fend off speculators and settlers. All struggles for land were difficult without proper representation, and those affected realized that Johnson was a powerful and sympathetic advocate. By 1765, those petitioning the Six Nations included men of considerable stature in colonial America, including New York's attorney general, powerful merchants, and members of the governor's council.[167] It is not unreasonable to think that the eastern Iroquois used the Indian deeds as a clever bribe to influence colonial leaders.

Writing ten years after the fact, Samuel Wharton remarked that Johnson informed the Six Nations that the Crown "had it in contemplation" to purchase a large tract of land in the trans-Appalachian region.[168] Two hundred years later, the essence of Wharton's message is still upheld by most historians. Jon Parmenter argues that Johnson was so "outraged over the participation of the Ohio Indians in Pontiac's War . . . [he] spent four years after 1764 pursuing an agenda of bolstering and extending the Confederacy's apparent control over the hostile Ohio nations." Furthermore, he suggests that during the land cession treaties of 1765 and 1768 Johnson "obtained his revenge on the Ohio Indians."[169] Parmenter's comments suggest that the matter was personal. It may have been personal, but there is reason to question that interpretation. By early 1764 it was clear that Johnson wanted freedom to negotiate with the Iroquois and did all he could to deter a swift and broad colonial-led attack against borderland tribes. He could have had revenge, if that was all he had in mind, just by standing aside and agreeing with General Gage. Furthermore, as we see in chapter 4, the eastern Iroquois encouraged Johnson to make arrangements for a treaty as settlement pressure mounted after the conclusion of the Seven Years' War and the 1763 Uprising. They were well aware that by ceding lands in the Ohio Valley they would relieve the strain on the Hudson River region and protect their homelands. Self-interest lay at the heart of their thinking, and Johnson lived among them.

Johnson has generally been depicted as a clever diplomat serving the British and colonial interests. He was that and more. His primary concern during the postwar era centered on holding together the Confederacy by deflecting imperial scorn away from the western Iroquois. By doing so, Johnson knew that future British claims to the trans-Appalachian region would likely receive support from his Iroquois allies. Meanwhile, the Iroquois were just as inclined to engage in a boundary dialogue by 1765 as Johnson. In fact, as the following chapter details, from 1766 to October 1768 Johnson was coerced and guided as he stressed the importance of securing a boundary. As Johnson worked to extend the empire into the northeastern borderlands, and thus his own place as superintendent of Indian affairs, his underlings and acquaintances manipulated the situation. Men such as Croghan knew well the potential benefits of brokering land. Croghan, too, encouraged Johnson to seek a boundary agreement, because that could increase the likelihood of gaining Crown confirmation of his Indian deeds. A moment of converging interests had arrived.

CHAPTER 4

Boundaries

By the mid-1760s, frontier expenses were becoming a topic of increasing interest at Whitehall and throughout the colonies. Britain had seized by war and retained by treaty a vast empire along with the burden of sustainability. The inability of the government at London to generate bullion "had a direct bearing on the Crown's efforts to fashion a western policy" in North America. The Grenville ministry's Stamp Act that intended to finance colonial costs was met with protest from Philadelphian row houses to Hudson Valley estates.[1] And as important as colonial reactions to parliamentary reforms in 1767 (the Townsend Acts) are to American revolutionary history, change during this time was not limited to historical categorizations. The borderlands of the English colonies in North America were, for instance, the scenes of ongoing alterations. A variety of problems confronted the Crown on account of the dynamic transformation. The Grand Council's insistence on Iroquois overlordship conflicted with the real level of sovereignty exercised by the Ohio nations, and settler interests clashed with imperial policy. The tonic that promised to transcend "the imperial-colonist dichotomy" and cure the rash of conflicting interests was land. Entrepreneurial ambition regarding land speculation may have "stirred on both sides of the Atlantic," but those who fostered and altered the basis of agreements in the latter half of the 1760s were not found in Whitehall or the provincial capitals but rather throughout northeastern borderlands.[2]

As 1765 came to a close, the verdict remained out on the future of the Indian Department and its activities. Although some encouragement had filtered back from Whitehall regarding William Johnson's earlier propositions, Crown indecision left many colonists wondering. The silence was broken after Christmas Day 1765 when General Gage sent Johnson a letter indicating that Whitehall was "tired of the Expense of Supporting Forts" and planned to reduce British presence up and down the frontiers.[3] Because Whitehall could not foot the colonial bill, it ordered a gradual withdrawal of troops and left trade regulation and the responsibility for borderland order in the hands of the colonial governments. As settlers pressed west, claims to indigenous lands increased, and violence followed close behind. With few enforceable regulations as a result of an impotent justice system, renegade traders engaged in the lucrative sale of liquor. Goods destined for tribal communities became scarce as French supplies ran out. Many English trading houses sought to take advantage of the market, but the hazards were many. British imperial presence was at best provisional, most Ohio Valley tribes were suspicious of English intensions, and most of the inhabitants of the Illinois Country remained anti-British.

By early 1766, William Johnson was well aware that the future of his operations as superintendent were in jeopardy. Although disheartened, he remained a devoted Crown agent who knew his livelihood depended on a strong imperial government. Thus, from late 1765 to October 1768, he worked to uphold Crown authority over the northeastern borderlands. But the situation could not have been less favorable. By 1768 the superintendent of Indian affairs was reduced to "the status of a frontier diplomatic corps." He was subordinate to the commander-in-chief, the home government was reliably unreliable, and money was in short supply.[4] As Johnson attempted to extinguish growing discontent throughout the borderlands, those around him, both indigenous and European, sought to exploit the situation. Croghan and the eastern Iroquois did their best to present the redrawing of a new boundary as a solution for securing future imperial involvement in North America. By that time, Johnson did not need much convincing. The one possible avenue to stability along the lines Johnson and his Iroquois associates would have wanted was a boundary between the colonies and the first nations. A new boundary promised to satisfy settlers, speculators, several colonial governments, and the eastern Six Nations.

The Ohio and Mississippi River valley lands remained prominent in the thinking of both enterprising Europeans and vexed tribes. From late 1765 to October 1768, Croghan and the Philadelphia merchant house of Baynton, Wharton and Morgan kept busy. Croghan almost always manipulated imperial assignments to settle personal debts and advance speculation in trade and land. The difference by 1766, however, was that imperial regulation had all but vanished west of the Susquehanna, so both tribes and colonists speculated in insecure places. From 1765 to the autumn of 1768, the pursuit of security and self-enrichment tied all parties. These years witnessed some of the most extensive jockeying throughout the northeastern borderlands as American Indians, land jobbers, and trading houses cued for position in anticipation of one of the largest land cessions in North America. They were not disappointed.

By 1766 "the colonial backcountry had become a locus for violence and disorder against all Indians."[5] European presence in the region was nothing new, but to the indigenous inhabitants the intentions appeared different. Trespassing occurred, game was hunted, and liquor was traded. By the mid-1760s, however, more and more permanent and illegal settlements had sprung up all over indigenous lands and the Crown could do little to curb the intrusions. More often than not, those charged with addressing squatting and trading problems were themselves shareholders in enterprises in land speculation beyond the Appalachians. The Ohio nations, which had previously tolerated infrequent run-ins with poachers and peddlers, loathed the influx of permanent settlements west of the mountains. Murders became frequent and vigilante justice threatened to erode what was left of Crown authority. Conflict fed rumors that the Ohio, Illinois, and Great Lakes nations were organizing in councils to plan for a combined offensive against the British.

Disagreement over land was not confined to the Ohio. On 12 August 1766, Governor Moore informed the Lords of Trade of recent riots in Massachusetts resulting from indigenous discontent over new settlements. Although the governor made it clear that he did not believe the claims of the Moheokunnuks (Stockbridge)—a people, he added, who were "looked upon by the Six Nations, to be a very despicable Tribe"—he insisted that it was the lack of investigation into their claims on the part of Crown Indian agents that was causing anger.[6] The eastern Iroquois, too, felt the squeeze. They complained to government authorities that their patience was running thin with regard to the continued hostilities their people encountered along the borderlands of Virginia and Pennsylvania. Warriors were killed by the English, and the eastern Iroquois remained convinced that the governor of Virginia sponsored the assaults. "I am sensible that your Excellency has wrote to the several Governors on the subject of murdering Indians," Croghan wrote to Gen. Thomas Gage in June. "I fear a Peace cannot be long preserved with those Nations, tho' at the same time I am fully persuaded that the Indians are very desirous of maintaining Peace with us."[7] Six Nations suspicions about Virginia's governor were close to the truth. In 1767, Gov. Francis Fauquier smugly commented that he "was in the dark as to the Sentiments of the Ministry by having never received His Majesty's Royal Proclamation of 7 October 1763."[8] That was hardly the case, but as settlers pushed north and west it was obvious that many provincial authorities did little to deter their provocative actions. Crown Indian agents informed Johnson of the frustrating situation, but he could do little but plead his case to Whitehall.

To make matters worse, trading practices had changed significantly, wreaking havoc on intercultural relations. The fur trade, although shrinking, remained a significant component of the local and transatlantic economies in the 1760s. After the suppression of the 1763 Uprising, trading houses once again targeted the Mohawk, Ohio, and Illinois River valleys. However, because game could be had only farther and farther west, few individuals could afford the increased transport costs and the greater risks of attack. Many experienced frontier traders, cleaned out by the previous hostilities, carried on as local agents for large trading houses based in New York, Philadelphia, and Montréal. The evolving economic landscape in the northeastern borderlands "ensured that only larger firms, with greater access to capital, credit, and a wide range of imported goods, would control [trade]." The absence of regulation also created a problem. Many traders brokered their own deals with the local indigenous inhabitants and many peddled liquor on the peripheries of empire. These factors created a volatile atmosphere as trading houses and rogue traders competed fiercely to recover previous losses by working to monopolize trade and push the liquor trade in new regions.[9]

"The English traders," Johnson wrote to the Lords of Trade in October 1766, are "imprudent, in giving each other the vilest of characters to the Indians and say whatever they think proper for promoting their private interests." To stop the trade abuses and contain the ill will of the remaining French inhabitants, Johnson remarked that the Lords of Trade should consider the establishment of forts to regulate trade and quell tensions.[10] Johnson longed for order. His remarks to London reveal that he grew discouraged as his powers waned: "My powers are very trifling, uncertain and in general disregarded and disputed here," he wrote, "insomuch that sundry persons do at pleasure call Indians together and transact any affairs they please with them, and thereby and by other misconduct and interested Stories do often overset all my transactions." Frustrated, Johnson made it clear to Whitehall that without proper authority he could not prevent disruptions to the delicate balance of power on the imperial fringe. Still steadfast in his support for the Plan of 1764, Johnson added, "until the plan is established beyond dispute and my powers fully ascertained and supported by proper authority it will not be in my power to render His Majesty or the public those services which it is my ardent desire to perform."[11]

Johnson was not the only one frustrated with backcountry events. On 11 November, Gov. Henry Moore of New York sent a scathing letter to London indicating the need for order, for "the whole nation suffers in the opinion of the Indians by a crime committed by a worthless individual." Moore suggested that, unlike New York, Pennsylvania did little to restrict its settlers from inhabiting lands beyond "the Limitts prescribed by His Majesty" at Red Stone Creek and beyond, which Moore insisted, infuriated the indigenous occupants.[12] The borderlands farther south were also a concern. In November 1766, the superintendent of Indian affairs for the southern colonies, John Stuart, warned South Carolina's governor George Johnstone that settler backlash from the recent murder of two Europeans must be avoided. Stuart argued that Crown assistance would be hard to come by if a war with the Creeks erupted, and "South Carolina would hardly be able to protect her own Frontiers, the Settlements and plantations of Georgia." All would have to be abandoned, and "the Inhabitants of the Two Floridas would be confined to their Stockades and Forts."[13] By the mid-1760s the situation looked bleak for those concerned with stabilizing borderland relations. Frontiers teetering on violence and anxious with fear, however, meant opportunities for a few.

Convinced of the inevitability of an Illinois colony and the promise of vast landed estates in the Ohio River valley as a consequence of a final settlement of the traders' claim, Croghan organized a scheme with the hope of capitalizing on the changing landscape. He pressed Johnson on the issue throughout late 1765 and early 1766, alleging that a permanent settlement in the Illinois was needed to protect Crown interests and a readjusted boundary to subdue local resentment. Writing to Baynton, Wharton and Morgan in January of 1766, Johnson reassured Croghan's creditors of the plan's validity and the special consideration they were to receive: "I have pursued as also your Expressions concerning demand I made of the Indians for a Tract of Land as a Resolution for the Traders Losses." Johnson stated that he could dictate the terms of settlement. "I have consulted the whole Six Nations thereon and found they could be induced thereto. . . . I will with pleasure contribute my Influence to Effect so reasonable a Demand." Johnson added, I will have "the power to deal with my Friends Amongst whom I shall particularly distinguish your house to which I am Sincere well Wisher."[14] He had become a close ally of the firm and occasionally directed business its way.[15]

Croghan corresponded with Benjamin Franklin in London in hopes of winning support for the scheme. On 25 February 1766 he noted that the nations desired to compensate the traders for their losses and urged Franklin to recognize the seriousness of the situation:

> This I thought then, as I do now, ought by no means to be refused, by his Majestys Ministers, as it is undoubtedly, a piece of Justice due to the sufferers and will be indulging the Natives in a scheme of retribution, that may ever hereafter, be rendered inexpressibly subservient, to His Majesty's Service. . . . William Johnson has, by this Months Packett . . . wrote to the Lords of Trade [DRCHSNY 7:809] and expressed to them, the Voluntary offer of the Shawnese and Delawares, and that the Six Nations,

had expressly Authorized him to confirm the Grant. . . . Therefore it is hoped—No time will be lost, before Sir William is authorized to complete it—when I dare say, you will Joyfully seize that opportunity of doing our distressed countrymen so much essential service, as to back Sir Williams request. . . . Indians are of a fickle, uncertain Temper, whereof their offers ought always to be accepted, as soon as possible, after proffer'd otherwise they are too apt, to construe a Delay, into a contemptuous refusal.[16]

Gov. William Franklin of New Jersey, Benjamin's son, was promised a significant share of any future land deeded to Croghan. Franklin Sr., as a result, supported the plan to compensate the Suffering Traders with land from a cession.[17] Well aware of the advantages of Benjamin Franklin's support, Croghan nevertheless believed it wise to deceive the Board of Trade about Franklin's complicity.[18] He advised Johnson: "Itt is preposed that itt is not to appear till ye success of our plan is known that your honor & Governor Franklin is concern[ed] as itts thought you Can be of more service by Nott being thought concern[ed]. . . . itt is Likewise proposed to apply for a grant of 120000 acerrs of Lands to the Crown in that Cuntry and to Take into this Grant two or three Gentlemen of fortune and influence In England, and Governor franklan. . . . Dr. Franklin [who they prepose to send the pre]posals to he is much [attended to by the ministry and] certainly can be of service [in this affair]."[19] Further correspondence between Johnson and William Franklin in June 1766 confirms Croghan's leading role in the scheme.[20] The only thing left to do was to get it all in writing.

On 29 April 1766, Croghan and his cronies gathered in Philadelphia and prepared for what appeared to be the inevitable establishment of an inland colony. Fourteen conspirators entered an agreement, including New Jersey governor William Franklin, Philadelphian merchants Baynton, Wharton, and Morgan and select relations, speculator and Indian agent John Hughes, Pennsylvania Assembly house speaker and lawyer Joseph Galloway, Sir William Johnson, and, of course, Croghan. The men agreed that,

Whereas it is expected that a civil government will be established by his Majesty in the Illinois country at or near Fort Chartres and that a sufficient

quantity of Land for the settlement of an English colony there will in a
short time by purchased of the Six Nations for that purpose, and Whereas
the said parties have agreed to apply to the Crown for a grant of Fourteen Hundred Thousand acres or more thereof if to be procured under
such Terms and Conditions as shall be obtained for the settlement thereof
[the parties agree] that they and each and every of them shall and will
form immediately after the Date of these presents, enter into and become
one joint Company and Partnership . . . that each and every of them shall
stand and beseized from and immediately after the time aforesaid of one
undivided equal twelfth part thereof the whole . . . provided always nevertheless that in Case should be thought Convenient or necessary in order
to obtain the said Grant, That any two other Gentlemen should be taken
into the said partnership by the said Company or by the person or persons
who shall be appointed to apply for and procure the said Grant, That then
and in such case the said Lands shall be equally divided between the said
parties and such two other persons . . . that is to say That each and every of
them shall stand and be seized of one equal undivided Fourteenth part.[21]

All participants were present to sign the written agreement, except
Johnson. Croghan signed for him. That fact is telling given the nature
of the agreement. Johnson wrote William Franklin four days later:
"I have been speaking to [Croghan] lately concerning the Advantages resulting from forming a settlement at the Illinois when he told
me that several Gentlemen were desirous of engaging therein. He
has now wrote to me on the subject and enclosed me a copy of the
scheme, and by his letter I find that your Excellency and myself are
intended to have shares." Johnson added, "I cannot refuse my consent,—although it has been always My Practice to avoid engaging in
Indian Lands. . . . neither have I a foot of land, but what I purchased
from the white Inhabitants."[22] Croghan knew he could act with the
weight of his superior behind him. Benjamin Franklin also backed the
plan.[23] By the fall of 1766 those involved in the venture had devised
a strategy to obtain an unidentifiable amount of land in a colony not
yet in existence. The risks were high, but in the 1760s speculating in
land and trade was just that: speculation.

Back in the Illinois Country as an official ambassador in January
1767, Croghan was keen to tie his own interests to the Crown's—and

Johnson was happy to let him. On 24 January he opened council with the Western Confederacy at Fort Charters. These nations agreed to peace terms, acknowledging the king of Great Britain as their "sovereign father." They agreed to let British troops occupy French forts to maintain trade but adamantly objected to the right of the Crown to cede or occupy any other part of their country without proper consideration. Our forefathers, they proclaimed, had occupied this land "many hundred years before any white man had crossed the great waters, wherefore they looked upon themselves as the sole owners of it and expected that no part of it should be taken from them before they were paid for it." The regional inhabitants also made it clear that they resented Iroquois claims to their lands and were determined to resist European settlement. Because the cost of maintaining their interests with annual gifts would be too great for the Crown, "they spare no pains to inflame their minds with the strongest prejudice against us." Not surprisingly, Croghan had a remedy: "From the best intelligence I could obtain . . . I am thoroughly convinced that the skins and Furs received there and shipped to France, are not worth less than eighty thousand pounds sterling one year with another." Croghan promised that the money from trade would defray the future cost of keeping the inhabitants tied to the Crown's interests. He urged that a fort be erected immediately at the mouth of the Illinois River and close to settlements on the Wabash. He concluded his report by emphasizing that "calamities of repeated Indian wars" would follow if the Crown did not quickly establish a strong trading network up and down the "Frontiers of all our Canadian conquests." Johnson, like Croghan, was not easily hoodwinked and understood borderland politicking. But considering their involvement in the recent secretive speculation scheme, Croghan felt it necessary to reassure Johnson and outline the steps necessary to win Crown support while keeping the interests of the company in mind. Croghan knew his superior well.[24]

Croghan's diplomacy on behalf of the Crown in the Illinois Country resulted in a sizable expenditure that he expected the Crown to cover. He was forced to visit New York in January 1767 to address such matters, and a partial account statement in excess of £8,400 attests to the scale of his spending.[25] General Gage complained to Johnson. When Croghan caught wind of a rebuke and a rejection of his accounts, he threatened, once again, to resign.[26] Meanwhile, to secure some money, he pressed Thomas Penn about the status of some unsettled Indian deeds he claimed and began to inquire once again about compensation for the trader's losses.[27] By early 1767, Croghan had been on the move for over two years. Alexander McKee, the agent left in charge of affairs at Fort Pitt, reported to Croghan about the increased unrest in the region. As a result, tribal hostility toward European presence increased. The murder and robbery of four tribespeople in February 1767 did not help.[28]

Johnson met Croghan in March 1767. For the second time in three years, Johnson convinced his underling to reconsider his decision to resign. The superintendent wrote Gage on his behalf, and the general reluctantly agreed to pay £1,372 in partial compensation for personal losses while in Crown service.[29] Croghan agreed to withdraw his resignation and use his influence to quell the increase in hostilities near Fort Pitt. After holding a council at Fort Pitt in May 1767, Croghan returned to New York in June still heavily indebted. In fact, most of his summer was spent embroiled in financial disputes. Unless resolved, he faced bankruptcy and debtor's prison.

Croghan's lawyer, Joseph Galloway, appeared in court on three separate occasions that summer to stave off creditors. Richard Hockley was demanding the £2,000 Croghan had promised him from the land he sold to Peters and Clark in 1763.[30] The barrage of legal activity and looming threat of prison kept Croghan in near seclusion. During the spring and early summer of 1767 even his closest friends were having a difficult time getting in touch with him.[31] But those who had invested in Croghan were in too deep to let their one link with the Ohio and Illinois nations rot in a debtor's cell. Croghan was well aware of this. As his housekeeping bills, for instance, were being settled by Baynton, Wharton and Morgan, Croghan spent his time scrounging for assets in order to secure a Crown title to land he held through Indian deeds. He petitioned Governor Moore for a patent to a 40,000-acre tract between Lakes Otsego and Canandaigua. Croghan used thirty-nine straw men for the memorial, and on 6 July 1767 he was granted title to the land. By the fall of 1767, however, Croghan's problems were many and his scheming had put his major creditors at risk. Baynton, Wharton and Morgan now had trouble securing credit.

Most likely low on cash, Croghan secured a £100 loan from Joseph Dobson on 8 October and returned to Philadelphia to meet Baynton, Wharton and Morgan to address their concerns. The Philadelphia merchants had been forced to stop payments to creditors on goods valued over £10,000 and consequently had to close accounts throughout the northeastern borderlands. The firm had heavily committed its capital and credit to Croghan's ambitions in anticipation of great return from the Ohio and Illinois River valley fur trade. It had not come. "I am sorry that Hans Thoulouse the Man whom Mr. Croghan recommended to me last year as worthy of any credit whatsoever has turned out so great a Rogue as to deceive," Wharton wrote his younger partner Morgan. "I have already acquainted you of the scarcity of Indian goods [and] all the Boats which have been loaded with wholly or principally with Liquors."[32]

Aware his livelihood and future rested with securing clear title to lands he claimed to hold in Indian deeds, Croghan pressed on with the land scheme once he arrived back at Fort Pitt in late summer. Using the tense situation in the borderlands to his advantage, he conspired to stir war panic—a panic in which his diplomatic skills would be required. With Samuel Wharton's help, Croghan sent letters to influential officials, warning of an impending war. Realizing that Whitehall would want to avoid a costly war, Croghan exaggerated hostilities to press home the completion of the major project of a boundary adjustment. According to Croghan, peace required the quick and speedy readjustment of the boundary.[33] Writing to Croghan in 1771, several years after the events, Wharton recalled their conspiracy. "Nothing will do," Wharton proclaimed, "but to act as you and I did about the boundary line. Mens passion must be alarmed and awakened."[34] Throughout late 1767 uneasiness throughout the northeastern borderlands complemented Croghan's effort to stir a panic. By January 1768, however, the threat of a major offensive by the Ohio nations in retaliation for frontier abuses appeared more real. The massacre of ten English-allied Native people near the banks of the Susquehanna fed the sense of urgency.

As the summer of 1767 drew to a close, there were many indications that all was not well: "Our forefathers held these lands as long as Death would let them live," Captain Amos complained to Johnson on

behalf of the Nanticokes on 12 August. "When Death took our forefathers away, they left these same Lands to their Children as long as
you and any of your Children is alive. We have followed their advice
which we find has been good and therefore until our Brothers of the
Six Nations can *show us* that it will be *our* Benefit to remove, we cannot think of destroying our town."[35] Captain Amos was responding
to the increased attempts of Crown deputies to buy the lands of the
Nanticoke nation to avoid further settler confrontations. But the Nanticokes, like other nations close to European settlements, often chose
to lease their lands instead of selling. Although lip service was paid
to the authority of the Grand Council, the Nanticokes also distrusted
Iroquois.

Murders and assemblies in the Ohio Valley revealed a precarious state of affairs for every party with an interest in that region. In
September 1767, eleven English traders murdered a band of Chippewas while they traveled through the Ohio Country.[36] On 28 October
while conversing with a Delaware confidant at Fort Pitt, Croghan was
informed that a party of Senecas "from the Six Nations Country" had
traveled to the region and summoned the Shawnees, Delawares, and
Senecas "of the two Creeks" to a council to discuss recent Iroquois
transactions with the British in the East. Referring to the 1765 meeting
with Johnson, the Seneca headmen told them that the British intended
to rob them of their land "lying between the Ohio river and the settlements of Virginia, Maryland and Pennsylvania." The nations were
told the English and Grand Council "had agreed with Sir William
Johnson to give up a Tract of country" and, as a result, intended to
unjustly take possession of their Ohio lands. The Senecas declared
that, because the English had cheated them of their lands so often,
they "were now determined to have justice therein, or bury every
warrior of their Nation." They requested the aid of the Shawnees and
Delawares in their endeavor to bring the English to a sense of the
injustice. The message delivered by the Senecas was also sent on a belt
to the Chippewas and Ottawas. Sometime thereafter, a party of Chippewas returned to the lower Shawnee town to inform the residents
that "the chiefs and principal warriors of twelve different nations
would collect themselves to a council in the Shawnee country." Two
weeks later a group of Mohicans and Wyandots confirmed that the

western nations had held council at the request of the Senecas.[37] The northeastern borderlands stirred.[38]

On 7 December 1767, Governor Moore wrote Shelburne in London: "Most of the letters which I have received from Sir William Johnson of the late have been fill'd with accounts of Uneasiness which now prevails among the Indian Nations." According to Johnson, Moore stated, "we are upon the eve of another Indian War." General Gage wrote a similar warning to the Pennsylvania governor the same day.[39] On 23 December, Lord Shelburne received an even stronger statement from the Lords of Trade. They had received a report that the western nations had held secret councils and that goods had been plundered throughout the Ohio. Their intelligence indicated "a design of a hostile and dangerous tendency." Not wanting to commit more resources to the American colonies, the Lords proposed enlisting the "Lord" of the frontier, Sir William Johnson, who had long argued that the "complaints of the Indians on account of encroachments upon their lands" could be resolved by "the expediency of the establishing a boundary line between their Country and the settlements of his Majesty's subjects." The line, the Lords argued, had already been negotiated by Johnson and was "received by the Indians with marks of the greatest satisfaction and approbation." Whitehall attached importance to the decisions of the Grand Council.[40]

A new cabinet-level office was also created in January to help matters. The new secretary of state for the colonies, Lord Hillsborough, avidly supported the idea of prompt boundary negotiations.[41] While London urged a boundary to be speedily settled to avoid war, tribes potentially affected by the proposal were planning to rebel if a line was confirmed. Many throughout the Ohio and Illinois Country, including Croghan, knew this well. Croghan, Johnson, and the eastern Iroquois promoted a solution to troubles that would help them but outraged some of the very people they claimed would be pacified by an end to uncertainty. They were perpetuating a grand deception. By the end of December the Board recommended to the king's ministers that no time should be lost in sending word to readjust the present boundary in order "to prevent the fatal consequences of an Indian war." According to the Lords, the boundary had been agreed to run from

Owegy, upon the Eastern branch of the Susquehannah, from whence, pursuing the coarse of that branch to Shamokin, it runs up the Western branch to the head thereof, and from thence to Kittaning on the Ohio, and so down that river to its influence with the Cherokee River ... as the line settled with the Cherokees falls in with a part of the Conohway River, communicating with the Ohio, it does seem to us that it would be *unadvisable*, that the line now proposed to be settled with the Six Nations and their allies, should be extended lower down the Ohio, than the mouth of the said Conohway River, as the carrying further might afford a pretence for settlements in a Country, which, however claimed by the Six Nations as part of their ancient dominion, is in fact actually occupied by the Cherokees as their hunting ground, and who would consequently consider such settlements as a direct violation of what has been agreed upon by them.[42]

Moreover, Lord Shelburne encouraged the Board of Trade to return control of indigenous affairs to the colonies.

"This Packet caries you his Majesty's Orders to settle the boundary with the Indians," Thomas Penn wrote Johnson on 7 January 1768. Penn urged Johnson to make the boundary as beneficial to the province as possible. "I hope you will get soon [some] of the Land in the Fork of the Susquehannah," Penn added, and noted that the orders to run the line would arrive shortly.[43] The following week the Pennsylvania Assembly and Governor Penn agreed to send a force once the snow cleared to remove illegal settlements near Red Stone Creek and Cheat River. As long as illegal settlements endured, the Assembly declared, the inhabitants would be motivated to form "a powerful Confederacy in the Spring" and threaten a devastating war. Assembly speaker Joseph Galloway remarked that "it is dread of exemplary Punishment, Steadily and uniformly inflicted on past Delinquents, that alone can deter the Wicked from the Perpetration of future Offenses." Galloway had more to gain than peace. His interest as a member of the Ohio Company must have also been on his mind. Squatter rights and Indian deeds would complicate a tidy land cession. He, too, had reason to tout the swift establishment of the boundary, and what better opportunity to voice concern.[44] "On this important Subject, permit us also to remark ... that a general

Boundary between the Natives and these Colonies has been some time past Negotiated with them by Sir William Johnson, in Obedience to his Majesty's Orders . . . that some Time has Elapsed since the Agreement was made with the Indians, and in the meantime the people on the Frontiers have been encroaching on their Lands, while this Boundary remains unconfirmed."[45]

Less than a week later, discussion of frontier problems in the Pennsylvania Assembly intensified. On 19 January the testimony of William Blyth made many in government shudder. After inebriating his visitors, Blyth testified, Frederick Stump murdered four indigenous men and two women at his house on 10 January. The following day Stump traveled fourteen miles up river and killed another woman and two children, and then set their camp ablaze. Later reports would indicate that Stump smashed in one victim's skull with the blunt end of a tomahawk and, while scalping the unlucky target, removed both ears.[46] A £200 reward for the apprehension of Stump and his servant was passed, and Governor Penn wrote to the local magistrates in Lancaster, Berks, and Cumberland counties calling for full cooperation. Johnson and Gage were informed of the details.[47]

Adding fuel to the fire were encroachments on lands not yet purchased.[48] Speaking on behalf of the Pennsylvania Assembly, Galloway again took the opportunity to demand a real boundary. "Founded on Mr. Croghan's Examination," he remarked, the other great reason for discontent remains the "non establishment of a Boundary. . . . nothing less, than the final Confirmation of this Boundary, can lay the foundation of a solid & lasting Peace."[49] From 23 to 28 January, the Assembly and Governor Penn settled on several initiatives to subdue tensions. They agreed that a boundary should be established as soon as possible, and the government restated its commitment to oust Europeans illegally squatting on tribal lands contrary to the Royal Proclamation of 1763 by passing a bill. Interestingly, the act did not apply to George Croghan's Fort Pitt lands. Actually, Joseph Galloway, Croghan's partner, proclaimed that the Assembly also decided not to restrict Croghan from making "Enlargement or Addition to the Improvements thereon" because it was not a cause of discontent. Because of "the Commission he holds, the Address and Fidelity with which he has always executed that Commission, and the eminent Services he has rendered the Nation . . . forbid the Suspicion," Galloway added, Croghan would not act in any way against the interests of the colonies or the tribes.[50] By 1768, Croghan's reputation was precarious at best, but a business partner found it expedient to sing his praises. Although the Stump affair appeared to work in favor of those wishing to finalize the boundary negotiations, the atrocity threatened to engulf the northeastern borderlands in a devastating war. Intelligence indicated growing hostilities, and by mid-February news that frontier settlers had kidnapped and detained several Tuscaroras in order to preempt retaliation over the Stump affair enraged the Iroquois.[51]

Johnson ordered Croghan to the region to contain the volatile situation. Writing to his superior in February, Croghan appeared comfortable with the current state of affairs. "I find the General has still the same fears of a rupter this spring with the Indians . . . & I have nott endaverd to lessen them, butt he seems much embarrassed as if he did nott know what to do."[52] Croghan recognized again that he would be needed, and that when there was a diplomatic mission to the nations there would be prospects for himself. Five days later he advised Johnson that the borderland hostilities would continue unless "Some Attonment Can be Made the Indians by Condoleing & presents Very Early this Spring."[53] Meanwhile, the Pennsylvania government agreed to raise £2,500 in addition to be used to cover the dead and "other Gifts for removing their Discontent and regaining their Friendship."[54] The gift was to be distinct from the king's presents in atonement for the province. It was determined that Johnson use over half of the sum to arrest Stump and distribute the rest at the forthcoming boundary negotiations. The remaining portion would be delivered to Croghan via two Pennsylvania representatives, John Allen and Joseph Shippen, for the upcoming conference he was to negotiate at Fort Pitt with the "western tribes." When word reached the frontiers that the Pennsylvania government was planning to distribute money to quell hostilities, the settlers were outraged.[55]

By February 1768 all roads to a peaceful resolution of borderland troubles converged at future boundary negotiations. William Johnson's "Vigilance & Attention to His Duty," Lord Hillsborough wrote Governor Moore of New York, "cannot be too much commended . . . [he] has not failed to communicate in the fullest manner the Apprehension." According to Johnson, Hillsborough continued, numerous tribes had repeatedly expressed that their greatest reason for discontent stemmed "from their not having received His Mâty's Determination upon the Proposition of a Boundary Line on the Plan suggested by them in 1765." Hillsborough remarked that indigenous complaints should be "examined with the greatest impartiality . . . as may restore mutual confidence."[56] Hillsborough agreed with the assessment. Nevertheless, those grievances emanating from the Ohio Country fell on deaf ears. Crown attention remained focused on the complaints of the eastern Six Nations, and Johnson made sure it did not stray. Moreover, on the general indication that the government favored a boundary adjustment, Croghan moved to sell some of his interests in western land. Presumably, any official indication of a land cession increased the value of interests in the lands in question. At least that was what Croghan told creditors.[57]

Meanwhile, Johnson was preparing for a congress with the Iroquois and Cherokees at Johnson Hall. He wrote the Pennsylvania Assembly and John Penn to inform them about his intention to speak highly of the province.[58] Before opening the council, Johnson spent the first day of March consulting his Mohawk allies on how to address the upcoming discussions in the "properest manner" possible. Meanwhile, the Cherokees were on peaceful terms with the Shawnees and working toward a resolution with the Delawares. That meant potential trouble for the Grand Council and eastern Iroquois communities. Depleted numbers, an insecure future, and rebellious Ohio Valley nations meant that those Iroquois delegates present at Johnson Hall in early March 1768 keenly sought to solidify peace with their traditional southern enemies in order to prepare for an Ohio Valley backlash.[59] On 2 March, shortly after Chief Tiadaroo spoke on behalf of the seven nations of Canada, the great Chief Attakullakulla (Little Carpenter) along with the Cherokee delegation entered Johnson Hall. The delegates present celebrated the occasion by returning to their quarters with pipes, tobacco, paint, and drams supplied by the superintendent.[60] On 5 March, Johnson reported to Gage that upwards of seven hundred tribal representatives had arrived. He believed peace would be concluded between the Cherokees and the Six Nations.[61]

Johnson would not be disappointed. Before the treaty concluded, on a belt a Iroquois speaker pulled up a pine tree and buried the axe of war. The speaker was careful to blow on the tree until it reached its former position, so "that the axe may no more be found." This metaphor, represented on a wampum belt, signaled the Six Nations' desire for peace. Ousonastota, a Cherokee chief who had visited England during the reign of George II, responded in similar fashion. In addition, Ousonastota urged that the Mohawks be placed in charge of subduing those who would seek to destroy the new alliance. The assembled Iroquois responded by thanking the "Great King for his intensions and for what he is going to do about the Boundary Line." They added, "but Brother we hear bad News the Cherokees have told us that the line was run in their Country last year, and that it has surrounded them so that they cannot Stir; We beg that you will think of this for our heads will be Quite turned if that is to be our Case, We therefore think that the line we talked of last should not go beyond Fort Augusta."[62] Within ten days Johnson concluded the negotiations and solidified peace. He wrote John Penn to inform him of the pains he took to quash indigenous hostilities towards Pennsylvanians. All went well, Johnson noted, and pledged his "readiness always to serve [John Penn] and [his] Family."[63] Meanwhile, Croghan wrote Johnson after celebrating Saint Patrick's Day with the Royal Regiment of Ireland at Peg Mullers in Philadelphia, "where there was no Want of good Beeff & Claret." He promised to depart for Fort Pitt on 18 March after a dinner celebration, with what Croghan feared would be "a very aching Head."[64]

In mid-March the Lords of Trade released their report on the state of affairs in North America. Heavily influenced by the events of the preceding months, the Lords stressed the importance of addressing indigenous concerns with regard to land and trade. The suggested method was through the superintendents and the boundary that had been proposed in the Plan of 1764, but a few notable differences were underscored: "The boundary line with the Six Nations and their allies is made upon the Map to terminate at that part of the Ohio, where it receives the Connahway River, instead of continuing it down the Ohio to the Cherokee River, and up that river to its source, as described in the Treaty [1765]; the reason for which is, that although the six Nations may have pretensions to the Dominion of the Country on the South side of the Ohio lower down than the Connahway River yet in fact it is more occupied by the Cherokees and other independent Tribes, as their hunting Ground."[65]

In addition to the boundary alternations to the 1765 negotiations, the Lords stated that "no one general Plan of Commerce & Policy is or can be applicable to all the different Nations of Indians." Wanting to wash their hands of the problematic backcountry, the Lords determined that the confining of trade to posts was ineffectual and even dangerous in the western parts of New York and Pennsylvania. In fact, the Lords declared that the Plan of 1764 would cost too much, becoming "both unreasonable and highly inconvenient" for the king and country. Therefore, the Lords suggested that trade policy be entrusted entirely to the colonies. The result would have been devastating to Johnson's office and the Grand Council. In fact, the office of the superintendent of Indian affairs would be made into little more than a ceremonial appointment.[66] On 15 April, Lord Hillsborough confirmed the new colonial strategy in an official message to the governors in America.[67] The Lords also rejected the proposed formation of an inland colony. The Ohio Company was dealt a critical blow.[68]

In sum, the Lords of Trade advised a reduction of the forts and soldiers to cut costs, the handing over of regulatory affairs in trade to local governments, and a dismantling of the office of the superintendent of Indian affairs. With all intelligence pointing to the fact that the frontiers could erupt into another war, the Crown opted to avoid financial responsibility for maintaining order throughout the northeastern borderlands over a long period of time. Interestingly, London retained control over land title and issuing of patents. As a result, even though the provincial governments were given control over trade, they were not given complete authority over the allotment of western lands and settlement. The establishment of a boundary was seen in London as the last Crown expense prior to devolving maintenance of a costly frontier empire onto the colonies. Colonial officials reasoned that the land ceded at the upcoming boundary negotiations would provide a buffer against further settlement problems, thus avoiding a war and its expense.[69] By the time the Ohio region became an issue again, the problem was in the hands of the provinces, not the Crown, and Lord Dunmore's army had laid waste to Shawnee villages in the heart of the northeastern borderlands.

Prompt readjustment of the boundary appeared inevitable in the spring of 1768 as tensions mounted. But at the same time, the Board of Trade had shelved the plan for an inland colony, British garrisons in North America were to be significantly reduced, some forts abandoned, and the Indian Department relegated to a diplomatic role. A mere £3,000 was allotted for annual maintenance of the department. The Iroquois were aware of the implications. The reduction of power in the department meant the future might not be so kind to their long-standing claims of overlordship. The standing peace with the Cherokee nation would undoubtedly help their quest for security if the Ohio Valley nations sought to rebel. So, too, would Croghan's presence in the region. By the spring of 1768, with dreams of a new colony temporarily dashed, much of Croghan's livelihood rested on the completion of the new boundary.

When William Johnson received word from Whitehall to hold a council and redraw the 1763 boundary, he wasted little time and ordered Croghan to convene a council with the Ohio nations at Fort Pitt.[70] When Croghan received Johnson's instructions, he responded and arranged a meeting with the superintendent at a tavern at New London Harbor. Croghan brought Samuel Wharton and William Trent. Johnson reassured the schemers that reparations for the 1763 traders' losses would be addressed at a planned council to be held at Fort Stanwix. In turn, Croghan organized the Indiana Company to centralize the interests of those concerned with the losses. The Suffering Traders of the Indiana Company consisted of men who had reportedly lost £86,000. Shares in the venture were allocated in proportion to each trader's losses in 1763. Croghan, William Franklin, William Trent, and Baynton, Wharton and Morgan paid off many others and held the vast majority of the shares. Given Croghan's debts, however, he was forced to transfer his shares valued at £2,250 to Joseph Galloway and Thomas Wharton. The transaction was characteristic of Croghan, who had long practiced the transfer of Indian deeds to cover debt, not to mention his role as a claimant was illegal. The pattern of giving creditors shares in unrealized assets and deeds that had no Crown title behind them was indicative of a man whose fortunes were precarious. The assets he surrendered to creditors, because of the potential rather than firm value, would have been discounted. Croghan was not just disposing of assets at a low value, he was surrendering a good portion of his future to dispose of debts incurred for previous ventures. What little hope he had for a windfall on western lands depended on the establishment of a new boundary.[71]

On Tuesday 25 April, a little more than a month after Croghan had cleared the cobwebs from his head as a result of the St. Patrick's Day celebrations, he began negotiations with over one thousand delegates at Fort Pitt. Those congregated included a who's who of Ohio Valley chiefs and warriors and eastern Iroquois representatives.[72] The proceedings began with the traditional Three Bare Words. Recording his message on wampum, Johnson's deputy proclaimed, "I clear your Eyes, and wipe away your Tears. . . . I clean the Sweat off your Bodies, and remove all evil Thoughts form your Minds, and clean the Passage to your Hearts. . . . I clear your Ears, that you may hear and consider well what is going to be said."[73] After the formalities of opening the council, negotiations were delayed three days while prominent representatives from both sides deliberated in private. Private, off-the-record negotiations were nothing new. Treaties were an art and were planned, recorded, and remembered with meticulous detail.[74] The negotiations at Fort Pitt in May 1768 were no different. The council reconvened on Friday, 29 April, and the first order of business was to address frustration with the horrific acts committed by frontiersman Frederick Stump. Crown translator Andrew Montour (known also as Sattelihu or Eghnisera) read Governor Penn's message to the assembled participants. The governor promised that justice would be delivered swiftly and strictly. On behalf of the province, Montour covered the dead with an array of condolence gifts and added a reminder of the recent killing of English traders on the Ohio. Croghan confirmed the message of the province and added that the Pennsylvanians were doing all they could to brighten the Covenant Chain.[75]

Tohonissahgarawa of the Six Nations then addressed the Ohio nations. Speaking on behalf of the Grand Council, he demanded "the Shawnese, Delawares, and Wyandotts . . . throw all evil Thoughts out of your Minds and Hearts; and to think of nothing but promoting a lasting Friendship with your Brethren the English, as we your elder

Brothers, the Six Nations, have determined to do." On Sunday 2 May, the Six Nations appealed to the colonial and Crown agents:

> Brother, It is not without Grief that we see our Country settled by you, without our Knowledge or Consent; and it is a long Time since we first complained to you of this Grievance; which we find has not yet been redressed; but Settlements are still extending farther into our Country. Some of them are made directly on our War Path, leading to our Enemies Country, and we do not like it. . . . You have Laws amongst you to govern your People by, and it will be the strongest Proof of Security of your Friendship to let us see that you remove the People from our Lands; as we look upon it, it will be Time enough for you to settle them when you have purchased them, and the Country *becomes yours.*[76]

The Iroquois claimed ownership of the Ohio Valley lands, and thus the right to dispose of them. But the Ohio nations had been acting independently from their "fathers" for decades. In fact, without the support of the English, the Iroquois had few resources to back their claims. When the Grand Council representatives took the opportunity at Fort Pitt to emphasize their right of conquest, Nymwha, the Shawnee speaker, was quick to respond. On 3 May in a speech worth quoting at length, Nymwha rose and blasted the Iroquois claimants and the English:

> Brethren, When you talked of Peace to us, at the Time we were struggling in War, we did not hearken to you at first. You mentioned it a second Time to us, we still refused to attend to you; but after repeating it to us several Times, we consented to hear you. We then looked at you, and saw you holding Instruments of War in your Hands, which we took from you, and cast them into the Air out of Sight. We afterwards desired you to destroy your Forts, as that would be the Way to make all Nations of Indians believe you were sincere in your Friendship; and we now repeat the Same request to you again.—We also desire you not to go down this River, in the Way of the Warriors, belonging to the foolish Nations to the Westward; and told you that the Waters of this River, a great Way below this Place, were coloured with Blood; you did not Pay any regard to this, but asked us to accompany you in going down, which we did, and we felt the Smart

of our Rashness, and with Difficulty returned to our Friends. We see you now making Batteaus, and we make no Doubt you intend going down the River again, which we now tell you is disagreeable to all Nations of Indians, and now again desire you to sit still at this Place. . . . They are also uneasy to see that you think yourselves Masters of this Country, because you have taken it from the French, who you know had no Right to it, as it is the Property of us Indians. We often hear that you intend to fight with the French again, if you do, we desire you will remove your Quarrel out of this Country, and carry it over the great Waters, where you used to fight, and where we shall neither see of know any Thing of it. All we desire is to enjoy a quiet Peace with you both, and that we should be strong in talking of Peace. . . . All we have to say to you now is to be strong, and let us agree to what we desire of each other. When you first talked of Peace to us, you desired us to sit over the River quietly at our Fires; but our Women and Children were frightened away by the Noise you made in repairing your Fort; but, if you do as we desired you, they will return without Fear. . . . We therefore desire you will put a Stop to your People going down this River, till we have spoken to the Nations living in that Country; which we intend to do with the Assistance of our Brothers the Six Nations, and our Grandfathers the Delawares.[77]

Nymwha had not only recounted Shawnee resistance to both English and Six Nations claims to the land and trade but demonstrated a stronger commitment to the advice of the Delawares over that of their Six Nation "brothers." Commotion over the address carried well into the next morning. All the cards were on the table.

The next afternoon, Tohonissahgarawa apologized for the words spoken by Nymwha and the "Difference which happened this Morning among themselves, as it was the Means of preventing our meeting them in the Forenoon, and desired that their Brethren, the English, and the Tribes of Indians present, would take no Notice of it." Tensions were high and the Six Nations needed to act fast. In response to the claims of the Shawnees, Kiasutha (Seneca) laid down a copy of the 1764 treaty negotiated with Colonel Bradstreet that claimed the Shawnees had given up their right to Ohio and Illinois lands. The Pennsylvania commissioners then addressed the Six Nations. By addressing indigenous concerns with European settlements via the

Iroquois, the commissioners not only acknowledged the authority of the Grand Council but also emphasized the subservient position of the Shawnees. It must be remembered that those speaking on behalf of the Six Nations, the Crown, and the province of Pennsylvania all knew about the 1765 boundary negotiations between Johnson and the eastern Iroquois. Those who had something to gain from recognizing Six Nations claims to the region simply trumped Shawnees discontent by addressing all concerns via the Iroquois.[78]

Meanwhile, on 5 March 1768, two months before Croghan convened the council at Fort Pitt, Johnson had sent his deputy detailed instructions for the upcoming congress. Johnson ordered Croghan to do all in his power to promote terms of general peace. He stressed that the Stump affair must be the first order of business and gave his consent to his deputy's use of Wharton's trading house to purchase the condolence gifts. Finally, he ordered Croghan to inform the delegates of the recent peace between the Cherokees and the Six Nations and pay attention to "the Relations and Friends of those lately killed as well as of those formerly Suffered in that Province," whom, Johnson added, "should receive particular favor on this occasion."[79] He was referring to the Ohio Country nations.

Croghan opened the council by addressing the Shawnees. He stated that they were the only nation complaining about the recent erection of forts and trading houses in the region. "I well remember that when the French first built a Fort here and passed down the River . . . you did not desire them to destroy their Forts, and leave your Country. We . . . took Possession of the Forts; after that we conquered them, [and with the Six Nations] opened the road of Peace through all this Country, from the Sun-rising to the Sun-setting, both by Land and Water . . . with all Nations of Indians to the Westward." Croghan then brought attention to his recent trip to the Illinois. He blamed the Shawnees for placing the hatchet of war in the hands of those who attacked his expedition. Instead of cautiously covering the bones of the dead, Croghan's actions threatened to stir further discontent. But diplomatic niceties were essential in concluding negotiations and cordial respect was paid to each attending party as all agreed to peace. In a private conference with Croghan, Kissinaughtha (Shawnee) apologized for the uneasiness his nation had caused but remained firm in his conviction that they were asked to speak their minds. In addition, Kissinaughtha remarked, it "is very true, Brother, we did send a Hatchet to those Nations in Time of War; but it was sent to us from the Senecas, to carry to them." Highlighting their responsibility in order to gain greater concessions, Croghan revealed the direct involvement of western Senecas. The Six Nations claim to the right of ownership was certain to be disputed.[80]

A flurry of activity followed the Fort Pitt negotiations. In anticipation of a successful council, Croghan and the Philadelphia merchants arranged for multiple shipments of goods to arrive at the fort to get a head start on trade. On 28 May, Joseph Rigby, the firm's Carlisle representative, reported to Baynton, Wharton and Morgan that their goods had arrived safely and would be divided, reorganized, and forwarded to Fort Pitt. Rigby warned that all incoming goods were "surrounded by Ja_b_t_s [likely Jacobites] who are continuously prying into every Waggon and package that comes to the gate to know its Contents, and often ask whether there is any powder or lead going back to kill the . . . Irishman." The local inhabitants loathed the idea that merchant houses like Baynton, Wharton and Morgan made money by selling illegal items of war to those who in turn often used them against settlements. As a result, the shipment of similar material was often done in secret. Croghan's involvement in such scheming was well known and resented.[81]

Word of the Fort Pitt negotiations was not the only thing creating a stir. As news spread that Johnson was given instructions from Whitehall to confirm a boundary, those with entrepreneurial interests prepared. A good account of the type of scheming that transpired appears in a letter from Joseph Shippen to David Jameson of York Town: "I should have told you long ago that Dr. Morgan and I had presented to the Governor the officers' Memorial for obtaining a Grant of Lands in the next purchase; and explained to him the whole Design of our Application." Shippen continued by declaring that the Pennsylvania governor fully supported the scheme. Those "Surveys which have been made on the unpurchased Lands," he added, will not threaten their plan because they run contrary to the Royal Proclamation and will "never be admitted in the office." Shippen suggested that there was no reason for concern, since he had reason to believe that he would be chosen to be sent as a representative of Pennsylvania in the upcoming negotiations. It was hoped, he later wrote, that Johnson and the commissioners could negotiate an alteration to the agreement, opening the land for purchase at the forks of the Susquehanna. If so, Shippen promised an investor, "I shall take the earliest Opportunity of applying to the Governor for an Order for them."[82] Private interest and meddling in boundary preparation was rampant—a fact that caused colonial elite in London much grief. "Private Persons in the City," Hillsborough wrote the American governors, often hear colonial intelligence long before it reaches Whitehall. The secretary of state for the colonies insisted that the governors send all forthcoming dispatches to London via the first available ship and a duplicate copy directly to his office.[83]

Hillsborough was not the only one struggling to control events. As of late April, Guy Johnson had taken over the majority of his father-in-law's duties as Sir William rested and recuperated on the east coast. Failing health had forced Johnson to make frequent and inconvenient trips to the seaside to be attended to by physicians at hot springs that seemed to alleviate his pain. His presence at Johnson Hall was missed. While traveling through Mohawk country, Governor Moore of New York wrote to Hillsborough, indicating among other things his inability to settle boundary disputes that concerned his province because Johnson was away in Connecticut attending to his health.[84]

The timing of Johnson's departure is important to note, given that Guy Johnson was largely responsible for addressing significant issues that related to the boundary negotiations in the early summer of 1768. Of particular concern was the path the boundary line might take through Mohawk territory. Hillsborough had recently rejected a line north through Mohawk and Oneida territory that would disrupt settlements and ran contrary to what was agreed upon in 1765. However, the eastern Iroquois had been pressing Johnson on the matter. In a series of letters to Hillsborough and Gage, Guy Johnson repeated Sir William's intension to extend the boundary north from Owego at the upcoming negotiations. On behalf of his father-in-law, Guy reasoned that the extension of the boundary would "give more permanency to the Transaction" because it was a natural boundary. He informed Gage that he would explain the reasons in further detail to Governor

Moore, who was scheduled to arrive in a few days. Gage was assured that "the contested grants from NY extending down the Susquehanna to Tionondadon [a branch of the Susquehanna near Lake Otsego] . . . need not . . . prevent the Continuation of the boundary Line this Way, for the satisfaction of the Six Nations and the obtaining a Cession of Territory to the Crown." Furthermore, Gage was told that Johnson intended to place great priority on establishing New York's provincial limitation and on "persuing the Transactions of 1765."[85]

Johnson expressed his ideas on 20 July in a letter to Gage. He observed that a "Mistake has been made by which the Line is not proposed by the Board of Trade to the Northward of Owegy." Johnson reasoned that when the nations met in 1765 the details of the northern extension of the boundary were not addressed at length. The Six Nations needed to convene and discuss the issue in greater detail before committing to a lasting agreement. They had done so, Johnson argued, and now if the "Boundary Between the Six Nations & New York . . . will not be secure[d] . . . the affair of the Boundary will be defeated in its principal Object." The boundary was a notable concern, but Johnson was even more concerned with the future course of indigenous affairs. The topic dominated his letter to Gage.[86] Johnson was not attempting to pull the wool over the eyes of his superiors in Whitehall. When his opinion conflicted with both Gage and Hillsborough, he made it clear what he planned to do toward establishing a boundary. The question is why?

A series of conferences were held at Johnson Hall throughout the summer of 1768. Growing tensions to the west and persistent Mohawk concern with the claims of the Kayaderosseras patentees took center stage. Maintaining the façade of unity was also clearly at stake for the Iroquois. Gage wrote Guy Johnson on 5 June that the "Belts which have been carried about far and near to raise the Indians against us as I understand . . . Originated amongst the Six Nations, at least amongst the Senecas, who make the largest part of the Confederacy."[87] From 8 to 28 June, a twenty-day heated discussion occurred at Johnson Hall over the issue of Mohawk lands. When Mohawk speaker Abraham pressed Peter Remsen and John McCrea, the Kayaderosseras patent claimants, to produce a copy of the contested patent, they "said that [they] had not brought it with [them]." Minutes later, the claimants produced a copy of the patent, dated 26 August 1702 and signed by chiefs Joseph and Hendrick. Abraham scoffed at the authenticity of the document, repeated the relevant oral history of his nation, and rejected once again the argument that his forefathers had ceded lands west of the Mohawk River. Disagreement ensued. "We now desire, that all Proceedings in this affair, and all surveys and pretensions may be stopped," Abraham concluded, "untill we hear further about it." The Mohawks also took the opportunity to emphasize that, since the reduction of the French, the English had been surveying and settling lands that had "never been conquered"—a practice that also infuriated the Mohawks. On 28 June, intelligence arrived that drew attention to instability in the Illinois and Ohio countries.[88]

A month later, Johnson met in secret with Abraham to let him know that he had recently been informed by New York governor Moore that two new applicants had applied for land within the contested Kayaderosseras patent. Unlike the other claimants, Johnson disclosed, these men had a convincing original proof of sale. When the claimants' representative arrived the following day and laid down the patent, "which had not been produced before," both Johnson and the Mohawks were likely surprised when the deed "appeared less favorable [for] the Patentees."[89] Johnson and the Mohawks were quick to act.

Increasing reports of unrest to the west and internal conflict among the Six Nations were pressing heavily by the summer of 1768.[90] It is not too speculative to assume that, when signs of changing winds appeared on the horizon, the Mohawks agreed to make concessions with regard to the loathed patent. Moreover, the most recent claim maintained European ownership over the least amount of land of any of the several rival claims, and Johnson's own claims in the region were not affected. After a few days of private deliberation with Johnson, Abraham addressed the council on 2 August:

We hope that the Gentlemen here present believe that we, though a Small Nation, have been, and are Still head of a powerfull Confederacy. . . . As we have now, with a view to peace, settled this matter and given up all pretensions to this Tract, and are at Present reduced to a very small scanty portion for our Subsistence, we now address you, Brother.—recommending it to you, to take this matter into consideration, & requesting you to procure some good Strong writing, as a Security for the Land we live upon, that we may no more be disturbed, or alarmed with apprehensions, and Storys, that this Land will be taken away from us.[91]

Before the conference concluded, Johnson assured the Mohawks that he would consider at length their recent concessions "and endeavour to the utmost of his power to have their Lands secured to them . . . in the most effectual manner."[92] It is difficult to imagine, given the events at Fort Stanwix, that Johnson was referring to anything other than the upcoming council.

On 17 August, less than a month before he departed for Fort Stanwix, Johnson wrote Hillsborough on the topic of the boundary. He stressed the need to have the freedom to conduct and conclude the negotiations in the best interest of the Crown. Johnson urged Hillsborough to accept a larger cession of land if the nations demanded such. "I believe it to be the most effectual means of preventing disputes," Johnson remarked. The superintendent added that those lands ceded must be viewed as extensions of the colonies and, thus, extensions of the Crown. The northeastern borderlands would naturally act as a boundary between original inhabitants and settlements. "But with this I apprehend I have nothing to do," Johnson surprisingly added, "and that my Deputy is solely to treat with, and obtain a Cession for and on behalf of the Crown of a Tract of Country along the Frontiers." Though Johnson prepared personally to secure Mohawks lands in the northeast, he intended to delegate the "western" cession to Croghan.[93]

Johnson ended the letter by inquiring about his recent suggestions regarding the Indian Department reforms and requested Hillsborough to send revised instructions for him for the impending conference. Hillsborough's response urged Johnson to cut as many costs as possible in the upcoming council and expressed hope that Johnson would be able to defray any expenses (aside from £10,000 to be used for the purchase) by persuading the colonies to cover any additional expenses. More important, Hillsborough confirmed, "His Majesty entirely approves the continuing the Boundary Northward from Owegy so as to include the Province of New York and thereby render the line perfect and complete." Furthermore, although Hillsborough instructed Johnson that the Plan of 1764 should not be considered "ripe for Execution," he encouraged Johnson that his suggestions would be further considered.[94]

Johnson was aware of the implications the recent colonial reforms had for his office and his future role. Yet, despite any disappointment he felt about the future reforms to his department, Johnson's actions leading up to the Treaty of Fort Stanwix suggest that he worked as diligently for Whitehall as he did for the eastern Iroquois. Instead of distancing himself from London, Johnson attempted to reorganize the department, worked toward gaining appropriate funds to pay his deputies, and held a series of councils with the Six Nations through-out the summer of 1768 with the hope of quelling hostilities. They were plays of a concerned and loyal subject, not a man willing to throw away friendships and allegiances in order to gain a few thou-sand acres of land.

From early 1766 to October 1768 the government in London had felt the pinch of limited resources while attempting to administer an expanded empire. The Chatham and Grafton ministries "were hard put to finance the everyday operations of government." Although historians have concentrated on the Townsend Acts of the sum-mer of 1767 as a great provocation to widespread colonial protest, a spirit of rebellion had grown throughout the Ohio River valley for entirely different reasons.[95] Disaffection was prevalent throughout the American frontiers. As Europeans pushed north and west and displaced the indigenous inhabitants, violence and vigilante justice ensued. From 1766 to 1768 small conflicts persisted, making the pros-pect of a costly and destructive war a constant concern. As a result, as Croghan's dealings illustrate, while those engaged in borderland bargaining maneuvered for position their very actions threatened disruption. All indicators pointed to growing discontent west of the Susquehanna, but the convergence of interests of the English-allied Six Nations and land-hungry merchants and colonial elites had cre-ated an atmosphere ripe for exploitation. It would not be long before the participants agreed to hold one of the most spectacular councils in early America at the Oneida Carry.

CHAPTER 5

THE 1768 TREATY OF
FORT STANWIX

In late September 1768, as summer in northeastern borderlands gave way to the chill of autumn, thousands of American Indians traversed the lake-dotted landscape of New York on their way to the English fort that straddled the well-worn portage between Wood Creek, the eastern tentacle of Lake Oneida, and the Mohawk River. Those congregating did not arrive in columns bearing arms in anticipation of battle but rather assembled amicably to participate in negotiations with selected provincial and Crown representatives, negotiations that promised to transform a continent.

Along with the smells and sights that accompanied hundreds of people that speckled the cleared portage, the unkempt log and earthen walls of Fort Stanwix greeted those who arrived at the Oneida Carry. Despite logistical setbacks and arguments over designs that plagued a timely completion of the new British palisade, by 1768 Fort Stanwix had been operational for about a decade.[1] In fact, even before its completion the emerging fort provided a safe haven for more than four hundred soldiers during the winter of 1758/9. But within only a couple years, as Fort Stanwix neared completion, its usefulness had already faded. By the end of the Seven Years' War, with the French defeated, the formidable fort had been relegated to providing an "imperial presence" in Iroquoia, "particularly among the Oneidas." By 1761 only fifty men garrisoned a complex that could house hundreds. The fort and those soldiers stationed at the Carry may have

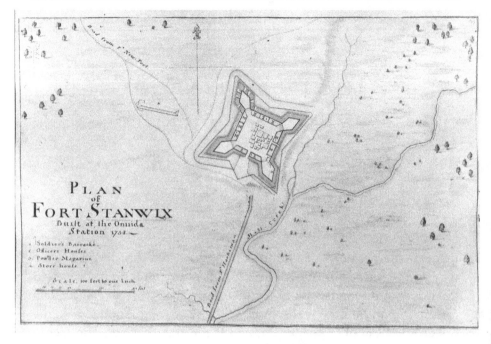

"Plan of Fort Stanwix, built at the Onnida Station, 1758." Courtesy of the Newberry Library, Chicago. Call # Ayer 136 H91 1907 Vol. 2.

escaped the fires of the Uprising of 1763, but by the summer of 1764
nature had taken its toll on the undermanned, underfunded post. By
the end of 1767, having evaded General Gage's recommendation that
the fort be abandoned to cut costs, "a half pay Officer, a Corporal &
his men" stood guard at Fort Stanwix. Despite still demanding admi-
ration in 1768, like the Crown's position in the American colonies,
the great fort at the Oneida Carry had been deteriorating rapidly
since the end of the war.[2] Nonetheless, for a brief moment in time
the Oneida Carry stood center stage of British imperial endeavors in
North America. As for Fort Stanwix, its walls provided shelter to the
chief negotiators of empire as whispers of the largest land cession in
early America soon traveled west.

Before Sir William Johnson formally opened the negotiations, several obstacles had to be addressed. The material and logistical requirements for the council were immense. By late October over three

thousand sachems, warriors, and their close associates had gathered at Fort Stanwix to witness the land cession and enjoy the largesse of Crown-sponsored diplomacy. This departed from many prior assemblies. "Occasioned by their staying at their Villages, to secure their Corn," Samuel Wharton later recorded, women and children did not accompany the men. Those in attendance still needed to be gathered, housed, and fed—feats that required significant planning and a touch of luck. Although the exact quantity of supplies consumed is difficult to determine, the number of occasions when Johnson stressed the need for ample provisions testifies to the importance he placed on the availability of supplies.[3]

Six months before the congress concluded, William Johnson's son-in-law and future superintendent of Indian affairs, Guy Johnson, wrote General Gage. While Sir William tended to his health, Guy Johnson informed Gage that the Crown must be prepared to cover the cost of fifty barrels of pork and "a proportion of Flour" per week, so long as the number being provisioned did not exceed one thousand.[4] In mid-July William Johnson submitted for approval a list of goods to Robert Adams, "a verry good Judge of such Articles," and Mr. Mortier, the deputy paymaster general. In addition to the supplies, at least £10,000 would be needed to secure the cession, William Johnson told Gage, £2,000 of which he figured would be used in private conferences with selected chiefs.[5]

William Johnson arrived at Fort Stanwix on 19 September 1768. In addition to "presents for the Indians consisting of divers Goods—ammunition Cash &ca. being prepared, and sent forward in 20 Boats," five boats packed with food stores arrived with Johnson. But by early October, Johnson sought more supplies. On 2 October he wrote Daniel Campbell of Schenectady, asking for "Sixty pounds Ster[ling] in Goods." Six days later Johnson dispatched two Mohawks with a letter and a wampum belt to hurry the tardy Ohio nations' delegates. As Johnson waited to open the negotiations formally, William Trent and Samuel Wharton used the interlude to advance the interests of the Suffering Traders. It should be remembered that before the Fort Stanwix congress Croghan, Trent, William Franklin, and Baynton, Wharton and Morgan had organized the Indiana Company in order to consolidate their land claims.[6]

According to the treaty records, on 19 September New Jersey governor William Franklin, William Trent, and Samuel Wharton accompanied Johnson as he arrived at Stanwix.[7] The record suggests that the men arrived two days after the superintendent, but it appears more likely that they informally presented their account of the traders' losses to Johnson and selected Iroquois headmen on 21 September.[8] Writing to Benjamin Franklin two months after the fact, Wharton recounted the events that preceded the negotiations. In July, after receiving news of the imminent council, Wharton, William Franklin, and Trent journeyed to Johnson Hall. The guests stayed for over a month before departing for the Oneida Carry. Wharton writes, "We were engaged, in using our best Interest with the Indians, to obtain a Reimbursement for the Losses, which we & others had sustained, by the Depredation of the Shawnanese and Delawares in the year 1763." On 15 September, after these preparations, it is likely that they *all* set off together for Fort Stanwix.[9]

During the three months before the treaty, George Croghan worked behind the scenes at Johnson Hall, and he remained active when he arrived at the fort.[10] Few records shed light on the clandestine dialogues that likely occurred late into many nights. We can assume that Croghan was well aware of the meeting between Johnson, Trent, and Wharton on 21 September, when they formally delivered their accounts of the trader's losses and their plan to obtain retribution. When news that a fellow disgruntled trader named Daniel Coxe was prepared to challenge the claims and tactics of the Suffering Traders, the men sought a meeting with Johnson. On 5 October, Wharton and Trent "delivered in a long State of their case" a rebuttal to Coxe's claims.[11] Trent requested that the Six Nations "make a compensation for the losses [the traders] incurred [in 1763]," and Johnson thereafter "reminded the Six Nations of their Promise and agreement as aforesaid in 1765, To give the Traders some land Near Fort Pitt."[12] The content of Coxe's request and the rebuttal have not survived; however, a series of related events are noteworthy.

Ten days after Wharton and Trent countered Coxe's claim, Governor Penn, Attorney General Benjamin Chew, and Chief Justice of Pennsylvania William Allen departed Fort Stanwix, leaving behind Richard Peters and James Tilghman as acting commissioners. Peters, an ordained clergyman from England who had run away from two marriages and a child, had an uncanny appetite for borderland property and an aptitude for dishonesty. A day before, on 14 October, Penn and his entourage had delivered a set of papers to Johnson. They had to adjudicate several claims for merchant losses, including those of the Wharton group and Coxe. After "persu[ing] the whole of the Papers," the committee ruled in favor of Wharton and Trent, stating that they had been the ones to apply for losses in 1763 and that the Iroquois had agreed to make future reparations to them during the council in 1765. No losses had been applied for before that time, and thus Coxe's claim could not be allowed now. The Pennsylvania delegation also dismissed earlier trader claims. These affairs, including Croghan's losses from 1754, "had been set aside in England." In other words, some claims for old losses were made void because no one had filed for restitution at the time, and other claims had been heard in London and rejected there. Penn's support for the Suffering Traders of 1763 and Croghan's willingness to set aside his earlier claims were both rooted in the prospect of a major land cession. Recall that Wharton, Trent, and Croghan had "secretly" bought out the right of claim of the other traders who lost goods in 1763 in anticipation of a private settlement. Penn was a shareholder in that venture. Wharton, Trent, and Croghan needed to negate other traders' claims if they were to corner the land cession opportunities at Fort Stanwix. Assured that the Suffering Traders cession would not interfere with his provincial claims over the region, Governor Penn prepared to depart. Thus, when the matter was settled with Coxe, and "Sir William assured them that he should have no [further] Objection," the governor and his closest advisors returned to Philadelphia.[13]

By mid-October over nine hundred tribesmen, largely those of the Six Nations, arrived at encampments around the fort. The death of a Seneca chief held up Ohio delegates at a Seneca village near Cayuga Lake.[14] Once the proper condolences were concluded at Cayuga, Johnson informed Gage that he expected their imminent arrival. While waiting, those already in attendance ate and drank heartily. Any one of them, Johnson wrote Hillsborough in London, "consumes daily more than two ordinary Men amongst Us."[15] Worried about the dwindling supplies, Johnson noted that the past four weeks "occasion[ed] such a Consumption of Provisions that had I not brought up sev[eral] head of cattle & a Quantity of Corn &c timelier we sho[uld] have been distressed on that account, before the Whole could arrive which . . . I hear will be near 3000."[16] Two days later Johnson's fears were confirmed when Lt. Achilles Preston arrived at Fort Stanwix from Cayuga. Preston alerted Johnson about a large delegation set to arrive from the Ohio. The next day, when another account arrived, a panicked Johnson wrote Schenectady resident John Glen. With the provisions near an end, Johnson requested enough pork and flour to feed three thousand for approximately three weeks. If the goods could not be procured, Johnson worried, it would negate the "design of this Congress, as it cannot be Supposed that Hungry Indians can be kept here, or in any temper without a Bellyfull." Johnson urged Glen to leave nothing "undone to procure provisions." This was unbridled diplomacy at its finest.[17]

When required, supplies could be mustered quickly. On 20 October, four days after Johnson appealed for additional goods from John Glen, John Bradstreet informed the superintendent that forty-eight of the requested sixty barrels of provisions had been sent. The other dozen barrels would follow as soon as he could locate additional supplies.[18] A day later Daniel Campbell informed Johnson that a quantity of blankets were on their way, but additional time would be needed to secure "two pair of Christian Blankets," four pairs of red strouds, and 1,000 Dollars.[19] As for edible necessities, Johnson must have breathed a sigh of relief when he received word from Bradstreet sometime shortly after 25 October that "about Seventy Barrells of Provisions arriv'd from New York which will be forwarded to you as soon as possible."[20] Well stocked, Johnson awaited the stragglers.

Meanwhile, as Croghan and Hugh Crawford traveled to Canajoharie to round up those still needed to open the negotiations, Johnson did his best to smooth over resentments that might hinder proceedings. On 18 October he met with Tiagawehe, a Tuscarora chief. Two years earlier Tiagawehe had visited Johnson Hall and lodged a seemingly trivial complaint. According to the chief, in 1766 some Pennsylvania settlers stole six horses from a large group of Tuscaroras traveling from North Carolina to the headwaters of the Susquehanna. He requested that Johnson write the Pennsylvania governor to seek compensation. Apparently nothing came of the matter—that is, until 1768. At Fort Stanwix, Tiagawehe approached Johnson. This time, however, the clever chief warned that "if any Sum [would] be allowed the Sufferers," he too "would be empowered" to receive something. Johnson responded by consulting the Pennsylvania commissioners. Soon thereafter, the superintendent informed the chief, "The Governor had Consented to make . . . Satisfaction," and the value of the horses was settled at "Sixteen half Johanne's," or approximately nine dollars.[21] Satisfied, Tiagawehe withdrew his complaint.[22]

Midday on 21 October, Croghan returned to Fort Stanwix from Canajoharie. He informed his superior of the imminent arrival of a large group of delegates. Johnson prepared by arranging an appropriate area for a large encampment. By early evening they had arrived. Johnson welcomed indigenous representatives in his private quarters and "gave them a strict Charge to keep their Young men sober & in Proper order." He then "drank Their healths & Ordered them Rum, Tobacco & 12 lb. of Paint for their young Warriors to dress with" and made sure a bullock was sent to feed the new arrivals until the next day when regular provisions would be available.[23] Two days later the treaty roster was completed when Gaustarax, the great Seneca chief, finally arrived along with a small contingent. Apologizing to Johnson for his lateness, the Seneca headman cited his old age, unexpected condolences, and "high-water." After the customary exchange of welcome, they and Johnson retired to their respective quarters and prepared for formal negotiations the following day.

In private, Johnson worried. Writing to Hillsborough the night before negotiations officially commenced, he brooded about the effects of a dwindling British presence in the region, which, according to Johnson's indigenous informant, illustrated English parsimonious neglect of the first peoples and were marks of Crown "injustice & disregard." Furthermore, if left unabated, the unregulated cheating practices of the traders signaled "characteristick proofs of [British] dishonesty & want of authority." Without a redress of grievances and the speedy conclusion of a boundary, the nations would remain "intoxicated with the Storys and promises of designing men." Johnson's paternalism is evident, but his lingering worries rested with the needs of the Iroquois. He conceded that the advantages of the boundary would not be felt by "any of the Indian Nations for some time, and are at best local, & confined to one Confederacy."[24] Evidently with Six Nations interests in mind, Johnson retired for the evening.

The sights must have been astonishing. Surrounded by makeshift lodging for more than three thousand visitors, at that moment Fort Stanwix took the leading role on the British imperial stage in North America. Collected were a who's who of colonial America, both European and indigenous. The fires that surrounded the English palisade no doubt cracked well into a night of customary song and dance. Guards kept a keen watch on the livestock, presents, and food stores inside and outside the fort. Chiefs as well as Crown and provincial representatives anticipated the completion of the most extensive land cession in early America. As dawn broke on Monday, 24 October 1768, the wait for those players who had long jockeyed for position came to an end.

That morning, after the commissioners representing Pennsylvania and Virginia announced their credentials to those assembled, Johnson addressed the gathering.[25] "Brethren, I take you by the hand and heartily bid you welcome to this place where I have kindled a Council Fire for affairs of importance. . . . I do now, agreeable to the ancient custom established by our Forefathers, proceed to the ceremony of Condolence." After allegorically rekindling the council fire and wiping away obstructions to their eyes, ears, and throats, Johnson addressed the assembled participants. Speaking on a wampum belt, he urged those gathered "warriors to pay a due regard to [their] Sachems and Councillors whose sage advise will seldom or never be amiss."[26] Johnson continued:

> Brethren, As I would deal with all people in their own way, and that your Ancestors have from the earliest time directed and recommended the observation of a Sett of Rules which they laid down for you to follow, I do now, agreeable to that custom, take of the clearest water and therewith cleanse your inside from all Filth and every thing which has given you concern. . . . In performing these ceremonies I can not omit this necessary part, which is, that as there are but two Council Fires for your confederacy, the one at my house and the other at Onondaga, I must desire that you will always be ready to attend either of them, when called upon, by which

means business will I hope, always be attended & properly carried out for our mutual Interest, and this I earnestly recommend to you all. . . . I must also advise you to be unanimous amongst yourselves & reside in your respective Countries, and not to think of scattering or settling amongst other Nations, as has been too much the Practice for some years past, to the great weakening of your confederacy.[27]

Johnson's comments reveal a subtle acknowledgement of borderland realities. By 1768 the independence exercised by the Ohio nations had opened a rift not easily ignored and potentially ruinous. It conflicted with long-standing protocols and the imagined place of the Grand Council. Johnson knew that well and sought to maintain order and control by reminding the prospective disgruntled tribes of acceptable behavior as outlined by years of tradition. After the chiefs "gave a Yo-hah at the proper places," Johnson's condolences ended. Those assembled dispersed until the next day.[28]

The following afternoon, Oneida chief Conoghquieson (Kanaghwaes, Kanaghqweasea, Kanongweniyah) addressed the assembly. After repeating Johnson's message from the previous day, he thanked the superintendent for the close attention he had paid to the ancient customs of the Six Nations—customs Conoghquieson considered to be "the cement of our union." At length, he promised Johnson that the chiefs would consult their young warriors as occasion may require. In addition, the Oneida speaker assured Johnson that all "the six nations, with the Shawanese, Delaware & all their dependents as far as great Plains of the Sioto," would observe whatever the superintendent decided to recommend to them. What Conoghquieson did not divulge, however, is that the recommendations he spoke of had been carefully negotiated over the past three years. Johnson's "decisions," as it would seem, would come as no surprise to those gathered at the Oneida Carry. The benefits to be had from such a personal relationship with Crown representative did not escape the eastern Iroquois. With the "clearest running stream," the chief then cleansed Johnson of his impurities and concluded his condolences, ending formal negotiations for the day.[29]

With the condolence ceremonies concluded, on Wednesday 26 October 1768 the council turned its attention to boundary details.

Speaking on the fifteen-row Covenant Chain wampum belt that had been used since the time of William Penn, Johnson first strengthened the peaceful union between the English and the Iroquois. He then reviewed the economic rewards that had benefited the tribes since time of contact and urged them not to molest future traders who traveled through their territory. "This will protect you from all dangers" Johnson maintained, "& secure to you the blessings of Peace, and the advantages of Commerce with a people able to supply all your wants."[30] Soon thereafter, Johnson departed from the "Usual Method of treating with [the Indians]" and had Chief Abraham, "who spoke & wrote both English & Mohock excellently well," translate his words into Mohawk in order to avoid misunderstandings.[31]

Johnson, a seasoned orator and multilinguist, knew the stakes were high. He recalled at great length and "in a verry full Council" the agreement reached in 1765 at Johnson Hall with regard to the readjustment of the boundary.[32] Remembering their previous discussions, he noted that settler encroachments would continue unless "some Bounds are agreed to, fixed upon and made public between us." Quick to assert Crown respect, Johnson added, "[as you can see,] His Majesty has directed me to give you a handsome proof of his Generosity proportion[e]d to the nature and extent of what Lands shall fall to him." After finishing, Johnson suggested that the tribal delegates retire to consider the subject before returning "fully prepared to give an agreeable answer." Chief Abraham informed Johnson that they would give him notice when they chose to reassemble and thanked him for giving them ample time "that our minds might not be burdened or diverted from it by attending to anything else." Before they retreated to their private camps, the Oneida chief, Conoghquieson, addressed the assembly in a bid to be granted a prominent role in the final consideration of the matter.[33]

That evening Johnson met with a delegation of Nanticokes to resolve a long-standing land issue with the province of Maryland. By 1768 only a few hundred Nanticokes remained, mostly scattered along the Susquehanna, having been allowed to jointly occupy Six Nations territory. A century of conflict with Maryland had left the Algonquian speakers few other choices. In 1768, however, the opportunity for redress was not lost. Utilizing a middleman, the Nanticokes obtained £166.2.3 for the "remainder of their land in Maryland."[34]

With the Nanticoke affair settled, the Crown waited while the nations deliberated.

On Thursday night, 27 October, Teyohaqueande, a respected Onondaga sachem and warrior, arrived at Fort Stanwix along with eighty-six fellows. An old acquaintance of Johnson, Teyohaqueande had been a prominent figure in Six Nations affairs since the mid-1750s. Johnson provided the new arrivals with "paint, Pipes, Tobacco & a dram" and turned his attention to the deliberating delegates.[35] For several days and nights, Samuel Wharton recorded, the Six Nations chiefs "were constantly sending for Sir William & Mr. Croghan to explain matters to them & remove their Doubts."[36] At approximately four in the afternoon on Friday 28 October, after being clothed by the Crown as a result of a cold snap, the Six Nations council emerged from their private quarters and addressed the superintendent. With reference to the boundary, they noted that "it would be for our mutual advantage if it were not transgressed" but added that "dayly experience teaches us that we cannot have any great dependence on the white People" and feared "that they will forget their agreement for the sake of our Lands." To help ease tensions, the speaker suggested, the boundary line detailed by Johnson in 1765 should be revised to take into consideration several of their concerns regarding recent settlements. The settlements in question were not on the Ohio but rather those increasingly surrounded by European settlers near the Finger Lakes. What would be the purpose of establishing "a Line between us & the country of Virginia & Pennsylvania," the speaker asked, if "our Towns" remained unprotected from settler excursions? According to the Six Nations, the remedy was simple: the boundary needed to be extended north from Owego. The Iroquois asked Johnson for his help in the resolution of the issue. With a prearranged answer at hand, Johnson replied: "I have attended to what you say and do admit that it is reasonable the Line should be closed . . . & I have prepared a Map on which the Country is drawn large & plain which will enable us both to judge better of these matters." After a brief exchange of words, the primary negotiators decided to retire to Johnson's private quarters for further deliberation.[37]

In a rare instance of note taking, a scribe recorded the content of the private deliberations. While pointing to the boundary map, Johnson noted that the Crown had yet to "fix upon any particular place" to continue the line northward from Owego. "It therefore remains for me to obtain a continuation of that Line which will be secure to you and advantageous to us on which subject we now meet."[38] In the months preceding the treaty, Thomas Gage had warned Johnson against any deviations from the 1765 agreement. The "matter [was] not to be done by any Persons on this Side of the Atlantick," Gage remarked in July, "and must be referred home for further Orders."[39] Johnson, however, did not hide the fact that he intended to make an appropriate concession to the Six Nations if it completed the boundary: "A Mistake has been made by which the Line is not proposed by the Board of Trade to the Northward of Owegy," Johnson replied to Gage on 20 July 1768, and unless solved "the affair of the Boundary will be defeated in its principal Object."[40] Johnson sought to establish security for the eastern Six Nations, the terms of which would be formalized before the conclusion of the treaty. Gage could do little more than caution Johnson against what he perceived to be the "needles Trouble" of attempting to resolve more than the boundary between the provinces and the nations.[41] But the Iroquois had much more sway over Johnson than did Gage.

Located on the Susquehanna River approximately fifty kilometers due south of the southern banks of Cayuga Lake, Owego marked the northern point of the boundary negotiated in 1765. But the termination of the line at Owego was not a settled matter. The Six Nations had had many good reasons for wanting an extension of the line northward. Without a northeasterly extension of the boundary from Owego, the Finger Lakes remained exposed to a swelling number of European land jobbers and squatters. In an attempt to protect the little land that remained, the Six Nations council pushed for a revision of the 1765 agreement and the establishment of an identifiable border between the province of New York and their ancient homelands.[42] In return, they arranged for an appropriate concession. Referring to a past agreement, Johnson mentioned that "the piece of Land in the Forks of the Susquehanna is very much desired by the Commissioners from Pennsylvania and would be more advantageous to them than to you." Besides, the land would likely soon be surrounded by settlements, making it difficult for any northward mobility, and the Pennsylvania governor had prepared "a large & handsome consideration" to compensate the Six Nations for ceding their interests in this tract. Johnson ended by suggesting the council retire for the night and consider the offer.[43]

The Iroquois sought security; however, that did not mean they were ignorant of, or about to be duped by, the pretreaty finagling that had taken place between European land jobbers. Before anyone could capitalize on the establishment of a new boundary, a cession had to occur. In fact, those Six Nations negotiators at Fort Stanwix were the ones who wielded the power to finalize the agreement. Thus, after Johnson concluded his speech to those assembled, Abraham responded that a reply would come from the Six Nations as soon as the Crown recognized the range of their land claim that extended well beyond the Kanawha River to the south and actually included a "very good & clear Title to the Lands as far as the Cherokee River." Based on the right of conquest, the Iroquois representative demanded Crown acknowledgment of the claim. The Six Nations had learned a difficult lesson over the preceding century of contact with land-hungry Europeans. It is evident that they had made a bid for as much as the Crown would recognize. "We were formerly generous & gave the white people in many places Lands when they were too poor to buy them, We have often had bad Returns. Nevertheless we would still act generously and mean to do as much as we can without ruining our Children." With Johnson's support behind them, the Iroquois vied for an extensive territorial claim. That night Johnson again hosted a council in his private quarters.[44]

Aware that an acknowledgement of Six Nations claims as far south as the Cherokee River meant deviating from Crown directions, Johnson backed the request. In fact, ten days prior to the Iroquois assertion of rights to the lands south of the Kanawha River, John Stuart, the superintendent of Indian affairs for the southern colonies, concluded the Treaty of Hard Labor with the Cherokees in South Carolina. On 14 October 1768, as Johnson engaged in pretreaty discussions at Fort Stanwix, the Cherokee nation agreed to cede its lands west of the Appalachian Mountains to the Ohio River running north to the Kanawha River. Half a decade of resistance to European expansion provided the Cherokees with a firm sense of territorial rights. It also provided aggressive Europeans with a glimpse of the prime settlement lands that would later include most of the states of Kentucky and Tennessee. Iroquois claims to the lands south of the Kanawha River later provided a serious point of contention at Whitehall and Charleston. The area in question also promised to redirect speculation well away from the Iroquois. In October 1768 the lands were part of a comprehensive assertion made by chiefs, who knew Johnson was eager for a major diplomatic agreement and thus realized they could push him.[45]

Interest in the northeasterly boundary was not limited to the Six Nations council. A significant amount of the land promised to Croghan fell on the eastern side of the would-be boundary. In fact, by 1768 Croghan had acquired more than 127,000 acres in deeds from Iroquois chiefs on Lake Otsego.[46] Like all such direct land sales by tribes, the buyer had not gained a defensible title unless the Crown confirmed the deeds. Croghan, of course, knew that a cession covering these lands would bring a confirmation of title closer to realization and thus increase the market value of the deeds. Without a confirmation of the boundary, the title rights to the deeds and all other prearranged grants to Croghan would remain imperfect. By erecting a legal boundary of settlement in New York, Croghan's deeds and grants would likely have been recognized by the Crown. It is difficult to believe that this fact did not registrar with Croghan as he tended to "Crown" business each night of the deliberations. The Iroquois, too, realized the weight of the confirmation.

On Saturday, 29 October, the Crown waited. The Six Nations remained in private council well into the afternoon as the chiefs and warriors consulted over the proposed boundary. The Oneidas, in particular, obstructed the proceedings. Johnson had allowed Presbyterian ministers Samuel Kirkland and Eleazar Wheelock into Oneida territory in the 1750s to combat the influence of the French Jesuits. Though Johnson and Wheelock held significantly different views about the local inhabitants, the men nevertheless maintained a cordial relationship until the mid-1760s. In 1766, Kirkland established a mission at Canajoharie. By 1768 his ministry had divided the Oneidas. Johnson was very displeased and had been increasingly wary of Kirkland's intensions. Making matters worse, in an attempt to secure land for further religious use the Presbyterian ministers decided to send a representative to Fort Stanwix.[47]

When Johnson found out that the "clergyman sent by Mr. Whee-lock from New England . . . was very busy amongst the Indians," he sent for the Mohawk and Onondaga chiefs. After clothing some of them "with whom he had several conferences," Johnson anxiously waited. Later that afternoon the Onondaga and Mohawk informants returned to the superintendent's quarters with a "Message from the whole" requesting additional time to deliberate. Johnson was impatient. He reasoned "that the security of their Lands depended upon their dispatch and the freedom of the Cession." Nevertheless, he had little choice but to wait until the next morning.[48]

That night a belt arrived from the Ohio Country carrying news that French and Spanish agents were stirring up trouble by spreading tales that warned the English intended to halt trade and remove tribes from their homelands. Believing these allegations, several nations planned to revivify an old pact to "unite and attack the English" but agreed not to engage in a general insurrection until the Stanwix negotiations had concluded. With every indication that the Ohio nations stood poised to revolt if the outcome of the deliberations threatened their territorial claims and livelihood, cession arrangements continued but with a hint of last-minute hesitation. On Sunday morning, after the warriors had been consulted regarding the proposed extension, four unnamed sachems voiced concern over ceding Ohio lands toward "Wioming or the Great Island, as they reserved that part of the Country for their Dependants." Johnson responded that much time had previously been spent negotiating the boundary. Then he warned that if the current opportunity was rejected and they insisted on drawing a new line that interfered with "Grants, or approach almost to our settlements," he could do little to initiate a more effectual method of preventing further encroachments. Thereafter, a series of arguments erupted. After the tension quelled, several alterations to the map were made and the sachems retired once again to their "Council Hutt for further consideration."[49]

Over the course of the next day, Johnson, Croghan, and Trent engaged in private negotiations with several chiefs. The latter held firm to their suggestions related to the extension of the boundary to the northeast. Although an Oneida chief informed Johnson that they continued to argue over the amount of time spent on discussing the northern extension, the matter nonetheless was not hurried. In fact, at nine in the evening six Oneida chiefs met Johnson in private, and in a bid to "shew their good intension" they suggested that the boat launch near Fort Stanwix would be an acceptable point of origin for the commencement of the line. Although thanking them for the concession, Johnson nevertheless asked that the line be extended much farther to the west. He offered $500 and a "handsome present for each chief" if the Oneida nation could convince the others to do so. The chiefs promised to do their best.[50]

On Monday morning the Oneida chiefs returned to Johnson's quarters. Because game had grown scarce in their country, they stated that their nation would likely have to depend on the revenue generated from the Carrying Place for survival in the future. As a result, "their people positively refused" to push the line any farther westward. Surprised at the obdurate refusal, Johnson encouraged reconsideration. Shortly thereafter the delegation returned. For the sum of $600, "over and besides the several Fees which were given in private," they agreed to extend the line slightly west to Canada Creek, reiterating that the new line would be forever binding. Johnson had no choice but to accept the final offer.[51] After a day of acquainting themselves with boundary details, the Iroquois headmen met Johnson on Wednesday and confirmed the line. The chiefs also insisted "on having 10,000 Dollars" for the lands relinquished to "Mr. Penns Gov't." After conferring with the Pennsylvania commissioners, Johnson informed the chiefs that the provincial representatives would agree to the terms.[52]

The Pennsylvania cession was immense. Bounded by the 1737, 1749, and 1754 land cessions to the east, the western edge of the tract stretched diagonally across the length of the province (northeast to southwest) from Owego to south of the Ohio forks.[53] Pennsylvania paid the Six Nations 10,000 Spanish dollars for the cession and, more important, for legal claim to the lands. As reviewed earlier, when Europeans did not have clear title to the land, there was a firm policy of recognizing the common law legal interests of people who *used* land but did not themselves have a Crown patent. These interests had to be cleared before patents could be issued from the Crown, or in the case of the colonies like Pennsylvania, from the proprietors.

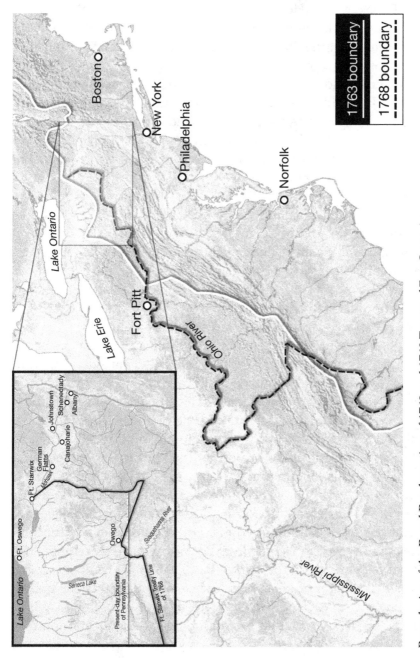

Boundaries of the Royal Proclamation of 1763 and 1768 Treaty of Fort Stanwix.
Courtesy of Stephen Otvos of Lookout Studio.

A complication arose with the purchase that pertained to the boundary of Pennsylvania. How far west and south could the Penn family claim to act with the powers of the Crown? The boundaries set by the treaty meant that the Six Nations had backed the Penns' claims to a jurisdiction over territory claimed by Virginia. In a struggle between two powerful colonies, the Iroquois supported Pennsylvania. According to the Board of Trade, the Ohio River southlands belonged to Virginia, and that province had previously allocated the lands to soldiers for services rendered in the Seven Years' War.[54] Johnson knew he was contributing to a clash of territory between Pennsylvania and Virginia, but his backing of Pennsylvania's bid for land, like his Iroquois counterparts', was strategic.[55] Thrilled by the news that a deal had been struck, Thomas Penn wrote Johnson thanking him for "doing everything in [his] power for the service of my family."[56] By assigning the lands to Pennsylvania, the Six Nations formally recognized Pennsylvania's provincial boundaries. Addressing the assembly on Tuesday, 2 November, the Iroquois affirmed that: "And as we know that Lydius of Albany did in the same of several persons lay claim to Lands in Pennsylvania, which we know to be unjust. . . . we expect that no regard will be paid to them or any such claims now hereafter, as we have fairly sold them to the proprietors of Pennsylvania."[57] The proprietors were not the only beneficiaries of the cession. Johnson, Croghan, and the Suffering Traders received particular distinction.

Having contemplated the current state of affairs, the Six Nations firmly endorsed Johnson's bid to maintain centralized authority. Rather than shedding the responsibilities of the superintendency by selling out his longtime allies, Johnson preserved the support of the Iroquois. As for the Iroquois, it was business as usual. Drawing attention to their contempt for the recent department changes, the Six Nations speaker announced that without the king's support the office of the superintendent of Indian affairs would be ill equipped to address their grievances properly. "We all know the want of this, and we make it a point of great consequence on which this our present Agreement is to depend." In a statement likely directed to Whitehall, the speaker concluded by cautioning the administration that, as injustices increased, so too would tensions between settlers and tribes. Without a capable Indian Department, "our Affairs will go wrong and our heads may be turned." The message could not have been more obvious.[58]

The Six Nations then turned to Croghan and the Suffering Traders. In "order to shew that we love justice, we expect the Traders who suffered by some of our dependants in the wars five years ago, may have a grant for the Lands we now give them down Ohio, as a satisfaction for their losses."[59] During the 1765 negotiations at Johnson Hall, the traders had gained indemnity from the Iroquois for goods destroyed in the Uprising (see chapter 4). The preferred method of compensation included a much-anticipated land grant. Although a system of reimbursement based on individual loses existed on paper, by 1768 the reality was that shares in the venture had been bought up and were held by a few scheming individuals. As noted earlier, to consolidate their claims Croghan, Trent, William Franklin, and Baynton, Wharton and Morgan had organized the Indiana Company before the congress at Fort Stanwix. By 3 November 1768 the Suffering Traders had been granted all the lands on the "southerly side of the mouth of Little Kanawha Creek, where it empties into the river Ohio, and running from thence south east to the Laurel Hill, thence . . . until it strikes the river Monongahela . . . to the Southern boundary line of . . . Pennsylvania, thence westerly . . . to the river Ohio, thence down the said river . . . to the place of beginning."[60] Elated, Trent later remarked on his complete satisfaction with the cession.[61]

In addition to his interests in the Suffering Traders' grant, Croghan received further consideration. Busy since 1764 circumventing restrictions set by the Royal Proclamation of 1763, he intended to make the most of the Stanwix negotiations. On 27 June 1767, Croghan and thirty-nine partners had petitioned Whitehall for 40,000 acres west of Lake Otsego. The Otsego patent actually contained more than 100,000 acres. To skirt limits imposed by the proclamation, Croghan worded the petition cleverly. Writing to the Board of Trade in 1767, the petitioners "humbly conceive that the Royal intention in said Proclamation was solely to prevent the defrauding the Indians in purchases made by Private Persons." Since the original owners were determined to give the claimants the land, Croghan reasoned, he would voluntarily cover the costs of the cession to avoid complications. Furthermore, because land transactions between the tribes and Europeans had to be sanctioned by a Crown agent, Croghan arranged for Governor Sir Henry Moore to purchase the land on behalf of the Crown on 10 June 1768 at Johnson Hall.

The financial benefits of speculation would not, however, be reaped until the owner could divide and sell the lands. As a result, it was imperative that the boundary be established west of the tracts. Thus, when the Six Nations speaker addressed the issue of Croghan's land on 3 November, it represented a culmination of almost five years of jockeying by Croghan. And in a moment his prospects were brightened. "Our friend Mr. Croghan," the speaker remarked, "long ago got a Deed for Lands from us, which may be considered and get as much from the King somewhere else, as he fairly bought it.—And as we have given enough to shew our Love for the King and make his People easy, in the next place we expect that no old claims which we disavow or new encroachments may be allowed of."[62]

The special considerations made by the Six Nations at Fort Stanwix served several purposes. The cession of legal interests in land to the Penns undercut the claims by Connecticut and Virginia to "Pennsylvanian" land by providing Six Nations support for provincial expansion west to the Ohio River. The Suffering Traders' Indiana grant along the Ohio, just south of Pennsylvania's southern border, satisfied a few well-connected speculators with a keen interest in expanding empire. Not only did Croghan manage to involve himself in the Suffering Traders cession, he was deeded more than 200,000 acres split between the Lake Otsego region in New York and Fort Pitt in the newly assigned lands of Pennsylvania. In the end, however, the Iroquois also used the cessions as a tool for securing their own future. The northern extension of the boundary to the Oneida Carry guaranteed, at least on paper, legal protection to most of the eastern Six Nations homelands in the Finger Lakes region. The Six Nations had washed their hands clean of the complications associated with controlling the increasingly hostile Ohio nations. Only a few issues remained. Before dealing with them, the Iroquois emphasized the significance of the Covenant Chain.

On Tuesday, 1 November 1768, with "Sentiments of Independancy, Justice & Finness, That would do honor to any Civilized Chieftans," the Iroquois speaker held the Covenant Chain wampum belt in his hand, recalling the ancient agreement.[63] When the English first reached the shores of North America, the inhabitants had done their best to accommodate and care for the beleaguered new arrivals. A peaceful agreement was made, binding the English and the Six Nations in a chain of friendship. Apprehensive that the bark that bound the agreement would break, they decided to make one of iron. "But perceiving the former chain was liable to rust," the Six Nations opted to replace it with a chain of silver. But silver tends to dull; as noted by the Iroquois speaker, it took both the energy of them and the "King's people" to polish and maintain the chain. In other words, the Six Nations had done their part and it was now time for the Crown to pay due regard to their needs. After the boundary details had been recited, to help commit them to the oral knowledge of the Iroquois the Six Nations insisted that "no further attempts . . . be made on our Lands" and desired that "one Article of this agreement be, that none of the Provinces or their People shall attempt to invade it under color of any old Deeds, or other pretences what soever." Furthermore, the warriors of every nation must be granted the liberty of hunting throughout the area, without interference from Europeans west of the line, for this was the only means of continued subsistence for many of their people.[64]

Finally, the Iroquois headmen turned to the particular security of the Mohawk nation. The northern extension of the boundary demarcated a clear line between European settlers and the Six Nations, but the traditional lands of the eastern gatekeepers of the League, the Mohawks, fell well within the region now formally on the settlement side. Divided and scattered among European communities, the primary Mohawk villages stretching along the Mohawk and Hudson rivers felt the sting of encroachments. Though the friendship forged between British agents and Mohawk chiefs, sachems, and warriors had provided a cordial and strategic alliance over the century, by 1768 there was no escaping the fact that most of the Mohawk ancestral lands had been consumed by European settlers, squatters, and speculators. The Mohawk nation, integral to the façade of Crown and Grand Council authority throughout the northeastern borderlands, demanded a resolution to its plight.

After outlining the course of the boundary, the Iroquois speaker mentioned the precarious situation of the Mohawks. Because their settlements are "now within the Line which we give to the King . . .

[and] they are the true old Heads of the whole confederacy," they must be given special consideration. The confirmed remedy was interesting. The speaker noted that the several villages and unpatented lands still in Mohawk possession, along with "the Residences of any others in our confederacy affected by this Cession[,] shall be considered as their sole property and at their disposal both now, and so long as the sun shines, and that all grants or engagements they have now or lately entered into, shall be considered as independent of this Boundary so that they . . . may not lose the benefit of the sale of it . . . with whom they have agreed, may have the Land."[65] The clause underscored Mohawk control over all the remaining lands east of the boundary yet unpatented and the unique authority to sell and transfer the lands to whomever they deemed. This addition to the agreement is nothing short of remarkable, for it illustrates not only the clout of the eastern gatekeepers but also their firm grasp of colonial land practices and legal rights.

With final concerns settled, the largest land cession in colonial North America was complete. The congress that prepared the transaction had provided the Six Nations an opportunity to put forward their grievances and anxieties; it gave them an occasion to bargain and negotiate long-overdue boundaries and guarantees. They negotiated skillfully. They had been adept at identifying their interests, at devising remedies, at putting pressure on other parties, and at stating matters eloquently. In diplomatic arts, they equaled the colonizers.

The next day, Wednesday, 2 November, it poured rain. Selected tribesmen were again provided blankets and additional clothing. During the day the assembled participants remained indoors. That evening Johnson again met with "the Mohocks and other Chiefs." After making few inroads in another attempt to persuade them to extend the line farther west in New York, Johnson informed the chiefs that the commander-in-chief, Thomas Gage, planned to reduce the number of occupants at Fort Ontario. The Six Nations did not take issue and retired until the next day.[66]

On Friday, 4 November 1768, after taking a day to prepare deeds and speeches, Iroquois and Europeans reconvened to conclude the treaty. After a condolence ceremony for the recent loss of the Oneida chief, Johnson rose and addressed the gathered participants. He requested them to protect the traders who were essential to continued trade and communication. After explaining that the king had done all in his power to address frontier abuses and compensate them, Johnson assured them that the line would be "duly observed by the English" and forever binding until a time the tribes felt it necessary to make "any future additions or alterations."[67] Had his promise been kept, the Treaty of Fort Stanwix would have been a fine pragmatic achievement of Six Nations diplomacy.

The superintendent then turned his attention to the Ohio nations: "Brothers the Shawanese & Delawares, I now particularly address you." According to Johnson, because they resided so far southward and away from the heads of the Confederacy, they had been susceptible to a variety of bad influences and poor intelligence, which resulted in mischief and poor judgment. Urging the Ohio nations to dismiss the rumors of a general revolution in America and the return of French fleets and armies, Johnson assured them "that those who were able to conquer Canada, & drive their enemies out of their country, will always have it in their power to defeat their future projects should they be weak enough to make any future attempts to regain what they lost." He further reminded them of their previous agreements with the English, the treaty of peace between the Iroquois and the Cherokees, and also their place in the Iroquois Confederacy. Johnson advised the Ohio nations to "pay due regard to the Boundary Line now made, & to make all your people acquainted with it."[68]

Johnson next recited the parting requests of Gov. William Franklin. Franklin, who had recently been honored with the name Sagorrihwhioughstha ("Doer of Justice") by the Six Nations, had little bother with treaty affairs now that his interests were secured. Before leaving, however, he made sure that Johnson reminded the Delawares of the agreement made at Easton in 1755, by which they had officially relinquished land in New Jersey such that the "Province [was now] entirely free from all Indian Claims."[69]

Concluding his address, Johnson urged the Ohio nations to avoid wandering and to return to their villages in the east, "after the manner of your ancestors." Instead of remaining disunited and confused by the ramblings of bad men, "bind you all together" under the protection of the Confederacy. By projecting an image of unification among the Iroquois, both Johnson and the Grand Council sought an order that gave legitimacy to their positions and strengthened their partnership in the extension of empire. Before executing the deed of cession, 500 Spanish dollars was paid to the Conestogas to give "full satisfaction of [their] Lands, which by the death of that People" became the property of Pennsylvania's proprietors. Johnson then called an end to the daily negotiations. Those assembled retired and awaited the formal reading of the cession.[70]

As the indigenous delegates entered the fort on the morning of 5 November 1768, they did so past the largest amount of currency and goods collected to date for an exchange between North American Indians and the British Empire. In the early morning hours workers carted and arranged more than twenty boatloads of gifts so that the "whole assembled in the Area [would] subscribe to the Deed & receive the consideration."[71] The Crown had spent an unprecedented amount of money to conclude the negotiations. In fact, Philadelphia merchant Samuel Wharton later recorded that he had never before seen such an enormous amount of money and added that the gifts were of the finest quality. In the middle and "circumvented by the Goods & Dollars on three Sides" sat Sir William Johnson. The chiefs, warriors, and "all other Indians standing on the Ramparts & ca pleasurably view[ed] the Goods."[72]

After reaffirming the treaty, the Six Nations speaker rose and addressed the Crown representatives:

> We the Sachems & Chiefs of the Six confederate Nations, and of the Shawanese, Delawares, Mingoes of Ohio and other Dependent Tribes on behalf of our selves and of the rest of our Several Nations the Chiefs & Warriors of whom are now here convened by Sir William Johnson Baronet His Majestys Superintendent of our affairs send greeting. Whereas . . . the Lands occupied by the Mohocks around their villages as well as by any other Nation affected by this our Cession may effectually remain to them and to their Property and that any engagements regarding Property which they may now be under may be prosecuted and our present Grants deemed valid on our parts with the several other humble requests contained in our said Speech. And whereas at the settling of the said Line it appeared that the Line described by His Majestys order was not extended

to the Northward of Oswegy or to the Southward of Great Kanhawa river
We have agreed to and continued the Line to the Northward on a suppo-
sition that it was omitted by reason of our not having come to any deter-
minations concerning its course at the Congress held in one thousand
seven hundred and sixty five and in as much as the Line to the Northward
became the most necessary of any for preventing encroachments at our
very Towns & Residences.[73]

Next, the Six Nations declared that the boundary was rightfully
extended to the southward to the Cherokee River, for the sum of the
"Ten thousand four Hundred and Sixty pounds seven shillings and
three pence sterling." The exact boundary line was read as follows:

Beginning the Mouth of Cherokee or Hogohege River where it emptys
into the River Ohio and running from thence by a direct Line to the South
side of said River to Kittaning which is above Fort Pitt form thence by a
direct Line to the nearest Fork of the west branch of Susquehanna thence
through the Allegany Mountains along the South side of the said West
Branch until it comes opposite to the mouth of a Creek callek [sic] Tiadagh-
ton [Pine Creek] thence across the West Branch and along the South side
of that Creek and along the North side of Burnetts Hills to a Creek called
Awandae thence down the same to the East Branch of Susquehanna and
across the same and up the East side of that River to Oswegy fro thence
East to Delawar River and up that River to opposite where Tianaderha
falls into Susquehanna thence to Tianaderha and up the West side of its
West Branch to the head thereof and thence by a direct Line to Canada
Creek where it emptys into the wood Creek at the West of the Carrying
Place beyond Fort Stanwix.[74]

The list of signatures confirming the treaty included six chiefs, one
from each of the Six Nations. The final treaty did not mention the
approval of any Ohio nation representatives, or of a single sachem or
chief of the western Senecas. Although George Knepper claims that
"the Ohio Indians . . . were prominently represented at councils leading to the Treaty of Fort Stanwix," the western nations had little representation or say in the final agreement.[75] They had been compelled
to take a loss. Adding insult to injury, the Ohio peoples would be sent

a mere twenty-seven pounds worth of goods.[76] Sealed and delivered in the presence of New Jersey chief justice Frederick Smyth, Virginian and Pennsylvanian commissioners, and Sir William Johnson, the 1768 Treaty of Fort Stanwix was concluded on 5 November 1768.[77]

Most historians have depicted the series of events at Fort Stanwix as the brainchild of William Johnson. He certainly had personal reasons for convening a congress and finessing a treaty. After all, Whitehall planned to reduce his position to that of diplomatic stature. The negotiations gave him an opportunity to show the usefulness of the office of superintendent of Indian affairs and his ability as a veteran cultural broker. Johnson, moreover, was no stranger to speculation. He had acquired approximately 200,000 acres in deeds from the Six Nations on two separate occasions prior to the Fort Stanwix treaty. According the Peter Marshall, he "had good reason to press for the abandonment of the [1763] Proclamation." Furthermore, as Jon Parmenter argues, by supporting the Six Nations claims to the Ohio, Johnson "obtained his revenge" on the delinquent confederate warriors for their conduct in 1755 and 1763.[78]

In concluding this treaty, those who signed the agreement deviated from royal instructions in three significant instances.[79] First, the agreed boundary extended south past the Kanawha to the Cherokee River. The additional area, "1107 3/4 miles in length, and about 100 miles in breadth," not only accounted for a significant portion of land but contained land already ceded by the Cherokees to the Crown at the Treaty of Hard Labor.[80] Second, the boundary also extended north past Owego to the Oneida Carry near Fort Stanwix. Third, Johnson and the Iroquois allowed personal transactions to occur simultaneously, which ran contrary to Crown instructions. By taking the liberty to adjust the royal instructions, the negotiators undoubtedly acted on their appraisal of the situation. That does not mean, however, that Johnson deviated from his responsibility as a loyal British subject and diligent Crown representative. In fact, Hillsborough was well aware of Johnson's intentions to adjust the boundary, and on at least one occasion he gave cautionary approval.[81]

Thus, despite claims of the opposite, Johnson's involvement in the "entire episode" was no "farce." The veteran weighed his options as a Crown representative and accepted that certain realities had to be addressed to achieve a diplomatic settlement. The northern boundary had to be settled to establish a new one in the south, and there were private interests which, unless settled, could impede harmony. Moreover, the Iroquois no doubt reasoned, it made more sense to guide, and thus benefit from, who would receive lands, and where. Consequently, the Suffering Traders and proprietors of Pennsylvania warmly greeted news of the treaty's terms, whereas Virginia and Connecticut speculators did not. Nor did the Ohio nations, whose lands had been sold from under their feet. When Philadelphia merchant and Suffering Traders powerhouse Samuel Wharton later recalled that no other treaty had ever been concluded with better judgment and satisfaction from the Six Nations than at Stanwix, his prejudice is easily identified.[82]

In the end, all signatories of the treaty were willing to sacrifice the fate of the independent-minded Ohio nations by promoting the authority of an empire that promised to protect their self-interests. That being said, those like-minded signatories who defined the boundaries of authority on pieces of paper in 1768 knew that their claims were increasingly tenuous without the presence of the Crown. Not long after the treaty concluded, Samuel Wharton suggested that the king should act swiftly to put colonists on the ceded lands because frontier settlements on the Ohio would be able to strike at traditional villages. If "delayed or disputed ... The most unhappy Consequences will instantly result."[83] Many borderland agents, traders, and interpreters had similarly played at raising anxieties about an Uprising in order to convince a government to act in a particular way. The sacrifice of the Ohio nations was a risky gambit, but it may have been the only path to regaining Crown control and Six Nations authority.

Much had changed over the course of a year that culminated in the Treaty of Fort Stanwix. Beginning with the cold blooded murder of Conestogas on the banks of the Susquehanna, 1768 seemed to confirm the apparent impotence of British law on the margins of empire. News that Whitehall sought to reduce colonial expenditures dramatically by scuttling the Plan of 1764 and stripping the Indian Department to a bare-bones operation further contributed to deteriorating relations between the two worlds. By spring of 1768, however, parties with converging interests had agreed on the need for a grand diplomatic initiative. In early November 1768 the previous efforts of the Iroquois appeared to have paid off. That being said, it would not take long before the beneficiaries of the treaty ran into trouble. Dorothy Jones has written that the "compromises that had been made . . . had the potential to destroy the agreements that were the purpose of the treaties."[84] In the end, for those attempting to project authority and capitalize on speculation, the Treaty of Fort Stanwix set the groundwork for the finale of a high-stakes game that had been unfolding since the end of the Seven Years' War.

CHAPTER 6

Prospects, and the Collapse
of Protocol

By opening the Ohio Country to settlement, the Six Nations' Grand Council collected a king's ransom at the treaty of Fort Stanwix, addressed contentious land claims, and momentarily alleviated European encroachment on eastern Iroquois homelands. In addition to the thousands of acres gifted in private negotiations, the Suffering Traders secured what would later become known as the Indiana grant.[1] As for the Pennsylvania proprietors, they gained invaluable Iroquois support for provincial endeavors west of the Appalachians. Sir William Johnson gave "the proceedings the color of legality" even though "the initiative, motivation, and rewards were wholly private." But unlike his speculating deputy, Johnson was primarily concerned with reasserting the authority of the Indian Department and the image of the Grand Council.[2] By the early 1770s, though, it was clear that the home government took a dim view of Johnson's willingness to overlook private interests for what he determined an important step in maintaining Crown control throughout the northeastern borderlands. By the middle of the decade the future of the Indian Department, and the Iroquois as a crucial component of British imperial design, waned.

From 1768 to 1774, Whitehall initiated a series of measures that significantly altered relations between tribes residing in the northeastern borderlands and European colonists, and thus the security of many indigenous communities. One of the first orders of imperial business for the new Pitt ministry concerning North America was the drawing of the new boundary. The ministry guaranteed the permanency of the Indian Department, but the abandonment of most western forts, the relocation of British regulars to the east coast, and the abandonment of the supervision of trade restricted the powers of the department and threatened to reduce the superintendency to little more than a symbolic position.[3] The unwillingness of Whitehall to uphold the many private clauses of the 1768 Fort Stanwix agreement created further tension. Crown discretion caused delay; the postponement of development eroded fortunes, jeopardized grand designs for an inland colony, and undermined Iroquois security. Finally, the Fort Stanwix treaty did not settle intercolonial boundary disputes, and the subsequent angst set those colonials jostling for control of the Ohio River valley on a collision course.[4]

Caught in the unfolding mayhem were the indigenous residents of the region. In October 1774, years of resistance to European encroachment erupted along the Scioto River and at Point Pleasant when Virginia forces under the command of the governor, Lord Dunmore, defeated Shawnee, Ohio Iroquois, Wyandot, and Delaware warriors in a series of clashes. In an attempt to lay claim to the contested region, the governor forced the Ohio tribes to acknowledge the Six Nations cession that occurred almost six years before at the Oneida Carry. The Stanwix agreement turned the ceded lands into a "racial killing ground . . . that rendered the Ohio River a battle line that Indians fought to defend and whites to breach for almost thirty years."[5]

Dunmore's play for control over the region was aided by an unsuspecting partner. By the spring of 1774, George Croghan found himself in a desperate state. Because of insurmountable debts and lack of resources, Croghan's ability to appear useful had quickly faded. That summer when William Johnson died he lost a crucial backer, and most of his clear title and Indian deeds had been mortgaged or absorbed by his sponsors in Philadelphia and New York so that he could tend to mounting legal battles and avoid imprisonment. He had been left behind in 1769 when Wharton and Trent departed for London to concentrate their efforts on borderland development with partners across the Atlantic. When the Pennsylvania proprietors began settling grants to clamoring settlers near Fort Pitt on what Croghan deemed his land, he turned in desperation to Virginia. In so doing, he chose to break with old allegiances in the Pennsylvania Assembly and at the council fires of the Six Nations.

The Crown's eroding power and Croghan's demise paralleled the collapse of Iroquois authority. By the time Dunmore marched on the Ohio, the Grand Council had other, more pressing problems to worry about. With an increase of colonial hostilities came an upsurge of speculating interests in Six Nations country. With Johnson dead and the Indian Department in disarray, the Grand Council struggled to exercise any tangible authority or project an image of a unified front. Consequently, as the continent tumbled toward open war, many indigenous leaders distanced themselves from the brewing conflict in a bid to safeguard their communities. At an emergency council held in Albany in 1775, the Grand Council declared Iroquois neutrality and Shawnee and Delaware leaders tried to calm their warriors as violence gripped the Ohio Country. Nevertheless, the scope of the American Revolution undermined indigenous attempts at neutrality and began to redefine the place of the Iroquois in the history of early America.

Within weeks of concluding the 1768 boundary negotiations at Fort Stanwix, William Johnson sent a copy of the agreement to Lord Hillsborough along with the treaty minutes. Johnson defended his choice to stray from Crown instructions. He insisted that if he had not granted terms for the Six Nations to claim the lands south of the Great Kanawha to the Cherokee River, the negotiations would have deteriorated and "prevented Settlement of the rest." He also claimed an inability to deter the Grand Council from continuing the line northward from Owego to Canada Creek. Actually, because the boundary divided several indigenous settlements and ran close to patented lands, Johnson maintained that only through great "pains & troubles" was an agreement reached. Furthermore, because the Nations were "not ignorant that the Colonies are governed by different Maxims and Politicks, and hav[e] been often disappointed in Matters where they apprehend they deserved redress," the Crown must act fast. They would not be "apt to repose a confidence a second time" should the Crown not honor all of the terms of the Fort Stanwix agreement. Those involved in the cession knew that bureaucratic bantering at Whitehall would be ruinous. As John C. Weaver remarks, "intrigues crossed the Atlantic, for the Board of Trade and the King in Council could bless or ruin a scheme."[6] The agreement required swift approval. Yet it did not take much investigation to uncover the complex array of private interests.

Only days after Johnson sent word to Hillsborough, he turned his attention closer to home. He distributed copies of the cession details to men of influence throughout colonial America. An accompanying message highlighted key agreements reached during the negotiations. The letter insisted that "the lands occupied by the Mohocks around their villages" must "remain to them and to their Posterity."[7] Gov. Henry Moore replied encouragingly to Johnson in early December. The governor insisted that "nothing will be omitted by the Legislature of this colony to secure to the Indians all the Rights they have reserved to the Eastward of the Line and to merit their confidence by making proper Laws for their protection."[8] It appeared that the Iroquois had carefully bent imperial directives in North America to meet their needs. News of land cession traveled fast, and Johnson did his best to uphold the interests of his Iroquois allies. By early 1769, however, the first signs of trouble began to arrive at Johnson Hall.

In response to the initial letter outlining the terms of the treaty of Fort Stanwix, an aggravated Lord Hillsborough wrote Johnson: "The King wishes . . . that you had not allowed the Six Nations" to claim the lands south of the Kanhawa River. Hillsborough remarked that the Commissioners for Trade and Plantations carefully considered the decision to conclude the line at the said river, and the deviation from the instructions was "considered by them as productive only of disadvantage and embarrassment, the worst of it is, that it will not only undo and throw into confusion those settlements and arrangements for the other part of the Boundary Line." After demanding that Johnson decline the southern cession of the Six Nations as diplomatically as possible, he ended his letter.[9]

The "other part" of the boundary Hillsborough referred to was the line settled by John Stuart, the superintendent of Indian affairs for the southern colonies, and the Cherokee nation at the Treaty of Hard Labor just prior to the opening of the Fort Stanwix negotiations. Hillsborough made no qualms about his opinion on that subject. Had

Johnson "discreetly avoided mixing any other matter, or suffering it to be clogged with any other conditions," he informed the king, "this difficult and embarrassing business would have been . . . brought to a happy Issue." Instead, the province of Virginia perceived the agreement as unjust and had since approached the Cherokee nation to run the southern line as far north as the Kanawha River. Subsequently, the Lords recommended to the king that Virginia be allowed to make an alteration to the southern line that would "begin at the point where the North Carolina Line terminates, and run thence a West Course to Holsteins River, where it is intersected by the Line, dividing the Provinces of North Carolina and Virginia, and thence in a North East by North Course to the Confluence of the Kanhaway & Ohio Rivers."[10] The situation continued to deteriorate.

Adding to the tension between Whitehall and Johnson Hall, the plan to strip the frontiers of any significant military presence and hand over the regulation of trade to each province appeared to be gaining momentum. A proposal to dismantle the Indian Department was laid before the Board of Trade in January 1769. According to Hillsborough, the cost of maintaining a formidable military presence in order to secure peace and trade throughout the borderlands had grown too high. After all, with the conclusion of the treaty at Fort Stanwix many policymakers across the Atlantic felt the matter somewhat finalized— or at least now not a Crown problem. Johnson viewed the matter differently. Annoyed that Hillsborough did not appreciate the fine balance needed between the Iroquois and the Crown to further imperial directives, Johnson warned his superior that the reduction of the western posts might result in "ill consequences" if the colonies did not first agree on trade regulations and provincial boundaries. He emphasized the important role of his office and urged Hillsborough to review his "sketch" of trade regulations. The governors and assemblies of New York, New Jersey, and Pennsylvania had all received a copy of his suggestions, but little progress would be made until the Crown decided to press the issue.[11] As for the boundary deviations, Johnson restated that he pursued the best avenue of negotiations on behalf of the king. If the provinces had been allowed to become the primary purchasers, the ensuing complications would have "greatly retarded the proceedings, & possibly have rendered the Congress abortive." In fact, because of the slew of private interests, "the Indians were verry far from being so unanimous as at first." According to Johnson, had he not been given the authority to act as a representative of the king, little would have been accomplished. He was right.[12]

Johnson chose his words carefully. As much as he loathed Hillsborough's limited grasp of borderland affairs, he knew that the strength of the Crown, the future of his post, and the security of the Six Nations depended on the support of the government in London. Nevertheless, by the end of March 1769 few steps had been taken to address the forthcoming withdrawal of Crown oversight throughout the northeastern borderlands. On 15 April, the Board of Trade ruled in favor of Hillsborough's suggestions and prepared to transfer power over relations with first peoples to the colonies. Gen. Thomas Gage worried about the lack of provincial directive. He supported Johnson's plan to divide provincial responsibility and pleaded with Governor Penn to have provincial agents ready to replace Crown personnel. So did the Pennsylvania Assembly.[13]

The Grand Council, too, fretted about the possibly of losing their control over borderland affairs. Hillsborough informed Johnson that "the wishes of the Indians to have their commercial as well as their political concerns managed in the manner suggested in the Plan of 1764" would not be met. He demanded that Johnson not fail in his endeavors to explain the matter to the Iroquois since already having "so fully explained . . . the reason and necessity for departing from that plan."[14]

But Hillsborough's distaste for how the Indian Department conducted business did not always translate into policy. By May the Grand Council's insistence on the right to run the boundary north from Owego paid off. In late April 1769, when the Lords of Trade made their final suggestions to the king regarding "Sir William Johnson's Treaty with the Indians," the Lords suggested that "the Mohawk Villages and all the Lands they occupy unpatented within the Line . . . shall be considered as their sole property, and at their own disposal." As for the lands south of the Kanawha River, the matter remained unsettled. In fact, the Lords criticized Johnson's role in the affair. The report stated that Johnson goaded the Six Nations into terms that complemented "the Plan proposed in 1764 . . . and [did] not correspond with what, which your Majesty has now adopted."[15] Whether or not Johnson had a hand in the final arrangement remains a trivial detail. As outlined in the preceding chapters, the eastern Iroquois had numerous reasons to push for the extensions, and they did so both prior to and during the first Fort Stanwix treaty. The Crown agreed to the continuations of the boundary because it wanted to begin withdrawing from the costly maintenance of indigenous affairs with the slate cleared of as many old grievances as possible. A rupture with the Iroquois, perhaps only rhetorically, risked a tidy break.

By the spring of 1769, months of disagreement over Connecticut settler claims to lands lying on and adjacent to the Susquehanna River had begun to boil over. The Pennsylvania proprietors fumed over the Connecticut-based Susquehanna Company's play for land they considered well within their territorial rights. Citing a private agreement made between Susquehanna Company representatives and Iroquois delegates during the congress at Fort Stanwix, Connecticut speculators William Logan, Benjamin Chew, Lynford Lardner, and James Tilghman informed the governor of Pennsylvania in February of their intension to establish inland settlements. By the end of the month, news of a "large body of New England men" determined to settle the Wyoming region by force if necessary filtered back to Governor Penn. In response, Penn wrote the Connecticut governor: "It is well known that the Indians never sell their Rights but in public Council, and it cannot be pretended that any Deeds made to the People of Connecticut were attended with that solemnity." In addition to informing the governor of the breach of treaty protocol, Penn issued a proclamation on 16 May 1769 that promised provincial interjection if the Connecticut settlers failed to halt their actions.[16] Tensions mounted.

Johnson worked to curb the expansionist designs of borderland settlers. Fear that westward-moving Virginian settlers would disregard the indigenous inhabitants in the newly ceded territory strained relations. Johnson informed Hillsborough that during the Fort Stanwix negotiations the chiefs "insisted in such warm terms on the justice of their claims to ye Cherokee River" to avoid an outbreak in hostilities with the Virginians.[17] Two months later he expressed the same sentiment in another letter to Hillsborough. In fact, by August

1769 Johnson conceded that much had changed with regard to indigenous dynamics in North America after the 1765 agreement with the Six Nations. By 1768 "the Northern Confederacy were more powerfull & more inclined to dispute, & their dispute of more dangerous consequence." Fearing Virginian aggression, Johnson insisted that he "could no longer hesitate . . . and had to act." With the Crown's well-being in mind, Johnson proclaimed that he labored over the negotiations often late into each night and in poor health.[18] In fact, he went as far as to defend the final written product. To avoid future ambiguity and obtain the most correct translation, Johnson paternalistically noted:

> I was aware that it might be liable to misconstruction unless due allowance be made for them as savages who have the most extravigant notions of freedom, property and independence, & who cannot as yet be persuaded to give up their hopes & expectations for the Crown, and any person who well understands & impartially represents them must admit that in all such treaties they endeavour to maintain their own importance by the most forcible expressions, to which I may with truth add, that, as their words for fear of offence have been often glossed over before they were committed to writing by many others, I was the first that in the most critical period took upon me to check them in their sallys of that nature.[19]

Though Johnson often used the voice of the chiefs to underscore the importance of his remarks, he did not do so in his capacity as enterprising speculator. That being said, men who pursued fortune within the confines of an orderly empire had lofty prospects. Johnson stated that he "had nothing to do" with the other private sales that occurred during the November deliberations, but he did note that no objections to the final agreement surfaced. As for what appeared to be excessive meddling on the part of his deputy, Johnson maintained that the land granted to Croghan "was only a confirmation of two former grants which the Indians particularly desired to make." The same went for the land granted to the Suffering Traders. Furthermore, Johnson had grown tired of hearing about the "ridiculous or partial" reports of those men without any competent ability to judge. They "are not easily refuted at 3000 miles distance . . . [and] there is scarcely one other subject where a man of sense and observation who has been on the spot cannot afford any remarks that may be of use." Candidly speaking, Johnson noted that it "is not during the period of a Governors residence at an American capital, of a commandant at an outpost, or a traveler in the country that this can be gained, it is only to be acquired by a long residence amongst them, a daily intercourse with them, & a desire of Information in these matters superseding all other considerations." In the end the disgruntled superintendent proclaimed, "It is easy for me to demonstrate that private interest governs none of my representations." In Johnson's empire private interests may have existed, but they only "flow[ed] from duty to the Crown & regard for the public security."[20]

By catering to the needs of the eastern Iroquois and a few close friends, the superintendent of Indian affairs sought to maintain Crown control throughout the northeastern borderlands and solidify his position in the larger imperial framework. Thus considered, independent-minded Virginians and Connecticutians had few opportunities in the colonial designs projected west from Philadelphia, Johnson Hall, and Onondaga.

Despite Johnson's attempts to smooth things over, clashes continued. In late June, Andrew, a Wyandot informant "of good sense," reported that tribes along the Mississippi River, throughout the Ohio River valley, and around Detroit planned to incite the western nations to unify and rise up against the British. By mid-July news reached Philadelphia that the "young Seneca George" had been shot by a settler named Peter Read near the forks of the Susquehanna River. Seneca George, the older, had been an important link between the English and the western Six Nations and Ohio nations. The unfortunate death of his son emphasized the deteriorating state of relations between the Crown and the nations.[21] In response and acting on behalf of the governor, James Hamilton agreed that the province act quickly and send "a Present of Condolance . . . to Old Seneca George, and the other Relations." On 19 July provincial authorities agreed to cover the body of the dead Seneca with the following articles: "1 Piece of Black Strouds; 1 Ditto of Black half thicks; 1 Ditto of Black Striped Duffills; 2 Ditto of Bandanoe Silk Handkerchiefs, dark Coloured; 1 Dozen of Shirts, Vizt 6 Ruffled and 6 Plain; 2 Pieces of Gartering, Scarlet and Star; 50 lbs of Tobacco; 4 Pair of Shoes, and 4 Pair of Buckles; 15 Gallons of Rum in 3 Keggs; 2 lbs of Vermillion; 1 dozen of Small Brass Kettles; and 2 Barrels of Pork." After informing Johnson of the mishap, provincial representatives began to organize and pack for a series of upcoming councils to quell rising tensions.[22]

On 19 August 1769, Seneca George arrived at Fort Augusta at the request of Col. Turbutt Francis. Last Night, a Conoy chief, and Genequant, an Onondaga chief, along with twenty-two others accompanied the bereaved Seneca "Captain." After concluding formal greetings, Seneca George requested that the English temporarily cease the distribution of all "Strong Drink" in order to engage in meaningful negotiations. All parties agreed, and a day later Seneca George and his retinue partook in the worship of the "White god" along with more than fifty European settlers of the region. When the council resumed, Colonel Francis ordered Peter Read to be sent to Lancaster prison "to be kept secure till he can be tried." The colonel then addressed the assembled Senecas. With the strouds brought from Philadelphia, Francis covered the body of young Seneca George "so deep" that no one's eyes could see it. The handkerchiefs metaphorically wiped "away tears to take sorrow from hearts," and the wampum belt scraped "up all the Blood that has lain on the Ground or stained the bushes." After distributing the gifts to the chief, Colonel Francis waited for a reply.[23]

On Wednesday, 23 August, a day after about fifty near-starving Delawares were restricted from attending the council, Seneca George rose and spoke to the assembled participants. Not a chief, George appointed the Conoy chief, Last King, to speak on his behalf. He assured the council that their words were as one. Subsequently, Last King denounced the excess of borderland injustices. Although they came in peace to settle the matter, Last King speculated about what would have happened had one of them committed "the like" against a European settler. According to Last King, the peaceful coexistence as arranged by their forefathers had been neglected. "We all came at first from one Woman . . . and our little Children when born have all the same Shapes and Limbs as yours, altho' they be of a different Colour." Unless both the tribes and Europeans again began to share resources and respect cultural differences, Last King continued, the road to council fire now kindled at Shamokin would remain blocked and the hearts of their peoples filled with perpetual sorrow. With those words, the chief assured Colonel Francis that the Nanticokes and Conoys had joined the English to wipe the eyes of Seneca George, clearing the "door to the Six Nations." Concluding his speech, Last King turned his attention to a matter a little closer to home. He expressed some anxiety over the fact that he had still not been compensated for the slaughter of a six-year-old steer used by Johnson during the Fort Stanwix negotiations. Because he planned to depart the next day, Last King hoped for swift and appropriate compensation. Before finishing, Last King also requested that "a Squaw [be sent] to keep [him] warm at Night." Unable to produce a female companion for the night, Colonel Francis nevertheless made sure Last King received a slaughtered cow, flour, and ample fluid. The chief left with a "walking stick as long and as tall as possible."[24]

While Colonel Francis was wrapping up negotiations at Shamokin, troubles throughout the northeastern borderlands brewed. The Grand Council worried about recent rumors that England, France, and Spain would soon again be at war. The tenuous hold that the Iroquois Confederacy and the Crown had on borderland affairs could perhaps not survive another conflict. As war belts circulated throughout their territories, many unhappy tribes prepared once again to raise the hatchet against the English. Reports of frontier violence, fraud, and abuses directed toward them found their way to Johnson Hall. Frustrated by what he thought was the misdirection of policymakers in London, Johnson did little to soften the tone of his report on the current state of affairs. In late August 1769, after returning from a council with the Senecas, he informed Hillsborough that the nations "were well assured that a war was near at hand, & they were courted to engage in it." Johnson added that the late "great present" given to the Six Nations may very well have caused jealously among the Ohio and Illinois nations. Rather than anxiously wait for a reaction, he urged that "a proper use may by made" to exploit their "spirit of discontent." News that settlers between Bedford and Fort Pitt were abandoning their homesteads had reached Johnson Hall. It would only be a matter of time before Whitehall received news of blocked trade and murder throughout the Ohio and Illinois.[25]

The threat of rupture lingered during the winter of 1770. By spring, British-sympathizing tribes maneuvered for position. The Cherokees sent twenty war belts to the Iroquois to strengthen their recent alliance. Many warriors of both nations agreed to wage war on the southwestern nations and looked to the Crown for its approval of the plan. Although it may appear irrational to sanction such a war, Johnson wrote Hillsborough, if the nations were not permitted to "cut each others throats" the Crown risked them "discharging their fury [on] our Traders and defenseless frontiers." Nevertheless, Johnson hoped to convince them otherwise. Hillsborough agreed and, while citing the security of the northeastern borderlands as his greatest concern, he requested that Johnson manage the affair without convening a general council in order to avoid unwanted expenses.[26]

Despite concerns regarding cost, by July more than six hundred first peoples had gathered near the upper settlement at German Flatts in anticipation of a congress. It had been a difficult year for them. The winter hunt produced little game; in early spring, caterpillars ravaged corn fields throughout New York and Pennsylvania; and the overall lack of goods at the undermanned Crown trading posts caused a serious need of provisions. They complained of having to travel over one hundred miles to arrive at posts unable to outfit them with blankets and basic articles of survival. In Philadelphia, starving western Senecas met with John Penn and commented about the horrible state of their villages. Moreover, the lack of trade goods and regulation caused grave disparity in prices and resulted in many traders trafficking rum only. Before they departed, Johnson promised to express the Crown's distaste with the cession to the south of the Kanawha River as agreed on during the Fort Stanwix negotiations.[27]

On 15 July 1770, Johnson opened the proceedings with more than 1,600 representatives from the Iroquois, Huron, Ottawa, and Cherokee nations. With the help of the Onondaga chief The Bunt (Chenaugheata), Johnson convinced some disenfranchised warriors to attend the council. It appears that the sachems failed to invite the warriors to the congress. After speaking with the principal warrior, Thomas King, Johnson soon found out why. Determined to strike at the "southern Indians," the warriors threatened to undermine the tentative peace advocated by the chiefs. But instead of disbarring them from the deliberations Johnson chose to attend to their concerns. After some careful maneuvering with the help of an old Mohawk friend, Chief Abraham, the warriors agreed to "stay all hostilities" until they attempted to use the Shawnees as conduits to convince the southerners of their folly.[28]

Johnson then directed discussion toward the southern boundary extension. After informing the Six Nations that the king "did not require the Lands so far to the Southward," he mentioned that the Crown worried that the Six Nations' "Dependents . . . who never had any Title to the soil" were dissatisfied, scoffed at the authority of the Iroquois, and sought to harm the English. That night during private deliberations with Johnson, Iroquois sachems expressed displeasure with his earlier message and stated that it appeared the king "intended to totally neglect, and disregard them." How could the king doubt the claims of the Grand Council, Chief Abraham later remarked during council, given the fact that he accepted the terms in front of thousands at Fort Stanwix? Addressing the Crown, Abraham did not mince his words: "You verry well know, that our Title has allways been Indisputable. . . . it was *our* property we justly disposed of." Little could be agreed on until they were given due recognition. Insulted, Abraham blasted the Crown. Since the Fort Stanwix cession, little had improved in terms of security in the northeastern borderlands. "Our people are frequently Robbed and murdered," Abraham proclaimed, "and no reparation made for all of this." Despite promises made, both trade and the availability of goods had worsened since the agreement. Trading houses were empty, violence had increased, and men of ill repute cheated and stole without consequence. The borderlands reeled from the lack of regulation and authority. Abraham made legitimate points, but he was also undoubtedly well aware of Johnson's approval of his message. As the world around them changed, men like Johnson and Abraham worked in concert to maintain the functionality of what they knew best.[29]

Before the congress ended, Johnson held a copy of the Fort Stanwix treaty in the air, reminded his indigenous brethren of the "the great, and valuable present [they] received upon that occasion," and in the name of his Britannic Majesty ratified and confirmed the "whole of the Treaty made at Fort Stanwix in 1768, and also the Deed of Cession to the King then executed." He had fulfilled his duty as the superintendent of Indian affairs by conveying Crown apprehension of the southern cession. Unable or unwilling to press the matter further, he also employed the same powers vested in his office and ratified the terms of the 1768 treaty—that is, with one exception.[30]

When Johnson publicly confirmed the treaty of Fort Stanwix in the summer of 1769, he did so with one slight variation. To please the Iroquois allies, the Crown agreed to the continuation of the line north from Owego and south below the Kanawha River. Even the cession to Pennsylvania received Crown approval. Croghan and the Suffering Traders were not so lucky. The failure of their grants to gain approval received particular mention in the official treaty minutes.[31]

The initial lack of acknowledgment likely came as no surprise to Johnson, Croghan, or the primary shareholders in the Suffering Traders scheme. Eyebrows rose in London almost immediately after Whitehall received a copy of the Fort Stanwix treaty in late 1768. In fact, Hillsborough was appalled at the play for land. Leading the charge against the traders' claims, Hillsborough urged the king to reject the private arrangements. The "foundation or extent of the claims of these persons have at any time been represented to Your Majesty . . . [the] transaction does so far as it relates to the Indians, stand upon no other ground than that of a proposition . . . [and] ought to be rejected." If confirmed, it would set a precedent in the colonies that would lead to "Frauds and Abuses."[32] Only weeks before Johnson departed to hold a council with Iroquois delegates in July 1769, Hillsborough informed him that the matter remained unsettled until further investigation. In other correspondence, Hillsborough sneered at the traders' claims and predicted that they would not see the light of day given the fact that they ran counter to the protocol established by the Royal Proclamation of 1763.[33]

Despite early signs of disappointment, Croghan remained high-spirited. After the Fort Stanwix treaty he had thousands of reasons to be optimistic. Besides the 250,000 acres he held in clear title in New York, he held 5,000 acres in Pennsylvania and anticipated a share of the hundreds of thousands of acres, if not millions, when the 1768 treaty received complete confirmation. With his name included in the treaty, and on several private agreements, the volatile world of

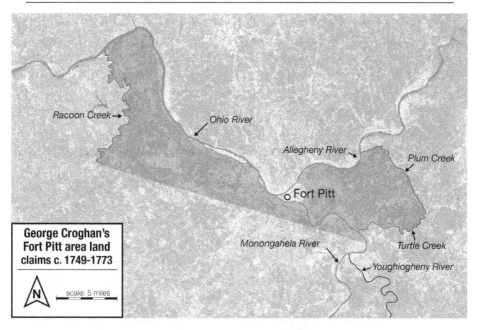

George Croghan's Fort Pitt area land claims, 1749–1773. Courtesy of Stephen Otvos of Lookout Studio, and David Croghan.

western speculation appeared a little less hazardous, and with a glimpse of opportunity Croghan acted quickly.

He began making plans to join the ranks of other great eighteenth-century landowners by arranging the construction of a grand manor at the foot of Lake Otsego in New York, a tract he held in clear title. To improve the land and construct a manor, Croghan needed money. He bonded his ideas for the west and mortgaged what property he could. In exchange for the deeds he held for land southwest of the Otsego tract, Gov. William Franklin secured £3,000 for him from a group of eight investors known as the Burlington Company. The skeptical men refused to deal with Croghan unless Franklin vouched for the loan and acted as a go-between. When the deed did not suffice to cover the costs of the loan, Croghan gave Franklin an additional 51,000 acres from his Otsego tract. Furthermore, on 10 December 1768, for the sum of £900, Croghan agreed to transfer 30 percent of his Suffering Traders' stake to Joseph Galloway and Thomas Wharton.

Croghan guaranteed to repay Galloway and Wharton £450 if the king did not confirm the land cession. Moreover, Croghan consented to give William Trent control over the management of the remaining 70 percent of his share in the Suffering Traders' grant. In turn, for the sum of £4,500 William Trent organized the transfer of 30 percent of the remaining 70 (21 percent of the original whole) to Galloway and Wharton. All together, then, within a month of the treaty Croghan relinquished claim to 51 percent of his shares in the land granted to the Suffering Traders at Fort Stanwix. Two days later, on 12 December 1768, he assumed responsibility for a £500 mortgage Thomas Wharton held on three houses and four acres of land in Philadelphia. The next day he bought fourteen acres of adjacent land and mortgaged both lots along with 40,000 more acres from his Otsego tract to Franklin for an additional £1,200. Croghan also sold and mortgaged some of his New York acreage to merchants Barnard and Michael Gratz for the sum of £1,800 and received additional loans from Goldsborrow Banyar of New York and John Morton and Dr. John Morgan of Philadelphia.[34] To avoid imprisonment, Croghan convinced Dr. Morgan to pay an outstanding bond in return for deeds for 4,000 acres in New York. Croghan told the doctor the land was worth in excess of £4,000, but Morgan was pressed to sell the land three years later for £1,000. A master manipulator and salesman, Croghan managed to secure over £10,000 in hard currency from 1768 to 1770. To pay back the loans, he banked on the stake he still held in the lands west of the Appalachians. The best hope for the opening of these lands was a scheme for the establishment of an inland colony, later called Vandalia.[35]

In January 1769, Samuel Wharton and William Trent departed for London in an attempt to win royal favor for the claimants with interests in the Suffering Traders' claim. By then the venture was known as the Indiana Company. Croghan did not lead the charge as he had in 1763. The situation had become too important for all parties involved in the private schemes conducted at Fort Stanwix to back a freewheeling negotiator like Croghan on a trip to London. The firm Baynton, Wharton and Morgan had been struggling to get out of receivership since 1767. Things got worse in July 1768 when William Murray, a trader with ties to the Philadelphia firm Franks-Gratz, and Lord Dunmore of Virginia arrived in the Illinois Country to compete with

Baynton, Wharton and Morgan for trade. When Lt. Col. John Wilkins decided to break a long-standing agreement with the firm and contract the rationing of his Illinois force to the firm of Franks-Gratz the same year, the situation deteriorated further. By the end of the year, James Rumsey, a slave trader and principal aide to the firm in the region, cut his ties with the men and decided to take a job as William Murray's secretary. In March 1769 the firm received word from John Campbell, an agent at Pittsburgh, that the influx of traders and lack of regulations had almost ruined their hold on trade. Many of the disgruntled employees cited issues with George Morgan, who had been sent to the region to oversee the firm's affairs.[36]

Meanwhile, Croghan's involvement with the firm of Franks-Gratz did little to alleviate tensions. He had borrowed from both Bernard and Michael Gratz and stood heavily indebted to the Burlington Company. Furthermore, when Trent and Wharton prepared to depart for London in early 1769, Croghan could not afford to pay his share for the mission.[37] While bed-ridden with gout, Croghan learned in May from Wharton that Lord Hillsborough did not intend to authenticate the private transactions Johnson had allowed at the Stanwix treaty.[38] On the brink of complete financial ruin, again, Croghan responded by traveling to Johnson Hall. He called on old tactics and suggested to Johnson that they announce the immanency of another war if the treaty of cession, in its entirety, was not approved by the government in London. Johnson, possibly sickened by Croghan's deviousness, refused. Writing to Wharton, Croghan's tone reflected his disappointment. Stooping to a new low, the agent scorned Johnson, likening his superior to Dr. Slop in *Tristram Shandy*.[39]

In an attempt to gain a financial footing, in November 1769 Croghan offered both Trent and Wharton first right of refusal and the "opportunity" for full control of his mortgaged New York lands if the men agreed to pay his outstanding debts to the Burlington Company. They turned down the offer, and Croghan's remaining patented tracts dwindled. In February 1770 he mortgaged his McKee patent and eventually surrendered to William Peters because he had been ordered by a court decree to pay a £5,739 outstanding debt. The same fate soon awaited his other clear title holdings. By the end of the year he had sold more than 150,000 acres in New York to cover legal fees.

Still heavily indebted, Croghan sought to postpone foreclosure on his remaining lands in New York by buying time with creditors with promises of fortune after the Crown sanctioned the establishment of an inland colony. No amount of bravado could now disguise his plight; he found it difficult to keep his head up. "Croghan is in town sure enough poor man," wrote John Wetherhead to William Johnson in February. "He . . . does nothing but pray and talk about the sufferings of the inner man."[40] In letters, however, Croghan downplayed his financial woes.[41] By the summer of 1770 he found himself captive at his estate near Fort Pitt. News of recent judgments against him reached the western post in October 1770. He was being systematically stripped of his possessions. Imprisonment likely awaited in Philadelphia, Lancaster, Carlisle, and Bedford. Croghan had no choice but to dig in and make himself comfortable on the edges of empire.[42]

Trusting Croghan proved difficult for Baynton, Wharton and Morgan at the best of times when they acted as his primary investors. Now that Croghan's allegiance to the firm's interest rested solely with the success of the Indiana grant, there was little room for error, and less for his antics.[43] Aware that Hillsborough had already taken critical aim at the newly formed Indiana Company, both Wharton and Trent moved with caution while in London. The Privy Council had overturned Hillsborough's decision to reject the boundary extension to the south of the Kanawha River, and there was hope that it might reconsider the claims of the Suffering Traders. To gain support for the venture, Wharton and Trent needed to bring a few men of persuasion into the fold. When Benjamin Franklin, who had been in residence in London since 1764, proved to be of little service, Samuel Wharton courted the interests of Thomas Pownall and also the London banker and member of parliament Thomas Walpole. When Walpole informed Wharton that he had strong reason to believe the Privy Council had tired of Hillsborough's policy toward the treaty at Fort Stanwix and would seek to confirm the entire agreement, Wharton and Trent rejoiced.[44]

But Walpole's interest in the affair came at a price. By the end of July 1769, the Indiana Company had been absorbed into a new cartel—sometimes called the Walpole Company or Associates—made up of men of stature in London.[45] In a larger bid for land, Walpole and his associates proposed to absorb the 2.4 million acres of the Indiana grant for an estimated £10,460, the approximate amount of currency used to finalize the Fort Stanwix treaty. The petition that called for the establishment of an inland colony in the recently ceded region south of the Ohio River stretching from Pittsburgh to the Scioto River and from the rivers' confluence south to the Cumberland Gap. The colony was to function under a proprietary system. Furthermore, Walpole and his associates would assume all expenses needed to establish civil authority until the colony could sustain itself. The proposal reached the Board of Trade on 20 December 1769, and much to the surprise of the claimants Lord Hillsborough appeared supportive of the plan. In fact, Hillsborough encouraged the group to petition the Crown for more land.[46]

In response, the Walpole group met at the Crown and Anchor tavern on 27 December and formed the Grand Ohio Company. Instead of severing their land claim at the Scioto River, the claimants revised the initial proposal to include all the land south of the Ohio River to its point of confluence with the Kentucky River, from there up the river toward the Cumberland Gap, hugging the western limits of Cumberland Mountains, thence northeast along the Greenbrier River back toward Pittsburgh. In total the tract amounted to a whopping 20 million acres of land and overlapped thousands of acres of land claimed by both Pennsylvania and Virginia. Despite the apparent grandiose nature of the petition, which Hillsborough later acknowledged he supported only because he thought it would serve to defeat the plan, on 4 January 1770 the Lords of Treasury agreed to the terms. For those with a stake in the Grand Ohio Company, the future looked promising.[47]

Almost immediately after the Lords of Treasury gave their approval to the Grand Ohio Company scheme, Virginia agents stationed in London lodged complaints. Arthur Lee, working on behalf of the Mississippi Company, submitted a petition on behalf of the Lees, George Washington, and others that challenged the Grand Ohio Company's claims to millions of acres lying "between the Alleghenies and the Ohio and between the thirty-eight and forty-second parallels." The Virginians long-standing claim to lands west of the mountains granted to Washington's soldiers by Governor Dinwiddie in 1754 also conflicted with the ruling. Nevertheless, the Grand Ohio Company managed to buy off George Mercer, the Ohio Company of Virginia's primary agent in London and the party ostensibly protecting the interests of the 1754 grantees. According to the agreement, the Ohio Company of Virginia was absorbed by the Grand Ohio Company for the price of two shares in the Vandalia venture, one of which went to Mercer directly. In addition, the company pledged to set aside 200,000 acres for Washington for the land Governor Dinwiddie guaranteed his regiment in 1754. The government of Virginia later rejected the deal, but no action was taken and the Ohio Company of Virginia and George Mercer remained shareholders in the scheme until the bitter end. By 8 May 1770, the Board of Trade had heard the second petition, and it "looked as though, with powerful politicians on its side, the Walpole Company would have clear sailing."[48]

The Grand Ohio Company's quest for an inland colony stands as one of the "most ambitious expansionist" activities in colonial North America. As Dorothy Jones indicates, the project reveals the extent of "what could be done by private initiative in dealing with the Indians."[49] The Vandalia project had its origins with Iroquois territorial claims and Croghan's earlier expeditions to the Illinois Country. In effect, the land bid for an inland colony in the Ohio was a direct extension of treaty protocol based on the cultivated partnership between the Grand Council and Crown Indian agents like Johnson and Croghan. Even with powerful backers, however, the speculative venture would meet a fatal end within a decade.

By late 1769, indigenous unrest persisted near Fort Pitt. The Fort Stanwix treaty had not done much to quash the Ohio nations' frustration with settlement. In fact, it did much to heighten anxiety in the area. For months, reports of animosity over the cession and poor trade had been filtering back to Albany and Philadelphia. Despite attempts by some Delawares led by Newcomer to calm the situation, large numbers of Wyandots, Delawares, and Shawnees pressed to raise the hatchet against the English once again. Residual debate caused the Ohio Iroquois residing at the Two Creeks to splinter. Many regional tribes resorted to plundering in an attempt to survive. Borderland settlers once again began to flee east, and even the respected middleman Andrew Montour prepared to pack up and head toward Albany to wait out the projected storm. Calls for Crown intervention became louder as fears of another conflict increased.[50]

Making matters worse, the Ohio nations had not received an ounce of the Crown gifts awarded to the Six Nations in compensation for the land ceded at Fort Stanwix. While in Philadelphia, Croghan wrote to General Gage to inform him of the situation: "A Party of the Ohio, Seneca, Shawanese and Delawares have been this fall at Detroit, and had a private Council in the Huron Village with the Hurons, Chipawas, Ottawas and Putiwatimies" and expressed great dissatisfaction with their "Fathers" to the east whom they considered the "Slaves of the White People." The disgruntled Ohioans denounced the Fort Stanwix treaty and pledged to align themselves with the Cherokees. Lead and powder stocks were already depleted, and Croghan warned of a rupture in the spring.[51]

In response, Johnson ordered his deputy back to the Ohio to attend to the problems near Fort Pitt. But Croghan excused himself from the call, citing illness. He was, however, well enough to travel to Philadelphia to answer creditors and to spend time at his estate in New York.[52] After settling what he could in Philadelphia, he departed for Lake Otsego. Travelers frequented Croghan's New York estate and gladly partook in his propensity to indulge. One visitor provided a rare glimpse of Croghan holding court: "Last Night a drunken Indian came and kissed Col. Croghan and me very joyously; here are natives of different nations almost continually; they visit the Deputy superintendent as Dogs to the Bone for what they can get."[53] Despite the delight he took in acting as the generous host and man of influence, Croghan was broke, indebted, and needed to work. By the summer of 1770 he found himself back at Fort Pitt attending to the increasing hostilities in the region.

According to Jon Parmenter, the Shawnee leader Red Hawk likened the Grand Council to an elder brother "who often offered good advice, but who exercised no power over" their affairs. By the time Croghan returned to the forks of the Ohio River in 1770, the Miamis, Piankashaws, Weas, and Misquetons residing on the Wabash and Miami rivers and the Creeks, Chickasaws, and Choctaws to the south had all been asked to form a lose confederacy by emissaries from the

Shawnees, Delawares, and Ohio Iroquois.[54] When word of the insubordination reached Iroquoia, the Grand Council responded by holding a meeting at German Flatts in July 1770, where they reiterated the terms of the treaty of Fort Stanwix and chastised their misguided "young Brothers."[55] But by the summer of 1770, Iroquois rhetoric carried little weight in the Ohio Country. In fact, by the end of the summer rumor had it that the aggrieved nations had organized a congress of their own on the banks of the Scioto River to discuss strategies to resist both the British and the Grand Council. No record of the congress has survived, but the fact that they assembled without the consent of the Six Nations was whispered throughout the northeastern borderlands.[56] "Although no grand Indian confederacy emerged," the Ohio nations nevertheless made the "Treaty of Fort Stanwix a dead letter for more than a decade."[57] Nevertheless, within only a few years of the first Scioto congress, the Ohio nations would be tested by a Virginia militia determined to seize their lands.

The unfolding British imperial policy, a poor harvest, and increased settlements west of the Appalachians also impeded the efforts of the participants of the Grand Council as they attempted to project their authority west. William Johnson reported to Hillsborough that the lack of trade regulation catered to rum peddlers who targeted assemblies. They ruined Crown initiative throughout the northeastern borderlands by getting the tribesmen drunk and trading liquor for all the goods bestowed on them by the king. "There was no longer any check on rapacious traders," and it soon became evident "that with the possession of the vast territory west of the mountains, imperial control of the Indian trade based on an act of Parliament was the only solution." Hillsborough responded by urging the governors of the American colonies to reign in those willing to disregard Crown interests and take appropriate action to regulate trade. But the provincial governments were no more able than the Iroquois to control the affairs along the Ohio River and throughout the Illinois Country.[58]

During the winter of 1771, Johnson pleaded with Hillsborough to take action. He warned that the Ohio nations were designing to unite in order to "check our advances into their Country." Rumors of an impending war had whipped the Ohio nations into a frenzy, but Johnson insisted that "if impowered to do so" he could save the colonies and the Crown from another devastating borderland conflict. By

May tensions continued, but apart from a small number of murders throughout the northeastern borderlands a full-scale war had yet to erupt. The British luckily maintained one important ally. Through a series of communications, the Delaware band led by Newcomer made it clear that they wished to avoid participating in the scheming against the English and sent messages and emissaries to Philadelphia to reiterate such sentiment. With a tentative foothold on the Ohio, Hillsborough encouraged Johnson to exploit jealousies among the nations.[59]

On 16 July 1771, Johnson hosted Six Nations representatives at Johnson Hall to discuss the deteriorating relations. He worried about recent intelligence that suggested the Senecas and Ohio Iroquois were both engaged in inciting war against the British. When Johnson detected signs of secrecy among some of those assembled, he confronted them with the allegations. In response, the speaker Tyorhansera insisted that if "any our People harbored any evil thoughts they were not propagated on this side of the Upper Seneca Villages." The remark was a criticism of the deceased Seneca chief Gaustarax. Tyorhansera continued, making the message from the Grand Council quite clear: "Sayenquarraghta has last night examined those of the farthest Castle, who are here, who have declared that any evil yet remaining proceeds from Gaustarax the Chief of the Chenussio, who is now under the ground, and was always a busy man, that privately and wickedly concerned himself in mischief in the name but without the Privity of the Six Nations." The Iroquois speaker blamed Gaustarax with conspiring to prepare the Ohio nations for war after returning from the treaty at Fort Stanwix. Rumors had it that in late 1768 the Seneca chief encouraged his young warriors to "apply themselves to hunting for three years, [and] to purchase the necessarys for war." In fact, Tyorhansera confessed that the Grand Council could no longer trust the western Senecas because of all the mischief they had caused during the last war. He also threatened to "remove the door of the six Nations which was formerly at his village at Chenussio." Maintaining an image of a unified Iroquois Confederacy had become increasingly difficult for the Grand Council.[60]

Reports of discontent continued throughout the winter and well into the summer of 1772.[61] Johnson defended the integrity of the Confederacy despite reports suggesting that the primary instigators of the continued unrest could be found in Seneca villages. Writing to

Hillsborough, Johnson cited the involvement of Chief Gaustarax and his few followers as an aberration from an otherwise loyal union of Iroquois. As was the case almost a decade before, however, the Shawnees could not be so readily excused and their loyalty could not be easily claimed. Johnson noted that Shawnee disappointment with the Fort Stanwix cession, in particular the lands north of the Kanawha River, had resulted in their continued efforts to undermine British interests west of the Appalachians. He again urged Hillsborough to empower him to address the situation properly: "I never coveted neither shall I ever wish for Authority, but, where the public requires it, to reach abuses that may not otherwise be easily removed. The attention wh[ich] the present duties of my Office require would rather incline me to wish that these important points could be effected in any other Channel, of which I express my doubts with real concern." Johnson knew that such misinformation often caused problems between Europeans and the nations on the fringes of empire. In April an illegal trader among the Chippewas and Mississaugas on Lake Erie murdered and scalped three men, one woman, and an infant. While being reprimanded at Fort Niagara for his actions, the trader stated that he brought the scalps to the fort for compensation because "he was told that War had been actually commenced between the English and Indians."[62] Aggravated by the continued troubles, Hillsborough lashed out at the colonial disorder he had helped create:

> Every day discovers more and more the fatal Policy of departing from the line prescribed by the proclamation of 1763, and the extension of it, on the ground of a cession made by the Six Nations of lands, their right to which is denied by other Nations, equally powerfull and more numerous, instead of being attended with advantage to this kingdom, & Security to the Colonies, is now likely to have no other consequence than that of giving a greater scope to distant settlements, which I conceive to be inconsistent with every true principle of policy & which I clearly see, from Your last letter, will most probably have the effect to produce a general Indian War, the expense whereof will fall on this Kingdom.[63]

Hillsborough blamed Johnson for the situation in the Ohio Country. Despite Johnson's efforts to achieve a diplomatic triumph at Fort

Stanwix in 1768, it was evident that the superintendent and his close advisors had made a serious error. As Johnson scurried for resources, the Ohio nations prepared once again to raise the hatchet against the English.

Despite Johnson's pleas, however, cutbacks continued. In the autumn of 1772, Fort Pitt was reduced to a mere skeleton of its previous glory and expenditures for the Indian Department in the northern district were capped at £5,000 annually, a fraction of what was typically spent in a year.[64] Meanwhile, European settlers streamed across the Appalachians in search of cheap land and a better life. From 1770 to 1773, Croghan could only observe as the Pennsylvania proprietors sold land around Fort Pitt to newcomers. Four months after the Penns opened their provincial grant to settlement on 3 April 1769, over one million acres had been sold. In Virginia, by the early 1770s over 6 million acres had been granted or petitioned for in the heartland of what both the House of Burgesses and the Grand Ohio Company considered theirs. Even Colonel Bradstreet, who had negotiated peace with the Ohio nations in 1764, scurried for a piece of the pie. Some was Croghan's land, bought from tribes but lacking Crown confirmation. In response, Croghan warned the settlers not to pay tax to the province of Pennsylvania. The land he claimed did not come within the province's boundaries and, he warned, could soon be a part of a new colony called Vandalia. Whether he believed this or hoped to deflect people away from territory where he still hoped to secure patents or both, we will never know. What we do know is that Croghan's actions were part of another scheme in the making. Not long thereafter, Croghan dismissed himself from service once again as deputy Indian agent and sold interests in 100,000 acres to the influx of settlers in the region based on the claims he held in the nonexistent Indiana Company. Not only did his claim to the area amount to a mere 23,800 acres, but the land had not been patented. It was a part of the greater Vandalia project.[65]

To avoid his creditors, Croghan decided to give Barnard Gratz full power of attorney over his patented holdings. Gratz, a fresh investor enthralled by Croghan's vision of the west and ignorant of the complicated ties he held with the Walpole group, met with Croghan's creditors. Gratz managed to stave off foreclosure on his New York lands until September 1773 based on the agreement that he would privately sell Croghan's holdings. Gratz advertised the sale of Croghan's land and met with prospective buyers from Albany to Johnstown throughout 1773. Few investors met the minimum asking prices, however, and by the summer Croghan again found himself in a desperate situation. When news arrived that Lord Hillsborough's initial decision to block the establishment of an inland colony had again been overturned and the Earl of Dartmouth had been appointed the new secretary of state for the colonies, Croghan's spirits soared. He ordered Gratz to delay the sale of any of his holdings for as long as possible. Once Wharton sailed from London, Croghan assured Gratz, "I am Certain in a mounth after his ariveal I shall be able to pay peters of, the Mordiges Likewise, and protected bills as he and Trent is fully prepaird to Do itt, this with what I can sell hear, on the Governts being Establishd will before Crismas Make me a freeman." Enamored by the possibility of fortune, Croghan once again begged for time.[66]

While Croghan sought time, settlers poured not only across the mountains into the newly ceded territory west of the Appalachians but also northwest from Albany onto the protected lands of the Mohawks. On 28 July 1772, William Johnson and the recently appointed governor of New York, William Tryon, met with disgruntled Mohawks from Canajoharie. Once again, land fraud related to the Kayaderosseras tract and trader abuses topped the list. A young Six Nations speaker indicated that their sachems had repeatedly appealed to the governor of New York, as instructed, but when their pleas fell on deaf ears they consented to hand the matter over to their young warriors. The Mohawk warrior Joseph reminded Governor Tryon that since the time of his forefathers his nation had served and fought to protect British interest in North America. He wondered why the Crown continued to ignore their complaints even after the Iroquois arranged to satisfy the European's thirst for land in 1768. Another Mohawk, Chief Hendrick, likewise expressed dissatisfaction and demanded that the province afford his people relief by surveying their lands so they "may know the exact quantity of [their] possessions." The following day, Governor Tryon could do little more than reassure the Mohawks that he would investigate their claims and cautioned them against disposing of their lands without properly recording the transactions. But, unless overturned or revised, both Johnson and the Mohawks knew that Hillsborough's policy would continue to hamper the efforts of the Indian Department and the threaten eastern Iroquois land security as stated in the terms of the 1768 treaty of Fort Stanwix.[67]

Starting in late 1772, William Johnson did his best to court the interests of the second secretary of state of the colonies, William Legge, Earl of Dartmouth. Dartmouth's appointment followed Lord Hillsborough's departure and briefly presented many enthusiasts concerned with North American affairs a new opportunity. In November, Johnson informed Dartmouth of the recent murders near Lake Erie and expressed concern over the lack of Crown control in the region. The Grand Council worked to stop Seneca factions from partaking in the troublesome politics of the Ohio Country. However, unless the Crown took decisive action the problem would persist. Johnson reiterated an old message. Trade must be regulated and speculation checked. He suggested to Dartmouth that the creation of an inland colony would help bring about order in the region and assured the secretary of state that the Iroquois agreed. As for the Ohio groups who quarreled and moaned about the 1768 cession, they "have not pretension or Title there," Johnson insisted, and should not be considered beyond the fact they were nuisances to British western policy. Again Johnson pressed for a course of empire that would benefit himself and his Iroquois allies. He also confessed that he agreed to the extension of the southern boundary during the Fort Stanwix negotiations to give the indigenous inhabitants of the region some breathing room from aggressive Virginian settlers. With the help of George Croghan, Johnson assured the new secretary, they could keep the Ohio nations in check, but it was essential for Whitehall to uphold the authority of the Iroquois Confederacy and approve the plans to form a new inland colony.[68]

The day after Christmas, 1772, Johnson again sent Dartmouth word of problems in the northeastern borderlands, or at least his biased assessment of the diplomatic and strategic situation. This time Johnson spelled out to the secretary of state the ramifications if the Confederacy did not receive Crown support. He explained that, if the colonies granted the Shawnees and Delawares a forum to complain about the abuses they had suffered at the hands of the Grand Council, the Ohio nations would be viewed as independent of the Iroquois Confederacy. As a result, the confederacies to the south and north would look upon the Grand Council as being weak and use the opportunity to strike both the Iroquois and the English. "The Plan for forming a secret alliance is pretty general amongst them, but this scheme for drawing in the Government as an Instrument . . . has been only as yet agitated by a few who of themselves are very inconsiderable." Until Dartmouth sent word, Johnson pledged to do what he could to subdue borderland animosity.[69]

Dartmouth did send word. In early February 1773 he noted that it seemed strange that Johnson sought to establish an inland colony given the fact the Ohio nations disagreed with such action and Seneca factions appeared to have already eroded the integrity of the Iroquois Confederacy. In fact, Dartmouth remarked that difficulties would inevitably "occur in carrying the intended Plan of Settlement into execution unless the other Tribes who reside within the Limits of the purposed Colony [could] be brought into the same measure which I fear will be impracticable." Notwithstanding Johnson's efforts to convince him otherwise, Dartmouth's apprehensions concerning the inland colony continued well into the spring of 1773. Johnson still did his best to help the Grand Council reign in the disobedient Senecas. He held council with the Six Nations to address the problem. After being assured by the Chenussio chief Seriohana that the western Senecas had come to their senses, Johnson informed Dartmouth that the Grand Council had "brought the Senecas to a sense of their misconduct."[70]

As Johnson tried to steer Dartmouth toward an understanding of the situation more in tune with his own, speculators on both sides of the Atlantic tried to push through the Vandalia project. Even Governor Tryon confessed to Dartmouth that, given the dubious nature of purchasing indigenous land and ignoring the fact that a few speculators often gained considerable fortunes from such grants, these ventures did not necessarily conflict with Crown policy. In fact, Tryon added, "for my own part, I should think it good policy rather to encourage than to check such spirit. . . . [It is] friendly to Govern[ment], and conducive to the strengthening the hands of the Crown, and perhaps it will prove the only counterpoize against levelling [the] Republican spirit."[71]

By late summer of 1773, with recent events of the northeastern borderlands in mind, Dartmouth perhaps gave Tryon's unsolicited advice more thought. Reports from America confirmed that some three hundred Virginian settlers led by Capt. Thomas Bullet had made their way up the Ohio River to the Scioto and surveyed the area. Alarmed, some Shawnees traveled northeast toward Fort Pitt to muster resistance. Rumor had it that Custaloga, the great Delaware chief, had retired below the falls of the Ohio River with a hundred warriors and talked about joining the western confederacies in an effort to strike at the English. By late summer Johnson's efforts appeared to be paying off. Convinced that aggressive Virginia settlers could spark a war, Dartmouth agreed to back the Vandalia project. By the time the winter snows started to gather in 1773, the colonies knew that the Vandalia scheme had received approval by the Lords of Trade and Plantations and the Privy Council.[72] The final step was the official charter. Things, again, looked hopeful.

An elated Croghan met Wharton and Trent when they returned from London and began to plan his financial revival. Although he remained considerably indebted, his services were once again required; for his assistance, he received additional shares in the Vandalia scheme. To earn his participation in the syndicate, Croghan reinstated himself as an Indian agent and planned to hold a private council at Fort Pitt to prepare the Western Confederacy and the Ohio nations for the establishment of Vandalia. He was making a conscious break from treaty protocol, thus undermining the authority of the Grand Council. As a result, the men agreed that the upcoming council should remain a private matter. Neither William Johnson nor Thomas Gage were informed of the plans. In anticipation of the meeting, Wharton reluctantly sent Croghan £160 to buy presents and provisions to placate the regional chiefs prior to the official congress. By late summer the tactics of a desperate Croghan appeared to be working. He informed Wharton that many chiefs had "returned to their Habitations with much good Will toward the Province." Croghan even managed to gain support for the new province from the Seneca chief Kayasutha. But news that the wily Indian agent was handing out gifts and preparing to hold a council spread fast, and by the autumn of 1773 hundreds tribal representatives had gathered at Croghan Hall near Fort Pitt. But, much to Croghan's chagrin, the Vandalia charter still had not been approved, and recent news indicated further problems. Left with inadequate resources and insufficient authority to conclude the council, Croghan wrote Wharton desperately asking for goods and money to sustain the visitors. When Wharton declined and the visitors departed without an agreement, Croghan once again faced ruin.[73]

Speculation remains as to why exactly the Vandalia charter did not receive swift approval in London. It appears most likely that mounting complaints from influential colonials against the prime movers of the scheme and their associates halted the process. Speculators from Virginia, New York, and Connecticut let it be known that their land claims and ambitions conflicted with those of the Walpole Company. Moreover, as Thomas Perkins Abernethy points out, after Benjamin Franklin admitted to drafting the famous Hutchinson letters, "how could the Ministry, without appearing to water the seeds of treason itself, grant a great proprietary government in the heart of its already reckless American dominion to this arch enemy, his son and associates?" Despite the fact that the Board of Trade called for a draft of the Vandalia charter on 28 October 1773 after approving the plans for an inland colony drawn up by Solicitor-General Alexander Wedderburn and Attorney-General Edward Thurlow, nothing more happened.[74]

Ambitious Virginian interest in the land around the forks of the Ohio River had a long history. Ever since Governor Dinwiddie had promised Col. George Washington and his soldiers land in the region in 1754 for services rendered during the defense of Ohio River valley in the Great Meadows campaign, the colony's claims to vast tracts of land west of the Appalachians were made well known. Not until the treaty of Fort Stanwix readjusted the 1763 boundary did Virginia claimants have a live prospect of applying their grants to a tract of land cleared of tribal interests. By late 1773 reports that Virginia settlers had pressed deep into the Ohio River valley had made their way east to the colonial capitals and to Johnson and Croghan. Like many eighteenth century borderland settlers, the Long Knives pushed west in search of land, paying little regard to ideas of Crown authority or the original residents of the region. By the end October 1773, stories of conflict and murder on the frontiers of Kentucky sparked the first tales about Daniel Boone, a man who inspired an American legend. As Colin Calloway notes,

> Kentucky became a battleground where two worlds and worldviews collided. Backcountry settlers hunted, supplementing their crops and livestock, and they adopted Indian hunting techniques, but they did not behave like Indian hunters or adopt the morality of Indian hunting values. They felt no kinship with animals; they ignored rituals that Indians believed were necessary to harvest plant and animal life and keep the world in balance, and they slaughtered game wastefully. The Indians fought to preserve their hunting territories; invading settlers fought to transform them into fields and pastures. They felled trees with fire and axes, fenced and plowed fields, brought in pigs and cattle, and tried to hold the land they seized as private property. They changed the landscape and many of its meanings. Colonists called the Indians savages; Shawnees called the invaders who disrupted the balance of their world "crazy people [who] want to shove us off our land entirely." . . . And the crazy people kept coming.[75]

Some of the first such conflicts materialized in what historians call Lord Dunmore's War.[76]

Similar borderland clashes between Ohio tribes and Virginia settlers occurred throughout early 1774 along the Little Kanawha and Scioto rivers. On 26 April after correspondence between the commander at Fort Pitt, Dr. John Connolly, and borderland trader and speculator Michael Cresap, an angry group of militiamen at Wheeling, West Virginia, declared war on the Ohio nations. Four days later, a group of them brutally murdered the relatives of the Ohio Iroquois chief Logan on the west bank of the Ohio River at Yellow Stone Creek. Alexander McKee recorded that the group killed a mother by shooting her in the forehead, and then before the Virginians "dashed [her infant's] brains out" they were stuck with remorse and collected her child. When news that Virginians had killed the family of Chief Logan, a promoter of peace throughout the region, scores of settlers fled east. On 5 May 1774, a Shawnee spokesman responded to pleas for a peaceful resolution: "It is you who are frequently passing up and down the Ohio, and making settlements upon it. . . . You tell us not to take notice of what your people have done to us. We desire you likewise not to take any notice of what our young men may now be doing." Further intelligence revealed that the Ohio nations were preparing to rid their lands of all English intruders.[77]

Within days, accounts of the flare-up reached Virginia governor Dunmore, who responded by organizing two militia forces with funds from the provincial government. Col. Andrew Lewis was assigned to lead one force from Camp Union, and Dunmore planned to march the other from Fort Pitt. Dunmore was well aware of the implications of staging a Virginian-led assault from the forks of the Ohio River. The region had long been considered by the Penns as the backyard of their proprietary province. Dunmore, however, had been invited onto the coveted land.[78]

During the summer of 1773, months after Pennsylvania established Westmoreland County and the regional seat of justice just thirty miles east of Fort Pitt, Lord Dunmore arrived at the recently reduced garrison at the forks of the Ohio River. He soon found common interest with Croghan and other men at the fort. For over three years Croghan had watched while settlers traversed the Appalachians and settled on lands near the fort that he considered his own. Croghan had few strategic ties to Pennsylvania and began to look elsewhere to capitalize on what he could. When Virginia created the district of West Augusta in response to Pennsylvania's Westmoreland County on 11 October 1773, Croghan subtlety aided the Virginia effort. Along with his cousin Thomas Smallman and half-brother Edward Ward, Croghan also agreed to serve as a justice of the peace for the Virginians. In return for his allegiance, Lord Dunmore privately pledged to uphold Croghan's Indian deeds in the region. But when Dunmore returned to Fort Pitt in January 1774 to raise a militia and hold court, the seasoned opportunist did not openly support the governor's bid to control of the region. When skirmishes between Pennsylvania and Virginia supporters ensued, Croghan remained on the sidelines—waiting for the right opportunity before placing his bets. Despite Croghan's apparent apprehension, by spring of 1774 few in Philadelphia doubted that he now worked for Dunmore and the Virginians. In fact, Alan Taylor is correct when he states that Croghan "provoked a frontier rebellion" in order to gain title to some 200,000 acres of land.[79]

Meanwhile, an ailing Johnson wrestled to bring order to a deteriorating situation. During a council at Johnson Hall in April, Seneca chief Sayenquaraghta agreed to "deviate from [the Seneca's] ancient customs" and hand over those accused of murdering a French trader. Moreover, Sayenquaraghta placed blame for his nation's recent misgivings with the Confederacy to messages circulated by the Shawnees. Only days after the council concluded, Johnson informed Dartmouth of the Senecas' compliance with English law but admitted that he held little hope that "that settlements can be restrained by any ordinary measures, where the multitude have for so many years discovered such an ungovernable passion for these lands, and pay so little regard to a fair title, or the Authority of the American Governments." By June, Johnson had no qualms about including the Virginians in his criticisms.[80]

On 6 July 1774, Dartmouth confirmed to Johnson that Virginians had marched on the Ohio and planned to settle "on a tract of land 30 leagues up the river." The secretary of state of the colonies confessed that he was privy to the plan because Dunmore himself had written him on that head. While news of the incident traveled from London, Guy Johnson sat in his father-in-law's house and wrote to Dartmouth. On the 11 July 1774, after persuading the assembled Iroquois to show patience toward the Crown and colonies with regard to regulating trade and speculation throughout the northeastern borderlands, Sir William Johnson outfitted his indigenous allies with smoking pipes, plenty of tobacco, and enough liquor to properly consider "the principal object of Congress." They were Johnson's last recorded words and acts as superintendent of Indian affairs for the northern colonies. That night, after retiring to his quarters exhausted and in pain, Guy wrote Dartmouth, his predecessor and mentor "was seized with a suffocation of which he expired in less than two hours." Johnson was dead.[81] Two days later, both Iroquois and Europeans carried his body from Johnson Hall to Johnstown, New York. Before a crowd of more than two thousand bereaved witnesses, Johnson's remains were put to rest in a family vault at the church he erected. The following day, Oneida chief Conoghquieson initiated the ceremony of condolence by uttering the three bare words, metaphorically covering the grave and body of the deceased with wampum.[82] News of the immense loss reverberated throughout the northeastern borderlands.

William Johnson's last acts as the superintendent of Indian affairs of the northern colonies illuminate his determination to uphold the protocols of cross-cultural diplomacy in a British North American empire. His primary interests rested with protecting his office, maintaining the Iroquois Confederacy, and flying the colors of his king on American soil. They were not just of equal importance, they were merged. From the mid-1760s until his death, however, Johnson's ability to adhere to Crown directives had become increasingly problematic. Cutbacks, an unautocratic policy, and a dysfunctional Confederacy meant that efforts to project authority and retain control over troublesome peoples in coveted regions often fell short. From 1763 to 1768, Johnson struggled to redress the wrongs of ineffective policy. He pressured Whitehall to readjust the boundary of 1763 and to adopt the Plan of 1764. As a result, when more than two thousand tribal representatives and colonial statesmen gathered at the Oneida Carry in the fall of 1768, astute diplomacy accompanied the greatest land cession in colonial America. Nevertheless, by the time of his death Johnson no doubt realized that the future of borderland affairs would soon look radically different.

Despite subsequent attempts to calm tensions in the Ohio Country throughout August and September, unchecked expansion by Virginians and the death of Johnson undermined the tribes' confidence and all but shattered any prospect of a peaceful resolution. On 15 September 1774 an Onondaga speaker relayed the following message from the Shawnees to Guy Johnson and the Six Nations: "Brothers, You are very much for making peace, and have sent your Messangers thro' all the nations for that purpose, and you have also taken the Ax from us, and buried it.—When you took this Ax, you desired us to promote peace with all about us; but whilst we are doing this, an Ax was struck into your Heads, and ours by the Virginians." The Onondaga speaker concluded by stating that the Shawnees now wished the Crown to place the ax back in their hands so they could properly defend themselves. By October 1774 few doubted the imminence of another war.[83]

The confrontation between Ohio nations and the Virginians exploded on 10 October 1774 when Shawnee and Ohio Iroquois forces led by Chief Cornstalk intercepted and attacked the 1,100-stong militia of Col. Andrew Lewis at the confluence of the Kanawha and Ohio rivers. The ensuing battle of Point Pleasant marked the only major conflict of Lord Dunmore's War. When night fell after hours of fighting, Cornstalk's force retreated over the river. The Virginians declared victory. By the end of October 1774, the Shawnees had been reduced "to reason," according to Dunmore, and forced to recognize the land cession of 1768 at the Treaty of Camp Charlotte.[84]

Notwithstanding the fact that historians have named the 1774 conflict "Lord Dunmore's War," Dorothy Jones is correct to point out that "it might better be called the War of the Stanwix Cession."[85] The 1768 agreement between the Grand Council and the Crown represented an essential step in Johnson's vision of maintaining an orderly empire, greater protection for Iroquois homelands in New York, and a key element in the plan for Croghan and his associates to cash out after years of speculation. But, in the end, the cession did little more than lay the seeds of future conflict by opening a vast territory to settlement during an era of unprecedented Crown cutbacks. Not unlike previous negotiations between Johnson and the Six Nations, the implementation of the agreement would depend less on regional realities and more on the ability of the Crown and the Grand Council to work in accord and project an image of hegemonic alliance. Without the weight of Crown resources after 1768, the office of the superintendent and the Grand Council simply could not function as primary agents in Ohio Country affairs. As a result, both colonials and indigenous peoples struggled to exert control and what they each considered their rightful claims over the region. When the Shawnees temporarily bowed to Virginian aggression in October 1774 and signed the Camp Charlotte treaty, the occasion marked the end of the Crown's ability to control western expansion. Moreover, by treating with the Shawnees directly, a colony rejected protocol by dismissing the authority of the Grand Council. It was a sign of unfortunate events ahead for the Iroquois.

EPILOGUE

Revolution and Redefinition

Whether working from the colonial capitals, the council fires of the Six Nations, or the frontiers of empire, by the mid-1760s those familiar with the colonial system sought to take advantage of personal politics and limited disorder. Chief among the forces guiding events and diplomacy on the North American continent was the Grand Council of the Iroquois Confederacy. As an increasingly impotent colonial system failed to stop squatters traversing the Appalachians and settling on Mohawk River valley lands despite the Royal Proclamation of 1763, the Iroquois maneuvered to resolve the problem. From 1763 to 1768, the Grand Council worked closely with the superintendent of Indian affairs, William Johnson, to devise a new boundary for their territory. By opening the Ohio River valley, thus steering settlers southwest, the Six Nations intended to protect their homelands and guarantee the continuation of their unique diplomatic status within the British empire. Therefore, when the Fort Stanwix proceedings ended in early November 1768, the Iroquois also watched closely as the terms of that treaty translated into policy. An Oneida speaker reminded Guy Johnson of the Crown's promise only a day after William Johnson's death: "With this Belt," Conoghquieson proclaimed, "we cause the Fire to burn clear as usual at this Place, and at Onondaga which are our proper Fire Places, & we hope the great King will approve and confirm it." Like William Johnson, however, the kismet of the Six Nations depended on a strong Crown commitment; and by the mid-1770s, having lost most of their diplomatic weight, the Iroquois watched as Virginians trampled across the Ohio Country and held council with the nations of that region.[1]

Lord Dunmore's War, Wilbur E. Washburn argues, "marked the beginning of the breakdown of the arrangements by which the seaboard colonies and the Indian nations of the interior were to be kept apart." But instead of realizing the primary role the Iroquois played in the opening of the Ohio, Washburn misleadingly suggests that they "demanded to know why whites were not honoring the former treaties and boundary lines and were moving beyond the mountains into the Ohio River valley."[2] In a bid to alleviate encroachments on their own lands, many Iroquois wanted, and in fact conspired, to direct the flow of European settlers into the Ohio Country. The events leading up to, and terms of, the 1768 Stanwix agreement confirm this point. Ever evolving and urged by the eastern tribes, the Grand Council agreed to cede the lands in order to solidify their partnership with the Crown and protect their communities. All parties present understood exactly what they were "selling," the mutually dependent authority on which the transaction rested, and the ultimate cost of their decision.

Accordingly, then, the ambiguities attributed to the "Iroquois Empire" are not as certain when we keep in mind how regional politics and imagined empire shaped continental events. The idea of empire remained critical to the anticipated well-being of both Crown officials and Iroquois headmen in continental affairs; without it, after 1763 they both faced an uncertain future. Consequently, we must not forget that those Europeans gathered at the Oneida Carry were not the only ones strategizing with the hope of sustaining or creating profit, protection, and empire. In spite of this, talk of colonial independence threatened to crush this mutually reinforcing vision of North America.

At the time of William Johnson's death, the American colonies and northeastern borderlands were spinning out of control. The pending imperial crisis assured Guy Johnson's speedy appointment as acting superintendent of Indian affairs. Helping matters, most Iroquois chiefs supported Guy's bid for the position. For the Iroquois, the reasons were simple. Guy may have lacked his predecessor's charm, charisma, and uncanny ability to bridge European and indigenous worlds, but he promised to "perpetuate the patronage and methods of Sir William." Given the unsettling pattern of events taking place within the colonies, the Grand Council no doubt felt they could work with Guy to protect their communities.[3]

Not long after the terms of the 1768 treaty became known in the colonies did settlers begin to pour into the Mohawk River valley. Unlike the troublesome Ohio Country, which stood at the center of the grand aspirations of budding land companies, the Mohawk River valley seemed relatively safe. By the end of 1772, the newly established Tyron (Montgomery) County that encompassed most Mohawk territory was helping funnel newly arriving Europeans into the heart of Iroquoia. Bearing the brunt was the Oneida Carry. Things were not going as planned.

Only years before, while gathered at Fort Stanwix, Oneida chiefs had consented to the extension of the northern boundary line up the Unadilla River to the juncture of Wood and Canada creeks—a location at the center of the Oneida nation and less than ten miles from Fort Stanwix. Despite promises from Johnson, settler pressure on their lands did not relent. Nor did the message from Rev. Samuel Kirkland, the protégé of Eleazar Wheelock and resident missionary at the Carry since 1766. Fueling Oneida discontent with the Crown was Kirkland. Even at the time of William Johnson's death, Kirkland encouraged the Oneidas to "reflect on the emptiness of all mortal accomplishments" instead of mourning the death of the superintendent. As the revolutionary spirit gripped the colonies, the New England–born Kirkland identified with the Patriot cause. This alienated old friends, like Joseph Brant, and other Iroquois who longed to uphold their relationship with the English Crown. But it did not stop Kirkland from making gains with the Oneidas and local Tuscaroras. By the time Patriot militia controlled Tyron Country, with the help of the local Palatine George Klock, Kirkland openly acted as a conduit of Patriot interests at the Carry. In fact, when Gen. John Sullivan laid waste to Iroquoia, Kirkland provided support, as both a brigade chaplain and an interpreter. Put simply, the path of empire in North America did not unfold as envisioned by those negotiators who gathered in 1768 at the Oneida Carry. As a result, by the time Dunmore's Long Knives took the forks at the Ohio in a Virginian bid for the region, the Grand Council had far more pressing concerns to attend to closer to home.

Rifts between Iroquois communities increased as land speculation in New York and talk of colonial rebellion gained ground.[4]

As insults turned to widespread revolution, most Iroquois sought to distance themselves from the turmoil. Since the end of the Seven Years' War, then, the Grand Council had struggled with borderland realities. Even with the aid of Johnson, their negotiating power had steadily slipped. The pressure of more and more settlers along the Mohawk River, Crown cutbacks, competing colonial interests among Six Nations communities, and the void left by Johnson's death all contributed to the destabilization of Iroquoia. These factors also led to a decrease in a people's confidence in their Council.

A similar fate awaited those Europeans able to scheme with the weight and resources of the Crown on the periphery of an imperial system that had a limited reach. With a history of shifting allegiances, close friends among the enemy, and lands coveted by all, George Croghan was left little room to maneuver during the revolutionary era. With the room he was given, the aged and indebted veteran was forced to traverse both Tory and Patriot camps in a last-ditch effort to capitalize on a lifetime of speculation. Nevertheless, as the war of independence laid ruin to Iroquois claims of vast continental territories, so too did the conflict extinguish Croghan's dreams of an inland colony.

On 7 June 1774, Dr. John Connolly informed George Washington that the "great Government Scheme is blown over; which like the Mountain in labor has bro't forth a Mouse." For those interested in the success of the Grand Ohio Company, news of the failed Vandalia venture brought an end to almost six years of political and economic jockeying. To the Virginians determined to speculate and settle in the Ohio River valley it meant fortunes won, but for the primary shareholders in George Croghan's vision of the west it marked disaster and continuation of financial woes. After having spent almost seven years in receivership, and without the projected presence of a centralized Crown authority, Baynton, Wharton and Morgan could do little other than withdraw its trade from the Illinois and Ohio regions. Notwithstanding George Morgan's frequent laments about the "unhappiness of Mr. Wharton's disposition" and "the shameful situation of their books," by 1774 the firm started to liquidate its assets to cover debts.

For the Philadelphia merchants, that meant joining the ranks of those grasping at the few remaining holdings of George Croghan.[5]

Like his superior, his creditors, and the Iroquois, Croghan depended on an active and flexible administration across the Atlantic. When the Crown failed to recognize the private transactions of the treaty of Fort Stanwix and withdrew its support for the Vandalia colony, Croghan was finished. As talk of revolution swept through the colonies, Croghan could not protect against the foreclosure of his coveted New York lands. "I main to Sell the ottsego Tract," a depressed Croghan wrote Gratz on 24 September 1774, "and gett Don with that part of the Country." He entered into agreements with William Franklin and Thomas Wharton, among other creditors, in order to meet outstanding judgments amounting to over £10,000. Although Bernard Gratz managed to save almost 29,000 acres of Croghan's Otsego tract, claims continued against Croghan and by April the following year it was likely he would never again set foot in New York.[6]

In the spring of 1775, battles at Lexington and Concord marked the beginning of the American Revolution. Croghan had long worked for the Crown, but he joined a pro-American committee in Pittsburgh in May 1775. The move was fueled by personal ambition, survival, and perhaps resentment, but not ideological convictions. Despite the overture, his recent alliance with Dunmore—and probably what was known of his entire career—put his trustworthiness in doubt. As a result, Croghan was soon strongly encouraged to pack up and depart for Philadelphia. He spent the next four years in Philadelphia, dodging imprisonment and charges of treason. After the British evacuation of the city in June 1778 he fled to Lancaster and then to Passyunk. He was a man now caught between two worlds.[7]

In 1780, as the war raged around him, for food and fuel for the winter an elderly and financially exhausted Croghan conveyed the last 26,634 acres of his Otsego patent to Joseph Wharton in lieu of an old debt of £2,100. By June 1782 he was bedridden and spiritually broken. Croghan wrote his will on 12 June, leaving his few worldly possessions and remaining deeds to his daughter Susannah. His personal estate was valued at £50 13s.6d. On 31 August 1782, age unknown, Croghan died. Soon thereafter, his "gardener brought his corpse to town, and it was interred in St. Peter's churchyard. . . . A marker with an inscription was set at Croghan's grave, but before long it yielded to the elements."[8]

As with speculators like Croghan, for the continent's indigenous peoples the colonial struggle for independence had as much, or more, to do with their lands as it did with competing notions of liberty. In response, and similar to their strategy in 1701, the Grand Council declared neutrality. But as the contest widened so too did the devastating effects on their communities throughout the northeastern borderlands. Regional leaders labored to balance the demands of their communities and those of their European neighbors. For the Iroquois, the war heightened regional divisions to the point of internal rupture. By 1777 many Iroquois warriors found themselves caught between opposing sides of the colonial conflict. In their own bid for independence, many Mohawks, Onondagas, Cayugas, and Senecas eventually fought alongside those Europeans who defended the British Crown. Most Oneidas and Tuscaroras, however, hedged their bets with the colonial rebels. Thus, not long after Oneida and Seneca warriors clashed at Oriskany in August 1777, the Great Peace that bound the Iroquois, Barbara Graymont maintains, "shattered."[9]

Peace between the Six Nations faltered, but it did not shatter. Most Iroquois maintained open to dialogue during the war, and few died at the hands of their brothers. Moreover, major disagreement among the Six Nations was nothing new. Since the middle of the eighteenth century alone, reports of clashing Iroquois factions accompanied news of the sacking of Fort Bull in 1756 when Akwesasne, Kanesetake, Kahnawake, and Oswegatchie Iroquois led French forces to the Oneida Carry; or after 1758, when rumors of widespread Oneida dismissal of the Grand Council's calls to arms filtered back to Johnson Hall; and again during the uprising of 1763, when Seneca warriors raised the hatchet against British garrisons and settlers. Just how often, or how many, Iroquois lost their lives as a result of regional interests and disagreements is next to impossible to establish with any degree of certainty. But it would be misleading to suggest that the Iroquois were impervious to the increasing tensions among indigenous communities during the eighteenth century as imperial enterprising engulfed the continent. In the end, there are reasons to question the notion that the 1777 Battle of Oriskany marked the beginning of a bloody civil war among the Iroquois. Still, a thorough explanation of those reasons is beyond the scope of this narrative, this epilogue. What is perhaps more important is that the authority of the Iroquois Confederacy, as understood by contemporaries, met its end.

The start of colonial rebellion marked the beginning of the end for those who struggled to maintain or guide imperial designs in the early American northeastern borderlands. The decade that followed the treaty of Fort Stanwix revealed an instance when tribespeople, agents, and speculators who worked to exploit and create opportunity within the confines of an empire fell victim to a despondent imperial apparatus and their own thoughts of grandeur. The ensuing rebellion against the Crown and American independence brought new players to the region. Seeking to curb borderland hostilities, publicly define national and state boundaries, and establish the protocol of a new continental order, in 1784 U.S. Indian agents began with the self-proclaimed indigenous overseers of Iroquois country. Within a year of the 1783 Paris agreement, Iroquois headmen again found themselves on a journey toward the Oneida Carry. But this time the terms of empire would be dictated, not negotiated.

In 1784 the issue of territorial rights, once again, took center stage at the Oneida Carry. In addition to laying claim over the lands ceded in 1768, Congress hoped to capitalize on the success of the recent war by demanding further cessions from indigenous peoples. If successful, Congress reasoned, state attempts to treat with American Indians directly and on a regional basis would be thwarted and unregulated settlement curbed. Consequently, increasingly problematic border and trade disputes could be resolved, and, more important, the federal government could generate thousands of dollars by clearing title and selling western lands. So important were the negotiations that the likes of Madison, Jefferson, and Lafayette all made their way to the Oneida Carry.

The Iroquois no doubt recognized the limits of negotiation with the arriving American representatives. Without imperial backers, the dysfunctional Grand Council could no longer sustain its claims to be the rightful overlord of vast territories. Colonial independence had extinguished Iroquois authority and undermined their future security. Left with few options, and knowing the toxic potential of state and settler aspirations, in 1784 Joseph Brant and his kinsmen began negotiating at the Carry by dismissing New York governor Clinton's attempts to finalize a direct land cession. Collective memory and treaty records warned of the complications that resulted from holding council only with regional players. With the last of Iroquois homelands up for grabs, Brant longed for delay to weigh his options. Accordingly, he encouraged the handful of gathered careworn sachems to wait to deal with the Indian commissioners on their way from Philadelphia. To be sure, rumors abounded as to what to expect from the arriving Americans. Many indigenous communities reasoned that it would not be long before hatred against them again received government sponsorship, even those who had proved to be indispensable allies of the new government. As a result, by the autumn of 1784 discontent and suspicion brewed among many indigenous communities.

There was reason to be concerned. On 22 October 1784, as stipulated by the terms of the treaty, the indigenous delegates present agreed to "yield to the United States, all claims to the country west of the [new] boundary."[10] Shortly thereafter, land-hungry speculators and settlers fanned across the northeastern borderlands. In fact, by January 1786, as Alan Taylor reminds us, frontier visionary William Cooper could be seen slugging though drifts of snow toward central New York with the aim of securing a grand tract of land at the source of the Susquehanna River on Lake Otsego. There, Cooper "looked out over a forest containing many trees marked 'GCCY1768.'" The initials of George Croghan and his surveyor Christopher Yates already represented a bygone era and the life of a largely forgotten fantasist whose schemes for western development illuminate the business of past speculators in empire. Subsequent forays, like those of Cooper, began to build over the colonial past, engulfing people and places into what would become a national narrative.[11]

Most commentators situate the 1784 treaty in a postwar narrative of nation building. In fact, in 1932 Henry S. Manley suggested that the treaty "marked consequences" for indigenous nations in the United States for the decade that followed: when new states emerged from the revolutionary war, not only did old provincial boundary disputes resurface, so did questions concerning state and federal jurisdictions over indigenous lands, trade, and treaty rights. Shortly after American representatives met at Fort Stanwix, the subsequent clash of interests temporarily "settled, for our national history, some of the phases of the peculiarly divided jurisdiction over the Six Nations Indians within New York State." In this light, the Oneida Carry is depicted as a battleground on which uncomfortable bedfellows vied to extend their respective domains.[12]

At the center of the power struggle were two legal remnants of the colonial past: the 1768 treaty of Fort Stanwix, and the Quebec Act of 1774. By recognizing the sovereignty of indigenous peoples and their territorial rights, both decisions built on the principles established by the Royal Proclamation of 1763. Seeking to sidestep the "tyrannical" legislation of empire, state politicians and land jobbers quickly claimed territorial and legal jurisdiction by way of retaining other, more convenient, "ancient" colonial rights. By 1784 correspondence between notable figures in New York, Pennsylvania, and Virginia confirm the remarkable degree of strategizing and positioning that took place as each state clamored to gain possession of new lands.[13]

Ultimately charged, then, with solidifying federal power throughout northeastern borderlands, Oliver Wolcott, Richard Butler, and Arthur Lee faced formidable obstacles as they made their way to the Oneida Carry. All factions did agree, however, that American Indians had to be punished, captives returned, and reparations given. Therefore, as Jack Campisi illustrates, the 1784 treaty terms had much in common with the five other subsequent treaties concluded between 1784 and 1786—marking a trend in the early republic's treatment of the land's early inhabitants. Campisi's observation is accurate in terms of identifying five common provisions: prisoner exchange, return of property, the offering of "peace and protection," the definition of boundaries, and the inclusion of punishment clauses. Others have made the same connection, stressing the geopolitical objectives of Congress. In fact, "even federal officials who had negotiated the purchase admitted that they knew they would be forced to also purchase Ohio from other tribes." To this point few distinctions have been made between the motivations of the U.S. officials who negotiated the terms at Fort Stanwix (1784), Fort McIntosh (1785), Hopewell, South Carolina (1785/6), and Fort Finney (1786). But there was more to the

1784 treaty than its punitive nature. In fact, by using the second treaty of Fort Stanwix as a lens to view the collapse of Iroquois-European relations, in addition to the beginning of a new chapter on such relations the events at the Oneida Carry take on additional significance.[14]

The 1784 treaty officially removed the Grand Council as a player in, and beneficiary of, empire. No longer could the Iroquois help orchestrate treaties with consequences of continental proportion. To this end, the second treaty held at Fort Stanwix underscored the new, restricted negotiating parameters for the Grand Council, thus redefining the place of the Iroquois Confederacy in early America. The revolution may have caused serious civil conflict, but it was the American marginalization of the Grand Council that snuffed out authority of the Iroquois in continental affairs. To realize their own North American aspirations, federal officials longed to bury the pesky legacies of the past, and the gathering of the Iroquois at the Oneida Carry in 1784 signaled the first step toward extending the boundaries of the new nation.

By relegating the Iroquois to the status of a defeated political identity at the second treaty of Fort Stanwix, U.S. officials made a strong statement on the very same grounds on which the gathered nations had achieved their greatest diplomatic feats only sixteen years before. By winter's end, the new proprietors of empire in North America made it clear that the place and protocol that sustained the authority of the Iroquois would no longer be integral to intercultural negotiations on the continent. And herein lies one of the most important aspects of the 1784 treaty held at Fort Stanwix. The treaty *was* "an auspicious beginning of treaty making by the independent United States," as Francis Prucha remarks, but not just because it "forced unilaterally upon the Indians the demands of the United States—in this case return of prisoners and, most important, land cessions."[15] By publicly demonstrating an unwillingness to maintain the façade of the Iroquois hegemony over the western nations, federal officials did much more than demand land and prisoners. By treating with the Six Nations as divided and conquered peoples, U.S. representatives emphasized the end of colonial traditions and the imagined place of the Iroquois in a new continental empire. By doing so, they redefined the Iroquois Confederacy while laying claim to a hotly contested region. If the British Crown initially sought to uphold the notion of indigenous sovereignty west of the 1768 boundary in an attempt to deter American expansion, in 1784 federal officials planned to begin absorbing western lands by confirming the land cession of 1768 and demanding further lands from the Iroquois. The treatment of the Six Nations as subjugated peoples announced the end of Iroquois authority and the end of British claims to the "Old Northwest" territory. Accordingly, the year 1784 should mark the conclusion of a notable chapter in early American history, even though it would take three more decades before the borders of the northeast and Great Lakes Region were solidified.

When Joseph Brant left the Oneida Carry in 1784, he did so in haste, and before the terms of the second council held at Fort Stanwix officially concluded. His intention to travel east toward London to seek confirmation of a tract of land in British Canada had been stalled by news of death and disease at Niagara. Doubling back to the Great Falls, Brant left Seneca chief Cornplanter with the arduous tasks of reconfirming their territory as outlined in 1768 and opposing any further land cessions to the Americans. Hardly a forum for celebration, a somber mood, no doubt, blanketed the indigenous people at the fort. Divided and displaced, the Iroquois did not receive lavish gifts worth thousands of pounds sterling as payment. In fact, during council the displaced peoples consented to further demands. The U.S. government used the opportunity to seize the remaining parts of New York, northwestern Pennsylvania, and northern Ohio. Unwilling to relinquish their sovereignty on the battleground, the Iroquois faced ruin through treaty. If the hatchet could not be buried, the power of the Grand Council would be by the strokes of a quill.

NOTES

ABBREVIATIONS

APS   American Philosophical Society

DRCHSNY   E. B. O'Callaghan and B. Fernow, eds., *Documents Relative to the Colonial History of the State of New York*

HSP   Historical Society of Pennsylvania

LCP   Library Company of Philadelphia

NAC   Library and Archives Canada

PA   William Henry Egle, ed., *Pennsylvania Archives*, 3rd Series

PCR   Samuel Hazard, ed., *Colonial Records of Pennsylvania: Minutes of the Provincial Council of Pennsylvania, from the Organization to the Termination of the Proprietary Government*

PHMC   Pennsylvania Historical and Museum Commission

WJP   Sullivan, James, et al., eds. *The Papers of Sir William Johnson*

INTRODUCTION

1. For the purposes of this book, the northeastern borderlands can be considered a zone of interaction inclusive of the area west of the Appalachian mountain range stretching from the Mohawk River valley southwest across New York, Pennsylvania, and West Virginia. Heading on an arched path northwest from the eastern borders of West Virginia, the area includes the northeastern limits of Kentucky, the state of Ohio, and the eastern regions of Indiana before returning again to the Detroit area and lands south of the Great Lakes. The individuals and groups studied here had rival visions for the future of this territory, and some had competing personal ambitions for the exploitation of sections of this area on the imperial fringe.

2. Griffis, *Sir William Johnson*, 193.

3. Barr, "Beyond the Pale."

4. Volwiler, *George Croghan*, 224.

5. Hurt, *Indian Frontier*, 12.

6. WJP 6:ix.

7. Wharton, *Facts and Observations*, 12 (available at LCP).

8. Billington, "Fort Stanwix Treaty," 182; Hurt, *Indian Frontier*, 13.

9. Marshall, "Sir William Johnson."

10. Hinderaker, "Liberty and Power," 229.

11. Mullin, "Personal Politics"; Parmenter, "Iroquois," 111.

12. Marshall, "Sir William Johnson," 149.

13. Wallace, *Death and Rebirth*, 251–52.

14. Parmenter, "Iroquois," 112.

15. Alvord, "British Ministry," 167; Griffis, *Sir William Johnson*, 193; Jones, *License for Empire*, 94.

16. Richter, *Ordeal*, 6–7.

17. Northern indigenous "empires" conveniently sprang forth in the regional discourse only when the inhabitants realized that they could both profit and protect themselves from the competing European newcomers. This is perhaps best exemplified in Jennings, *Ambiguous Iroquois Empire*.

18. Preston, *Texture of Contact*, 7–11.

1. EXCHANGES AND TRANSFORMATIONS

1. William Fenton Papers, Ms Coll. 20, Series 3, "Indian Treaty Protocol: The Crucible of Indian-White Relations," 24 February 1979, APS.

2. Treaty records leave details regarding what the transcribers believed important, but little evidence survives to outline the physicality of those assembled and the metaphorical language employed to convey ideals and observe tradition. To grasp the extent of the events, argues William Fenton, scholars must be willing to depict the past by embracing the present. "Upstreaming," therefore, is the ethnological exercise of 'proceeding from the known and observable present to the unknown historical past.'" See Foster, Campisi, and Mithun, *Extending the Rafters*, 14; Johnston, "To the Mohawk Station," 65. William Fenton Papers, Ms Coll. 20, Series 3, "Indian Treaty Protocol: The Crucible of Indian-White Relations," 24 February 1979, APS.

3. Cadwallader, *History*, 19. As early as 1744, Benjamin Franklin published the advice of Canaestoga, an influential Onondaga speaker who urged the English colonists to bind together as the Five Nations had before. Furthermore, Bruce Johansen maintains that at the Albany Plan of Union in 1754 Franklin advised Americans to unite under a "tree of peace," using Six Nations diplomacy as a model to emulate. Since Johansen, a few scholars have used these and other passing references as evidence of direct indigenous influence on the U.S. Constitution. The "Influence thesis" as championed by Johansen, Donald Grinde, and Vine DeLoria enjoyed shock-value success during the early 1990s, but it carries little weight among most Iroquois and early American scholars. For a review of the debate, see Payne, "Iroquois League"; Tooker, *Iroquois Sourcebook*; Johansen, *Debating Democracy*, 9.

4. During the late nineteenth century, scholars interested in recording the history and traditions of the Six Nations visited the Grand River Six Nations, near present-day Brantford, Ontario. After the American Revolution, a significant proportion of the English-allied Six Nations followed Thayendanegea (Joseph Brant) to British Canada. In 1784, Gen. Frederick Haldimand ceded a tract of land six miles on either side of the Grand River, from its mouth to source, to the nations that fought against the Americans during the war of independence. This land was granted in lieu of the Six Nations territory lost to the Americans in New York State. During the spring of 1784/5, approximately 450 Mohawks, 380 Cayugas, 200 Onondagas, 25 Tuscaroras, 75 Senecas, and a few Oneidas settled the Grand River area. Believing that the inhabitants of the Grand River reserve had maintained the "most authentic" oral histories of the Iroquois nations since their dispersal from their ancestral lands in the late 1770s, such scholars as J. N. B. Hewitt, Arthur C. Parker, Horatio Hale, Duncan Campbell Scott, and A. A. Goldenweiser attempted to record the oral history of the "Iroquois," their founding legends and procedures involved in the "traditional" maintenance of the Great Laws. By 1900 the Confederacy Council, following a series of rejections of earlier manuscripts, had sanctioned an "official" written version of the Great Laws. Within twelve years Chief John Gibson, who had earlier been appointed by the Council to lead the committee instructed to write the Laws, challenged the "official" version with a revised publication. Both versions have since been consider the most authentic by inquisitive academics. For further reading, see Campbell, "Seth Newhouse," 183–202; Fenton, *Great Law,* chaps 4 and 5.

5. Hale, *Hiawatha.* Hale's findings were later recorded in the widely circulated *Iroquois Book of Rites.* Francis Jennings remains more skeptical, suggesting that the Laws were written sometime between 1400 and 1600; see Jennings, *Ambiguous Iroquois Empire.*

6. Fenton, *Great Law,* chaps. 1–4.

7. Richter, *Facing East,* 135. Furthermore, negotiations were to always be conducted in ritual "Indian speech"; see Sturtevant, "Structural Sketch," 138.

8. Johnston, "To the Mohawk Station," 82. Also see Fenton, *American Indian,* 21–22.

9. Graymont, *Iroquois,* 14.

10. William Fenton Papers, Ms Coll. 20, Series 3, "Indian Treaty Protocol: The Crucible of Indian-White Relations," 24 February 1979, APS; Foster, "Who Spoke First," 183–85; Richter, *Facing East,* 134–35; Graymont, *Iroquois,* 13–15.

11. As anthropologist William Engelbrecht notes, "these moieties are often incorrectly referred to as Elder Brothers and Younger Brothers. Groups within the same moiety are 'younger brothers;' literally 'they are younger brothers to themselves.'" Engelbrecht, *Iroquoia,* 129.

12. Johnston, "To the Mohawk Station"; William Fenton Papers, Ms Coll. 20, Series 3, "Indian Treaty Protocol: The Crucible of Indian-White Relations," 24 February 1979, 82, APS.

13. Jacobs, *Dispossessing,* chap. 4; Jacobs, *Wilderness Politics,* 12–17. For a revised account of the tools involved in indigenous-European relations, see Miller and Hamell, "New Perspective."

14. Fenton quotes from Foster, "Who Spoke First," 183–85.

15. William Fenton suggests that the evolution of indigenous-European diplomatic protocol stems from the Iroquoian Condolence Ceremony for the mourning of dead chiefs; see Foster, "Who Spoke First," 183.

16. Prucha, *American Indian Treaties*, 24–25; for summary of treaty protocol, see 25–26.

17. Richter and Merrell, *Beyond the Covenant Chain*, 22.

18. Richter, *Facing East*, 134–37.

19. Jacobs, *Dispossessing*, 12–17; Calloway, *Scratch of a Pen*, 67–69; White, *Middle Ground*, 112–19.

20. Jacobs, *Wilderness Politics*, 12.

21. Lee, "Peace Chiefs," 701–702; Anderson, *War*, 3–6.

22. Richter, *Facing East*, 51–60; Hopkins, "Impact."

23. For a study that challenges the primary motivator of the Beaver Wars as being economic in nature, see Starna and Brandão, "From the Mohawk-Mahican War."

24. Hinderaker and Mancall, *At the Edge*, 33–35.

25. Richter, "War and Culture," 540.

26. For information on the depopulation of the Ohio, see White, *Middle Ground*, chap. 1. On the Iroquois loss of firearm advantage, see Richter, *Facing East*, 87, 147–80; and "War and Culture," 528–59.

27. Although neglectful of the central role Iroquois diplomats played in colonial affairs, for a detailed account of French-Iroquois diplomacy during the seventeenth century see Goldstein, *French-Iroquois Diplomatic*, 170–97; also see Richter, *Facing East*, 156–58; Wallace, *Death and Rebirth*, 45–50, 111–13; Hinderaker and Mancall, *At the Edge*, 62–68; Richter, "War and Culture," 551.

28. Wallace, *Death and Rebirth*, 44–48.

29. Richter, *Facing East*, 158.

30. For a detailed account of the settlement, see Havard, *Great Peace*.

31. Richter, *Facing East*, 157; Richter and Merrell, *Beyond the Covenant Chain*, 6–7.

2. THE CARRYING PLACE, WAR, AND THE OHIO COUNTRY

1. Jennings, *Ambiguous Iroquois Empire*, 12, 42–43; Jones, *License for Empire*, 20–22.

2. Jennings, *Ambiguous Iroquois Empire*, 10–24; Jones, *License for Empire*, 21–35; Shannon, *Indians and Colonists*, 20.

3. Richter, *Ordeal*, 262.

4. For van den Bogaert's journal, see Snow, Gehring, and Starna, *In Mohawk Country*, 1–13; Hagerty, *Massacre*, 13.

5. Roberts, *New York's Forts*, 414.

6. Römer's journal quoted in Sherman, "Six Nations," 491.

7. Hagerty, *Massacre*, 13.

8. Hagerty, *Massacre*, 13; Luzader, *Fort Stanwix*, 3.

9. Luzader, *Fort Stanwix*, 4.

10. Richter, *Ordeal*, 262.

11. Shannon, *Iroquois Diplomacy*, 1–10; Garratt and Robertson, *Four Indian Kings*; Richter, *Facing East*, 165; Wallace, *Death and Rebirth*, chap. 1.

12. Jennings, *Ambiguous Iroquois Empire*, 12–15.

13. For further discussion of middlemen and cultural mediators, see Adelman and Aron "From Borderlands," 814–41; Szasz, *Between Indian and White*; Faragher, "More Motley"; Knepper, *Ohio*; White, *Middle Ground*, 105–10, 129; Merrell, *Into the American Woods*.

14. For notable published references see, Griffis, *Sir William Johnson*; Flexner, *Mohawk Baronet*; and Flexner, *Lord of the Mohawks*. For an excellent summary of Johnson, see Taylor, *Divided Ground*, 3–15; and Mullin, "Personal Politics." For a recent alternative reading of Johnson's life, see O'Toole, *White Savage*. For what is perhaps the best rebuttal to O'Toole's thesis, see Taylor, "Collaborator." Notable unpublished works on Johnson include Dunn, "Western Commerce," chap. 5; Inouye, "Sir William Johnson"; McKeith, "Inadequacy of Men"; and Marshall, "Imperial Regulation."

15. Flexner, *Mohawk Baronet*, 7–39.

16. Taylor, "Collaborator."

17. Shannon, "Dressing for Success," 367.

18. Gwyn, "Sir William Johnson."

19. Flexner, *Mohawk Baronet*, 52; Gwyn, "Sir William Johnson."

20. In August 1755, commenting on the mid-century perception of Johnson, the Philadelphia *Gentlemen's Magazine* published the following (Historical Chronicles, 426, Fort Pitt Museum Collection, Roll 4608, PHMC):

Major General Johnson (an Irish gentleman) is universally esteemed superior to any we have in our parts, for the post he sustains. Besides his skill and experience, as an old officer, he is particularly happy in making himself beloved by all sorts of people, and can conform to all their manners and customs, and suits himself to all companies and conversations. He is very much of the fine gentlemen in general company. But as the inhabitants next to him are mostly Dutch, he sits down with them, smokes tobacco, drinks flip, and talks of improvements, bears and beaver skins. Being surrounded with Indians, he speaks several of their languages well, and has always some of them with him. His house is a safe and hospitable retreat for them from the enemy. He takes care of their wives and children when they go out on parties, and even wears their dress. In short, by his honest dealings with them in trade, his courage, which has often been successfully tried to them, and his courteous behaviour, he has endeared himself to them, that they chose him one of their chief sachems or princes, and esteem him as their common father.

21. *Aouapou* was an indigenous word used by French Canadians to denote the proper gift package to be delivered to representatives at council. The quality and size varied with the status of the recipient; Jacobs, *Dispossessing*, 52. For a 1747 account

of such goods, see WJP 9:15–30. For a detailed account of Johnson's ties with the Mohawks, see Shannon, *Indians and Colonists*, 38–48, and on Mohawks as middlemen, 24–39; Mullins, "Personal Politics," 350–358; and White, *Middle Ground*, 53–60, 105–110. For reference to Johnson's expenditures on Indian affairs while in office, see New York Assembly to Governor Clinton, 9 October 1747, DRCHSNY 6:619–20. For a description of Johnson's estate, see Flexner, *Mohawk Baronet*, 287–310.

22. Taylor, "Collaborator."

23. Graymont, "Koñwatsiātsiaiéñni."

24. Hurt, *Ohio Frontier*, 12–20.

25. Charles Thompson and Jasper Yeates, "Causes of the Alienation of the Delaware and Shawanese Indians," [?1759] MG 193, Box 1, Fort Pitt Museum Collection, PHMC. For migration of nations to the Ohio Country and increased independence, see McConnell, *Country Between*, 5–20, 69–72; and Jennings, *Empire of Fortune*, 28–30.

26. Charles Thompson and Jasper Yeates, "Causes of the Alienation of the Delaware and Shawanese Indians," [?1759] MG 193, Box 1, Fort Pitt Museum Collection, PHMC.

27. For Walking Purchase details, see Jennings, "Scandalous Indian Policy;" and Jennings, *Empire of Fortune*, 25–28.

28. Charles Thompson and Jasper Yeates, "Causes of the Alienation of the Delaware and Shawanese Indians" [?1759] MG 193, Box 1, Fort Pitt Museum Collection, PHMC.

29. The Ohio Iroquois, or "Mingos," were of Iroquois decent and had migrated to the Ohio Country around the 1740s with the Delawares. The cultural and political bond that existed between these populations and the eastern Six Nations was gradually replaced by regional ties with the other Ohio nations—Shawnees and Wyandots included. The Chenussios were the most westerly body of Senecas and had, as a result of geography, more in common with the western and Ohio nations than with their eastern brethren. Furthermore, French influence on the western Senecas was much greater than British during the time of the French colonial network that spanned the Pays d'en haut and the Mississippi and Ohio river valleys.

30. Richter, *Facing East*, 184.

31. Hurt, *Ohio Frontier*, 35.

32. The pronunciation of "Croghan" seems to be as unpredictable as the life of the man who bore the name. Based on a few linguistic observations, Robert G. Crist concludes that given the Gaelic origins of the surname it was most likely pronounced "Crow-an." This is confirmed in a letter from the governor of Canada, Marquis de Vaudreuil, to the minister, 8 August 1756, in which Vaudreuil refers to "George Craon's fort"; Stevens and Kent, *Wilderness Chronicles*, 94. For a more detailed explanation, see Crist, "George Croghan," 3.

33. Cave, "George Croghan," 2; McConnell, *Country Between*, 67–94.

34. Croghan's name first appeared in the records in 1742. He was listed as a transporter of goods from Edward Shippen to Peter Tostee; see Crist, "George Croghan," 9.

35. Volwiler, *Westward*, 32; Wainwright, *George Croghan*, 9; Crist, "George Croghan," 9.

36. Cave, "George Croghan," 2; Crist, "George Croghan," 9–10.

37. Richard Hockley to Thomas Penn, February 15, 1749/50(?), Penn Family Papers, Official Correspondence, 4, HSP.

38. Cave, "George Croghan," 3. The same line of argument is noted in Volwiler, *George Croghan*, 21, and Crist, "George Croghan," 10–12.

39. Quoted from Shirai, "Indian Trade," 11.

40. Wallace, *Conrad Weiser*, 335.

41. Conference at Albany, 6 July 1751, DRCHSNY 6:717–26.

42. Ibid.

43. Quote from Charles Thompson and Jasper Yeates, "Causes of the Alienation of the Delaware and Shawanese Indians," [?1759] MG 193, Box 1, Fort Pitt Museum Collection, PHMC.

44. Only two years before at a council in Philadelphia, Canasatego belittled the Delaware representative, Nutimus, by ordering his people to disperse from the Walking Purchase lands to either Wyoming (present-day Wilkes-Barre, Pa.) or Shamokin (present-day Sunbury, Pa.). The Shamokin sect, led by Teedyuscung, maintained a friendly but tentative relationship with the English. Weslager, *Delaware Indians*, 190–92.

45. Also see conference between Lt. Governor Clarke and Six Nations, Albany, 16 August 1740, DRCHSNY 6:173–99.

46. Van Doren and Boyd, *Indian Treaties*, 73–79.

47. Pennsylvania currency. Charles Thompson and Jasper Yeates, "Causes of the Alienation of the Delaware and Shawanese Indians," [?1759] MG 193, Box 1, Fort Pitt Museum Collection, PHMC.

48. John Baynton (1726–73) was at various times a member of the Pennsylvania Assembly, provincial commissioner (1756), and member of the board of trustees for the state house and trustee of Provincial Island. In 1757 he partnered with Samuel Wharton (1732–1800). The firm engaged in global trade, primarily exchanging local products like hay, onions, cord wood, and lumber for rum, sugar, bottled beer, and gunpowder. Their trading network was extensive, reaching Québec, Detroit, Fort Pitt, the West Indies, Portugal, London, and even China. George Morgan married John Baynton's daughter Mary and partnered with the firm in 1763. See Baynton, Wharton and Morgan Sequestered Papers, PHMC.

49. Shirai, "Indian Trade," 12–13; Van Doren and Boyd, *Indian Treaties*, 73–79.

50. For a detailed analysis of indigenous concepts of land ownership and use, see Tooker, *Iroquois Sourcebook*, 80–86.

51. DRCHSNY 10:159.

52. Galbreath, *Expedition of Celoron*, 110–111; PRC 5:510:

L'AN 1749 DU REGNE DE LOUIS XV ROY DE FRANCE, NOUS CÉLORON, COMMANDANT D'UN DETACHEMENT ENVOIE PAR MONSIEUR LE MIS. DE LA GALISSONIERE, COMMANDANT GENERAL DE LA NOUVELLE FRANCE POUR RETABLIR LA TRAN QUILLITE DANS QUELQUES VILLAGES SAUVAGES DE CES CANTONS, AVONS ENTERRE CETTE PLAQUE AU CONFLUENT DE L'OHIO ET DE TCHADAKOIN CE 29 JUILLET, PRES DE LA RIVIERE OYO

AUTREMENT BELLE RIVIERE, POUR MONUMENT DU RENOUVELLEMENT DE POSSESSION
QUE NOUS AVONS PRIS DE LA DITTE RIVIERE OYO, ET DE TOUTES CELLE~ QUI Y TOMB-
ENT, ET DE TOUTES LES TERRES DES DEUX COTES JUSQUE AUX SOURCES DES DITTES
RIVIERES A'NSI QU'EN ONT JOUY OU DU JOUIR LES PRECEDENTS ROIS DE FRANCE' ET
QU'ILS S'Y SONT MAINTENUS PAR LES ARMES ET PAR LES TRAIT TES, SPECIALEMENT
PAR CEUX DE RISWICK D'UTRECHT ET D'AIX LA CHAPELLE.

53. Hurt, *Ohio Frontier*, 35–36.
54. "Summons to British troops at the Monongahela," DRCHSNY 6:842; Dowd, *Spirited Resistance*, 23–25.
55. Gipson, *British Empire*, 5:3–112.
56. Albany Congress, 6 July 1751, DRCHSNY 6:717–37.
57. "The Present state of Indian Affairs, with British and French Colonies in North America . . . promoting trade among them." DRCHSNY 6:738–73.
58. White, *Middle Ground*, 233–34; McConnell, *Country Between*, 66–101.
59. Shannon, *Indians and Colonists*, 46–48.
60. "Conference between Gov. Clinton and the Indians," Fort George, New York, 12 June 1753, DRCHSNY 6:781–88.
61. Shannon, *Indians and Colonists*, 50. For "dog" reference, see 1746 Albany congress with Governor Clinton, DRCHSNY 6:294.
62. Mullins, "Personal Politics," 350–52.
63. DRCHSNY 6:808–11.
64. Journal of Conrad Weiser's Visit to the Mohawks, 11 August 1753, DRCHSNY 6:797. Weiser recorded that Mohawk chief Kanadakayon confirmed Abraham's sentiments.
65. DRCHSNY 6:813–16.
66. Dr. Shuckburgh to Thomas Pownall, 30 October 1753, "Memorandum," DRCHSNY 6:805.
67. See Journal of Conrad Weiser's Visit to the Mohawks, 1753, DRCHSNY 6:797–804.
68. Merritt, *At the Crossroads*, 174; White, *Middle Ground*, 240–41.
69. Earlier that year Croghan and Trent secured fifteen depositions from traders in April, May, and June for losses suffered prior to 1754. The group, which was headed by Croghan and represented by Trent (attorney), became known as the "Suffering Traders". Wainwright, *George Croghan*, 111.
70. Penn Family Papers, Indian Affairs, 1687–1801, vol. 1, *Croghan's Journal*, "Speech of Half King," 28 January 1754, Logstown, HSP.
71. Penn to Peters, May 29 1755, Penn Letter Book, 4, 38, 89–90, HSP.
72. Peckham, *George Croghan's Journal*, 4.
73. DRCHSNY 6:800–801. For Croghan quote, see Croghan to Governor Penn, 14 May 1754, PA 2:144–45.
74. Quotes from Shannon, *Indians and Colonists*, 10–13, and, for details on the Plan of Union, 83–105. For traditional interpretations of the congress, see Mullin, "Albany

Congress"; Hackett, "Social Origins"; and Jezierski, "Imperii in Imperio." Gipson described the congress as a piece of statecraft that promised to hold the empire together if enacted; see *British Empire*, vol. 5.

75. Albany Congress, 19 June 1754, DRCHSNY 6:854–56.

76. 28 June 1754, DRCHSNY 6:866–70.

77. DRCHSNY 6:870.

78. DRCHSNY 6:872–73.

79. DRCHSNY 6:888; Dixon, *Never Come*, 29. For detailed account of contested provincial boundaries, see "Virginia Claims to Land in Pennsylvania," PA 3:483–574.

80. DRCHSNY 6:875–92; Shannon, *Indians and Colonists*, 221.

81. Shannon, *Indians and Colonists*, 223.

82. "Colonel Johnson's Suggestions for defeating the designs of the French," July 1754, DRCHSNY 6:897.

83. DRCHSNY 7:270. Washington, on the other hand, criticized Croghan, remarking shortly after the Fort Necessity debacle: "Croghan (who by vainly boasting of [his] interest with the Indians, involved the country in great calamity, by causing dependence to be placed where there was none) . . . never could induce above 30 fighting men to join us." Quotation cited from Wainwright, *George Croghan*, 65.

84. Cave, "George Croghan," 4.

85. Peter Wraxall, "Some Thoughts upon the British Indian Interest in North America more particularly as it relates to the Northern Confederacy commonly called the Six Nations," Memoir on North American Indians c. 1755–1760: Secretary of State Miscellaneous. Microfilm: B-618, 1Ref: MG11-C05, NAC. William Johnson earlier confirmed the same sentiment in a letter to the Lords of Trade, July 1754, DRCHSNY 6:897. Hendrick quote from Jennings, *Ambiguous Iroquois Empire*, 14. In 1755 cartographer Lewis Evans's "General Map of the Middle British Colonies in America" furthered the myth of an Iroquois empire. Evans depicted the boundaries of the Six Nations extending to the Mississippi River.

86. Minutes of Council of War Held at Albany, 25 May 1756, and William Alexander to William Shirley, 27 May 1755, in Lincoln, *Correspondence*, 2:453–55; Luzader, *Fort Stanwix*, 5; Hagerty, *Massacre*, 21–22.

87. Hagerty, *Massacre*, 22.

88. William Shirley to Sir Thomas Robinson, 20 June and 20 December 1755, Lincoln, *Correspondence*, 2:200, 355. For instructions to Williams, see William Shirley to William Williams, 12 August 1755, Lincoln, *Correspondence*, 2:235; Hagerty, *Massacre*, 23.

89. William Shirley to William Johnson, 24 September 1755, and William Eyre to William Shirley, 10 September 1755, Lincoln, *Correspondence*, 2:280–82, 259–60; Luzader, *Fort Stanwix*, 5; Anderson, *Crucible of War*, 94–201; Hagerty, *Massacre*, 26.

90. William Shirley to William Johnson, 24 September 1755, Lincoln, *Correspondence*, 2:280–82; Luzader, *Fort Stanwix*, 4.

91. Anderson, *Crucible of War*, 94–201; Hagerty, *Massacre*, 26–29.

92. William Shirley to John Bradstreet, 17 March 1756, Lincoln, *Correspondence*, 2:419–22.

93. Anderson, *Crucible of War*, 94–201; Parkman, *Wolfe and Montcalm*, 374–76; Mac-Cloud, "Franco-Amerindian Expedition."

94. William Shirley to James Abercrombie, 27 June 1756, Lincoln, *Correspondence*, 2:470–71.

95. Luzader, *Fort Stanwix*, 6.

96. Richard Peters to William Shirley, 6 May 1756, Lincoln, *Correspondence*, 2:438–42.

97. "Council held in Philadelphia," Penn Family Papers, Indian Affairs 1687–1801, 1:39, HSP.

98. Croghan to Johnson, Philadelphia, 14 March 1757, DRCHNY 7:266.

99. Cave, "George Croghan," 6.

100. "At a Council held in Philadelphia" Tuesday, 30 August 1757, Penn Family Papers, vol. 3, HSP.

101. Quoted from Luzader, *Fort Stanwix*, 7.

102. McConnell, *Country Between*, 128.

103. Luzader, *Fort Stanwix*, 8–10, 14.

104. Ibid., 10.

105. Stanwix to Abercrombie, 7 September 1758, and Abercrombie to Stanwix, 12 September 1758, James Abercrombie Papers, Huntington Library. Quoted from Luzader, *Fort Stanwix*, 11.

106. White, *Middle Ground*, 249–51.

107. Wainwright, *George Croghan*, 129–30.

108. Wallace, *King of the Delawares*; Weslager, *Delaware Indians*, 235–47; White, *Middle Ground*, 251.

109. Wainwright, *George Croghan*, 151. For the 1758 Treaty of Easton, see WJP 2:752–54.

110. Richter, *Facing East*, 186.

111. Long, *Lord Jeffrey Amherst*, 187.

112. Luzader, *Fort Stanwix*, 14.

3. CONVERGING INTERESTS

1. Jones, *License for Empire*, 74–75.

2. Calloway, *Scratch of a Pen*, 49.

3. White, *Middle Ground*, 292, suggests that it was never made clear why peace overtures from the Wyandots, Chippewas, and Ottawas were likely to prevent further conflict but the same could not be said for the Shawnees and Delawares.

4. For a referenced list of studies on William Johnson, see chap. 2, n. 14.

5. Jennings, *Empire of Fortune*, 441.

6. Calloway, *Scratch of a Pen*, 15.

7. Ibid., 48–63. In 1763 the British-allied Six Nations had been reduced to a population of approximately 160 fighting men and a total population of perhaps six hundred to eight hundred. The western Senecas, however, had a population of about four thousand in twenty villages that largely remained anti-British; ibid., 35–44.

8. Ibid., 67–69.

9. For report of Shawnees at Pitt, see Slick, *William Trent*, 109–25. For Croghan reports, see WJP 3:964–65 (1762); WJP 4:62, 97, 98 (1763); WJP 10:534–35 (1763). For Johnson to Amherst, see WJP 3:185–86, 530–31.

10. Calloway, *Scratch of a Pen*, 66–71. For a detailed discussion concerning Neolin and other prophets, see Dowd, *Spirited Resistance*, chap. 2, esp. 33–35.

11. Quoted from Anderson, *Crucible of War*, 809n. Also see White, *Middle Ground*, 288; and Dixon, *Never Come*, 152–53.

12. For details on the progression of events related to the infectious material, see Volwiler, "William Trent's Journal." For further commentary on the Uprising with reference to the siege of Fort Pitt, see Anderson, *Crucible of War*, 541–42; Dowd, *War under Heaven*, 190; McConnell, *Country Between*, 195; and Peckham, *Pontiac*, 226.

13. Calloway, *Scratch of a Pen*, 72–76.

14. For Pontiac's War, see Dixon, *Never Come*; Dowd, *War under Heaven*; Nester *"Haughty Conquerors"*; and White, *Middle Ground*, chap. 7.

15. Proclamation and Peace Treaty (1763), Johnson Family Papers, MG19-F2, NAC. For quotation, see Volwiler, *George Croghan*, 271; and Richter, *Before the Revolution*, 408–14.

16. Proclamation and Peace Treaty (1763), Johnson Family Papers, MG19-F2, NAC; Peter Wraxall, "Some Thoughts upon the British Indian Interest in North America more particularly as it relates to the Northern Confederacy commonly called the Six Nations," Memoir on North American Indians: Secretary of State Miscellaneous, Microfilm: B-6181, MG11-C05, NAC.

17. Calloway, *Scratch of a Pen*, 14.

18. In 1893, the historian Frederick Jackson Turner delivered a paper ("The Significance of the Frontier in American History") at the American Historical Association in Chicago that suggested that the origins of distinctive American characteristics could be traced to a frontier experience. As early pioneers pressed westward, Turner argued, they not only shed the traditions of their European ancestors but, more important, developed a uniquely innovative, competitive, and democratic society. Only when prewar and interwar American scholars began to test the degrees of applicability of Turner's Frontier Thesis did the Royal Proclamation of 1763 and related eighteenth century land treaties assume significance in the study of American history. In 1919, Clarence W. Alvord suggested that whenever the British ministries deliberated the colonial problem their primary concern rested not with the revolutionary centers in the east but rather with the policy of the west. Central to Alvord's argument was the Peace of Paris in 1763. Historians, Alvord maintained, could understand the successive plans of the English ministries for the newly acquired territories only insofar as they approached these programs with an understanding of the political situation of 1763, and of the proclamation issued on 7 October of the same year. See Turner, "Significance"; Alvord, *Mississippi Valley*. Also see Bolton, *Wider Horizons*. For other notable examples, see Paxson, *History*; and Branch, *Westward*.

In 1926, Albert Volwiler's book *George Croghan and the Westward Movement, 1741–1782* suggested that Pennsylvania and New York Indian agents such as Croghan and

William Johnson contributed the most to the opening of the west. Volwiler mounted an unwavering defense of the loyalty and dedication of the colonial agents in the northern district of the Indian Office to the development of America. According to Volwiler, the land-hungry tyranny of Virginian speculators coupled with the impact of "Pontiac's Rebellion" hastened the declaration of the 1763 proclamation and the new boundary. Thereafter, Crown agents such as Croghan and Johnson "advocated an Indian policy" based on friendship and fair dealings while land speculators coerced and cheated in an attempt to sidestep the proclamation boundary.

In contrast to Volwiler, in 1937 Thomas Perkins Abernethy staunchly defended Virginian gentry and militia claims to land west of the trans-Appalachian range. Citing prewar land incentives offered by Virginia governor Robert Dinwiddie, Abernethy contended that George Washington, Thomas Cresap, James Mercer, and others had legal title to land west of the mountains in spite of the 1757 declaration at Easton that forbade such settlements. Furthermore, Abernethy acknowledged the commercial interests of land speculators and conceded that many prominent settlers were connected in one way or another to land schemes. He depicted Croghan as a criminal and his superior, William Johnson, as a fat lord who "lived in feudal magnificence." Nevertheless, according to Abernethy, this "individualistic [and] hardy generation" of frontiersmen helped establish an early American identity. Though the birthing of an American identity from the intrepid "evils of the ancient forest" remains suspect, the agency of those players on the frontiers of empire continues to be relevant. See Abernethy, *Western Lands*, 16, 21–23, 70, 111. For a similar line of argument, see Bailey, *Ohio Company*, and Billington, *Westward Expansion*.

In 1961, Jack M. Sosin challenged the dominant opinion that the Royal Proclamation of 1763 was a hastily imposed imperial policy. Sosin's *Whitehall and the Wilderness* suggests that the costs of the Seven Year's War had such a devastating effect on provincial ability to sustain colonial ambitions that the Crown had little choice but to implement the proclamation in order to attempt to reduce conflict by curbing settlement. Therefore, the "proclamation of 1763 stemmed directly from the experience of the British officials in prosecuting the war in America." Sosin also argued that the most pressing problem that faced the colonies in 1763 was the dilapidated relationship with the nations that had led directly to the Uprising. According to him, the British government hoped that the proclamation would stabilize the backcountry and minimize the expense of aiding the defense of the colonies or financing retaliatory expeditions against first peoples who drove out unwanted settlers. Though Sosin did not challenge the notion that the boundary remained ineffectual in curbing settlement, *Whitehall and the Wilderness* reoriented colonial history by underscoring the impact of the 1763 decree. It would take almost a decade and a half before historians turned from the high politics of the proclamation to evaluate the effectiveness of the boundary. See Sosin, *Whitehall and the Wilderness*, 25–28, 77, 110.

Although the evidence Eugene Del Papa uses to argue that Virginia's House of Burgesses remained steadfastly loyal to Crown directive during the 1760s remains questionable, his 1975 article "The Royal Proclamation of 1763: Its Effects upon Virginian Land Companies" makes an important observation. From 1763 to 1768, the grand land companies of Virginia were unable to capitalize on land development because of the restrictions imposed by the proclamation. As a result, the primary shareholders in the Loyal Company and Ohio Company of Virginia, which included prominent statesmen, faced foreclosure and financial ruin. Building on these revisions, historian Mark Egnal, in *A Mighty Empire*, explains that the proclamation drove the landed gentry to revolution. Egnal contends that western settlement and legal land title, and thus the overthrow of the boundary, remained of utmost importance to colonial gentry. Land bred loyalty, and only when the gentry could secure title to land could they control politics. According to Egnal, historians have incorrectly attributed a long tradition of libertarian and democratic principles to both colonial settlers and gentry when really the acquisition of land and political power remained the central motivation behind the actions of the revolutionary leaders.

In addition to arguing that the Virginia gentry exercised unparalleled control over the lower classes in the colony, a decade later Woody Holton declared that the "assumption that the Proclamation was an imaginary line that did not halt settlement is incorrect." His *Forced Founders*, esp. 7–30, emphasizes the authority imperial declarations carried, especially those that restricted the securing of indigenous lands. Regardless of the number of Indian deeds speculators may have held, they could not sell a clear title to land until the Crown authorized a root title. Indian deeds were not completely worthless, but they had only a speculative value worth a fraction of a valid title. Although Holton acknowledges that at the 1758 treaty of Easton the Crown insisted that settlement west of the Appalachians was forbidden, because of the Seven Years' War the matter remained in legal limbo until the Royal Proclamation of 1763. Subsequently, land jobbers such as George Washington and Arthur Lee were denied access to land they hoped to claim with Virginia land certificates. To make matters worse, renegade settlers poured across the boundary and established legal interests by squatters rights while the hands of speculators remained tied unless they engaged settlers to work with them and hold the land. In the end, Holton maintains, Virginia's gentry found the stifling of liberty to speculate, trade, and swindle grounds for revolt.

19. Calloway, *Scratch of a Pen*, 93–100.

20. On Pontiac at Ouiatenon and Detroit, see White, *Middle Ground*, 303–305. Amherst to Johnson, 10 September 1763, New York, WJP 4:201. Also see Cave, *French and Indian War*, 91.

21. McConnell, *Country Between*, 236.

22. Johnson to Colden, 20 September, 1763, WJP 4:205.

23. The Board of Trade expressed its disapproval of Amherst's policies as early as September 1763. By November it was evident in Johnson Hall that the direction of policy was to be seriously reconsidered; Richter, "Native Americans," 9. The text of the Plan of 1764 is printed at PA 4:182–89.

24. Johnson to Gage, 17 November 1763, PA 4:137. Johnson's reference to the Seneca settlements in the Ohio is implicit in the letter.

25. PA 1:143.

26. PCR 9:91.

27. Johnson to Colden, 30 December 1763, WJP 4:281. Johnson's opinion was most likely influenced by intelligence reports throughout the autumn of 1763. For one example, see Johnson to Amherst, 6 October 1763, PCR 9:63.

28. On 19 December 1763, Colden wrote the Lords of Trade: "It is not long since SW [Sir William] gave me a very different account of the Disposition of the Five Nations. . . . I advise SW to be cautious in supplying the Indians with Ammunition, and I am confident, they will at all times be willing to give intelligence to the Enemy as to us. . . . I am humbly of opinion, that we can never be secure against that fierce, cruel and rapatious spirit, natural to the Indians, without makeing them afraid of punishment, and this may be done by chastising the most obnoxious and ungratefull nation the Sinnekes." DRCHSNY 7:589.

29. Johnson to Colden, 24 December, 1763, WJP 4:273–74.

30. Gage to Johnson, 12 January 1764, WJP 4:291.

31. Johnson to Gage, 12 January 1764, WJP 4:294. The same sentiments were stressed in a second letter to Gage a week later; see Johnson to Gage, 20 January 1764, WJP 4:300.

32. Johnson to Colden, 27 January 1764, WJP 4:306.

33. PA 4:162.

34. Johnson was convincing. On 10 March 1764, Governor Colden wrote to the Earl of Halifax: "This plainly evinces the great influence which Sir William had among the six Nations: for it has been at all times difficult, to make one Indian nation attack another, when the quarrel was not their own. . . . The Five Nations formerly subdued the Delawares, & in the Indian phrase put Petticoats on them, that is, the Delawares were never afterwards to make war as a Nation. In the last war with France they revolted, joined the Shawenese, & told the Five Nations that We are Men." WJP 4:361. McConnell, *Country Between*, 237.

35. Johnson to Bradstreet, 2 March 1764, WJP 4:349; to Colden, 4:350; to Gage, 4:351–52.

36. Johnson to Gage, 1 March 1764, in Day, *Calendar*, 347–48: "[The Senecas] have even desired to be employed against the Shawanese & Delawares, and sent to call away all their People from amongst them, and are to leave three of their Chief Men Hostages for the performance of the Several Articles of Peace, all which, plainly shews that they repent of their late conduct, & their desire to regain our Esteem." Also see Johnson to Colden, 6 April 1764, WJP 4:387.

37. Quoted in Jennings, *Empire of Fortune*, 451. Also see White, *Middle Ground*, 291–94.

38. In fact, I have uncovered only a few references to conflict. On 16 March 1764, Johnson indicated to Governor Colden that he had heard a report that the war party led by Thomas King had scalped one Delaware and taken three prisoners; Johnson to Colden, WJP 4:365. In a letter to General Gage the same day, Johnson noted that "many of the Indians were desirous of going the length of the Scioto & falling upon the Shawanese who are scattered along that River but I have been unwilling to let them until they had first drove away the Delawares & few Shawanesees from all

the branches of the Susquehanna & Cleared that Quarter of such Villains." Gage responded to Johnson on 26 March, stating that Scioto and Muskingham "are part of the Plan." WJP 4:372–78. Both letters suggest that Johnson was not inclined to send warriors en masse against the Ohio nations. Quote from Ward, *Breaking the Backcountry*, 241. Merrell, "Cast of His Countenance," and Parmenter, "Iroquois," 111, both note that a war party led by Andrew Montour burned the Seneca-Delaware town of Kenestio in February 1764.

39. DRCHSNY 7:621–23. Also see WJP 4:383; and Wharton-Willing Papers, Box 1, 1669–1766, 2014, 73:24, HSP.

40. White, *Middle Ground*, 305.

41. Ward, *Breaking the Backcountry*, 241.

42. "I fear [we] will not find it an easy Matter to punish those Who realy deserve it, and the falling upon those yet our friends, and who are consequently not aware of any such Design would . . . be imprudent . . . since it must inevitably involve us in a general Quarrel." See Johnson to Colden, 12 January 1764, WJP 4:287–90.

43. "They repent of their late conduct," Johnson argued, "likewise have taken up the War Axe against our Enemies." See Johnson to Colden and Johnson to Gage, 6 April 1764, WJP 4:386–92.

44. Gage to Johnson, 22 April 1764, WJP 4:401–402. For an example of Gage's reliance on Johnson in terms of the intricacies of Indian Department affairs, see Gage to Johnson, 4 April 1764, WJP 4:385; 1 October 1764, WJP 4:550–51.

45. Gage to Johnson, 22 April 1764, WJP 4:401–402. Gage's attitude was again confirmed on 16 May when he wrote to the superintendent in response to recent news of peace overtures (WJP 4:424–26):

Those villains (Delawares and Shawnees) have received more of our Favors and done us more Mischief than all the Indians together. The Terms of Peace I send them are, That they shall deliver up the Ringleaders of the War, and the Murderers of Clapham [Col. in Penn] & the Traders, to be put to Death for their Crimes. That they deliver up all White men, & Negros whether Prisoners or adopted, French or English. That they renounce their Alliances, with any other Indians than the Six Nations. That they renounce in Favor of the Crown all Rights and Claims which they ever had, to the Lands on the East side of the Ohio, from the head of the River to the Sea (In this Case the Claims of so many Tribes to those Lands might be reduced to those of the Six Nations) That, if they have fallen on any of our Traders & plundered them, they shall repay the Losses of such Traders, at a certain Number of Skins Pr. year. . . . You will be pleased to add such other Articles as you see Necessary.

46. WJP 4:426.

47. Interestingly, Johnson remained transfixed with separating the Six Nations from the Ohio nations, at least in the mind of Gage, well after British "offenses" had ceased. See Johnson to Gage, 8 November 1764, in Day, *Calendar*, 243. Johnson went

so far as to ask Gage his opinion of further action, if any, that needed to be taken with the Senecas considering their recent help and "humanity towards soldiers"; Johnson to Gage, 6 December 1764, ibid., 247.

48. White, *Middle Ground*, 291.

49. Ibid.

50. For the Niagara conference proceedings, see 17 July–4 August, 1764, WJP 11:285; for uncertainty of the alliances, see Gage to Johnson, 15 August 1764, WJP 4:509.

51. In numerous letters to Gage, Colonel Bradstreet made it clear that he desired to punish the rebel tribes by attacking them. White, *Middle Ground*, 291.

52. White, *Middle Ground*, 291–92. Also see conference references for 7–10 September 1764 and 29 September 1764, in Day, *Calendar*, 237–38.

53. Gage blasted Bradstreet, indicating that the peace with the Shawnees and Delawares was "unauthorized and derogatory to the honor of his Majesty's arms." Gage to Johnson, 2 September 1764, in Day, *Calendar*, 234.

54. White, *Middle Ground*, 291–92. Also of interest is that Bradstreet and Bouquet did have orders from Gage allowing them to attack Shawnees and Delawares. The Senecas were not, however, on his list.

55. "Magazines, 1755, 1759, 1766," Fort Pitt Museum Collection, Roll 4608, PHMC, 182; White, *Middle Ground*, 294. Thomas Wharton to Ben Franklin, 13 November 1764, Benjamin Franklin Papers, FG1106, APS.

56. Dixon, *Never Come*, 237–38.

57. For full version of the council, see Waddell, *Papers of Henry Bouquet*, 17–20 October 1764, 6:669–674; and 17 October 1764, WJP 4:439–36.

58. Many captives did not wish to return to colonial society. For more on the dynamics of captivity, see Axtell, "White Indians"; and Ward, "Redeeming the Captives."

59. Dixon, *Never Come*, 240–41; White, *Middle Ground*, 300–305.

60. Dixon, *Never Come*, 242.

61. McConnell, *Country Between*, 233–34; White, *Middle Ground*, 289.

62. Ward, *Breaking the Backcountry*, 251.

63. See Wallace, "Origins."

64. Gage to Johnson, 24 December 1764[?], WJP 4:269.

65. Thomas Gage to Johnson, 26 December 1763, WJP 4:278–80. On the tribes under Pontiac, see Gage to Johnson, 12 January 1764, WJP 4:292. Gage also noted five weeks later that he believed the Detroits sought peace to trade as much as the English wished for it: "These Considerations may possibly induce many Nations to join with us to put a Speedy end to a War." Gage to Johnson, 20 February 1764, WJP 4:334.

66. Johnson to Gage, 12 January 1764, WJP 4:296.

67. WJP 4:331–33.

68. Gage to Johnson, 28 May 1764, WJP 4:432.

69. Johnson to Colden, 9 June 1764, WJP 4:442–44.

70. "To the Kings Most Excellent Majesty in Council From Ben Franklin, agent appointed by the Assembly of Pennsylvania, 1759," Penn Family Papers, Indian Affairs 1687–1801, vol. 3, 69, HSP.

71. DRCHSNY 2:454–55.

72. McConnell, *Country Between*, 234. Shannon, *Indians and Colonists*, 208–12, suggests that the Albany agreement was largely ignored.

73. White, *Middle Ground*, 289; Croghan to Johnson, 24 February 1763, WJP 4:339.

74. Richter, "Native Americans"; PA 4:182–89. Also see McConnell, *Country Between*, 234–35.

75. Richter, "Native Americans," 2–5.

76. Paxton was a settlement on the east bank of the Susquehanna River. See Jacobs, *Paxton Riots*, 2; and Vaughan, "Frontier Banditti," 3–4.

77. For accounts of the riots, see Edward Shippen to Gov. Penn, and Lancaster Sheriff John Hay to Gov. Penn, 27 December, 1763, PCR 9:103; Jacobs, "Paxton Riots," 3–4; and Dixon, *Never Come*, 246–48.

78. Gov. Penn to Johnson, and Gov. Penn to Gage, 5 January 1764, PCR 9:111–12.

79. PCR 9:133.

80. PCR 9:138–42.

81. 17 February 1764, PCR 9:142–45.

82. On "sectional antagonisms," see Jacobs, "Paxton Riots," 2, 15–17. Also see Hindle, "March."

83. Plan for Future Management of Indian Affairs, 1764; see points 1–6, PA 4:182–83.

84. Comm. of Trade to John Stuart, 10 July, 1764, PA 4:190, emphasis added.

85. McConnell, *Country Between*, 234. Shannon, *Indians and Colonists*, 13–15, 33–35.

86. PA 4:183; Richter, *Facing East*, 209.

87. The only clause that was to restrict the power of the superintendents included "in Cases of great Exigency, or when . . . the Superintendent may be in some remote part of his Distrct." PA 4:183.

88. McConnell, *Country Between*, 235–36.

89. Wainwright, *George Croghan*, 199–200.

90. WJP 4:208.

91. Bouquet to Gage, 22 December 1764; Stevens, *Papers of Henry Bouquet*, 6:342.

92. Testifying further to Croghan's self-interest were actions in Philadelphia on his way to London. Croghan lost no time engaging in several shady deals to finance his trip to London. He sold 30,000 acres in Cumberland County that he held in Indian deed only to Daniel Clark, his cousin, and Richard Peters of the Land Office. Croghan arranged to accept £1,000 as a down payment and an additional £2,000 within twelve months. Clark and Peters agreed to pay Croghan £17.10.0 per hundred acres of the tract. The land he sold, however, was from an Indian deed released to him by Thomas Penn for the sole purpose of selling and repaying outstanding funds Croghan owed merchant Richard Hockley. Even more scandalous was the fact that 2,000 of the acres were of the highest quality, previously owned by Hockley

and deeded to Croghan for the purpose of luring in potential buyers. Most of the other land was worthless for agricultural purposes, and Hockley would have to wait almost twenty years before receiving payment. In August 1763, Croghan sold additional lands, then at the heart of the 1763 Uprising, to his longtime creditors and erstwhile friends John Baynton, Samuel Wharton, and George Morgan. See Wainwright, *George Croghan*, 200–201.

93. Present at the tavern meetings were David Franks, Jeremiah Warder, Samuel Burge, George Croghan, John Coxe, Abraham Mitchell, William Trent, Robert Callender, Joseph Spear, Thomas McGee, Philip Boyle, and Samuel Wharton. See "Proceedings of a Meeting of Traders," WJP 4:264. Also see Slick, *William Trent*, 128.

94. It is important to note that the focus of the "Suffering Traders" was shortly thereafter centered on the losses incurred from the events of 1763. This decision was made by the primary investors (Baynton, Wharton, Croghan, and Trent), who had more to gain seeking restitution for losses in 1763 rather than 1754.

95. Abernethy, *Western Lands*, 54, contends that Croghan's trip to London was financed by New Jersey governor William Franklin. This connection is challenged by Mariboe, "Life of William Franklin," 278. Both authors fail to provide evidence to support their claims. What is known is that Croghan secured some money—the exact amount was never disclosed—from the Burlington Company of New Jersey, in which Franklin held interest. See Byars, *B and M Gratz*, 762.

96. Baynton, Wharton and Morgan: 1763–1768, George Croghan Papers, d. 1782, 1754–1808, Section 10, 1763, HSP.

97. For the text of the proposal, see *Pennsylvania Gazette*, 21 April 1763. For colonial reaction, see Benjamin Franklin to Richard Jackson, 10 June 1763, in Labaree, Boatfield, and Hutson, *Papers of Benjamin Franklin*, 10:286; Shirai, "Indian Trade," 193; and Johnson, DRCHSNY 7:959.

98. Alvord, *Mississippi Valley*, 1:94–95.

99. Ibid.; Barr, "Contested Land," 198–200.

100. Merchants to Moses Franks and George Croghan, Philadelphia 12 December 1763, WJP 4:267, 269, 270–71:

A Traffick with the Savages, being entirely in the way of Barter without the Use of Books, renders it very difficult, To furnish Accounts with that regularity, which may be expected by the Lords of Trade, We would therefore recommend to you, To prevail [upon] their Lordsships, if they should induce his Majesty to grant us Redress, To appoint Commissioners in this Government, To exam[ine] and liquidate the respective Traders Accounts.—perhaps, They may be influenced, to name Gentlemen in this City; If they can, Mr Croghan will recollect such, As will be proper. . . . We beg leave to request, That you will all Dispatch After Mr. Croghans arrival, converse with as great Number of Merchants, trading to this city & New York, As possible, and explain to Them How essentially their Trade is interested, in supporting Our Memorial to the Lords of Trade & what Advantages will result to Them, By having it favourably received.

101. Shirai, "Indian Trade," 157–58.

102. Ibid., 158.

103. Croghan to Johnson, 24 February 1764, WJP 4:339–41.

104. Croghan to Johnson, 10 March 1764, WJP 4:362.

105. Croghan lobbied Mr. Rice, a member of the Lords of Trade. On 14 April he sent word to Johnson updating his superior on the state of affairs. He indicated to Johnson that his recent efforts had not been in vain and that the Lords of Trade appeared happy with the news of Johnson's efforts against the Shawnees and Delawares. In addition, Croghan misleadingly assured Johnson that he is working tirelessly for his benefit, stating that he had "Don Nothing in My own affairs as yet Nor Do I See any Greatt probability of getting any thing in Restitucion for ye. Greatt Loss My Self & others Sustaind. ye. Beginning of ye. Late War." Croghan to Johnson, 14 April 1764, WJP 4:396–98.

106. Croghan to the Lords of Trade, 12 July 1764, DRCHSNY 7:602–605.

107. Ibid.

108. Shirai, "Indian Trade," 158.

109. Croghan to Johnson, 14 April 1764, WJP 4:399. Also see Croghan to Johnson, 11 May 1764: "P S: yr. Honour was plesd. To Write Me that if you Could you wold Take part of ye. Goods from Baynton & Wharton wh. I Menshond. To you in My Leter by Mr. MaKee wh. If you Can will greatly oblidge Me." WJP 4:422.

110. Johnson first learned his Indian deed did not meet with favor in London in early April 1764 via Croghan. On 6 April the superintendent sought advice on the tract of land he was given by the Conajoharee Mohawks in 1760. "Altho this Tract is as a free Gift from the Indians," Johnson wrote Governor Colden, "yet I gave them above 1200 Dollars after Signing & delivering me the Deed . . . Who from thence forward consider it my property." The superintendent asked Colden to accept his proposal to remit 10,000 acres of patent fees and deemed it necessary to have another meeting with the Iroquois "previous to taking out the Pattent. . . . as I understand the Proclamation, Affairs of this Nature remain with each governour & consequently can be soon Settled." Johnson to Colden, 6 April 1764, WJP 4:424–25.

111. Croghan to Johnson, 12 July 1764, WJP 4:462–66.

112. The Plan of 1764 was issued on 10 July 1764.

113. McConnell, *Country Between*, 237.

114. Jones, *License for Empire*, 78. This interpretation challenges Barr's view, *Contested Lands*, 195, of Croghan's time in London.

115. Croghan to Johnson, 10 March 1764, WJP 4:363.

116. Wharton-Willing Papers, Box 1, 1669–1766, 73:24, HSP. Marshall indicates in "Sir William Johnson," 161, that Croghan's debts ranged from £8,000 to £12,000 after the 1763 Uprising.

117. Col. John Armstrong to Gov. Penn, 17 July 1764, PA 4:193.

118. Wainwright, *George Croghan*, 209.

119. Pennsylvania currency. Baynton, Wharton and Morgan: 1763–1768, George Croghan Papers, d. 1782, 1754–1808, Section 10, 1763, 4–12, HSP.

120. Baynton, Wharton and Morgan: 1763–1768, George Croghan Papers, d. 1782, 1754–1808, Section 10, 1763, HSP. Also see Shirai, "Indian Trade," 164.

121. Baynton, Wharton and Morgan: 1763–1768, George Croghan Papers, d. 1782, 1754–1808, Croghan Papers, Section 10, 1763, HSP.

122. WJP 11:566.

123. Samuel Wharton to Ben Franklin 23 November, 1764 (FG 1104), Benjamin Franklin Papers, APS.

124. BWM to SWJ, Phil 24 April, Baynton, Wharton and Morgan Sequestered Papers, 1757–1787, Reel 2237, Roll 4, "General Correspondence" MG-19, 723, PHMC. A brief reference to this item is also listed at Day, *Calendar*, 218–19.

125. For Croghan's offer to Johnson, see Croghan to Johnson, 18 December, 1764, in Day, *Calendar*, 194. Although the exact whereabouts of the suggested tract is not disclosed in the reference, the illegal suggestion itself sheds light on Croghan's freedom of action while serving under Johnson. For "desire of Five Nations," see Johnson to Gage, 23 December 1764, ibid., 194–95, referenced from WJP 4:272.

126. Joseph Galloway to Benjamin Franklin, 25 January 1765, in Labaree, Boatfield, and Hutson, *Papers of Benjamin Franklin*, 12:26–27; Wainwright, *George Croghan*, 214; Cave, *Ohio*, 9–11.

127. The massacre of the Conestoga Susquehannocks in December 1763 tipped off a series of provincial debates in Pennsylvania that left the authorities at a political impasse by March 1764. The Assembly, or "Quaker" party, maintained that the proprietors were to blame, having monopolized western lands for a future market, which drove up prices of land and in turn pushed settlers to other colonies and left the "frontier" thinly populated and exposed to attacks. In March 1764, the Assembly agreed to pursue a policy to royalize the proprietary colony and sent Benjamin Franklin to London to petition the Crown. The proprietary government, on the other hand, argued that the Assembly had failed on multiple instances to provide adequate supplies to the backcountry inhabitants at times of distress. For further reference to the royal campaign, see Hutson, *Pennsylvania Politics*.

128. Wainwright, *George Croghan*, 216.

129. Mariboe, "Life of William Franklin," 279–84; Ward, *Breaking the Backcountry*, 254.

130. For Baynton, Wharton and Morgan's concern, see Samuel Wharton to Johnson, 14 April 1765, WJP 4:712–16. For General Gage's reaction, see Gage to Johnson, 15 April 1765, WJP 4:717–18. Also see Thomas Wharton to Benjamin Franklin, 27 April 1765, in Labaree, Boatfield, and Hutson, *Papers of Benjamin Franklin*, 12:113–17.

131. Quoted in Wainwright, *George Croghan*, 217; Gage to Johnson, 27 April 1765, WJP 4:732–33.

132. Gage to Johnson, 15 April 1765, WJP 4:715–18. For the second letter, see Gage to Johnson, 21 April 1765, WJP 4:721–23.

133. For defense of Croghan, see Johnson to John Penn, 12 April 1765, WJP 4:710–11. For the forewarning, see Johnson to Croghan, 4 April 1765, WJP 4:706–707.

134. Johnson to Gage, 27 April 1765, WJP 4:732–33. Johnson also went as far as to blame Samuel Wharton for the mishap, suggesting that he "deserves to be Condemned [for sending] goods without a pass." See Johnson to Gage, 4 May 1765, WJP 4:735.

135. After this Croghan incident, borderland settlers near Fort Loudon insisted on inspecting all goods passing through the area. In May, Joseph Spear, a trader from Carlisle, was attacked at the fort by approximately thirty men disguised by blackened faces. The drivers of the merchandise, which included liquors and "warlike" goods, were whipped and five of their horses killed. See PCR 9:269. Also see Calloway, *Scratch of a Pen*, 76–80.

136. Etting Collection, no. 38, "Croghan-Gratz Papers," Vol. 1, File 38–2: "George Croghan Letters/Journal 1765," HSP.

137. Ward, *Breaking the Backcountry*, 256.

138. Slotkin, *Regeneration*, 5–16.

139. George Croghan Papers, Series 4, Box 8. no. 6, Croghan Private Journal, Fort Pitt to the Illinois Country, 1765, 1766, Cadwalader Collection, HSP.

140. The instances of Croghan's awareness are numerous throughout the march. On 15 June he recorded the following after arriving at a French settlement on the Wabash: "The country is level and clear and the soil is very rich, producing Wheat and tobacco. . . . the inhabitants here-abouts are an idle lazey people . . . much worse than the Indians." For 18–19 June a similar tone can be noted: "We traveled through a prodigious large Meadow, called the Pyankeshas hunting grounds—here is no woods to be seen, and the country appears like an ocean—the Ground exceedingly rich and partly overgrown with wild hemp the lands are well watered and full of Buffaloes, Deer and all kind of Wild Game." Cadwalader Collection, George Croghan Papers, Series 4, Box 8, no. 6, "Croghan Private Journal, Fort Pitt to the Illinois Country, 1765, 1766," HSP.

141. "Journal of Colonel Croghan's Transactions with the Western Indians," 4–8 July 1765, DRCHSNY 7:780–82.

142. William Franklin to Benjamin Franklin, 17 December 1765, in Labaree, Boatfield, and Hutson, *Papers of Benjamin Franklin*,12:403–406. WJP 4:743; Calloway, *Scratch of a Pen*, 29.

143. Croghan to Johnson, [?] November 1765, DRCHSNY 7:787–88.

144. Croghan to Johnson, 27 December 1765, WJP 4:886–89; Wharton-Willing Papers, Box 1, 1669–1766, HSP.

145. Croghan to Ben Franklin, 25 February, 1766, Cadwalader Collection, George Croghan Papers, Series 4, Box 8. no. 6, Croghan Private Journal, Fort Pitt to the Illinois Country, 1765, 1766, HSP. Also see WJP 5:37–38.

146. Croghan to Johnson, 27 December 1765, WJP 4:888.

147. For Johnson's message to the Board of Trade, see WJP 5:37–38, 196–97. For Illinois Company details, see "Articles of Agreement" for the first Illinois Co.," 29 March 1766, Cadwalader Collection, George Croghan Papers, HSP. Also, Samuel Wharton

to Thomas Wharton, 11 August 1766, Wharton-Willing Papers, Box 1, 1669–1766, HSP.

148. Volwiler, *George Croghan*, 191.

149. Wainwright, *George Croghan*, 212. Volwiler, *George Croghan*, 177, also views Croghan's excursion to the Illinois as an admirable venture on behalf of the English Crown.

150. The letter indicates that Croghan left a parcel of goods "in our Hands . . . expecting, you would be kind enough, to purchase them from us for his Account. . . . As we have not had the honour of hearing from you, on the Subject, we suppose Mr. Croghan's Letter must have miscarried & Therefore we presume to trouble you upon the occasion." Baynton, Wharton and Morgan to Johnson, 4 April 1764, WJP 4:384.

151. Croghan Papers, Section 10, 1763, 10–12, 16, HSP.

152. On 5 January 1765, the Trent and Levy Co. (of which Croghan held primary interest) was joined by Robert Callender, Alexander Lowrey, Thomas Mitchell, and Thomas Smallman (Croghan's cousin). The newly formed consortium of traders sent a memorial to General Gage to ask to recommend to Sir William Johnson that he organize an upcoming council with the Six Nations in order to grant the traders restitution for their losses in 1754/5 and 1763. Johnson agreed to do so, but he decided that restitution would be sought only for 1763 losses. See Slick, *William Trent*, 129.

153. Johnson informed Robert Leake, a senior colonial government agent from Albany, of the capture of Captain Bull of the Delawares and added: "The people in N York no doubt are too selfish to admit persons readily into their Land schemes Except where it may be of little value. There is a good deal of Land about the Western parts of this province unlocated, but at the same time such as the lands. would not readily dispose of." Regarding the Kayaderosseras patent, Johnson also noted that it was "fraudulently obtained in Q Annes time . . . had given great disgust to the Mohawks & been the occasion of their present dislike to selling Lands." Finally, Johnson offered to purchase land on behalf of Leake. Johnson to Robert Leake, 9 March 1764, WJP 4:359–60.

154. On the Mohawk protests, see Johnson to Colden, 21 September 1764, in Day, *Calendar*, 237. Also see DRCHSNY 4:853–92.

155. See Johnson to the Lords of Trade, DRCHSNY 7:670–75, and Johnson to Gage, WJP 4:624. On resistance to renegotiating the patent as noted in the New York Assembly, see 3 November 1764, Johnson to Colden, in Day, *Calendar*, 243.

156. Johnson to Colden, 27 February 1765, WJP 4:653–54. For Johnson's repeated concern over the Kayaderosseras patent, see letters from Johnson to Colden marked "private," WJP 4:655–56; Johnson to Colden, 27 February 1765, in Day, *Calendar*, 257; Johnson to Gage, 9 March 1765, WJP 4:665.

157. Colden to Johnson, 15 March 1764, WJP 4:681–82. For Colden to Lords of Trade, see WJP 4:711–12. For a record of the discussion at Fort George, see "The Kayaderosseras Patent," WJP 4:683–85.

158. Johnson to Colden, 21 March 1764, WJP 4:693–94.

159. Johnson to Gage, 22 March 1764, WJP 4:699, emphasis added.

160. On 17 December 1764, Johnson wrote Lt. Col. Charles Lee in London, indicating that he believed that if the Kayaderosseras region was vacated it would result in the sale of almost 200,000 acres of land. Day, *Calendar*, 244.

161. DRCHSNY 7:718: "there were many conferences previous to [the opening] day."

162. DRCHSNY 7:724–25. Also see William Trent Journal, 1759–1763, 2–4, HSP.

163. DRCHSNY 7:728.

164. DRCNSNY 7:729–30.

165. DRCHSNY 7:730.

166. Lt. Gov Colden to Lords of Trade, 8 June 1765, DRCHSNY 7:744.

167. For detailed description of the petitioners, see Nammack, *Fraud*, chap. 5.

168. Wharton, Facts and Observations.

169. Parmenter, "*Iroquois*," 111.

4. BOUNDARIES

1. Hinderaker and Mancall, *At the Edge*, 141–42.

2. Jones, *License for Empire*, 74–75.

3. Gage to Johnson, WJP 11:987.

4. McConnell, *Country Between*, 237; Marshall, "Colonial Protest"; Sosin, *Whitehall*, 110–17.

5. Ward, "Indians Our Real Friends," 76.

6. Governor Moore to the Lords of Trade, 12 August 1766, DRCHSNY 7:849.

7. Croghan to Gage, 17 June 1766, "Transcript of Correspondence," 12 March 1763–12 June 1808, George Croghan Papers, HSP.

8. Quoted from Ward, "Indians Our Real Friends," 77.

9. Ridner, "Relying on the 'Saucy' Men," 136–37. For further discussion on trade ca. 1750–70, see Auth, *Ten Years' War*; Hinderaker, *Elusive Empires*, 147–70; Merritt, *At the Crossroads*, 60–86; White, *Middle Ground*, chap. 7; McConnell, *Country Between*, 162; Richter, *Facing East*, chap. 5; Usner, "Frontier Exchange Economy, 217–39.

10. Johnson to the Lords of Trade, Johnson Hall, 8 October 1766, DRCHSNY 7:871.

11. Ibid., 7:872–73.

12. Gov. Moore to the Earl of Shelburne, 11 November 1766, DRCHSNY 7:877–78.

13. Stuart to Johnstone, 13 and 17 December 1766, Indian Affairs Correspondence, 1755–1830, Microfilm, A-612, 118–19, NAC.

14. Johnson to Baynton, Wharton and Morgan, 30 January 1766, WJP 5:16–17.

15. On 5 January 1766, Johnson wrote to John Baynton indicating that in Charlestown people had inquired about purchasing local lands. Johnson sent word to Baynton that he informed the individuals of Baynton's ownership of the land and directed all such queries to him. General Correspondence, 1758–1787, Baynton, Wharton and Morgan Sequestered Papers, 1757–1787, Reel 2234, Roll 2, PHMC.

16. Croghan to Franklin, 25 February 1766, WJP 5:38–39.

17. Croghan to Johnson, 30 March 1766, WJP 5:128–29. Also see Wharton-Willing Papers, Box 1, 1669–1766, 29 April 1766, "Articles of Agreement," HSP.

18. George Croghan to Benjamin Franklin, 25 February 1766, in Labaree, Boatfield, and Hutson, *Papers of Benjamin Franklin*, 13:171–73.

19. Croghan to Johnson, 30 March 1766, WJP 5:128–29. Also see Wharton-Willing Papers, Box 1, 1669–1766, 29 April 1766, "Articles of Agreement," HSP.

20. See Johnson to William Franklin, 3 May 1766, and William Franklin to Johnson, 7 June 1766, Wharton-Willing Papers, Box 1, 1669–1766, HSP. Also see William Johnson to Benjamin Franklin and William Franklin to Benjamin Franklin, 10 July 1766, in Labaree, Boatfield, and Hutson, *Papers of Benjamin Franklin*, 13:330, 333.

21. Articles of Agreement, 29 April 1766, Box 1, 1669–1766, Wharton-Willing Papers, HSP.

22. Johnson to William Franklin, 3 May 1766, Box 1, 1669–1766, Wharton-Willing Papers, HSP.

23. Benjamin Franklin to Joseph Galloway, Benjamin Franklin to William Franklin, 10 May 1766, in Labaree, Boatfield, and Hutson, *Papers of Benjamin Franklin*, 13:276.

24. Record of journey later submitted to Johnson, 15 January 1767, Croghan Papers, File 5, 1766–1768, HSP. The following nations signed the Fort Charters treaty: "Pecrins, Kaskaskeys, Mitchigamis, Cahokias, Pyankichaas, Wawiatanons, Kikapoos, Masgrtamis, Poutewatemis, Sackees, Outagamis, _____wees[?]."

25. New York currency.

26. Gage to Johnson, 5 October 1766, WJP 5:386; Wainwright, *George Croghan*, 239.

27. Penn to Croghan, 11 April and 12 September 1767, Penn Letter Book 9:107, 118, HSP.

28. Nelson, *Man of Distinction*, 55–57.

29. Johnson to Gage, 3 April 1767, in O'Callaghan, *Documentary History*, 2:846. 30. Wainwright, *George Croghan*, 244–50.

31. William Trent to Baynton, Wharton and Morgan, 1 April, 21 April, and [?] June 1767, Baynton, Wharton and Morgan Sequestered Papers, Roll 5, Reel 2235, PHMC.

32. For housekeeping bills, see Irwin to Baynton, Wharton and Morgan, 3 June 1767, Baynton, Wharton and Morgan Sequestered Papers, General Correspondence, 1758–1787, Roll 2, Reel 2235, PHMC; Receipt of Loan, File 38–14, Croghan-Gratz Papers, vol. 1, Etting Collection 38, HSP.

33. See Croghan to Johnson, 25 September 1767 and 1 March 1768, WJP 5:700–702, 6:129; Samuel Wharton to Ben Franklin, 30 September 1767, and Croghan to Penn, 1 October 1767, Cadwalader Collection, HSP; DRCHSNY 7:985–86.

34. Wharton to Croghan, 21 July 1771, Cadwalader Collection, HSP.

35. Amos to Johnson, 12 August 1767, Superintendent of Indian Affairs, Series I, Lots 657–58, NAC, emphasis added.

36. McKee to Johnson, 20 September 1767, WJP 5:686–87; Nelson, *Man of Distinction*, 56.

37. Croghan Private Journal, no. 8, 28 October and 6 November 1767, George Croghan Papers, Ser. 4, Box 8, Cadwalader Collection, HSP.

38. For further reference to heightened Ohio Country affairs, see Samuel Wharton to Benjamin Franklin, 20 September 1767, in Labaree, Boatfield, and Hutson, *Papers of Benjamin Franklin*, 14:257–60.

39. Moore to Shelburne, 7 December 1767, DRCHSNY 7:1003. Gage to Governor Moore, 7 December 1767, PCR 9:403.

40. [Citation to be added in Proofs.]

41. Jones. *License for Empire*, 88.

42. Moore to Shelburne, 7 December 1767, DRCHSNY 7:1004–1005, emphasis added.

43. Thomas Penn to Johnson, 1 January 1768, WJP 12:405–406.

44. 13 January 1767, PCR 9:405–11; Wharton, *Facts and Observations*, 6.

45. PCR 9:411.

46. A Letter to the Governor from James Galbreath and John Hoge, Esqs., East Pennsborough, 29 February 1768, PCR, 9:487. On the Stump affair, see Reis, "Rage."

47. PCR 9:414–16.

48. On 22 January, Billy Champion (Delaware) complained to the provincial government that Newoleeka (a Delaware chief) was "much displeased that five white men had lately been marking Trees and Surveying Land in the Forks of the Susquehanna, as yet not been purchased from the Indians." Council with Government in Philadelphia, 22 January 1768, PCR 9:426.

49. Pennsylvania Assembly to Benjamin Franklin and Richard Jackson, 19 January 1768, WJP 12:417–18.

50. PCR 9:427–33; Documents Relative to the Wyoming or Connecticut Controversy FG 1003, APS.

51. Croghan to Baynton, Wharton and Morgan, [?] February 1768, Baynton, Wharton and Morgan Sequestered Papers, General Correspondence, 1758–1787, Roll 2, Reel 2235, PHMC. On Six Nation discontent, see Johnson to John Penn, 18 February 1768, WJP 12:431–32.

52. Croghan to Johnson, 2 February 1768, WJP 6:91–92.

53. Croghan to Johnson, 7 February 1768, WJP 12:425.

54. Pennsylvania currency.

55. On the allotment of funds, PCR 9:462, 468; Thomas Wharton to Benjamin Franklin, 9 February 1768, Benjamin Franklin Papers, FG 1817, APS; Johnson to Croghan, 5 March 1768, WJP 6:107; John Penn to Johnson, 18 February 1768, WJP 12:432–34; instructions for Shippen and Allen, PCR 9:493–95; testimony of angered backcountry inhabitants, PCR 9:462.

56. Earl of Hillsborough to Governor Moore, 25 February 1768, DRCHSNY 8:11.

57. On 10 March, Croghan signed over 70 percent of his shares of the "soon to be land" to fellow Ohio Company member William Trent, who paid John Hughes (one of Croghan's creditors) £4,500. See Indenture, 10 March 1768, Deed of George Croghan to William Trent, Wharton-Willings Papers, HSP.

58. Johnson to Penn, 29 February 1768, WJP 12:453–54; Johnson to Joseph Galloway, 1 March 1768, WJP 12:544–46.

59. Writing to Croghan on 16 March 1768, Johnson prepared his deputy for the arrival of the outgoing Cherokee delegation at Fort Pitt, Little Carpenter included, and noted, "I must say, I never See the Six Nations so hearty in any thing, as in this Peace." WJP 12:472.

60. Journal of Indian Affairs, Johnson Hall, 1–3 March 1768, WJP 12:456–58.

61. Johnson to Gage, 5 March 1768, WJP 12:459–60.

62. Treaty with the Six Nations and the Seven Confederate Nations of Canada and the Deputies of the Cherokee Nation, DRCHSNY 8:38–53.

63. Johnson to John Penn, 15 March 1768, WJP 12:467–69.

64. Croghan to Johnson, 18 March 1768, WJP 12:473–74.

65. Lords of Trade on State of Indian Affairs, 17 March 1768, DRCHSNY 8:22.

66. Ibid., 8:19–27.

67. Earl of Hillsborough to the Governors in America, 15 April 1768, DRCHSNY 8:55–56.

68. On adverse sentiment, see William Franklin to Johnson, 23 May 1768, WJP 12:511.

69. Lord Hillsborough to Johnson, 12 March 1768, DRCHSNY 8:35:

The Fixing the Boundary line will I trust remove the first great Foundation of Jealousy and Discontent from the minds of the Indians and be solid proof to them of the Sincerity of his Majesty's Intentions; And I flatter myself I shall very soon be enabled to signify his Majesty's pleasure with regard to the conduct of the Indian Trade in general; the unjustifiable occupancy of their Lands; the Posts that are to be maintained; and the particular Duties of your Office. . . . I have the honour to inclose to you a Map, whereon is delineated the Boundary Line proposed by the Board of Trade to be Settled with the Six Nations in conformity to what was agreed upon at the Congress in 1765, and also those lines settled with the Choctaws, Creeks and Cherokees, by the Superintendent for the Southern District. This Map may possibly be of some us as it will shew in what manner the several lines are meant to be united.

70. "That no time be lost at this critical Juncture, I would have you dispatch a Message immediately to the Six Nations living along the Ohio, the Shawanese, Delawares, and such other tribes in that part of the Country as have had any of their People killed by ours since the Peace, to meet you at Fort Pitt, as soon as possible." Johnson to Croghan, 29 February 1768, "Transcript of Correspondence" (March 12, 1763–June 12, 1808), George Croghan Papers, 1754–1808, HSP.

71. For Croghan's business transactions both before and after Stanwix, see Deed of Croghan to William Trent, 10 March 1768; "Bond," George Croghan to Joseph Galloway and Thomas Wharton, 10 December 1768; "Indenture" and "Deeds," George Croghan to William Trent and Joseph Galloway and Thomas Wharton, 31 January 1769; Deeds, Samuel Wharton to Thomas Wharton, 31 January 1769, Wharton-

Willings Papers, Box 2, 1767–1771, HSP; Croghan to Benjamin Franklin, 12 February 1768, in Labaree, Boatfield, and Hutson, *Papers of Benjamin Franklin*, 15:42–44.

72. *Minutes of Conferences Held at Fort-Pitt, In April and May 1768, under the direction of George Croghan, Esquire, Deputy Agent for INDIAN Affairs, with the Chiefs and Warriors of the Ohio and other Western INDIANS* (Philadelphia: William Goddard, 1869), LCP:

> Six Nations (Chiefs): Keyashuta, White Mingo, Soneno, Allyondongo, Onaughkong, Gettyqueaye, Onondagago, Cadedonago, Soggoyadentha, Thonissagarawa, Oyanay, Toeaughquottet, (Chief Warriors): Toeageda, Toedassaho, Kennissoen, Thagonneyesus, Dawatdehough, Awanneynatha; Delawares (Chiefs): Custettoga, Beaver, Latourt, Spawagassa, Nessicuthethem, Cascatehon, Kekiwenum, Washawanon, Mahetoaughkong, Loyalaughaland, Tugasso, (Chief Warriors): Cpt. Jacobs, Winganum, Cpt. Pipe, Cpt. Johnny, Grey Eyes, White Wolf, Theckhoton, Opemalughim, Killaykhehon, Wiesahoxon. Shawnees (Chiefs): Kaysinnaughtha (Hard Man), Etawakissaho, Maughkatethwa, Maykypuckathey, Maughkatemawaywa, Nymwha, Bennoxcumma, Naynichtha, Wassaynametha, Wethawathocks. (Chief Warriors): Thethawgay, Waughcomme, Othawaydia, Mawaydia, Munnena, Kawcomme, Shilleywathetha, Quighbya. Munsies (Chiefs): Auttemaway, Kendasseong, Wassawayhim, Quekquahim, Waughellapo. Mohickons (Chiefs): Wennighjalis, Kelleigheon, and seven Wyandots.

Also see PCR 9:515–544.

73. *Minutes of Conferences*, 4, LCP.

74. As James Merrell remarks, although significant differences can be noted in treaty records depending on who was speaking, translating, and recording, historians have been left with a rich source detailing deliberations. Both Europeans and the nations were aware that the record of events could and most likely would be used in the future as reference. As a result, days would often pass as the prime movers of negotiations hammered out the details of the subsequent deliberations before having them "officially" recorded. James Merrell, informal discussion, McNeil Center for Early American Studies, March 2006. Also see Merrell, "I desire."

75. Hagedorn, "Faithful, Knowing, and Prudent," 53–60.

76. *Minutes of Conferences*, 9, LCP, emphasis added.

77. Ibid., 12.

78. Ibid., 14. The terms of Bradstreet's treaty negotiations are explored in chapter 3. For an expanded summary of the events, see chapter 2, and Jones, *License for Empire*, 90–91. The subservience of the Ohio Valley nations to the Six Nations was also being underscored in other venues; see An Indian Conference at Guy Park, 16 May 1768, WJP 12:507.

79. Johnson to Croghan, 5 March 1768, and Instructions to George Croghan, 5 March 1768, WJP 12:461–62, 462–64.

80. *Minutes of Conferences*, 13–18, LCP.

81. Joseph Rigby to Baynton, Wharton and Morgan, 28 May and 11 June 1768, Baynton, Wharton and Morgan Sequestered Papers, Roll 5, Reel 2238, PHMC.

82. Shippen to David Jameson, 20 June 1768, and Shippen to William Mackay, 29 June, 1768, Joseph Shippen Letterbook, Edward and Joseph Shippen Papers, American Indian Manuscripts, APS.

83. Hillsborough to the Governors of America, 11 July 1768, DRCHSNY 8:82.

84. Moore to Hillsborough, 4 July 1768, DRCHSNY 8:78.

85. Guy Johnson the General Gage, 30 May 1768 and 16 June 1768, WJP 12:519–21, 525–27; Guy Johnson to Hillsborough, 20 June 1768, DRCHSNY 8:76.

86. Johnson to Gage, 20 July 1768, WJP 12:552–56.

87. Gage to Guy Johnson, 5 June 1768, WJP 12:522–23; also see Guy Johnson to Gage, 5 July 1768, WJP 12:543–45.

88. An Indian Congress at Johnson Hall, 8 to 28 June 1768, WJP 12:529–43.

89. An Indian Conference with the Mohawks at Johnson Hall, 28 July 1768, WJP 12:555–56.

90. On Indian unrest, see "An Indian Congress" with Chippewas at Guy Park, 10 to 16 July 1768, and Johnson Hall, 22 to 27 July 1768, WJP 12:548–50, 558–63.

91. An Indian Conference with the Mohawks at Johnson Hall, 2–4 August 1768, WJP 12:578.

92. Ibid., 12:579.

93. Johnson to Hillsborough, 17 August 1768, DRCHSNY 8:94–95.

94. Hillsborough to Johnson, 17 August 1768, DRCHSNY 8:100–101.

95. Jones, *License for Empire*, 87–88. Sosin, *Whitehall*, 128–64.

5. THE 1768 TREATY OF FORT STANWIX

1. Luzader, *Fort Stanwix*, 8–16.

2. Ibid., 17.

3. Wharton (Thomas? Samuel?) to Ben Franklin, 2 December 1768, Benjamin Franklin Papers, FG 1109, APS.

4. Guy Johnson to General Gage, 4 May 1768, WJP 12:489.

5. Johnson to Gage, 20 July 1768, WJP 12:555.

6. Congress at Fort Stanwix, WJP 12:617–19.

7. WJP 8:111.

8. The treaty as recorded in the DRCHSNY indicates that Wharton and Trent arrived at Fort Stanwix on 21 September with Governor Penn. Evidence suggests, however, that the 21st marked only the first day they spoke, on record. They had arrived with Johnson two days earlier; see WJP 12:618.

9. Wharton (Thomas? Samuel?) to Ben Franklin, 2 December, 1768, Benjamin Franklin Papers, FG 1109, APS; Johnson to Gage, 12 September 1768, WJP 6:363.

10. Croghan is identified as present at a Six Nations council at Johnson Hall as early as 22 June 1768; see An Indian Congress, WJP 12:558.

11. WJP 12:618–19.

12. William Trent Journal, 1759–1763 AM 170, HSP.

13. "Congress at Fort Stanwix," WJP 12:619–620; Calloway, "Pen and Ink Witchcraft."

14. The chief in question was later identified as Onoghkaridawey; see WJP 12:621.

15. Johnson to Hillsborough, Fort Stanwix, 23 October 1768, DRCHSNY 8:104.

16. Johnson to Gage, 13 October 1768, WJP 6:436.

17. Johnson to John Glen, 16 October 1768, WJP 12:607–608.

18. John Bradstreet to Johnson, 20 October 1768, WJP 6:445.

19. Daniel Campbell to Johnson, 21 October 1768, WJP 6:446.

20. John Bradstreet to Johnson, 25 October 1768, WJP 6:449.

21. WJP 12:623–24.

22. WJP 12:624–25.

23. WJP 12:625–26.

24. Johnson to Hillsborough, 23 October 1768, DRCHSNY 8:104–106.

25. Those chief negotiators assembled at Fort Stanwix on Monday 24 October included Sir William Johnson; New Jersey governor William Franklin; Chief Justice of New Jersey Fred Smith; Virginia commissioner Thomas Walker; Pennsylvania commissioners Peters and Tilgham; Indian agents George Croghan, Daniel Claus, and Guy Johnson; interpreters John Butler, Andrew Montour, and Philip Philips; Mohawk chiefs Abraham, Aroghiadecka, Onahario, Kanadagaya, Kayenqueregoa, Kendrick, and Tobarihoga; Onondaga chiefs The Bunt, Diaquanda, Tawawshughti, and Tewawmit; Seneca chiefs Guastrax and Odongot; Oneida chiefs Ganaghquieson, Senughsis, Tagawaron, Nicholasera, and Cajuheta; Cayuga chiefs Tagaaia, Atrawawna, and Skanarady; Tuscarora chiefs Saquarcesera, Kanigot, and Tyagawehe; and select "Mingoes of Ohio." Benevissica stood for the Shawnees; Killbuck and Turtleheart spoke on behalf of the Delawares. See DRCHSNY 8:111–12.

26. DRCHSNY 8:114

27. "Proceedings of Sir William Johnson with the Indians at Fort Stanwix to settle a Boundary Line," DRCHSNY 8:114.

28. Ibid.

29. DRCHSNY 8:116–17.

30. DRCHSNY 8:118.

31. Wharton (Thomas? Samuel?) to Benjamin Franklin, 2 December 1768, Benjamin Franklin Papers, FG 1009, APS.

32. Ibid.

33. DRCHSNY 8:118–19.

34. DRCHSNY 8:119.

35. Ibid. On Teyohaqueande history, see "Deiaquande," *Dictionary of Canadian Biography*, www.biographi.ca/EN/ShowBio.asp?BioId=36309&query=Deiaquande.

36. Wharton (Thomas? Samuel?) to Ben Franklin, 2 December 1768, Philadelphia, Benjamin Franklin Papers, FG 1009, APS.

37. DRCHSNY 8:120.

38. DRCHSNY 8:120–21.

39. Gage to Guy Johnson, 11 July 1768, WJP 12:546.

40. Johnson to Gage, 20 July 1768, WJP 12:552–57.

41. Gage to Johnson, 14 August 1768, WJP 6:394.

42. To avoid their settlements between Owego and Oswego, they demanded that the "Line should run up the Delaware to the Swamp & from that run across to the Governors (Cosbys Land) and then go away to lake George which we can not but think a fair offer." DRCHSNY 8:122.

43. DRCHSNY 8:121.

44. DRCHSNY 8:121–22.

45. For a record of the Treaty of Hard Labor, see University of Nebraska–Lincoln, Envisioning the West, http://jeffersonswest.unl.edu/archive/view_doc.php?id=jef.00092.

46. Wainwright, *George Croghan*, 256–57.

47. O'Callaghan, *Documentary History*, 4395.

48. DRCHSNY 8:122–23.

49. DRCHSNY 8:123–24. The four sachems were Tyaruruante, Ganaquieson, Tyeransera, and Tagawaron.

50. DRCHSNY 8:124.

51. DRCHSNY 8:124–25.

52. DRCHSNY 8:126.

53. A. F. Wallace, "Iroquois Indians: Treaties and Treaty Journals, 1701–1857," A. F. Wallace Papers, Misc. Coll. 64, Series 9, APS:

On the east side of the east branch of the River Susquehannah, at a place called Owegy, and running with the said boundary line, down the said branch on the east side thereof till it comes opposite the mouth of a creek called by the Indians Awandac (Tawandee) and across the river and up the said creek on the south side thereof, along the range of hills called Brunette Hills by the English, and by the Indians, on the northside of therein, to the heads of a creek which runs into the west branch of the Susquehannah, which creek is by the Indians called Tiadughton (Pine Creek—as noted in 1784), and down the said creek on the south side thereof, to the said west branch of Susquehanna, then crossing the said river, and running up the same on the south side thereof, the several courses thereof to the fork of the same river which lies nearest to place on the River Ohio called the Kittanning, and from the said fork by a straight line to Kittanning aforesaid, and then down the said river Ohio by the several courses thereof to where the western bounds of the said Province of Pennsylvavnia cresses the same river, and then with the said western bounds to the south boundary aforesaid to the east side of the Allegheny hills, and with the said hills on the east side of them to the west line of a tract of land purchased by the said proprietors from the Six Nation Indians, and confirmed October 23d, 1758, and then with the northern bounds of that tract of land purchased of the Indians by deed (August 22d, 1749) and then with that northern boundary line to the river Delaware at the north side of the mouth of a creek called Lechawaachasein, then up the said river Delaware on the west side thereof to the intersection of it, by an east line to be drawn from Owegy aforesaid to the said river Delaware, and then with that east line to the beginning at Owegy aforesaid.

54. A report of the Board of Trade of 7 March 1767 states: "Your Majesty will be pleased to observe that altho on the one hand the Settlements in the new established Colonies to the South are confined to very narrow limits; yet on the other hand the middle Colonies (whose state of population requires a greater extent) have room to spread much beyond what they have hitherto been allowed and that upon the whole one uniform and complete line will be formed between the Indians and those antient Colonies, whose limits not being confined to the Westward has occasioned that extensive settlement." Clarence Walworth Alvord, "The British Ministry and the Treaty of Fort Stanwix," Proceedings of the State Historical Society of Wisconsin at its 56 annual meeting, 15 October 1908, Madison, Published by the Society, 1909, LCP.

55. See Johnson's letter 26 June 1769, quoted in Jones, *License for Empire*, 89.

56. Thomas Penn to William Johnson, 2 November 1768, David Library of the American Revolution Collection, APS.

57. DRCHSNY 8:127–28.

58. Ibid.

59. Ibid.

60. Wharton, *Facts and Observations*.

61. William Trent Journal, 1759–1763, 4–5, HSP.

62. DRCHSNY 8:127–28.

63. Wharton (Thomas? Samuel?) to Benjamin Franklin, 2 December 1768, Philadelphia, Benjamin Franklin Papers, FG 1109, APS.

64. DRCHSNY 8:127.

65. DRCHSNY 8:127–28.

66. DRCHSNY 8:129.

67. DRCHSNY 8:129–30.

68. DRCHSNY 8:131–32.

69. DRCHSNY 8:131–33.

70. Ibid.

71. DRCHSNY 8:134.

72. Wharton (Thomas? Samuel?) to Benjamin Franklin, 2 December 1768, Philadelphia, Benjamin Franklin Papers, FG 1109, APS.

73. DRCHSNY 8:135–36.

74. DRCHSNY 8:136.

75. Knepper, *Ohio*, 33. For a detailed recounting of the events, also see Samuel Wharton to Benjamin Franklin, 2 December 1768, in Labaree, Boatfield, and Hutson, *Papers of Benjamin Franklin*, 15:275–79.

76. Parmenter, "Iroquois." For account of goods sent to the Ohio, see DRCHSNY 8:132–34.

77. The Six Nations chiefs to sign the treaty and deed were Abraham (Mohawk), Conoghquieson (Oneida), Sequarusera (Tuscarora), Bunt or Otsinoghiyata (Onondaga), Tegaaia (Cayuga), and Guastrax (Seneca). The Virginian commissioners were Thomas Walker and Richard Peters, and James Tilghman represented Pennsylvania. For Λ. F. Wallace's brief reference to the event, see "Iroquois Indians: Treaties and Treaty Journals, 1701–1857," A. F. Wallace Papers, Misc. Coll. 64, Series 9, APS.

78. In August 1751, Johnson acquired approximately 130,000 acres on the Charlotte River from the Mohawks for £300. Furthermore, in December 1760 he purchased 80,000 acres from the Canjoharee Mohawks on the Mohawk River for $1,200. See Marshall, "Sir William Johnson," 159–161; Flexner, *Mohawk Baronet*, 112.

79. Marshall, "Sir William Johnson," 149; Jones, *License For Empire*, 89.

80. Wharton, *Facts and Observations*.

81. Hillsborough to Johnson, 12 October 1768, DRCHSNY 8:101.

82. Wharton (Thomas? Samuel?) to Benjamin Franklin, 2 December 1768, Benjamin Franklin Papers, FG 1109, APS. For reference to "farce," see Shannon, *Iroquois Diplomacy*, 168–69.

83. Wharton, *Facts and Observations*.

84. Jones, *License for Empire*, 94.

6. PROSPECTS, AND THE COLLAPSE OF PROTOCOL

1. The deed to the Suffering Traders was issued to William Trent (the assigned power of attorney) on 7–12 January 1769. Present were the mayor of Philadelphia, Isaac Jones, and Richard Peters. The deed read as follows:

Whereas: Robert Callender, David Franks, Joseph Simon Levy, Andrew Levy, Phillip Boyle, John Baynton, Samuel Wharton, George Morgan, Joseph Spear, Thomas Smallman, Samuel Wharton, Administrator of John Welch, deceased. Edward Moran, Evan Shelby, Samuel Postlethwait, John Gibson, Richard Whiston, Dennis Cronon, William Thompson, Abraham Mitchell, James Dundas, Thomas Dundas and John Ormsby . . . [have appointed] William Trent of the County of Cumberland and Province of Pennsylvania . . . their lawful attorney and agent . . . to receive from the Sachems, Councellors and Warriors of the said united nation[s], a grant of a tract of land, as a compensation. satisfaction or retribution for the Goods, Merchandise and Effects of the said William Trent and the Traders aforesaid which the Shawese, Delaware and Huron tribes, tributaries of the said six nations (contrary to all good faith and in violation of their repeated promises of safety and protection to their persons, servants and effects (whilst trading in their country), did in the spring of the year One Thousand, Seven Hundred and sixty-three, violently seize upon and unjustly appropriate to their own use, and Whereas are now convened in full Council by order of our Father the King of Great Britain and France and Ireland, defender of the faith, etc., at Fort Stanwix, in the province of

New York in order to agree for asertain and finally fix and settle a permanent and lasting boundary line . . . and whereas the said Sir William Johnson, Baronet has now at this present Congress reminded the said Six United Nations of their said promise, and at the earnest desire of the aforesaid Traders by their said attorney strongly recommended to the Six United Nations to make them a restitution by a Grant of a Tract of Land to his said Majesty . . . to and for the only Use, Benefit and Behalf of the said William Trent in his own right and as Attorney as aforesaid . . . [the Six Nations] therefore by these presents signify, publish and declare that notwithstanding the grant and gift hereby made and given by them unto his said Majesty . . . and Behalf of the said William Trent in his Own Right and as Attorney . . . will be included within the Cession Sale and Boundary Line which the said United Six Nations shall and will make, sell and grant. . . . yet, nevertheless the said Six United Nations have neither asked, demanded, nor received . . . consideration for the hereby given and granted premises. . . . And for and in consideration of the sum of Five Shillings . . . all the Tract or Parcel of Land beginning at the Southerly side of the Mouth of Little Kanahawa Creek, where it empties itself into the river Monongahela, then down the stream of the said River Monongahela, according to the several courses thereof to the southerly boundary line of the Province of Pennsylvania, thence westerly along the course of the said Province Boundary Line as far as the same shall extend and from thence by the said course to the River Ohio, thence down the said River Ohio according to the several courses thereof t the Place of beginning, together with and all singular, the Trees, Weeds, and Under-Woods, Mines, Minerals, Oares, Waters, Water Courses, Fishings, Liberties, Privileges, Herditaments and Appurtenances, whatsoever, to the said Tract or Parcel of Land. . . . And also all the estate, right, title Interest, Property claims and demands whatsoever, whether native, legal or equitable, of us, the said Indians.

The deed was signed and validated on 12 January 1769 in Philadelphia by Abraham ("The Steel"), Sennghois ("The Stone"), Sagaurisera ("The Cross"), Choaugheata ("The Mountain"), Tagaaia ("The Pipe"), and Gaustarax ("The High Hill"). See Deed at Fort Stanwix for Traders Losses—Iroquois Indians to William Trent and Others, 3 November 1768, American Indian Manuscripts, Misc. Mss. FG 1718, APS.

2. Jones, *License for Empire*, 117–18.

3. Volwiler, *George Croghan*, 224.

4. Maxey, "Honorable Proprietaries," 367.

5. Calloway, "Pen and Ink Witchcraft."

6. Johnson to Hillsborough, 18 November 1768, DRCHSNY 8:110–11; Weaver, *Great Land Rush*, 190.

7. Letter to Henry Moore from William Johnson, 24 November 1768, William Fenton Papers Relating to Indian Affairs, 1709–1797, Mss. Film 637, APS.

8. Sir Henry Moore's Message, 6 December 1768, William Fenton Papers Relating to Indian Affairs, 1709–1797, Mss. Film 637, APS. Moore also helped Johnson by writing to Hillsborough to urge that the Crown act swiftly to ratify the boundary in New York; see Moore to Hillsborough, 27 January 1769, DRCHSNY 8:149.

9. Hillsborough to Johnson, 4 January 1769, DRCHSNY 8:144–45.

10. The Lords of Trade to the King, DRCHSNY 8:160–62. For discussion of the Treaty of Hard Labor, see ibid. The text describes the various boundary lines negotiated by Mr. Stuart with the Cherokees during the 14 October to 12 November 1768 negotiations.

11. For discussion of trade regulation in the Pennsylvania Assembly, see PCR 9:554 55.

12. Johnson to Hillsborough, 15 February 1769, DRCHSNY 8:150–52.

13. Assembly to Governor, 24 May 1769, PCR 9:592:

His Majesty having thought proper to take the Management of the Trade with the Indian Nations out of the Hands of His Superintendents of Indian Affairs, and to leave the Management of the Provinces concerned in said Trade, Sir William Johnson finds himself under the Necessity of discharging immediately the Commissaries, Interpreters, and Smiths appointed by him in the Posts and Forts in the interior Country. . . . If the Provinces will appoint Officers to superintend the Trade in such parts of the Indian Country where they appear from their Situations to enjoy the chief Benefit of the Trade, Pennsylvania will appoint at Fort Pitt and the Illinois, New York at Niagara and the Detroit, and Quebec at Misilimakanak.

Gage to Governor Penn, 24 March 1769, PCR 9:581–82: "Our Laws for regulating the Trade with [the Indians] appear to be deficient. . . . our attempting to extend the Laws of this Province beyond the Limits thereof, would be in vain and ineffectual to regulate and restrain the Traders from the adjunct Colonies." For discussion of the transfer of power to the colonies, see Council held at Philadelphia, 15 January 1770, PCR 9:645.

14. Hillsborough to Johnson, 13 May 1769, DRCHSNY 8:165–66.

15. Lords of Trade to the King, "Representation of the Board of Trade to the King upon Sir William Johnson's Treaty with the Indians," 25 April 1769, DRCHSNY 8:158–60.

16. Connecticut council with Governor Penn, 13 February 1769, PCR 9:569–70. On news of settlers, see A Letter to the Governor from Lewis Gordon, ESQ., Easton, 7 February 1769, PCR 9:572. Penn letter to Connecticut governor, PCR 9:574. For Penn's proclamation details, see PCR 9:588.

17. Johnson to Hillsborough, 26 June 1769, DRCHSNY 8:172–73.

18. Johnson to Hillsborough, 21 August 1769, DRCHSNY 8:179–81.

19. Ibid., 8:181.

20. Ibid., 8:181–82.

21. Merrell, *Into the American Woods*, 302.

22. 18–19 July 1769, PCR 9:603–604.

23. Minutes of the council held with Indians at Shamokin with Colonel Francis, 19 August 1769, PCR 9:610–14.

24. Ibid., 9:614–20.

25. Johnson to Hillsborough, 26 August 1769, DRCHSNY 8:183–86.

26. Johnson to Hillsborough, 10 February 1770, DRCHSNY 8:203–204; Hillsborough to Johnson, 14 April 1770, DRCHSNY 8:211.

27. Johnson to Hillsborough, 12 July 1770, DRCHSNY 8:222. For grievances, also see John Penn in council with Seneca Indians, 22 August 1770, PCR 9:604–607.

28. Proceedings of Sir William Johnson with the Indians, July 1770, DRCHSNY 8:227–31.

29. Ibid., 8:231–44.

30. Ibid.

31. Ibid.

32. Excerpt of the Lords of Trade to the King in Johnson the Hillsborough, 15 February 1769, DRCHSNY 8:163.

33. Hillsborough to Johnson, 13 May 1769, DRCHSNY 8:165–66; Hillsborough to Governor Moore, 13 May 1769, DRCHSNY 8:165.

34. New York currency.

35. For a record the Croghan-Galloway-Wharton-Trent transactions, see "Bond— George Croghan to Joseph Galloway and Thomas Wharton" and "Deed 'Indenture' made between William Trent and Joseph Galloway and Thomas Wharton," 10 December 1768, Wharton-Willing Papers, HSP. For record of Thomas Wharton's debt to John Hughes, see "To Thomas Wharton from John Hughes," 16 November 1768, Wharton-Willing Papers, HSP. For reference to the Croghan's dealings with the Burlington Company and William Franklin, see Volwiler, "George Croghan." For agreements between Croghan and Gratz, record of land sale for 9,050 acres lying on the south side of the Mohawk River, 1 November 1770, Croghan-Gratz Papers, vol. 1, Etting Collection, no. 38, HSP. Of additional note, on 13 December 1768, William Trent thereafter sold John Hughes 5,000 acres he was granted by the Suffering Trader shareholders for his services as an attorney for the sum of £1000; see "William Trent article for 5000 acres on the Ohio," 13 December 1768, Hughes Papers B-116, no. 302, HSP. Also see "Indenture" Thomas Stevenson to George Croghan, 25 December 1769, Croghan-Gratz Papers, vol. 1, Etting Collection, no. 38, HSP; and "Indenture 1770— Croghan et al. . . . New York Lands, 1768, 1770," George Croghan Papers, Ser. 4, Box. 8, no. 15, Cadwalader Collection, HSP. Furthermore, brothers Thomas and Samuel Wharton made land and money exchanges based on a series of post–Fort Stanwix transactions with Croghan. Thomas Wharton paid Samuel Wharton £800 for "1/5 of 50,000 acres of land on the River Susquehannah"; see Wharton "Deeds," 28 January and 31 January 1769, Wharton-Willing Papers, HSP. Wainwright, *George Croghan*, 261; Taylor, *William Cooper's Town*, 13, 46.

36. Abernethy, *Western Lands*, 40–41. For evidence of financial difficulties, see John Campbell to George Morgan, 20 March 1769, and George Morgan of Baynton, Wharton and Morgan, Evidence of Bond Transaction with John Hughes, N. D. Baynton, Wharton and Morgan Sequestered Papers, 1757–1787 Microfilm MG-19, Roll No. 5:851–69, PHMC.

37. Abernethy, *Western Lands*, 42–43.

38. "I trust no countenance or attention either has been or will be given to any application for those lands . . . upon the ground of private agreements with the Indians, contrary to the directions of the Proclamation of 1763." Hillsborough to Moore, 13 May 1769, DRCHSNY 8:165.

39. Dr. Slop is a character in Laurence Sterne's nine-volume *The Life and Opinions of Tristram Shandy, Gentleman*, first published in 1759. Slop was an ill-humored and devious male midwife of Catholic persuasion. Given the Irish ancestry of both Croghan and Johnson, this was a notable insult. Wharton to Croghan, 18, 27, 28 May 1769, Cadwalader Collection, HSP.

40. Wetherhead to Johnson, 12 February 1770, WJP 7:388.

41. Croghan to Johnson, 10 May 1770, WJP 7:651–54.

42. Volwiler, "George Croghan," 32–33. For discussion detailing the division of Croghan's possessions, see Ben Chapman to George Morgan, 26 May and 30 August 1770, Baynton, Wharton and Morgan Sequestered Papers, 1757–1787, MG-19, Roll 5, PHMC.

43. Croghan to Trent, 30 November 1769, Croghan-Gratz Papers, vol. 1, Etting Collection, no. 38, HSP.

44. Trent to Croghan, 11 June 1769, WJP 7:16–17.

45. In addition to Pownall and Walpole, notable members of the new lobby group included Lord Hertford; member of the Ministry Lord Camden; Richard Jackson, counselor to the Board of Trade and former secretary to George Grenville; George Grenville; Privy Council members Lord Gower and Lord Rochford; Parliament member Lachlan Macleane; John Robinson, under-secretary of the treasury; Grey Cooper, joint secretary of the treasury; and Thomas Pitt, British post-master general. Taking a back seat to the Londoners were men of influence in British North America, including the Whartons, Trent, Johnson, Croghan, Galloway, the Franklins, and the Franks. For further detail on the Walpole Company, see Abernethy, *Western Lands*, 44–58; Marshall, "Lord Hillsborough."

46. Wharton, *Facts and Observations*; Cadwalader, *History*.

47. Abernethy, *Western Lands*, 46. A record of the Walpole petition can be seen in the Records of the Proprietary Government 1629–1828, Pennsylvania Land Grants, 1681–1806, Penn Family Papers, vol. 9, HSP.

48. Abernethy, *Western Lands*, 47–49.

49. Jones, *License for Empire*, 110, 117.

50. John Campbell to George Morgan, 20 March and 15 April 1769; John Finley to James Rumsey, 1 November 1769; James Rumsey to George Morgan, 10 October 1769, Baynton, Wharton and Morgan Sequestered Papers, 1757–1787, MG-19, Roll 5:851–69, 24–27, 11–12. PHMC.

51. Croghan to Gage, 1 January 1770, Croghan Papers, 1754–1808, HSP; WJP 12:406–408, 488.

52. Croghan to Johnson, 16 November 1769, DRCHSNY 4:420.

53. The visitor was Richard Smith, 26 May 1769. Quoted from Volwiler, "George Croghan," 29.

54. Parmenter, "Iroquois," 111.

55. "Proceedings of the Congress at German Flatts," July 1770, DRCHSNY 8:239. Jennings, *Invasion of America*, 120–22; Jones, *License for Empire*, 95.

56. Johnson to Hillsborough, 14 August 1770, DRCHSNY 8:224–27; Jones, *License for Empire*, 102.

57. Hurt, *Indian Frontier*, 14

58. Johnson to Hillsborough, 14 August 1770, and Hillsborough to Governors of America, 15 November 1770, DRCHSNY 8:224–27, 254. Quotes from Volwiler, *George Croghan*, 229.

59. Johnson to Hillsborough, 18 February 1771, DRCHSNY 8:262–63; Edward Shippen to Joseph Shippen, 25 April 1771, Shippen Papers, vol. 2, APS; Hillsborough to Johnson, 4 May 1771, DRCHSNY 8:270.

60. For July treaty details, see Johnson to Hillsborough, 6 August 1771, DRCHSNY 8:280–83.

61. At the second congress at Scioto in 1771, the Shawnees acknowledged their past subordination to the Grand Council but declared that, since the Six Nations neglected them, they now had the right live as they pleased, where they pleased. See Jones, *License for Empire*, 107–108.

62. Johnson to Hillsborough, 4 April and 29 June 1772, DRCHSNY 8:290–92, 300.

63. Hillsborough to Johnson, 1 July 1772, DRCHSNY 8:302.

64. For a list of Johnson's expenses post-1768, see "William Johnson's accounts from 1768 to1773," Superintendent of Indian affairs in the northern district of north America fonds, c. 1753–1829, Microfilm H 2943, NAC, and Volwiler, *George Croghan*, 229.

65. Document dated 10 December 1771, Land Transactions, Cadwalader Collection, HSP; Volwiler, *George Croghan*, 223–24. For Bradstreet's claims, see Lord Dunmore to Hillsborough, 2 April 1771, and Johnson to Bradstreet, 23 December 1771, DRCHSNY 8:267–68, 287.

66. Croghan to B. Gratz, 7 July 1772 and 8 September 1773, Croghan-Gratz Papers, vol. 1, Etting Collection, no. 38, HSP; Volwiler, "George Croghan," 33–34; Earl of Dartmouth to Johnson, 2 September 1772, DRCHSNY 8:311.

67. Proceedings of Sir William Johnson with the Mohawks, 28 July 1772, DRCHSNY 8:304–308.

68. Johnson to Dartmouth, 4 November 1772, DRCHSNY 8:311–14.

69. Johnson to Dartmouth, 26 December 1772, DRCHSNY:340–41.

70. Dartmouth to Johnson, 3 February and 10 April 1773, DRCHSNY 8:348, 360; Johnson to Dartmouth, 22 March and 30 April 1773, DRCHSNY 8:361, 368; Proceedings of William Johnson with the Six Nations, 7–10 April 1773, DRCHSNY 8:362–67.

71. Tyron to Dartmouth, 2 June 1773, DRCHSNY 8:374.

72. Dartmouth to Johnson, 4 August and 1 December 1773, DRCHSNY 8:393, 404; Johnson to Dartmouth, 22 September and 16 December 1773, DRCHSNY 8:395, 405.

73. Wharton to Croghan, 3 November and 24 December 1773, Cadwalader Collection, HSP. Thomas Wharton to Thomas Walpole, 27 December 1773, Thomas Wharton Letterbook, 1773–1784, Wharton-Willing Papers, HSP.

74. Abernethy, *Western Lands*, 55–58, quote on 57.

75. Calloway, "Pen and Ink Witchcraft."

76. Abernethy, *Western Lands*, 78–90; Dowd, *Spirited Resistance*, 40–46. For more on Daniel Boone, see Lofaro, *Daniel Boone*.

77. McKee met with White Mongo at Croghan's house, 3 May 1774; Meeting with principle inhabitants of Pittsburg with several six Nations and Delawares [and] Shawanese, 5 May 1774, DRCHSNY 8:465–67.

78. Extract from the Journal of Alexander McKee, Sir William Johnson's Resident on the Ohio & Ca., 1 May 1774, DRCHSNY 8:464. Abernethy, *Western Lands*, 97, 113.

79. Wharton to Croghan, 17 and 21 March 1774, Wharton Letter Book, Wharton-Willing Papers, HSP. Abernethy, *Western Lands*, 96–97; Croghan to Dunmore, 9 April 1774, Cadwalader Collection, HSP. Volwiler, *George Croghan*, 300–301; Taylor, *William Cooper's Town*, 49.

80. Johnson with Indians at Johnson Hall, 18 April 1774, DRCHSNY 8:424–29; Johnson to Dartmouth, 2 May 1774, DRCHSNY 8:421–24; Johnson to Earl of Dartmouth, 20 June 1774, DRCHSNY 8:459–60.

81. Dartmouth to Johnson, 6 July 1774, and Guy Johnson to Dartmouth, 12 July 1774, DRCHSNY 8:471, 486.

82. Johnson's last council with Indians, June and July 1774, DRCHSNY 8:474–80.

83. Guy Johnson to Earl of Dartmouth, 6 October 1774; 'Proceedings of Col. Guy Johnson with the Six Nations,' Johnstown, September 1774, DRCHSNY 8:495, 496–506, quote on 499.

84. Hurt, *Indian Frontier*, 15, 57–58.

85. Jones, *License for Empire*, 107.

EPILOGUE. REVOLUTION AND REDEFINITION

1. Council with Six Nations, 14 July 1774; and Guy Johnson to Dartmouth, 14 December 1774, DRCHSNY 8:480–82, 516.

2. Washburn, "Indians."

3. Taylor, *Divided Ground*, 72.

4. Ibid., 72–82; Preston, *Texture of Contact*, epilogue.

5. Volwiler, "George Croghan," 32–35; Regarding Baynton, Wharton and Morgan's relationship with Croghan, written by George Morgan [n.d.], George Croghan Papers, 1754–1808, Section 10, 2, HSP.

6. Volwiler, "George Croghan," 43.

7. Croghan's bills were covered by Barnard Gratz, an old merchant friend and creditor of the agent. Gratz, in return for his services, was awarded more than one hundred thousand acres of Croghan's Indian deeds. See George Croghan Estate, 1747–1816, vol. 43, Croghan-Gratz Deeds, Etting Collection, 1558–1917. HSP.

8. PA, Series 1, vol. 10: 250; Bothwell and Scott, "George Croghan;" Wainwright, 304–306.

9. Graymont, *Iroquois*, 142 ; Bilharz, *Oriskany*, chap. 3.

10. Treaty with the Six Nations, 22 October 1784, in Kappler, *Indian Affairs*, 5–6.

11. Taylor, *William Cooper's Town*, 45.

12. Manley, *Treaty*, 10, 113.

13. Hauptman, *Conspiracy*, 63.

14. Edmunds, "Northeast," 247; quote from Campisi, "Colonial," 71.

15. Prucha, *American Indian Treaties*, 42–46.

Bibliography

ARCHIVES

American Philosophical Society, Philadelphia, Pa.
  A. F. Wallace Papers
  American Indian Manuscripts, Misc. Mss.
  Benjamin Franklin Papers
  David Library of the American Revolution Collection
  Documents Relative to the Wyoming or Connecticut Controversy
  Shippen Papers
  William Fenton Papers Relating to Indian Affairs
David Library of the American Revolution, Washington Crossing, Pa.
Historical Society of Pennsylvania, Philadelphia, Pa.
  Cadwalader Collection
  Croghan-Gratz Papers
  Frank M. Etting Collection
  George Croghan Papers
  Penn Family Papers
  Wharton-Willing Papers
  William Trent Journal
Library and Archives Canada, Ottawa, Ont.
  Indian Affairs Correspondence
  Superintendent of Indian affairs fonds
Newberry Library, Chicago, Ill.
Pennsylvania Historical and Museum Commission, Harrisburg, Pa.
  Baynton, Wharton and Morgan Sequestered Papers
  Fort Pitt Museum Collection

PUBLICATIONS

Abernethy, Thomas Perkins. *Western Lands and the American Revolution.* New York: D. Appleton-Century Company, 1937, 1959.

Adelman, Jeremy, and Stephen Aron. "From Borderlands to Borders: Empires, Nation States, and the Peoples in between in North America History." *American Historical Review* 104:3 (1999): 814–81.

Alvord, Clarence W. "The British Ministry and the Treaty of Fort Stanwix." Proceedings of the State Historical Society of Wisconsin, 56th annual meeting, 15 October 1908. Madison: State Historical Society of Wisconsin, 1909.

———. *The Mississippi Valley in British Politics: A Study of Trade, Land Speculations and Experiments in Imperialism Culminating in the American Revolution,* 2 vols. Cleveland, Ohio: Arthur H. Clark, 1917; New York, 1959.

Anderson, Fred. *Crucible of War: The Seven Years' War and the Fate of Empire in British North America, 1754–1766.* New York: Alfred A. Knopf, 2000.

———. *The War That Made America.* New York: Viking, 2005.

Auth, Stephen. *The Ten Years' War: Indian-White Relations in Pennsylvania, 1755–1765.* New York: Garland, 1989.

Axtell, James. *The Invasion Within: The Contest of Cultures in Colonial North America.* New York: Oxford University Press, 1985.

———. "The White Indians of Colonial America." *William and Mary Quarterly* 32:1 (1975): 55–88.

Bailey, Kenneth P. *The Ohio Company of Virginia and the Westward Movement, 1748–1792.* Glendale, Calif.: Arthur H. Clark Company, 1939.

Barr, Daniel P. "Beyond the Pale: An Overview of Recent Scholarship pertaining to the Colonial Backcountry." *Early America Review* 2:4 (1998/1999).

———, ed. *The Boundaries between Us: Natives and Newcomers along the Frontiers of the Old Northwest Territory, 1750–1850.* Kent, Ohio: Kent State University Press, 2006.

———. "Contested Land: Competition and Conflict along the Upper Ohio Frontier, 1744–1784." Ph.D. thesis, Kent State University, Ohio, 2001.

Bellesiles, Michael. *Revolutionary Outlaws: Ethan Allen and the Independence on the Early American Frontier.* Charlottesville: University of Virginia Press, 1993.

Bilharz, Joy. *Oriskany: A Place of Great Sadness: A Mohawk Valley Battlefield Ethnography.* Boston: National Park Service, 2009.

Billington, Ray A. *America's Frontier Heritage.* Albuquerque: New Mexico University Press, 1972.

———. "The Fort Stanwix Treaty of 1768." *New York History* 25:2 (1944): 182–94.

———. *Westward Expansion: A History of the American Frontier.* New York: Harper and Row, 1949.

Bolton, Herbert E. *Wider Horizons of American History.* Notre Dame, Ind.: Notre Dame University Press, 1939.

Bothwell, Margareth Pearson, and Margery Shore Scott. *George Croghan: Pioneer.* Pittsburgh, Pa.: Pittsburgh Chapters of the American Revolution, n.d.

Branch, E. D. *Westward: The Romance of the American Frontier.* New York: Appleton, 1930.

Byars, William, ed. *B and M Gratz, Merchants in Philadelphia, 1754–1798.* Jefferson City, Mo.: Lewis, 1916.

Cadwallader, Colden. *The History of the Five Indian Nations of Canada, Which Are Dependent on the Province of New-York in America.* London: Published for T. Osbourne, 1747.

Calloway, Colin. "Pen and Ink Witchcraft." Preliminary draft of a book to be published by Oxford University Press, 2012.

———. *The Scratch of a Pen: 1763 and the Transformation of North America.* Oxford: Oxford University Press, 2006.

Campbell, William J. "An Adverse Patron: Land, Trade, and George Croghan." *Pennsylvania History* 76:2 (2009): 117–40.

———. "Converging Interests: Johnson, Croghan, the Six Nations, and the 1768 Treaty of Fort Stanwix." *New York History* 89:2 (2008).

———. "Seth Newhouse, the Grand River Six Nations and the Writing of the Great Laws." *Ontario History* 96:2 (2004): 183–202.

Campisi, Jack. "Colonial and Early Treaties, 1775–1829." In Donald Fixico, ed., *Treaties with American Indians*, vol. 1. Oxford: ABC-Clio, 2008.

Cave, Alfred. "The Delaware Prophet Neolin." *Ethnohistory* 46:2 (1999): 265–90.

———. *The French and Indian War.* Westport, Conn.: Greenwood Press, 2004.

———. "George Croghan and the Emergence of British Influence on the Ohio Frontier." In Warren Van Tine and Michael Pierce, eds., *Builders of Ohio.* Columbus: Ohio State University Press, 2003.

Cooper, James Fennimore. "William Cooper and Andrew Craig's Purchase of Croghan's Land." *Quarterly Journal of the New York State Historical Association, New York History* 12:4 (1931).

Crist, R. G. "George Croghan of Pennsboro." Paper presented before the Cumberland County Historical Society and Hamilton Library Association, May 7, 1964. Harrisburg, Pa.: Dauphin Deposit Trust Company, 1965.

Cronon, William. *Changes in the Land: Indians, Colonists, and the Ecology of New England.* New York: Hill and Wang, 1983.

Cronon, William, et al., eds. *Under an Open Sky: Rethinking America's Western Past.* New York: W. W. Norton, 1992.

Day, Richard E., ed. *Calendar of the Sir William Johnson Manuscripts.* Albany: New York State Library, 1909.

Deloria, Philip J. "What Is the Middle Ground, Anyway." *William and Mary Quarterly,* 3rd ser., 63:1 (2006): 15–22.

Del Papa, Eugene. "The Royal Proclamation of 1763: Its Effects upon Virginian Land Companies." *Virginia Magazine of History and Biography* 83:4 (1975): 406–11.

Dixon, David. *Never Come to Peace Again: Pontiac's Uprising and the Fate of the British Empire in North America*. Norman: University of Oklahoma Press, 2005.

Dowd, Gregory, *A Spirited Resistance: The North American Indian Struggle for Unity, 1745–1815*. Baltimore: Johns Hopkins University Press, 1993.

———. *War under Heaven: Pontiac, the Indian Nations, and the British Empire*. Baltimore: Johns Hopkins University Press, 2002.

Dunn, W. S. "Western Commerce, 1760–1774." Ph.D. thesis, University of Wisconsin, Madison, 1971.

Edmunds, R. David. "Northeast and the Great Lakes." In Donald Fixico, ed., *Treaties with American Indians*, vol. 1. Oxford: ABC-Clio, 2008.

Egle, William Henry, ed. *Pennsylvania Archives*, 3rd series. Harrisburg: State Printer, 1894.

Egnal, Mark. *A Mighty Empire: The Origins of the American Revolution*. Ithaca, N.Y.: Cornell University Press, 1988.

Engelbrecht, William. *Iroquoia: The Development of a Native World*. Syracuse, N.Y.: Syracuse University Press, 2003.

Faragher, John M. *"More Motley than Mackinaw."* In A. R. L Cayton and F. J. Teute, eds., *Contact Points: American Frontiers from the Mohawk Valley to the Mississippi, 1750–1830*. Chapel Hill: University of North Carolina Press, 1998.

Fenton, William. *American Indian and White Relations to 1830: Needs and Opportunities for Study*. Chapel Hill. N.C.: UNC Press for the Institute of Early American History and Culture, 1957.

———. *Great Law and the Longhouse: A Political History of the Iroquois Confederacy*. Norman: University of Oklahoma Press, 1998.

———. "Indian Treaty Protocol: The Crucible of Indian-White Relations." American Philosophical Society. 24 February 1979.

Fischer, Joseph. *A Well-Executed Failure: The Sullivan Campaign against the Iroquois, July–September 1779*. Columbia: University of South Carolina Press, 1997.

Fisher, David Hackett, and James C. Kelly. *Bound Away: Virginia and the Westward Movement*. Charlottesville: University of Virginia Press, 2000.

Fixico, Donald, ed. *Treaties with American Indians*, vol. 1. Oxford: ABC-Clio, 2008.

Flexner, James T. *Lord of the Mohawks: A Biography of William Johnson*. Boston: Little and Brown, 1979.

———. *Mohawk Baronet: Sir William Johnson of New York*. Syracuse: Syracuse University Press, 1959.

Foster, Michael K. "Who Spoke First at Iroquois-White Councils: An Exercise in the Method of Upstreaming." In Michael K. Foster, Jack Campisi, and Marianne Mithun, eds., *Extending the Rafters: Interdisciplinary Approaches to Iroquoian Studies*, 183–85. Albany: State University of New York Press, 1984.

Foster, Michael K. Jack Campisi, and Marianne Mithun, eds. *Extending the Rafters: Interdisciplinary Approaches to Iroquoian Studies*. Albany: State University of New York Press, 1984.

Galbreath, Charles. *Expedition of Celoron to the Ohio Country in 1749*. F. J. Heer Printing Co., 1921.

Ganter, Granville, ed. *The Collected Speeches of Sagoyewatha, or Red Jacket*. Syracuse, N.Y.: Syracuse University Press, 2006.

Garratt, John G., and Bruce Robertson. *The Four Indian Kings*. Ottawa: Public Archives of Canada, 1985.

Gipson, Lawrence Henry. *The British Empire before the American Revolution*. 15 vols. Idaho, and New York: Caldwell, 1936–1970.

Glatthaar, Joseph T., and James Kirby Martin. *Forgotten Allies: The Oneida Indians and the American Revolution*. New York: Hill and Wang, 2006.

Goldstein, Robert A. *French-Iroquois Diplomatic and Military Relations, 1609–1701*. The Hague: Mouton, 1969.

Graymont, Barbara. *The Iroquois in the American Revolution*. Syracuse, N.Y.: Syracuse University Press, 1972.

———. "Koñwatsiàtsiaiéñni." Dictionary of Canadian Biography Online. Toronto: University of Toronto Press, 1988.

Griffis, William Elliot. *Sir William Johnson and the Six Nations*. New York: Dudd, Meadows and Co., 1891.

Gwyn, Julian. "Sir William Johnson." Dictionary of Canadian Biography Online. Toronto: University of Toronto Press, 1988.

Hackett, David G. "The Social Origins of Nationalism: Albany, New York, 1754–1835." *Journal of Social History* 21:4 (1988): 659–81.

Hagerty, Gilbert. *Massacre at Fort Bull: The De Lery Expedition against Oneida Carry, 1756*. Woonsocket, R.I.: Mowbray, 1971.

Hagedorn, Nancy Lee. "'Faithful, Knowing, and Prudent': Andrew Montour as Interpreter and Cultural Broker." In Margaret Connell Szasz, ed., *Between Indian and White Worlds: The Cultural Broker*. Norman: University of Oklahoma Press, 1994.

Hale, Horatio. *Hiawatha and the Iroquois Confederation: A Study in Anthropology*. Salem, Mass.: Private printers, 1881.

———, ed. *Iroquois Book of Rites*. Philadelphia: Brinton, 1883.

Hamilton, Milton W. *Sir William Johnson, Colonial American, 1715–1774*. Port Washington, N.Y.: Kennikat Press, 1976.

Hauptman, Laurence M. *Conspiracy of Interests: Iroquois Dispossession and the Rise of New York State*. Syracuse, N.Y.: Syracuse University Press, 1999.

Havard, Gilles. *The Great Peace of Montreal of 1701*. Montreal: McGill-Queen's University Press, 2001.

Hazard, Samuel, ed. *Colonial Records of Pennsylvania: Minutes of the Provincial Council of Pennsylvania, from the Organization to the Termination of the Proprietary Government*, 16 vols. Harrisburg, Pa.: Theodore Finn and Co., 1851.

Hinderaker, Eric. "Liberty and Power in the Old Northwest, 1763–1800." In David C. Skaggs and Larry L. Nelson, eds., *The Sixty Years' War for the Great Lakes, 1754–1814*. Lansing: Michigan State University Press, 2001.

Hinderaker, Eric, and Peter Mancall. *At the Edge of Empire: The Backcountry in British North America*. Baltimore: Johns Hopkins University, 2003.

Hindle, Brooke. "The March of the Paxton Boys." *William and Mary Quarterly*, 3rd ser. (1946):461–86.

Holton, Woody. *Forced Founders: Indians, Debtors, Slaves and the Making of the American Revolution in Virginia*. Chapel Hill: University of North Carolina Press, 1999.

Hopkins, Kelly. "The Impact of European Material Culture on New York Ecologies, Economies, and Diplomacy, 1700–1730." *New England Journal of History* 62:1 (2005): 40–72.

Hurt, R. Douglas. *The Indian Frontier, 1763–1846*. Albuquerque: University of New Mexico Press, 2002.

———. *The Ohio Frontier: Crucible of the Old Northwest, 1720–1830*. Bloomington: Indiana University Press, 1996.

Hutson, James. *Pennsylvania Politics, 1747–1770: The Movement for Royal Government and Its Consequences*. Princeton, N.J.: Princeton University Press, 1973.

Inouye, F. T. "Sir William Johnson and the Administration of the Northern Indian Department." Ph.D. thesis, University of Southern California, 1951.

Jacobs, Wilbur. *Dispossessing the American Indian: Indians and Whites on the Colonial Frontier*. New York: Charles Scribner's Sons, 1972.

———. *The Paxton Riots and the Frontier Theory*. Chicago: Rand McNally, 1967.

———. *Wilderness Politics and Indian Gifts: The Northern Colonial Frontier, 1748–1763*. Lincoln: University of Nebraska Press, 1967.

Jennings, Francis. *The Ambiguous Iroquois Empire*. New York: W. W. Norton, 1984.

———. *Empire of Fortune: Crowns, Colonies, and Tribes in the Seven Years' War in America*. New York, W. W. Norton, 1988.

———. *The Invasion of America: Indians, Colonialism, and the Cant of Conquest*. Chapel Hill, University of North Carolina Press, 1975.

———. "The Scandalous Indian Policy of William Penn's Sons: Deeds and Documents of the Walking Purchase." *Pennsylvania History* 37:1 (1970): 19–39.

Jezierski, John V. "Imperii in Imperio: The 1754 Albany Plan of Union and the Origins of the American Revolution." *North Dakota Quarterly* 42:3 (1974): 18–35.

Johansen, Bruce E. *Debating Democracy: Native American Legacy of Freedom*. Santa Fe. N.M.: Clear Light, 1989.

Johnston, Charles M. "To the Mohawk Station: The Making of a New England Company Missionary—the Rev. Robert Lugger." In Michael K. Foster, Jack Campisi, and Marianne Mithun, eds., *Extending the Rafters: Interdisciplinary Approaches to Iroquoian Studies*. Albany: State University of New York Press, 1984.

Jones, Dorothy V. *License for Empire: Colonialism by Treaty in Early America*. Chicago: University of Chicago Press, 1982.

Kappler, Charles J., ed. *Indian Affairs: Laws and Treaties*, Vol. 2: Treaties. Washington, D.C.: Government Printing Office, 1904.

Knepper, George W. *Ohio and Its People*. Kent, Ohio: Kent State University Press, 1989.

Labaree, Leonard, Helen C. Boatfield, and James H. Hutson, eds. *The Papers of Benjamin Franklin*, 18 vols. New Haven, Conn.: Yale University Press, 1968.

Lee, Wayne E. "Peace Chiefs and Blood Revenge: Patterns of Restraint in Native American Warfare, 1500–1800." *Journal of Military History* 71:3 (2007): 701–41.

Limerick, Patricia Nelson. *Legacy of Conquest: The Unbroken Past of the American West.* New York: W. W. Norton, 1987.

Limerick, Patricia Nelson, Clyde A. Milner II, and Charles Rankin, eds. *Trails: Toward a New Western History.* Lawrence: University Press of Kansas, 1991.

Limerick, Patricia Nelson, et al. "Why the Past May Be Changing." *Montana: The Magazine of Western History* 40:3 (1990): 50–76.

Lincoln, Charles H., ed. *Correspondence of William Shirley.* New York: MacMillan, 1912.

Lofaro, Michael. *Daniel Boone: An American Life.* Lexington: University Press of Kentucky, 2003.

Long, J. C. *Lord Jeffrey Amherst: A Soldier of the King.* New York: Macmillan, 1933.

Luzader, John F., et al. *Fort Stanwix.* Washington, D.C.: Office of Park Preservation, National Park Service, U.S. Department of the Interior, 1976.

MacCloud, D. Peter. "The Franco-Amerindian Expedition to the Great Carrying Place in 1756." Paper read at the 18th annual meeting of the French Colonial Historical Society, McGill University, Montreal, 23 May 1992.

Manley, Henry S. *The Treaty of Fort Stanwix, 1784.* Rome, N.Y.: Rome Sentinel, 1932.

Mariboe, Herbert. "The Life of William Franklin, 1730(1)–1813, Pro Rege et Patria." Ph.D. thesis, University of Pennsylvania, 1962.

Marshall, Peter. "Colonial Protest and Imperial Retrenchment." *Journal of American Studies* 5 (1971): 1–17.

———. "Imperial Regulation of American Indian Affairs, 1763–1774." Ph.D. thesis, Yale University, New Haven, Conn., 1959.

———. "Lord Hillsborough, Samuel Wharton and the Ohio Grant, 1769–1775." *English Historical Review*,80:317 (1965): 717–39.

———. "Sir William Johnson and the Treaty of Fort Stanwix, 1768." *Journal of American Studies* 1:2 (1967): 149–79.

Martin, Calvin. "Ethnohistory: A Better Way to Write Indian History." *Western Historical Quarterly* 9:1 (1978): 41–56

Maxey, David W. "The Honorable Proprietaries v. Samuel Wallis: 'A Matter of Consequence' in the Province of Pennsylvania." *Pennsylvania History* 70:4 (2003): 361–95.

McConnell, Michael. *Army and Empire: British Soldiers on the American Frontier, 1758–1775.* Lincoln: University of Nebraska Press, 2004.

———. *A Country Between: The Upper Ohio Valley and Its Peoples, 1724–1774.* Lincoln: University of Nebraska Press, 1992.

McKeith, D. S. "The Inadequacy of Men and Measures in English Imperial History: Sir William Johnson and the New York Politicians, a Case Study." Ph.D. thesis, Syracuse University, Syracuse, N.Y., 1971.

Merk, Frederick. *History of the Westward Movement.* New York: Alfred A. Knopf, 1978.

Merrell, James. "The 'Cast of His Countenance': Reading Andrew Montour." In
    Ronald Huffman, Mechal Sobel, and Fredrika Teute, eds., *Through a Glass Darkly:*
    Reflections on Personal Identity in Early America. Chapel Hill: University of North
    Carolina Press, 1997.

———. "'I Desire All That I Have Said . . . May Be Taken Down Aright': Revisiting
    Teedyuscung's 1756 Treaty Council Speeches." *William and Mary Quarterly*, 3rd
    ser., 63 (2006): 743–77.

———. *The Indians' New World: Catawbas and Their Neighbors from European Contact*
    through the Era of Removal. Chapel Hill: University of North Carolina Press, 1989.

———. *Into the American Woods*. New York: W. W. Norton, 1999.

Merritt, Jane T. *At the Crossroads: Indians and Empires on a Mid-Atlantic Frontier, 1700–*
    1763. Chapel Hill: University of North Carolina Press, 2003.

Miller, Christopher L., and George R. Hamell. "A New Perspective on Indian-White
    Contact: Cultural Symbols and Colonial Trade." *Journal of American History* 73:2
    (1986): 311–28.

Minutes of Conferences Held at Fort-Pitt, In April and May 1768, under the direction of
    George Croghan, Esquire, Deputy Agent for INDIAN Affairs, with the Chiefs and War-
    riors of the Ohio and other Western Indians. Philadelphia: William Goddard, 1869.

Mullin, Michael J. "The Albany Congress and Colonial Confederation," *Mid-America*
    72:2 (1990): 93–105.

———. "Personal Politics: William Johnson and the Mohawks." *American Indian*
    Quarterly 17:3 (1993): 350–58.

Nammack, Georgiana C. *Fraud, Politics, and the Dispossession of the Indians: The Iroquois*
    Land Frontier in the Colonial Period. Norman: University of Oklahoma Press, 1969.

Nash, Gary. *The Unknown American Revolution: The Unruly Birth of Democracy and the*
    Struggle to Create America. New York: Viking, 2005.

Nelson, Larry L. *A Man of Distinction among Them: Alexander McKee and the Ohio Fron-*
    tier, 1754–1799. Kent, Ohio: Kent State University Press, 1999.

Nester, William. *"Haughty Conquerors": Amherst and the Great Indian Uprising of 1763*.
    Westport, Conn.: Praeger, 2000.

O'Callaghan, E. B., ed. *The Documentary History of the State of New York*. 4 vols. Albany,
    N.Y.: Weed and Parsons, 1849–51.

O'Callaghan, E. B., and B. Fernow, eds. *Documents Relative to the Colonial History of the*
    State of New York. 10 vols. Albany, N.Y.: Weed, Parsons, and Co., 1853–87.

Olwell, Robert, and Alan Tully, eds. *Cultures and Identities in Colonial British America:*
    Anglo-America in the Transatlantic World. Baltimore: Johns Hopkins University
    Press, 2006.

O'Toole, Fintan. *White Savage: William Johnson and the Invention of America*. New York:
    Farrar, Straus and Giroux, 2005.

Parkman, Francis. *Wolfe and Montcalm*. New York: Collier Books, 1962.

Parmenter, Jon W. "After the Mourning Wars: The Iroquois as Allies in Colonial
    North American Campaigns, 1676–1760." *William and Mary Quarterly*, 3rd ser., 64
    (2007): 39–82.

———. "At the Wood's Edge: Iroquois Foreign Relations, 1727–1768." Ph.D. thesis, University of Michigan, 1999.

———. "The Iroquois and the Native American Struggle for the Ohio Valley, 1754–1794." In David C. Skaggs and Larry L. Nelson, eds., *The Sixty Years' War for the Great Lakes, 1754–1814.* Lansing: Michigan State University Press, 2001.

Payne, Samuel. "The Iroquois League, the Articles of the Confederation, and the Constitution." *William and Mary Quarterly* 53:3 (1996): 605–20.

Paxson, F. L. *History of the American Frontier, 1763–1893.* New York: Houghton Mifflin, 1924.

Peckham, Howard H., ed. *George Croghan's Journal of His Trip to Detroit in 1767.* Ann Arbor: University of Michigan Press, 1939.

———. *Pontiac and the Indian Uprising.* Chicago: University of Chicago Press, 1947.

Preston, David L. *The Texture of Contact: European and Indian Settler Communities on the Frontiers of Iroquoia, 1667–1783.* Lincoln: University of Nebraska Press, 2009.

Prucha, Francis Paul. *American Indian Policy in the Formative Years.* Cambridge: Harvard University Press, 1962.

———. *American Indian Treaties: The History of a Political Anomoly.* Berkeley: University of California Press, 1994.

Ray, Arthur J. *Indians in the Fur Trade: Their Role as Trappers, Hunters, and Middlemen in the Lands Southwest of Hudson Bay, 1660–1870.* Toronto: University of Toronto Press, 1974.

Ray, Arthur J., and Conrad E. Heidenreich. *The Early Fur Trades: A Study in Cultural Interaction.* Toronto: McClelland and Stewart, 1976.

Reis, Linda A. "The Rage of Opposing Government: The Stump Affair of 1768." *Cumberland County History* 1:1 (1984): 21–45.

Richter, Daniel K. *Before the Revolution: America's Ancient Pasts.* Cambridge: Belknap/Harvard University Press, 2011.

———. *Facing East from Indian Country: A Native History of Early America.* Cambridge: Harvard University Press, 2001.

———. "Native Americans, the Plan of 1764, and a British Empire that Never Was." In Robert Olwell and Alan Tully, eds., *Cultures and Identities in Colonial British America: Anglo-America in the Transatlantic World,* chap. 11. Baltimore: Johns Hopkins University Press, 2006.

———. *The Ordeal of the Longhouse: The Peoples of the Iroquois League in the Era of European Colonization.* Chapel Hill: University of North Carolina Press, 1992.

———. "War and Culture: the Iroquois Experience." *William and Mary Quarterly* 40:4 (1983): 528–59.

Richter, Daniel K, and James Merrell, eds. *Beyond the Covenant Chain: The Iroquois and Their Neighbors in Indian North America, 1600–1800.* Syracuse, N.Y.: Syracuse University Press, 1987.

Ridner, Judith. "Relying of the 'Saucy' Men of the Backcountry: Middlemen and the Fur Trade in Pennsylvania." *Pennsylvania Magazine of History and Biography* 129:2 (2005): 133–62.

Roberts, Robert B. *New York's Forts in the Revolution*. Rutherford, N.J.: Fairleigh Dickinson University Press, 1980.

Shannon, Timothy. "Dressing for Success on the Mohawk Frontier." In Peter C. Mancall and James H. Merrell, eds., *American Encounters: Natives and Newcomers from European Contact to Indian Removal, 1500–1850*. New York: Routledge, 2000.

———. *Indians and Colonists at the Crossroads of Empire: The Albany Congress of 1754*. Ithaca, N.Y.: Cornell University Press, 2000.

———. *Iroquois Diplomacy on the Early American Frontier*. London: Penguin, 2008.

Sheehan, Bernard W. "Indian-White Relations in Early America: A Review Essay." *William and Mary Quarterly*, 3rd ser., 26:2 (1969).

Sherman, Daniel. "The Six Nations." In William W. Williams, ed., *Magazine of Western History*, vol. 1. Cleveland, Ohio: n.p., November 1884–April 1885.

Shirai, Yoko. "The Indian Trade in Colonial Pennsylvania, 1730–1768: Traders and Land Speculation." Ph.D. thesis, University of Pennsylvania 1985.

Silver, Peter. *Our Savage Neighbors: How Indian War Transformed Early America*. New York: W. W. Norton, 2009.

Silver, Timothy. *A New Face on the Countryside: Indians, Colonists, and Slaves in South Atlantic Forests, 1500–1800*. New York: Cambridge University Press, 1990.

Sleeper-Smith, Susan. "Introduction" (Middle Ground Revisited forum). *William and Mary Quarterly*, 3rd ser., 63:1 (2006).

Slick, Sewell. *William Trent and the West*. Harrisburg: Archives Publication Company of Pennsylvania, 1947.

Slotkin, Richard. *Regeneration through Violence: The Mythology of the American Frontier, 1600–1860*. Middletown, Conn.: Wesleyan University Press, 1973.

Snow, Dean R., Charles T. Gehring, and William A. Starna, eds. *In Mohawk Country: Early Narratives About a Native People*. Syracuse, N.Y.: Syracuse University Press, 1996.

Sosin, Jack. *Whitehall and the Wilderness: The Middle West in British Colonial Policy, 1760–1775*. Lincoln: University of Nebraska Press, 1961.

Starna, William A., and José António Brandão. "From the Mohawk-Mahican War to the Beaver Wars: Questioning the Pattern." *Ethnohistory* 51:4 (2004): 725–50.

Steele, Ian K. "Exploding Colonial American History: AmerIndian, Atlantic, and Global Perspectives." *Reviews in American History* 26:1 (1998): 70–95.

———. *Warpaths: Invasions of America*. New York: Oxford University Press, 1994.

Stevens, Sylvester, and Donald Kent, eds. *Wilderness Chronicles of Northwestern Pennsylvania*. Harrisburg: Pennsylvania Historical Commission, 1941.

Stevens, S. K., et al., eds. *The Papers of Henry Bouquet*. 6 vols. Harrisburg: Pennsylvania Historical and Museum Commission, 1951.

Sturtevant, William C. "Anthropology, History, and Ethnohistory." *Ethnohistory* 13:1–2 (1966): 1–51.

———. "A Structural Sketch of Iroquois Ritual." In Michael K. Foster, Jack Campisi, and Marianne Mithun, eds., *Extending the Rafters: Interdisciplinary Approaches to Iroquoian Studies*. Albany: State University of New York Press, 1984.

Sullivan, James, et al., eds. *The Papers of Sir William Johnson.* 14 vols. Albany: State University of New York Press, 1921–1963.

Swinehart, Kirk. D. "William Johnson among the Mohawks." Ph.D. dissertation, Yale University, 2002.

Szasz, Margaret Connell, ed. *Between Indian and White Worlds: The Cultural Broker.* University of Oklahoma Press: Oklahoma, 1994.

Tanner, Helen. *Atlas of Great Lakes Indian History.* Norman: University of Oklahoma University Press, 1986.

Taylor, Alan. "The Collaborator." *New Republic,* 11 September 2006.

———. *The Divided Ground: Indians, Settlers, and the Northern Borderland of the American Revolution.* New York: Alfred A. Knopf, 2006.

———. *William Cooper's Town: Power and Persuasion on the Frontier of the Early American Republic.* New York: Alfred A. Knopf, 1995.

Tillson, Albert, Jr. *Gentry and Common Folk: Political Culture on a Virginia Frontier, 1740–1789.* Lexington: University of Kentucky Press, 1991.

Tiro, Karim. "A Civil War? Rethinking Iroquois Participation in the American Revolution." *Explorations in Early American Culture* 4 (2000): 148–65.

Tooker, Elisabeth. *An Iroquois Sourcebook.* New York: Garland, 1985.

Trigger, Bruce G. *The Children of Aataentsic: A History of the Huron People to 1660.* Montreal: McGill-Queen's University Press, 1976.

Turner, Frederick Jackson. "The Significance of the Frontier in American History." In Martin Ridge, ed., *Frederick Jackson Turner: Wisconsin's Historian of the Frontier.* Madison: State Historical Society of Wisconsin, 1986.

Usner, Daniel H., Jr. "The Frontier Exchange Economy of the Lower Mississippi Valley in the Eighteenth Century." In Peter C. Mancall and James H. Merrell, eds., *American Encounters: Natives and Newcomers from European Contact to Indian Removal, 1500–1850.* New York: Routledge, 2000.

Van Doren, Carl, and Julian P. Boyd, eds. *Indian Treaties Printed by Benjamin Franklin, 1736–1762.* Philadelphia, Historical Society of Pennsylvania, 1938.

Vaughan, Alden T. "Frontier Banditti and the Indians: The Paxton Boys' Legacy, 1763–1775." *Pennsylvania History* 51:1 (1984): 1–29.

Vecsey, Christopher, and William A. Starna, eds. *Iroquois Land Claims.* Syracuse, N.Y.: Syracuse University Press, 1988.

Volwiler, Albert T. "George Croghan and the Development of Central New York, 1763–1800." *Quarterly Journal of the New York State Historical Association (New York History)* 4:1 (1923): 21–40.

———. *George Croghan and the Westward Movement, 1741–1782.* New York: AMS Press, 1926, 1971.

Volwiler, Albert T., ed. "William Trent's Journal, June 24, 1763." *Mississippi Valley Historical Review* 11 (1924): 390–413.

Waddell, Louis, et al. *The Papers of Henry Bouquet.* Harrisburg: Pennsylvania Historical and Museum Commission, 1984.

Wainwright, Nicholas B. *George Croghan, Wilderness Diplomat*. Chapel Hill: University of North Carolina Press, 1959.

Wallace, Anthony. *Death and Rebirth of the Senecas*. New York: Vintage Books, 1972.

———. *King of the Delawares: Teedyuscung, 1700–1763*. Salem, N.H.: Ayer, 1970.

———. "Origins of Iroquois Neutrality: The Grand Settlement of 1701." *Pennsylvania History* 24 (1957): 223–55.

Wallace, Paul A. *Conrad Weiser, Friend of Colonist and Mohawk*. Philadelphia: University of Pennsylvania Press, 1945.

Ward, Matthew C. *Breaking the Backcountry: The Seven Years' War in Virginia and Pennsylvania, 1754–1765*. Pittsburgh, Pa.: University of Pittsburg Press, 2003.

———. "The Indians Our Real Friends: The British Army and the Ohio Indians, 1758–1772." In Daniel Barr, ed., *The Boundaries between Us: Natives and Newcomers along the Frontiers of the Old Northwest Territory, 1750–1850*. Kent, Ohio: Kent State University Press, 2006.

———. "Redeeming the Captives: Pennsylvania Captives among the Ohio Indians, 1755–1765." *Pennsylvania Magazine of History and Biography* 125:3 (2001): 161–89.

Washburn, Wilcomb. "Indians and the American Revolution." AmericanRevolution. org, www.americanrevolution.org/ind1.html.

Weaver, John C. *The Great Land Rush and the Making of the Modern World, 1650–1900*. Montreal: McGill-Queen's University Press, 2003.

Weslager, C. A. *The Delaware Indians*. New Jersey: Rutgers University Press, 1972.

Wharton, Samuel. *Facts and Observations respecting the Country Granted to His Majesty by the South-East Side of the River Ohio in North America; The Establishment of a New Colony There; and the Causes of the Indian War, Which, Last Year, Desolated the Frontier Settlements of the Provinces of Pennsylvania, Maryland and Virginia*. London, 1775.

White, Richard. *The Middle Ground: Indians, Empires, and Republics in the Great Lakes Region*. New York: Cambridge University Press, 1991.

INDEX

References to illustrations are in italic type.

Abercrombie, James, 59, 62–63
Abraham: addressing German Flatts council (1770), 179; on division among Six Nations, 47; at Fort Stanwix, 151; and Kayaderosseras dispute, 135–36; as translator, 148
Adams, Robert, 141
Albany, N.Y.: central role played by, 50–51; Congress (1754), 50–53, 85, 103; council (July 1751), 44; emergency council (1775), 169; and Oneida Carry, 32–33, 55
Allen, John, 124
American Revolution: and Battle of Oriskany, 4, 207; beginning of (spring 1775), 206; and Croghan's ruin in era of, 205, 206, 250n7; and Iroquois Confederacy demise, 3–4, 13, 169; 1768 treaty eclipsed by, 9
Amherst, Jeffrey: and collapse of career, 85; Croghan ordered to return to Fort Pitt by, 89; made clear Crown need not maintain costly assurances after reduction of New France, 75; and order to withdraw New Wales proposal, 91; and plan for retribution after Uprising of 1763, 76–78; tensions fueled by, 65, 71–72
Andros, Edmund, 23
Atotarho, 15
Attakullakulla (Little Carpenter), 125

Bacon, Anthony, 96
Battle of Oriskany (6 August 1777), 4, 207–208
Battle of Point Pleasant, 168, 201
Baynton, Wharton and Morgan (Philadelphia firm): central to supply of goods, 42, 219n48; and Croghan, 90, 95, 97, 102–103, 111, 118–19, 184; and further deterioration of situation, 182–83; and Indiana Company, 157; and inland colony agreement in Philadelphia, 115–16; Johnson as close ally of, 114, 235n15; and liquidation of assets by 1774, 205–206; reassurance by Johnson of plan's validity, 114; selling illegal items of war by, 133; shares allocated to, 128; Wharton angered by Croghan, 96. *See also* Morgan, George; Wharton, Samuel
Beaver Wars, 21–22, 36, 216n23
Blyth, William, 123
Boone, Daniel, 197
Boundaries, 109–38, 133–34; and absence of regulation by Crown, 112–13; atonement payments from Pennsylvania, 124; and boundary negotiations urged, 110, 121, 128; and British imperial presence, 110; and change in trading practices, 112; council convened at Fort Pitt for

Boundaries (*continued*)
  redrawing, 128–32, 238n70, 239n72,
  239n74; and encroachments on
  lands not purchased, 123, 237n48;
  and frontier expenses as Whitehall
  concern, 109, 110, 127–28, 238n69;
  and grand deception perpetuated,
  121–22; and Illinois scheme
  organized by Croghan, 102–103, 114;
  and Johnson's reduced status, 110,
  113; and Kayaderosseras claims,
  135–36; and letter to Hillsborough
  from Johnson on boundary, 137–38;
  and Mohawk concerns, 134–35; and
  mounting borderland hostilities,
  124; and peace in jeopardy, 112; and
  Proclamation of 1763 ignored in
  1767, 112; and speculation and self-
  enrichment, 111; and squatting and
  trading problems, 111; and unrest
  and rebellion in frontier (1766–1768),
  138; and unrest in Ohio country
  (Sept. 1767), 120–21; and war panic
  created by Croghan (1767), 119.
  See also Croghan, George; Illinois
  scheme; Johnson, William; Nymwha
Boundaries of the Royal Proclamation
  of 1763 and 1768 Treaty of Fort
  Stanwix, 155
Boundary negotiations with Crown, 4,
  74, 91, 93, 213n1. *See also* Boundaries
Bouquet, Henry, 78, 80, 81, 82, 89
Braddock, Edward (general), 54, 56, 60
Bradstreet, John: and Fort Frontenac,
  62–63; as land speculator, 191;
  peaceful overtures to Ohio Iroquois
  made by, 80–81; peaceful resolution
  sought in 1764, 69; relief column
  organized for supply trip to
  Oswego, 58
Brant, Joseph (Thayendanegea)
  (Molly's brother): and 1784
  journey, 3; education by Johnson,
  36; and Kirkland's influence, 204;
  leaving Oneida Carry in 1784, 212;
  negotiations at Carry (1784), 209;
  relocation in British Canada, 9
Brant, Molly (Konwatsi'tsiaienni and
  Degonwadonti). *See* Johnson, Mrs.
  William (Molly Brant) (second wife)

Brant, Mrs. Joseph (Catherine
  Adwontishon Croghan) (third wife),
  9–10
Burlington Company, 181, 183
Butler, Richard, 3, 4, 210

Callender, Robert, 95, 96
Callière, Louis-Hector de, 23
Campbell, Daniel, 144
Campbell, John, 59, 183, 247n36
Canadagara, 51
Canagaraduncka, Brant, 36
Canassatec, 41–42
Carrying Place, war, and the Ohio
  country, 26–66; and Abercrombie's
  expectation of fort lodging four
  hundred, 63; and abuse at the Carry
  reported to DeLancey, 56; and
  Albany congress in 1754, 50; and
  Albany council in July 1751, 44;
  and Albany negotiations during
  first three decades of eighteenth
  century, 26; and Albany's central
  role by seventeenth century, 50;
  arrival of Johnson and Seven
  Years' War, 27; and bleak outlook
  for British by end of 1757, 61; and
  Braddock's Enterprise, 54; and
  Bradstreet's trekking supplies
  over Carry in mid-March 1756, 58;
  and breaking of Covenant Chain,
  27; British prestige suffered in
  northeastern borderlands, 60; and
  Canadian governor's aggressive
  action (June 1749), 43–44; "Carte
  de l'Amerique Septentrionnale,"
  30–31; and construction of Fort
  Stanwix, 28; construction of two
  forts to safeguard portage ordered
  by Shirley, 57; and Covenant
  Chain rupture (and Hendrick at
  Johnson Hall), 46–48; Croghan
  and Teedyuscung, 61; Croghan
  dispatched to conduct peace
  talks between Pennsylvania and
  Delawares (April 1756), 60; Croghan
  had forged strong trading alliances
  in Ohio Country, 48; Croghan's
  commitment to Crown selective,
  65; and Croghan's diplomacy,

48–49, 60–61; and Croghan's loss of independence because of debts in need of new patrons, 64–65; Croghan's marriage to daughter of Mohawk chief gave access to trade, 39; curbing French expansion sought by Crown, 33–34; demands made that Johnson be appointed conduit between indigenous and white worlds, 40; earthworks at Oneida Carry burned to ground, 60; and eastern Iroquois support needed by Crown, 49; and Easton agreement, 27; and Easton, Pa., meeting in October 1758 for treaty turning tide for British, 63; and erection of Fort Bull on Wood Creek, 27–28; European negotiators in fleeting agreement at Easton, Pa., (1758), 64; and fall of Niagara, 64; and first Europeans traversed Oneida Carry, 28–29; Forbes assumed control of Fort Pitt without firing a shot, 65; Forbes prepared move against Fort Duquesne, 62; and formalization of alliance at Treaty of Easton (1758), 27; Fort Stanwix as point of contention among Iroquois, 65–66; Fort Stanwix delayed for three years, 63; and French-allied Iroquois opting to take Carry by surprise, 58–59; and French negotiations with Grand Council, 27; French presence in Ohio River valley threatened to hem in English colonies, 38; French prestige eroded by trade arrangements between Pennsylvania proprietors and Ohio Country traders, 43; and George Croghan's arrival in Ohio, 38–39; and gifts disappeared as Johnson was no longer New York Indian agent, 45–46; and Grand Council could not project hegemony over region, 41; Hendrick and Mohawks on 28 June 1754, 51–52; and illegal squatting on increase alienating pro-British factions of Iroquois, 45; Indian Department cut frontier costs, 65; Iroquois-British relations were strained by early 1750s, 44; and

Iroquois Kings arrival in London (1710), 33; Iroquois prominence recognized settling conflict between Virginia and Iroquois, 42; Iroquois pushed hard to have Johnson commissioned (1751), 44; Iroquois recognized as primary players, 26; and Johnson, 36–37; and Johnson's appointment in 1755 as superintendent of Indian Affairs, 54; and Johnson's marriage to Molly Brant, 35–36; and Johnson's orders to construct fort at Oneida Castle, 60; and Johnson's reinstatement urged, 53; and July 1751 meeting with Governor Clinton and Six Nations, 39–40; King George II declared war against King Louis XV on 17 May 1756, 59; and Lancaster, Pa., meeting on 4 July 1744, 41–42; and land ownership complex in early eighteenth century, 42–43; and Louisbourg fall in May 1758 hurt French, 61; Mohawks and special relationship with British, 49; and Mohawks cited Kayaderosseras claim, 51; Mohawks unhappy with reinstated Indian commissioners (1753), 46–47; Montréal surrendered on 8 September 1760, 65; and myth of "Iroquois Empire" set back by Five nations' defeat, 26; and Niagara attack delayed, 58; and obstacles plaguing construction of new fort at Oneida Carry, 62; and Ohio Country provided security to first peoples (e.g., Hurons), 36–37; and Ohio Delawares weary of European presence, 48; Oneida Carry crucial to supply lines, 27, 28–29; Oneidas and other Iroquois communities fostered closer ties with British in 1727–54 period, 27; Oneidas hostile to construction at Carry, 56; Oneidas once again in charge of Carry, 65; opening of new frontier would benefit converging interests, 66; Oswego fell to French (15 August 1756), 59; and Oswego River trading post (1727), 32–33;

Carrying Place (*continued*)
and Penn's dislike of Croghan,
60; Pennsylvania presented Ohio
nations gifts in return for pledge
of allegiance, 42; and petition for
trade route to Albany (July 1702),
32; Pickawillany village sacked 21
June 1752 as onset of Seven Years'
War in North America, 45; and
Plan of forts at Oneida Carry, 1754,
55; and proposed Plan of Union
negotiations (3 July 1754), 52; and
publication of Colden's *The History
of the Five Nations* (1747), 33–34; and
refortifying the Carry as Shirley
goal, 59; and Sassoonan's complaints
on settler encroachments, 37; and
scalp bounty as source of animosity,
60; and Shawnees' refusal to leave
Ohio Country, 37; and shining of
Covenant Chain by English, 45–46,
47–48; and Shirley's aspirations to
march on Niagara, 57; and Shirley's
recognition of Oneida Carry
importance between Albany and
Oswego, 55–56; and Sir William
Johnson, 34–35; Stanwix ordered to
reoccupy the Carry (summer1758),
62; and starvation and scurvy at
Oneida Carry in Feb. 1756, 58; and
St. Lawrence River controlled by
English (summer 1758), 62; and
strategy to combat French expansion,
50–51; and Teedyuscung's distrust
of Croghan's minutes, 64; and Treaty
of Utrecht in 1713, 26; and tribes
within English orbit by late 1740s,
38; and van den Bogaert, Harmen
Meyndertsz, 28–29; and Walking
Purchase scandal of 1737, 37–38,
60; and War of Austrian Succession
(1740–48) (aka King George's War),
35; and Washington's failures, 53;
and work started on Fort Craven, 59.
See also Römer, Wolfgang William
"Carte de l'Amerique Septentrionnale"
(Franquelin), *30–31*
Cayugas: in bid for independence,
207; at council, 17; and problems
with confederacies to the west, 15;
returning wampum to speaker, 17;
and spring of 1784, 215n4; and ten
representatives at council, 16
Céloron, Pierre-Joseph, 43–44
Charles II, 23
Chenussios, 77, 189, 194, 218n29
Cherokees: congress of Iroquois and,
125–28; land ceded to Crown by, 164;
and Ohioans aligning themselves
with, 187; and peace between Six
Nations and, 132.; on peaceful terms
with Shawnees, 125; and rumors of
potential enslavement by British,
100–101; sense of territorial rights
of, 151; and treaty of peace between
Iroquois and, 161; war belts sent to
Iroquois to strengthen alliance, 178
Chew, Benjamin, 173
Chippewas, 80, 120, 187, 190, 222n3
Clinton, George (NY governor): and
Albany council of 1751, 44; and
attempt to move Shawnees, 37;
Indian commissioners reappointed
by, 46; Johnson sent to Onondaga
(1746) by, 35; and news of trader
abuses, 37; warning to Six Nations of
French, 39–40
Colden, Cadwallader: *History of the Five
Nations*, 33; on Iroquois diplomacy,
15; Johnson's letter on behalf
of Iroquois, 76, 225n23, 226n27;
Johnson's report to, 93; plea to
Crown for reinstatement of Johnson,
44; skepticism of, 77, 226n28
Condolence ceremonies, 18, 132, 147,
160, 199–200, 216n15
Connolly, Dr. John, 197, 205
Conoghquieson (Kanaghwaes,
Kanaghqweasea, Kanongweniyah),
147
Converging interests, 67–108;
and boundary established
by Proclamation, 74, 91; and
Bradstreet's peaceful overtures,
80; and British imperial policy, 85;
concession by Gage of satisfaction
with actions taken against Ohio
Iroquois, 79, 227n45, 227n47;

Croghan as Johnson's right-hand man, 67, 70; and disaffection of western nations toward English, 71–72; and disputes over trade and land policies, 85–86; and eruption of Pontiac's Rebellion, 67–68; and fragmentation of Confederacy, 69; and Gage's pressure on Johnson, 70, 77, 78; and inconsistencies of administration, 68; and increase in squatters, 86; Iroquoi reaped benefits as British allies, 69; Johnson and trade (1764), 84–85; Johnson figures prominently in, 67–70; and Johnson's efforts in behalf of Iroquois, 76–78; land speculation undercut by Proclamation, 74–75; and Neolin's message of resistance, 72; North America reeling from devastation after Seven Years' War, 67–68, 76; Paxton riots in December 1763, 86–88; and Peace of Paris, 70–71, 222n7; peace terms offered Ohio nation by (1764), 81; and Pontiac's attack at Fort Detroit, 72; and Pontiac's Rebellion, 72–73; and The Royal Proclamation of 1763, 73–74; and success of Johnson's diplomacy, 78–79, 226n36, 226n38, 227n42; and temporary conclusion to hostilities from 1763 Uprising, 82; and tensions fueled by Amherst, 71; and Turner's Frontier Thesis, 75, 223n18. *See also* Croghan, George; Johnson, William; "1764 Plan for the Future Management of Indian Affairs"
Council convened at Fort Pitt for redrawing boundaries (1768), 128–32, 239n72, 239n74
Council fires of Iroquois, 13, 18, 35, 169, 202
Covenant Chain (Iroquois-English alliance): brightening of, 48, 52, 53, 129; erosion of, 45, 46–47, 103; and Johnson, 27; and shifting strategy, 70; and unity image, 12; wampum belt of, 148, 158
Coxe, Daniel, 142, 143
Craven, Charles, 59

Crawford, Hugh, 144
Cresap, Michael, 197
Croghan, George: atonement payments urged to stop borderland hostilities, 124; background of, 38–39, 218n32, 218n34; and Braddock's campaign, 54; on brink of financial ruin, 183–84, 247n35; captive of French forces, 49; character assessment of by Bouquet, 89; collapse of enterprises, 49; and complaints to Johnson, 91–93, 108, 231n109; and criticality of new boundary to, 128–29; death of (1782), 206–207; diplomacy of, 48, 220n69; distrust of by Teedyuscung, 61, 63–64; and Fort Charters treaty (Jan. 1767), 116–17; Fort Pitt area land claims of (1749–1773), *181*; frontier policy directed by, 68; Gratz given power of attorney by, 191–92; holding court as generous host, 187; Johnson's instructions before Fort Pitt council, 132; as Johnson's right-hand man, 67, 70; as justice of the peace, 198; land sold by before boundary change, 125, 237n57; message to board on Indian policy, 92, 231n105; and misled creditors, 102, 234n150; and mission to Illinois, 97, 232n125; new scheme of, 94–95; optimism despite Crown's rejection of claims, 180–81; payments delivered by Pennsylvania representatives, 124; and peace talks between Pennsylvania and Delawares, 60–61; and peace terms negotiated by after own capture by Indians, 100, 233n140; and Pontiac, 100–101; in praise of Grand Council, 60; reinstatement as deputy by Johnson, 94; reputation as schemer, 61–63, 64, 96–97, 124, 133; resignation threatened by, 118; and return to Illinois a hero, 101; and ruin in revolutionary era, 205, 206, 250n7; and scheme to claim land, 89–90, 229n92; and second resignation from service for land grab, 191; and significance of boundary to, 152;

Croghan, George (*continued*)
significance of story, 10–11; and
Stanwix negotiations, 157; strong
British presence in Illinois advocated
by, 101–102; submission of "suffering
traders" memorial to Board of Trade,
91, 230n100; Teedyuscun's distrust
of, 63–64; and trade violation scandal
revealed, 97–98; trading network
established by, 39, 45. *See also*
Croghan, George, legal problems of;
Illinois scheme; Vandalia project
Croghan, George, legal problems of:
assets surrendered to creditors,
128–29; on brink of financial ruin,
183–84, 206; illegal plan presented
to merchants, 95; land sold to
avoid imprisonment, 181–82; major
creditors put at risk, 118–19; and
mounting legal battles, 168–69;
transfer of stock to Galloway, 181–82;
and war panic created by (1767), 119
Cutbacks in funding of Indian
Department. *See under* Indian
Department

Dartmouth, 192–95, 199
Dekanawidah, 15
DeLancey, James, 49, 51
Delawares: and 19 April 1765 treaty
negotiations, 104–106; and dislike
of European presence, 48; near-
starving, 176; and Newcomer,
186–87; open to throwing off yoke,
41; peace sought by, 82; and peace
talks with Pennsylvania, 60–61; and
Sassoonan, 37–38; and scalp bounty,
60; and Shawnees, 120, 125, 129,
131, 142, 161–62; and Shawnees as
target for Amherst's call to arms,
76–78, 79–80; subversion of Iroquoi
claims by, 37–38; and Teedyuscung's
distrust of Croghan's minutes,
63–64; weary of European presence,
48, 54
De Léry, Gaspard-Joseph Chaussegros,
58
Denny, William, 61
Deo-Wain-Sta (Oneida Carry), 28
Dinwiddie, Robert, 91, 185, 196

Exchanges and transformations,
18–25; and Condolence Ceremony,
18, 216n15; and French-Iroquois
diplomacy, 23–24; and gift giving,
20; and "Grand Settlement of
1701," 23–24; Indian perspectives,
14–15, 214n2; and Iroquois oral
history, 15–16; and rise of Iroquois
Confederacy, 25; and Six Nation
diplomacy, 15–16, 214n3, 215n4;
and tensions leading to conflict,
20–21; and trade impact, 21–22. *See
also* Grand Council of the Iroquois
Confederacy

Fairservice, James, 59
Fauquier, Francis, 112
Field, Robert, 95, 97
Forbes, John, 62, 65
Forest diplomacy, 18
Fort Bull, 27, 28, 58, 207
Fort Charters treaty, 116–17, 236n24
Fort Duquesne, 53, 62, 64, 65
Fort Michilimackinac, 72
Fort Niagara, 3, 55, 57–58, 61, 64, 78,
190, 212
Fort Pontchartrain, 37
Fort Stanwix: construction of, 28;
council meeting at, 3; council
meeting planned, 128; deterioration
of, 139–40; point of contention
among Iroquois, 65. *See also* Oneida
Carry
Fort Williams, 57
Francis, Turbutt, 175–76
Franklin, Benjamin: and Albany
Congress of 1754, 50; and
Hutchinson letters, 196; and Illinois
scheme, 114–15, 116; on Indian
retaliation, 85; Johnson more
prominent than, 35; and Paxton
riots, 87
Franklin, William: and agreements
with Croghan, 206; honored as
Sagorrihwhioughstha ("Doer of
Justice"), 161; and Illinois scheme,
115, 116; and Indiana Company,
128, 141–42, 157; loan secured for
Croghan by, 181. *See also* Suffering
Traders

Franks, David, 89–90
Franks-Gratz firm, 182–83
Franquelin, Jean-Baptiste Louis, 29, 30–31
French and Indian War, 67. *See also* Seven Years' War
Frontier Thesis by Turner, 75, 223n18

Gage, Thomas: anger at Croghan's trade violation, 98–99; and concession to Johnson that administration satisfied with compromise, 79, 227n45, 227n47; and Johnson's letter on behalf of Iroquois, 77; pressure placed on Johnson by, 70, 150; and renunciation of Bradstreet's peace overtures, 80–81, 228nn53–54; strategy followed by Johnson, 83–84, 228n65; in support of plan to divide provincial responsibility, 172
Galloway, Joseph: and agreement at Philadelphia (April 1766), 115–16; as assembly speaker on illegal settlements, 122–23; and backing of Croghan, 23–24; as Croghan's lawyer, 118; Croghan's shares transferred to, 128; Croghan's Suffering Traders shares transferred to, 181–82
Gaustarax (Kayendarua), 105, 145, 189, 190
"George Croghan's Fort Pitt area land claims c. 1749–1773" (map), *181*
Grand Council of the Iroquois Confederacy: and appointed councilors, 17, 215n11; assembly to resolve dispute, 16–18, 215n7; authority bolstered by Croghan and Johnson, 64; basic rules for, 19, 216n15; claim over lands east of Mississippi, 68–69; colonial independence, 208; control over borderland affairs in jeopardy, 172; diminished power of, 103, 187–88, 205; double-agent nature of, 83; and English Crown, 34; German Flatts meeting (July 1770), 188; as guiding force on North American continent, 202; and Iroquois diplomacy, 25;

and irreplaceable importance of, 26; and Johnson as facilitator, 27, 34, 167; and king's ransom at treaty of Fort Stanwix, 162, 167; and lack of dominance over region, 41, 219n44; neutrality of in death of Piankashaw chief, 45; removed as player by 1784 treaty, 211, 212; seen as politically dysfunctional by some, 8; and Seven Years' War, 69; and shared power, 16; Tohonissahgarawa at Fort Pitt council (1768), 129–30
Grand Ohio Company, 185–86, 205. *See also* Ohio Company of Virginia; Walpole Company or Associates
"The Grand Settlement of 1701," 23–24
Gratz, Bernard, 182, 183, 191–92, 206
Gratz, Michael, 182, 183
Great Laws of Peace (He Gayanashagowa), 15–16, 215n5
Guerre de la Conquête, 67–68

Hamilton, James, 175
He Gayanashagowa (Great Laws of Peace), 15–16, 215n5
Hendrick (Theyanoquin): and Albany congress of 1754, 51; Covenant Chain recognized as broken by, 46–47; demand the province survey lands, 192; Johnson's reappointment urged by, 40; land survey demanded by, 192; pledged to brighten Covenant Chain, 52
Hiawatha, 14, 215n5
Hillsborough, Lord: anger at colonial disorder, 190; awareness of Johnson's intentions on boundary, 164; and boundary negotiations urged by, 121; commendation for Johnson, 124–25; courted by Croghan, 91, 93; and Fort Pitt negotiations, 134; and Fort Stanwix treaty agreement received by, 169; letter from Johnson on boundary, 137–38; new colonial strategy confirmed by, 127; private transactions rejected by, 180, 183, 248n38; and Privy Council decision against, 184; rejection of path through Mohawk territory, 134; response to Fort Stanwix treaty

Hillsborough, Lord (*continued*)
agreement, 170; in support of
Walpole proposal, 185
History of the Five Nations, The (Colden),
33
Hockley, Richard, 118
Hujnnhuj, no longer New York Indian
agent, 45–46
Hurons, 21, 36, 37, 58, 187
Hutchinson letters (B. Franklin), 196
Hyde, Edward, 32

Illinois scheme: agreement at
Philadelphia (April 1766), 115–16;
backed by Dr. Franklin and son, 114,
115, 116; Croghan's and Johnson's
interest in, 102–103; and Croghan's
diplomacy (Jan. 1767), 116–17. *See
also* Croghan, George
Indiana Company, 128, 141, 157, 158,
182, 184. *See also* Suffering Traders;
Walpole Company or Associates
Indiana grant, 167, 244n1
Indian commissioners, 46
Indian Department: and changes
in borderland strategy, 83; and
cutbacks in funding, 13, 65, 165–66,
171, 191, 200, 201, 205; in disarray
after Johnson's death, 169; future
uncertain in 1765, 110; Johnson's
efforts for future of, 138–39, 157–58,
167; proposal to dismantle, 171;
relegation to diplomatic role in
1768, 128; and significance of new
boundary, 75, 89, 91, 92, 93; waning
powers of, 167, 168
Indian hatred, rise of, 99
Iroquois-British relations (mid-1700s),
43–45
Iroquois Confederacy: agency
regarding treaty, 7; collapse of, 3–4,
114–17, 169, 207–208; factors leading
to destabilization of, 204–205;
fragmentation of, 69; image of
unification increasingly difficult,
189; and Johnson, 108; and relations
with British, 8, 44–45, 76, 214n17;
rise of, 25; and rumors of war (1769),
177; and sectionalism, 8–9; status

redefined by 1784 treaty, 211–12. *See
also* Iroquois Empire
Iroquois Empire, myth of, 10, 26, 33, 203
Iroquois League, 16–18, 28

Jameson, David, 133
Johnson, Guy (son-in-law of William):
acting in place of father-in-law,
134–35; on father-in-law's death,
199; future superintendent of Indian
Affairs, 141; message from Shawnees
to, 200; Oneida speaker to, 202; as
successor to father-in-law, 203–204
Johnson, Mrs. William (Catherine
Weisenberg) (first wife), 36
Johnson, Mrs. William (Molly Brant)
(second wife), 35–36
Johnson, Peter Warren (son), 36
Johnson, William: 1768 treaty as
brainchild of, 164–65, 244n78;
background of, 34–35; death of
(1774), 168, 199–200, 203, 250n82;
failing health of, 134, 141, 174, 199;
and Joseph Brant, 36; legacy of,
34, 199–200; and marriages and
children of, 35–36; motivations of,
6–7; paternalism of, 145, 174. *See
also* Brant, Joseph (Thayendanegea)
(Molly's brother); Johnson, Mrs.
William (Molly Brant) (second wife)
Johnson, William, Indian agent and
speculator: advantages of proposed
plan to, 89; and Albany congress of
1754, 51–52; arrival at Fort Stanwix
for council (Sept. 1768), 141–42,
240n8; baronetcy awarded to, 35;
centralization of power urged by, 88;
close ally of Baynton, Wharton and
Morgan, 114, 235n15; and concern for
provisions for Fort Stanwix council,
143–44; deal struck with Oneidas, 56;
in defense of straying from Crown
instructions, 169, 171–72, 174; as
devoted Crown agent, 7, 110, 138,
164–65, 167, 200, 223n18; and eastern
Six Nations, 27, 35, 217nn20–21; and
efforts to modify Amherst's plans
of retribution, 76–78; explanations
on boundary to Whitehall, 135;

following Gage's strategy, 83–84, 228n65; frontier policy directed by, 68, 69–70; and German Flatts council (1770), 178–80; and gift of Mohawk land, 106–107; and Hillsborough's commendation of, 124–25; illicit trade practices overlooked by, 97, 232n125; and Illinois scheme, 102–103, 115–16; instructions to Croghan before Fort Pitt council, 132; Iroquois delegates appeal to crown for reinstatement of, 44; as land speculator, 6–7, 93, 106–107, 136, 164; and outrage at hostile Ohio nations, 107; plea to Hillsborough for authority to deal with situation, 190; and reduction of status by 1766, 110, 113; report to Hillsborough of imminent war, 177; secret meeting with Abraham, 136; in support of Iroquois, 27, 34, 64, 76, 78, 83, 167, 225n23, 226n27, 226n34; traders' losses from 1763 addressed by, 103, 234n152; void left by death of, 205; waning powers of, 110, 113; workers ordered to "Oneida Castle" to build fort, 60. *See also under* Boundaries; Croghan, George; Johnson Hall; Mohawks; Prospects, and collapse of protocol; 1768 Treaty of Fort Stanwix
Johnson Hall: conferences in summer of 1768, 135; council with Senecas (3 April 1764), 78; Johnson's manor, 19; and July 1753 meeting, 47; and March 1768 congress of Iroquois and Cherokees, 125–26, 238n59
Johnstone, George, 113

Kaské, Charlot, 82
Kayaderosseras dispute: and Abraham, 135–37; and claims of patentees, 135–36, 234n153; and Johnson, 104, 106–107, 136; land fraud related to, 192; and Mohawk claim, 51; original patents for, 103–104, 235n160
Kentucky frontier (1773), 197
Kiasutha, 81
Kickapoos, 100
King, Thomas, 178

King George's War, 33, 35, 38, 41
Kirkland, Samuel, 152, 204
Klock, George, 204

La Galissonière, Roland-Michel Barrin de, 43–44
La Mothe Cadillac, Antoine Laumet de, 36–37
Lancaster, Pa. (4 July 1744), council held for resolution of land disputes, 41–42
Land speculation: Crown's attempt to control, 67, 111; and Johnson, 6–7, 93, 106–107, 136, 164; and new boundary, 91; and struggles for sovereignty codependent, 11; undercut by Proclamation, 74–75. *See also* Croghan, George; Kayaderosseras dispute; Squatters, European; Suffering Traders; Vandalia project
Lardner, Lynford, 173
Last King, 178–79
Lecroix, Jeronimus de, 28
Lee, Arthur, 3, 4, 185, 210
Legge, William (Earl of Dartmouth), 192–95, 199. *See also* Dartmouth
Levy & Trent and Co., 95
Logan, Chief, attack on family of, 197–98, 250n77
Logan, William, 173
Long Coat (Anindamoaken al), 105
Long Knives, 52, 196, 204
Lord Dunmore of Virginia, 182–83. *See also* Dunmore, Lord
Lord Dunmore's War, 197–99, 201, 203
Loudoun, the fourth Earl of. *See* Campbell, John
Louisbourg, fall of, 61
Louis XIV, 22, 23
Lowry, Alexander, 95
Lydius, John, 52

Manawkyhiekon, 37–38
Mascoutens, 100
McCrea, John, 135–36
McKee, Alexander, 71, 197
Mercer, George, 186
Mississippi Company, 185
Mohawk River valley, location of, 3

Mohawks: and Albany congress of 1754, 51–53; assurance of fairness in concessions by Johnson, 137; and boundary negotiations, 106, 134–35; Catholic settlements of, 26; dislike of negotiating with Indian commissioners, 46; eastern Iroquois leaders, 8, 45; and the English, 45, 49; grievances of, 104; growth of influence in seventeenth century, 18; reaffirmation of allegiance to Crown, 47; and reliance on Johnson, 34, 35, 45–46, 53; settlers invading protected lands of, 192–93; and weaponry, 21. *See also* Johnson, William; Kayaderosseras dispute

Montcalm-Gozon, Louis-Joseph de, 59–60

Montour, Andrew, 129, 187

Moore, Henry, 113, 158, 170, 245n8

"Moor's Indian Charity School" (later Dartmouth College), 36

Morgan, Dr. John, 182

Morgan, George, 90, 95, 183, 205. *See also* Baynton, Wharton and Morgan (Philadelphia firm)

Morton, John, 182

Murray, John, 4th Earl of Dunmore. *See* Dunmore, Lord

Murray, William, 182–83

Nanticokes, 119–20

Neolin, message of spread by Pontiac, 72

Newcomer, 186, 189

New Wales, proposal for, 90–91

Niagara carrying place, 78, 84

Nymwha, on resistance to land claims at Fort Pitt council (1768), 130–31

Ohio and Muskinggum Rivers country (map), *81*

Ohio Company of Virginia: absorbed by Grand Ohio Company, 186; and Galloway, 122; and inland colony rejected by Lords, 127; patents petitioned for on behalf of, 91; Washington as shareholder, 53. *See also* Grand Ohio Company

Ohio Country: and benefits to Ohio nations, 38, 218n29; and Céloron's "Lead Plate" expedition, 43–44; changes after fall of Louisbourg, 38; Clinton's warning of French designs on, 39–40; competing claims to, 49; controlled by French at end of 1757, 61; and Crown seeking control over, 41; European settlers directed to boy Iroquois, 203; French presence in, 38, 45; gifts presented to by Pennsylvania, 42; as Iroquois refuge, 36, 69; and lands ceded to Pennsylvania by Hendrick, 52; and March 1768 congress of Iroquois and Cherokees, 125–26, 238n59; Mohawks and English disagreement on, 51–52; opening of new frontier in, 64; opening to settlement after Fort Stanwix treaty, 167, 203; and resentment of English presence, 82; and strengthened ties with traders, 41; and temporary truce, 82–83; unrest in (Sept. 1767), 120–21; and violence eruptions, 169

Oneida Carry (Deo-Wain-Sta): abuses at, 56; clearing of by Hyde, 32; congregation in September 1768, 139; and convergence of interests, 12–13, 29, 203; crucial trading route link, 27–28; de Léry attack on, 58–59; description of, 3; and French takeover of, 59–60; and importance to Albany, 32–33, 55; and Iroquois bartering away birthright, 5; Joseph Brant leaving in 1784, 212; and negotiators, 11; and past struggles, 13; Plan of forts at (1754) (map), *55*; scene in 1768, 4–5; Stanwix's reoccupation of (1758), 62; and territorial rights issue (1784), 208. *See also* Fort Stanwix; 1784 Treaty of Fort Stanwix

Oneidas: agreement for new fort at Carry, 62; and clearing of Carry, 32; closer ties with British fostered by, 27; compensation for use of Carry received by, 33; deal struck with Johnson, 56; first peoples to control the Carry, 28; Fort Stanwix as imperial presence after war, 65–66; and hostility to construction, 55–56; obstruction to 1768 Treaty of Fort Stanwix council, 152

Onondagas: and dedicated council fire, 16; as defectors, 22; and extended war, 15; as firekeepers, 17, 19; Johnson sent to (1746) by Clinton, 35; Mohawk representatives sent by Johnson, 35; and "Onondaga Castle," 29

Orontony, Nicholas, 37

Otsego patent, 157, 206

Ottawas: dissatisfaction shown by, 187; and 15 July 1770 meeting with Johnson, 178; and Pontiac, 72, 80, 100; as principals in war, 97

Ousonastota, 126

Paxton riots in December 1763, 86–88, 229n76

Peace of Paris, fragmentation of, 70–71

Penn, John, 177

Penn, Thomas: address to provincial assembly (Dec. 1763), 77; adjudication of claims in 1868 Fort Stanwix treaty, 143; on boundary to Johnson, 122; and dislike of Croghan's betrayal of protocol, 60; and Johnson's Fort Stanwix deal, 156; principal proprietor in Pennsylvania, 49; proclamation on 16 May 1769, 173; Shawnees declined protection of, 37; solutions to tensions sought by, 87; and support for Suffering Traders, 143

Pennamite Wars, 53

Peters, Richard, 142–43

Peters, William, 183

Petri, Marcus, 55, 56–57, 60

Piankashaws, 45

Pickawillany, 41, 45, 59

Pisquetomen, 64

Plan of 1764. See "1764 Plan for the Future Management of Indian Affairs"

Plan of forts at Oneida Carry (1754) (map), 55

"Plan of Fort Stanwix, built at the Oneida Station, 1758" (map), 140

Plan of Union (1754), 50, 52, 214, 220n74

Pontiac: Neolin's message spread by, 72; peace offers accepted by Johnson, 83; peace solidified by and on pipe sent to Johnson, 100–101; terms of peace and trade offered to, 68, 73. See also Uprising of 1763 (Pontiac's Rebellion)

Pontiac's Rebellion. See Uprising of 1763 (Pontiac's Rebellion)

Post, Christian Frederick, 64

Pownall, Thomas, 184

Preston, Achilles, 144

Prospects, and collapse of protocol: and American Revolution, 169; and Camp Charlotte treaty, 201; ceded lands as "racial killing ground," 168; clashes continued (e.g., killing of young Seneca George), 175–76; and collapse of Iroquois authority, 169; and Connecticut-based play for land, 173; and Croghan's troubles, 168–69, 181–82; Crown control sought by Johnson, 175; Crown response to terms of treaty, 170–71; and discontent continued into summer of 1772, 189–90, 249n61; and European settlers streaming in (1770–73), 191; and German Flatts council (1770), 178–80; and Grand Council meeting at German Flatts (July 1770), 188; and indigenous unrest near Fort Pitt (late 1769), 186–87; intercolonial boundary disputes not settled by Fort Stanwix agreement, 168; and Johnson Hall meeting of Six Nations (July 1771), 189; Johnson's activities following Fort Stanwix agreement, 169–70; and Johnson's concluding remarks, 179; and Johnson's death and legacy, 199–200; Johnson's plan to divide provincial responsibility, 172, 246n13; Johnson's report to Hillsborough of imminent war (1769), 177; and

Prospects, and collapse of protocol
(*continued*)
lack of trade regulation, 188; and
Lord Dunmore's War, 197–99, 201,
203; and Moore's encouragement to
Johnson, 170, 246n8; opening Ohio
Country to settlement, 167; Penn's
proclamation on 16 May 1769, 173;
and Pennsylvania proprietors,
173; proposal to dismantle Indian
Department, 171; and waning of
Indian Department power, 167;
war among tribes sanctioned by
Johnson, 178; Whitehall's measures
to alter relationships, 167–68.
See also Croghan, George; Indian
Department; Johnson, William;
Suffering Traders; Vandalia project;
Walpole Company or Associates

Quebec Act of 1774, 210

Read, Peter, 175
Reade, James, 57–58
Remsen, Peter, 135–36
Rigby, Joseph, 133
Römer, Wolfgang William, 24, 29–31, 32
The Royal Proclamation of 1763, 73–74,
103, 123, 210, 223n16
Rumsey, James, 183

Sassoonan, 38
Sayenquaraghta, 199
Scalp bounty, 60, 87, 98, 232n127
Seneca George, 175–77
Senecas: authority of, 18; and
compliance with English law,
199; council representatives, 16;
disobedience of, 194; felt cheated
by English, 120–21; and fighting
to defend British Crown, 207;
as gatekeepers of metaphorical
longhouse, 17; and Johnson Hall
meeting on 16 July 1771, 189; and
Johnson's council with, 177; and
Seneca George, 176; and wars, 15
1784 Treaty of Fort Stanwix, 13, 208–12
1768 Treaty of Fort Stanwix, 139–66;
and Abraham as translator, 148;

arrival of tribesmen by mid-October,
143; and attendees represented
who's who of colonial America, 146,
241n25; Boundaries of the Royal
Proclamation of 1763 and 1768 Treaty
of Fort Stanwix (map), *155*; boundary
line questions of Six Nations council,
149; changes culminating in, 165–66;
and collapse of fragile system, 13;
and complaint of Tiagawehe, 144–45;
and Conoghquieson's response to
welcome, 147; and Covenant Chain
emphasized by Iroquois, 158–59;
and Croghan's negotiations at,
157–58; and deviations from royal
instructions, 164, 169; as diplomatic
feat, 7; and divergent strategies, 9;
and dwindling British presence, 145;
and events preceding negotiations,
142; and exact boundary line, 163;
and Fort Stanwix's deterioration,
139–40; and Gage's pressure on
Johnson, 150; and gifts exchanged,
162, 167; intention of, 6; Iroquois
assured own future at, 151,
158–59; and Johnson's arrival at
Fort Stanwix, 141–42, 240n8; and
Johnson's assurances of binding
agreements, 160–61; as Johnson's
brainchild, 164–65, 244n78; and
Johnson's concern for provisions,
143–44; and Johnson's concluding
remarks, 161–62; and Johnson's
support of Iroquois, 151–52, 156;
and Johnson's welcome, 146–47;
as largest land cession in colonial
North America, 160; logistical
requirements for Crown-sponsored
council, 140–41; and Mohawk
nation security, 159–60; and Oneida
obstruction to, 152–54; and Penn's
adjudication of claims, 143; and
Pennsylvania cession, 154, 242n53;
and Pennsylvania complication,
156, 243n54; "Plan of Fort Stanwix,
built at the Oneida Station, 1758"
(map), *140*; preparations for, 145;
and private deliberations recorded
by scribe, 149–51; and sacrifice

of Ohio nations, 165; signatures confirming, 163–64; and significance of boundary to Croghan, 152; and Six Nations speaker, 156–57, 162–63; and Suffering Traders, 142, 157, 165; and Teyohaqueande, 149; Wharton's suggestions to Crown, 165; and William Franklin's parting requests, 161

"1764 Plan for the Future Management of Indian Affairs": declared too costly, 127; and Hillsborough, 137–38, 172; Johnson's support for, 113, 172–73, 200; new European policy after Uprising of 1763, 85; reconfiguration of, 88; and report from Lords of Trade, 126; scuttling of by Whitehall, 165–66; terrain of North America not reflected in, 103; on verge of confirmation, 94, 95

Seven Years' War: and British monopoly on borderland trade, 85; devastation following, 67, 76; emergence from, 65; onset of in North America, 45; and William Johnson, 27

Shawnees: and Bradstreet's negotiations with, 80; Camp Charlotte treaty signed, 200–201; Cherokees on peaceful terms with, 125; as conduits, 179; disappointment with Fort Stanwix cession, 190; at Fort Pitt to express frustration, 71–72; and Ground Council's influence, 83; message on 15 September 1774, 200; relocation of, 62; right to Ohio and Illinois lands given up, 131–32; in 1740s, 37–38

Shelburne, Lord, 75, 121, 122

Shingas (Delaware leader), 48

Shippen, Joseph, 124, 133–34

Shirley, William: delay of expedition against Niagara, 57–58; and hostility of Oneidas, 55–56

Sidling Hill mishap, 98, 104

Smallman, Thomas, 97, 198

Smith, Matthew, 87

Squash Cutter (Yaghkapoose), 105

Squatters, European, 66, 74, 86, 123, 202

Stamp Act, 108

Stanwix, John, 28, 62–63

Stuart, John, 88, 113, 151, 170

Stump, Frederick (Stump affair), 123, 124, 129, 132

Suffering Traders: and Benjamin Franklin's support, 115; Coxe's challenge to, 142; failure of grants to gain approval, 180, 184; and favor for claims sought in London (1769), 182, 184; formation of, 90; and Indiana grant, 167, 244n1; lands granted to, 156, 157–58; and new petitioners, 96; and Penn's support for, 143; Stanwix treaty approved by, 165. See also Croghan, George; Franklin, William; Indiana Company

Sullivan, John, 204

Susquehanna Company, 71

Susquehanna massacre, 119

Teedyuscung ("Delaware King"), 61, 63–64

Teyohaqueande, 149

Thomas, George (Pa. governor), 42

Thurlow, Edward, 196

Tiagawehe, 144–45

Tilghman, James, 173

Tohonissahgarawa, 129–30, 131

Tomassen, Willem, 28

Townsend Acts, 109

"Treaty," defined, 19

Treaty negotiations (spring 1765), 104–106

Treaty of Aix-la-Chapelle (1748), 44

Treaty of Camp Charlotte, 201

Treaty of Easton (1758), 27

Treaty of Hard Labor, 151, 170

Treaty of Paris (1783), 3, 208

Treaty of Utrecht (1713), 26

Treaty of Westminster (1674), 28

Treaty provisions, common, 210

Tree of Peace, 15

Trent, William: arrival at Fort Stanwix for council (Sept. 1768), 142; and Croghan's shares of land, 182; and Indiana Company, 157; and Suffering Traders, 90, 128, 141; and trip to London, 182

Tryon, William, 191–92, 194
Turner, Frederick Jackson, and Frontier
    Thesis, 75, 223n18
Tuscaroras, 17, 124, 144, 204, 207
Tyorhansera, 189

Uprising of 1763 (Pontiac's Rebellion):
    brief account of, 72–73; British
    imperial system exposed in, 85;
    diminished power of Six Nations
    revealed by, 69; eruption of, 67–68;
    and evolution of policy toward first
    peoples, 70; and gift-giving failure,
    20; inconsistencies following, 68,
    222n3; problems following, 65–66;
    revenge of Ohio nations for, 7; and
    temporary conclusion to hostilities
    from, 82. See also Pontiac
U.S. Indian agents (1784), 208

Vandalia project: backed by Dartmouth,
    195; charter not approved for, 196;
    and Grand Ohio Company, 186,
    205; as part of Croghan scheme, 191;
    scheme for establishment of inland
    colony, 182; and speculators, 194
Van den Bogaert, Harmen Meyndertsz,
    28–29

Wabash nations, 100, 117, 187
Walking Purchase, 37–38, 60
Walpole, Thomas, 184–85
Walpole Company or Associates,
    184–85, 248n45. See also Indiana
    Company
Wampum: belts of, 16, 17, 45, 100, 126,
    141, 146, 176; Covenant Chain belt,
    148, 158; covering grave and body
    of deceased with, 200; as mnemonic
    record, 16, 17, 18, 129; as valued
    gift, 20
Ward, Edward, 198
War of Austrian Succession (1740–48).
    See King George's War
War of the League of Augsburg, 23

Washington, George: and dispute with
    Shingas, 48; failure to construct
    fort, 53; Johnson more prominent
    than, 35; as land speculator, 91; as
    shareholder in Ohio Company of
    Virginia, 51
Wassong, 80
Webb, Daniel, 59–60
Webb, Thomas, 91
Wedderburn, Alexander, 196
Weiser, Conrad, 47, 52
Western Confederacy, 101, 117, 195
Western Senecas: and Croghan, 133;
    and Johnson's efforts in behalf
    of, 69, 76, 78–79, 97; meeting with
    John Penn, 178; no longer trusted
    by Grand Council, 189; refusal
    to engage French, 47–48; and
    Shawnees, 54
Westmoreland County, Pa., 198
Wharton, Samuel: arrival at Fort
    Stanwix for council (Sept. 1768),
    142; and distrust of Croghan, 96–97;
    message upheld by historians, 107;
    reassurance of reparation for 1763
    losses, 128; recommendations to
    Crown after Fort Stanwix Treaty, 165;
    sent to Fort Pitt to oversee return of
    goods, 102; and Suffering Traders,
    90; and warning of impending war,
    119. See also Baynton, Wharton and
    Morgan (Philadelphia firm)
Wharton, Thomas, 181–82, 184
Wheelock, Eleazar, 36, 152, 204
Wilkins, John, 183
William III, 23, 29
Williams, John, 63
Williams, William, 56
Wolcott, Oliver, 3, 210
Wraxall, Peter, 54, 221n85
Wyandots: and Bradstreet's
    negotiations with, 80; council
    held at request of Senecas, 120–21;
    establishment of, 37; in mid-1740s,
    38; and unrest by late 1769, 186

CPSIA information can be obtained
at www.ICGtesting.com
Printed in the USA
LVHW110901100922
728068LV00003B/34